THE OFFICIAL
Arsenal
ENCYCLOPEDIA

Acknowledgements

The publisher would like to thank Julian Flanders, Kathie Wilson, Laura Sandell
and Jem Maidment for their help throughout this project.

Produced for Hamlyn by Flanders Publishing

An Hachette Livre UK Company
www.hachettelivre.co.uk

This revised edition published in 2008 by Hamlyn, a division of
Octopus Publishing Group Ltd, 2-4 Heron Quays, London E14 4JP
Originally published in Great Britain in 2006
www.octopusbooks.co.uk

ISBN 978-0-600-61888-1

A CIP catalogue record for this book is available from the British Library

Printed and bound in Italy

10 9 8 7 6 5 4 3 2 1

Executive Editor Trevor Davies
Project Editor Julian Flanders
Design Kathie Wilson
Production Martin Croshaw and Nick Heal

All images copyright © Arsenal Football Club Plc/Stuart MacFarlane except the following:
PA Photos 8, 10, 11, 15, 19, 20, 21, 23, 24, 26, 27, 32, 33, 35, 37, 38, 40, 45, 47, 49, 53, 55, 60, 64, 69,
72, 74, 76, 84, 91, 94, 95, 97, 101, 103, 105, 109-115, 119, 120, 122, 124, 126, 134, 136, 137, 141, 143, 144, 151,
152, 155, 157, 159, 160, 166, 167, 169, 171, 173, 175, 180, 183, 185, 186, 189, 191, 193-195, 203, 206, 207;
Getty Images 92; Illustrated London News 79; Offside Sports Photography 93

All statistics for domestic and international fixtures are correct to 31 May 2008

CONTENTS

FOREWORD

In September 2006 I celebrated my tenth anniversary as manager of Arsenal Football Club. It has been a true privilege to have served this Club every single day since I first arrived a decade ago. It is a wonderful institution to work for, with an illustrious history and an exciting future. And that sums up Arsenal; tradition allied with vision, and this is reflected in *The Official Arsenal Encyclopedia*.

In these pages you will find all the important figures and dates that have shaped our history, making Arsenal a world-renowned name. The achievements of my predecessors, such as Herbert Chapman, Tom Whittaker, Bertie Mee and George Graham, make impressive reading. Now a new chapter is beginning at Emirates Stadium.

It was a wrench to leave Highbury, a place with so many fond memories for us all. I still remember my first visit, and my shock when I discovered it 'tucked away' among the terraced streets of Highbury. It was a truly unique stadium with its Art Deco stands and marble halls. But I am sure you will all agree that our magnificent new home is a fitting arena to watch football and for the Club to continue to develop.

It was an important move for us, made with the same foresight, aspirations and determination that Sir Henry Norris showed back in 1913 when he moved the Club from Woolwich, in south-east London, to Islington. It was a brave decision, but one that has reaped heavy dividends over the past 93 years.

I am a keen student of this Club, and Herbert Chapman, rightly, figures higher than most in Arsenal's past. His methods fascinate me; again, here was a man with true vision years ahead of his time. Where would Arsenal be today without his extraordinary work?

I am also struck by how the club breeds loyalty. Thierry Henry was really torn before departing for Barcelona. Regardless of where he is, I know he will always remain Arsenal through and through. Patrick Vieira too spent nine years at Highbury, which is a magnificent and increasingly rare achievement in this day and age. Cesc Fabregas, who I believe is the future of this club, signed the longest contract in the club's history. I know Arsenal has an irresistible pull on you. It enjoys magnificent support which demands continued success.

We often hear of players who have long since departed still calling themselves 'Arsenal men'. I know how they feel. Why else would so many ex-players return here? Liam Brady – a true legend – is now the head of the Club's Academy. Pat Rice, of course, has been a fantastic assistant to me throughout my time here. Believe me, Pat lets every single player know just what the Club means. And there are people like Steve Bould, another fine servant, who is now starting out in his coaching career at our Shenley training complex with our Academy side.

It has been a wonderful experience coming to England and learning about this Club. Arsenal is special to us all, and you can rest assured that I, and all the players and staff, will do our utmost to win more trophies and strive for new successes – and add yet more pages to this book.

Arsène Wenger,
June 2008

INTRODUCTION

The summer of 2006 marked one of the most important chapters in the glorious history of Arsenal Football Club with the opening of the state-of-the-art 60,000-seat Emirates Stadium. It has proved a sensational success. The move once again put the Club at the forefront of innovation, a precedent set repeatedly throughout its 120-year existence. With fans saying a tearful farewell to Highbury, it seemed entirely appropriate to compile a directory of the Club, that chronicles the key events and personnel of this wonderful footballing institution from its humble origins as a works' team in south-east London to its first appearance in the UEFA Champions League final and the dawn of a new era in a new home.

There was the move from Plumstead to Islington and the construction of Highbury in 1913, and then the Chapman years, when Arsenal won their first major trophy and became the biggest, and most famous, Club side in world football. Those heady days in the inter-war years cemented the Gunners' standing from Belgium to Brazil, and more successes came after hostilities ceased with Tom Whittaker guiding Arsenal to two more titles in 1948 and 1953. Bertie Mee's young side then ended 17 years in the footballing wilderness in spectacular fashion with European glory for the first time in 1970 before the hitherto elusive Double followed the very next season. At the end of the decade Terry Neill's Gunners appeared in four cup finals in three seasons before former player George Graham reinvigorated the Club when he returned as manager in

1986, winning six trophies in eight years. The title-winning match against Liverpool at Anfield in 1989 and European glory in Copenhagen five years later, stand out during another golden period for the Gunners. Graham had kick-started a sustained period of success which continues 20 years after his arrival in the hot seat.

But Arsène Wenger's appointment in 1996 could still prove to be the most important in a history dripping with achievement. With it a French revolution began in N5 which took the Club on to new levels with football of the highest calibre and yet more trophy success to reiterate Arsenal's standing as the premier club in the south of England – and the only one to consistently challenge the Lancastrian dominance of Manchester and Liverpool. The new Emirates Stadium – just a short walk from the once mighty Highbury – has further cemented that status. The move to a new home has proved a magnificent success. The Gunners are now enjoying the largest aggregate crowds in their history, regularly filling the new arena – in 2007/08 Arsenal had more sell-out home games than any other club in the UK. Profits, revenues and turnover are at an all-time high, taking a massive leap since leaving the physical and financial confines of Highbury. Emirates Stadium, now undoubtedly the new home of football, should provide many more entries for this encyclopedia over the coming years.

Jem Maidment,
June 2008

KEY

 League or Cup Competition

 Place or Stadium

 Player (past or present)

 Records/ Statistics

ACADEMY, The

Arsenal was one of the first clubs to attain Academy status in 1998 and since then over 50 graduates have gone on to play professional football, with numerous others forging a career at non-league level. The most famous former pupil reared by head of youth development Liam Brady and his team is Spain midfielder Cesc Fabregas. Others to have come through and are now playing Premiership football include Ashley Cole, Jermaine Pennant, Steve Sidwell and David Bentley. The Academy produced FA Youth Cup-winning sides in 2000 and 2001, and the Under-17s and Under-19s Academy League championship-winning teams of 1999/2000 and 2000/01 respectively.

Based just a few miles north east of Islington, at Hale End in Walthamstow, E17, the Academy opened in the summer of 2001, and hosts all of Arsenal's schoolboy sides, from Under-9s to Under-16s. It develops the youngsters on a day-to-day basis until they are ready to join the scholars at the Club's main Hertfordshire training base at London Colney Training Centre.

At any one time there are in excess of 100 footballers based at Hale End, and the man responsible for running the centre is Roy Massey, a former centre-forward who played for Rotherham, Leyton Orient and Colchester before injury cut short his career. Roy, a qualified teacher, answers to Liam Brady.

Since its opening the Academy has earned a reputation throughout Europe for its excellence. In recent years its sides have chalked up some impressive results at other notable clubs home and abroad, winning 7-1 at Manchester United, 5-0 at Liverpool and beating Feyenoord in the Netherlands.

Under FA rules, Academy youngsters have to be local to Arsenal FC. Under-9s to Under-12s must live within an hour of Islington, while Under-12 to Under-16s must live within 90 minutes. Members train twice a week with the Club and then play fixtures on Sundays.

There are seven pitches at Hale End; two full size, one junior 11-a-side pitch, and three small 8-a-side grass pitches, comparable to the playing surface at Emirates Stadium, along with one floodlit artificial pitch.

Former Gunner Steve Bould coaches the Under-18s side and led them to the semi-finals of the FA Youth Cup in 2007. During that run, the Gunners beat Manchester United in the first-leg of the semi-final, in front of a competition record crowd of 38,187 at Emirates Stadium. In the previous round of the competition Jay Simpson, 18, became the first player to score a hat-trick at the new arena in a 3-1 win over Cardiff.

Below is a list of former Academy graduates now playing professional football:

Jeremie Aliadiere	Forward	Middlesbrough
Alex Bailey	Defender	Chesterfield
Graham Barrett	Forward	Falkirk (Scotland)
Nicklas Bendtner	Forward	Arsenal
David Bentley	Forward	Blackburn Rovers
Adam Birchall	Forward	Barnet
Tommy Black	Midfielder	Unattached
Jay Bothroyd	Forward	Wolves
Stephen Bradley	Midfielder	Falkirk (Scotland)
Lee Canoville	Defender	Notts County
Liam Chilvers	Defender	Preston North End
Ben Chorley	Defender	Tranmere Rovers
Ashley Cole	Defender	Chelsea
Matthew Connolly	Defender	QPR
Patrick Cregg	Midfielder	Falkirk (Scotland)
Johan Djourou	Defender	Arsenal
Giorgos Efrem	Midfielder	Glasgow Rangers
Cesc Fabregas	Midfielder	Arsenal
Ryan Garry	Defender	Bournemouth
Kerrea Gilbert	Defender	Arsenal
Ben Gill	Midfielder	Cheltenham Town
Julian Gray	Midfielder	Coventry City
David Grondin	Defender	Excelsior (Belgium)
John Halls	Defender	Unattached
James Harper	Midfielder	Reading
Justin Hoyte	Defender	Arsenal
Neil Kilkenny	Midfielder	Leeds United
Sebastian Larsson	Midfielder	Birmingham City
David Livermore	Midfielder	Hull City
Peggy Lokando	Midfielder	Southend United
Arturo Lupoli	Forward	Fiorentina
Dean McDonald	Midfielder	Unattached
Fabrice Muamba	Midfielder	Bolton Wanderers
Nicky Nicolau	Midfielder	Unattached
David Noble	Midfielder	Bristol City
Guillaume Norbert	Defender	Nantes (France)
Joe O'Cearnill	Defender	St Patrick's Athletic (Rep of Ireland)
Stephen O'Donnell	Midfielder	St Mirren (Scotland)

Nicklas Bendtner: the latest in a long line of first team players to come up through the ranks of the Academy.

 7

Sam Oji	Defender	Leyton Orient
Jo Osei-Kuffour	Forward	Bournemouth
Quincy Owusu-Abeyie	Forward	Spartak Moscow (Russia)
Carl Parisio	Defender	AS Cannes (France)
Jermaine Pennant	Midfielder	Liverpool
Dean Shiels	Forward	Hibernian (Scotland)
Steven Sidwell	Midfielder	Reading
Frankie Simek	Defender	Sheffield Wednesday
Jay Simpson	Midfielder	Arsenal
Ryan Smith	Midfielder	Millwall
John Spicer	Midfielder	Burnley
Graham Stack	Goalkeeper	Reading
Anthony Stokes	Forward	Sunderland
Sebastian Svard	Midfielder	B M'gladbach (Germany)
Stuart Taylor	Goalkeeper	Aston Villa
Jerome Thomas	Midfielder	Charlton Athletic
Moritz Volz	Defender	Fulham
Rhys Weston	Defender	Walsall
Chris Wright	Goalkeeper	Boston United

ADAMS, Tony (MBE)

Born Romford, 10 October 1966
Arsenal appearances 673
Arsenal goals 49
International caps (England) 66 (5 goals)

He started his career with his shorts back to front – and ended it as the most decorated captain in the Club's history. One of Terry Neill's final acts as manager before he was sacked was to give 17-year-old Anthony Adams his first-team debut against Sunderland at Highbury in November 1983. Few people, least of all Neill, could have possibly imagined the heights the Romford-born stopper would reach, especially as his defensive colleague Kenny Sansom had to point out to the teenager that he was wearing his shorts the wrong way round during the 2-1 defeat. 'You just knew that he was

special,' said Don Howe, his next manager, years later.

His appearances were sporadic over the next few seasons, but he became a first-team regular in 1986/87 on the arrival of George Graham. 'The fact was,' said midfielder Steve Williams, 'that the reserves were brimming with players more talented than most in the first team. George realised that and immediately put them in, Adams especially.'

In February 1987, Adams made his England bow in a 4-2 success against Spain at the Santiago Bernabeu in Madrid, and a Littlewoods Cup winners' medal followed two months later. Now, forging a reputation as a tough, uncompromising customer, he was dubbed the 'new Bobby Moore'. He won the PFA Young Player of the Year award that year.

His first big setback came in Euro 88 when Holland's Marco van Basten gave him a torrid time in a 3-1 defeat, but true to his nature – and with the chants of 'Donkey' from opposition fans ringing in his ears – he fought back to skipper Arsenal to their first

title in 18 years with that famous 2-0 win over Liverpool at Anfield. Another title followed in 1991, when Arsenal lost just one game all season, although he was to miss two months of the season after being sent to prison in December 1990 for drink driving.

The trophies continued to come with double success in 1993 when the Coca-Cola and FA Cups came to Highbury, although Adams enhanced his unwelcome reputation for clumsiness – earned due to his ungainly manner – by dropping match winner Steve Morrow in the post-match celebrations of the first Final, breaking his shoulder. In the FA Cup that year Adams scored a memorable Wembley winner in the semi-final over Tottenham Hotspur, avenging a defeat to the old enemy at the same stage two years before.

In 1994 came another trophy when he led a magnificent rearguard action as Arsenal overcame AS Parma 1-0 in the Cup-Winners' Cup Final in Copenhagen, the famous back four's finest hour.

Tony Adams (right) scores as Everton's Craig Short (left) looks on helplessly on 3 May 1998. It was a majestic day for the Club as a first Premiership trophy came to Highbury.

By now Adams was also skippering his country with increasing regularity and led England to the semi-final of Euro 96. It was after defeat to Germany on penalties – and a two-week drinking spree – that he admitted his alcohol addiction, which coincided with the arrival of Arsène Wenger. The new manager stuck by Adams who reinvented himself as a cultured footballer and human being and two years later was captain as Arsenal won the Double – the first side to do so in separate decades.

Injuries began to take their toll and his final season was in 2001/02, when he led the Club to another Premiership and FA Cup Double, skippering the side to a 2-0 win over Chelsea in Cardiff. His second Premiership title also saw him become the first captain in English football to lift a title in three different decades, a feat that may never be beaten. Adams' habit of emerging triumphant through adversity earned him hero status among the North Bank, as did his loyalty to the Club, staying with Arsenal throughout his entire playing career, despite much interest in his services, notably from Manchester United manager Sir Alex Ferguson.

In 2004, Adams' excellent service was recognised when he was inducted into the English Football Hall of Fame.

He later had a brief spell as manager at Wycombe Wanderers and even shorter stints coaching at Dutch clubs Feyenoord and FC Utrecht. Adams has devoted large amounts of time and money to his Sporting Chance clinic in Hampshire, which aids sporting figures who have addiction problems.

In June 2006 he took up the offer to become Harry Redknapp's assistant at Portsmouth and in 2007/08 they led the club to eighth in the Premiership, the club's highest league position since the 1950s, and won the FA Cup beating Cardiff City 1-0 in the Final. This was the second time the club were FA Cup winners, the first being back in 1939.

AFRICA

No English club has had more African players representing it, with the first Gunner from the continent joining as far back as 1957. That was South African winger **Danny Le Roux**, who arrived at Highbury in February of that year after impressing when he toured the UK with his country three years before. First-team appearances were limited to just five outings, although he netted 15 times in 25 appearances for the second string.

Another 40 years would pass before the next African – **Christopher Wreh** – arrived. The Liberian striker, signed from AS Monaco, is a cousin of former World Footballer of the Year George Weah and made a sizeable impact with vital goals in the 1997/98 Double-winning season, including the winner in the FA Cup semi-final against Wolves at Villa Park. He later moved around Europe and the English lower leagues and has settled in Buckinghamshire with his young family. 'My children can always tell their friends that daddy played for Arsenal,' he says proudly.

Nigerian striker **Nwankwo Kanu** became the next African Gunner when he was signed from Inter Milan in 1999 and he remains perhaps the most popular. His sublime skills and unique style made him a firm favourite and his finest hour came in his first season at the Club, when he scored a memorable hat-trick against Chelsea as Arsenal came back from 2-0 down to win 3-2 at Stamford Bridge in a game voted by supporters as the ninth greatest in the Club's history.

Guinea striker **Kaba Diawara** made 15 appearances in red and white while **Jehad Muntasser** remains the only Libyan to play in English top-flight football after playing just one minute of a League Cup tie against Birmingham in 1997. In 2006 he played in all three African Nations Cup group games for his country. Another forgotten African is **Carlin Itonga** – who once scored a record seven goals for Arsenal's Under-19s side against Ipswich Town – and, like Muntasser, played just one senior fixture for the Club, coming on as a substitute in a 4-0 Carling Cup triumph over Manchester United at Highbury in 2001.

In more recent times the defence has a strong African core with the presence of **Laureano Bisan-Etame Mayer**, otherwise known as **Lauren** (Cameroon), and Ivory Coast pair **Emmanuel Eboue** and **Kolo**

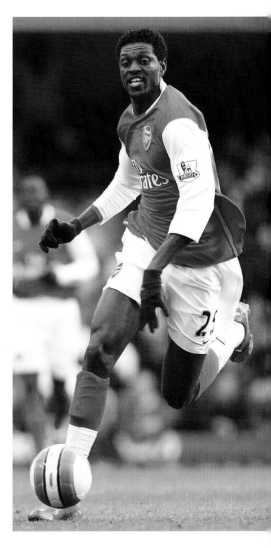

Born in Lome, the capital of Togo, Emmanuel Adebayor was first spotted playing at Under 15 level at a training ground in the city by French club FC Metz.

Toure, the latter two picked up courtesy of Arsenal's superb scouting system in the country. Eboue and Toure played for Arsenal's Belgian feeder club KSK Beveren before moving to London. Lauren, however, was an established international when he was signed from Real Mallorca in 2000. Born in Londi Kribi, Cameroon, his family fled Equatorial Guinea and eventually arrived in Spain, settling near Seville – all by the time of little Lauren's third birthday. In fact, when Jose Antonio Reyes signed from Sevilla, Lauren was immediately appointed interim translator for the young Spaniard and was even coveted by Spain before choosing to represent Cameroon. Cameroon midfielder **Alex Song** has made sporadic appearances while Togo international striker **Emmanuel Adebayor**, who made a scoring debut in a 2-0 win at Birmingham in February 2006, has taken over the mantle of Thierry Henry as the club's main striker after he scored more than 20 times in the 2007/08 season.

And there are also many players past and present with African connections. Take Club legend Patrick Vieira, a Frenchman on the international stage bought up near Paris, but who was born in Senegal capital Dakar to parents from Cape Verde Islands and Guinea Bissau. Two other Frenchmen also have their roots in Africa: Jeremie Aliadiere, another Les Bleus star, has an Algerian mother, and midfielder Abou Diaby's family are originally from the Ivory Coast, as is the case with Swiss defender Johan Djourou. Former goal-keeper Rami Shaaban was brought up in Sweden, but has an Egyptian father and British citizen Fabrice Muamba was born in the Democratic Republic of Congo.

Up to the end of the 2007/08 season, 16 Africans from nine different countries had represented Arsenal.

AISA

The Arsenal Independent Supporters Association was formally established in October 2000 as a campaigning organisation run by and for Arsenal supporters. It is an independent voice for Gunners fans and holds fund-raising events and dinners and meets with the Club on several initiatives. Meetings are generally held at the Hen and Chickens theatre bar on Highbury Corner. Its website is www.aisa.org

ALLISON, George

MANAGER 1934/47
Born **Darlington, 1885**
Died **13 March 1957**

Originally a journalist hailing from Durham, Allison moved south in 1905 and became Woolwich Arsenal's programme editor. He then worked for BBC radio, for whom he was the commentator on the very first FA Cup Final to be broadcast, between Arsenal and Cardiff City in 1927, but he gave up the microphone to take over as Club secretary at Highbury before becoming the shock choice to take the manager's job after the death of Herbert Chapman in 1934, despite his lack of managerial experience. It was a brave move for the Club, but one that it would replicate years later with Bertie Mee.

Allison's first signing for the Club was swashbuckling centre-forward Ted Drake, who had been a target of Chapman's the previous season, and he seamlessly fitted into the Arsenal hot-seat, winning two more titles in 1935 and 1938 and an FA Cup in 1936, to continue his great predecessor's fine work.

He also made an appearance in the 1939 movie *The Arsenal Stadium Mystery*, along with most of the first team, playing himself as manager and commentator. It was a fascinating insight into the inter-war years at Highbury, and he concluded his half-time team talk to Drake, Bastin and co. by coining a famous phrase, 'It's one-nil to the Arsenal. That's the way we like it.'

After the war Allison found the job of building another great Arsenal side – not to mention the stadium which had been bombed several times during hostilities – too much and after a disappointing 13th-place finish in 1946/47 he stepped down to be replaced by Tom Whittaker.

He died of a massive heart attack in March 1957, aged 73, just a few months after his old pal and successor Whittaker had passed away in similar circumstances.

ALLISON'S STARS

It speaks volumes for Herbert Chapman that much of the side he built remained in the years after his death. Allison, in truth, just needed to tinker with his squad.

His first signing, however, would become a true Gunners great: **Ted Drake** become the finest centre-forward of his age, plundering 136 goals in 182 appearances. Alongside Chapman's favourite son, **Cliff Bastin**, another Allison buy – **Alf Kirchen** – also went on to be a big star for the Gunners, with his lightning pace, endless supply of crosses and eye for

George Allison was a shock managerial appointment after Herbert Chapman's death in 1934. But the former journalist and broadcaster proved any sceptics wrong by steering the Gunners to two league titles and an FA Cup during the second half of the 1930s.

goal making him a big favourite with the Laundry End.

The reliable full-back partnership of **George Male** and **Eddie Hapgood** was as solid and dependable as ever and played through until the Second World War, the former even staying on for another title medal in 1948.

Wilf Copping, the Iron Man, signed in the summer following Chapman's death, became a frequently important – and popular – figure as the decade wore on, with his robust challenges greeted with whoops of delight from the crowd.

However, Allison's biggest star signing was probably the worst decision he made. **Bryn Jones** was seen by many as an unmitigated, and costly, disaster after flattering to deceive following a £14,000 switch from Wolves. The Wales international inside-forward failed to live up to the huge fee or the tag of Alex James' replacement and became a target for the boo-boys, rarely reproducing his Molineux form.

AMATEUR GUNNERS

In the pre-Highbury days, prior to the beginning of the First World War, it was the norm for many players to remain as amateurs because they had well-paid jobs or businesses outside the game. Perhaps the best example of this was Edinburgh-born **Thomas Fitchie**, who joined Woolwich Arsenal as a teenager in 1901 and netted nearly a goal every other game in 63 appearances during the next eight years. During that time, due to his amateur status, he also turned out for Fulham and Tottenham Hotspur as well as returning to his native Scotland for two years to play for Queen's Park in Glasgow.

One of Fitchie's team-mates, centre-half **Percy Sands**, was also one of the Club's greatest ever amateurs, spending 17 years with Arsenal after joining in 1902 and being one of the few players, like the legendary Charlie Buchan, who played for the Gunners in both south and

north London. A teacher by profession, he did not turn professional for another three years and held the Club's appearance record until it was broken by Wales international defender Bob John.

Bernard Joy is perhaps Arsenal's most famous amateur player – and the last to play for England in March 1936 – who skippered the Great Britain side at the Berlin Olympics later that year. During his time at Highbury he remained a player of the famous amateur side Corinthians, who changed their name to Corinthian Casuals in 1939.

The most remarkable amateur, however, was **Dr Kevin O'Flanagan** who was a dual international at football and rugby for Ireland. His work as a doctor at a north London hospital meant he could rarely be considered for away games but he still managed to turn out for Arsenal on 16 occasions during a four-year period after the end of the Second World War.

The last recognized amateur to play for the club was keeper **Bob Wilson**, who was originally on the books of Wolverhampton Wanderers while studying to be a PE teacher at Loughborough University. He eventually got a job at Holloway School, close to Highbury, where he taught future team-mate Charlie George before joining the Gunners in July 1963, making his debut later that year and playing several times as an amateur before signing professional forms at Highbury the following March.

ANDERSON, Viv

Born **Nottingham, 29 August 1956**
Arsenal appearances **150**
Arsenal goals **15**
International caps (England) **30**

Viv Anderson was a marauding figure down the right flank for three seasons during the 1980s. The England defender broke Highbury hearts when he moved to Manchester United prior to the start of the 1987/88 season.

A lively right full-back who always demanded nothing short of 100 per cent from his team-mates, Viv Anderson led by example with fantastic fitness levels and a thirst for victory.

Anderson – the first black player to represent England – signed from hometown club Nottingham Forest in 1984 and would become a member of

George Graham's first defensive unit, along with David O'Leary, Kenny Sansom – his full-back partner at international level too – and his young protégé Tony Adams.

There was real shock – and genuine sadness – when he departed for one last big move to Manchester United shortly after the 1987 Littlewoods Cup Final. It had come out of the blue. Many fans felt betrayed, but they should not forget his wholehearted commitment, as well as a knack of scoring goals, in his three years at Highbury.

He would play on until 1994, later representing Sheffield Wednesday, Barnsley and Middlesbrough, where he worked with former United and England team-mate Bryan Robson.

ANELKA, Nicolas

Born **Versailles, France, 14 March 1979**
Arsenal appearances **90 (17)**
Arsenal goals **28**
International caps (France) **48**
(11 goals)

The *enfant terrible* of Arsenal's Gallic invasion joined Arsenal in November 1996 after he was spotted by Arsène Wenger playing for Paris Saint-Germain. He broke into the team in 1997/98 when Ian Wright suffered a long-term injury, and was in superb form for much of the campaign as Arsenal won the Double, Anelka scoring the second goal in Arsenal's 2-0 win over Newcastle United in the FA Cup Final.

The next season he continued where he left off with his electric pace and natural finishing terrorising opponents as he won the PFA Young Player of the Year Award, although Arsenal narrowly failed to defend their title.

Anelka became unsettled at the Club and eventually transferred to Real Madrid in the summer of 1999 despite pleas from Arsène Wenger to stay at Highbury. He failed to settle in Madrid, scoring only four goals in 29 appearances, leaving in the summer of 2000 to begin his second spell at Paris Saint-Germain.

Anelka soon returned to the English Premiership, signing a one-year loan deal with Liverpool. He then joined newly promoted Manchester City before leaving after three years for Turkish Superliga outfit Fenerbahce. He later moved to Bolton before signing for Chelsea in January 2008.

ANFIELD

Liverpool FC's home will remain, for most Arsenal fans, the venue for the Club's greatest ever triumph: a 2-0 win on 26 May 1989 which gave the Gunners their first Division One title for 18 years. That famous Friday night drama – beamed live to an estimated worldwide TV audience of 600 million – is, without question, the most dramatic ending to a domestic league campaign in history.

Liverpool were three points clear at the top with Arsenal second as the two sides prepared to meet for the league decider. Arsenal had to win by two clear goals – a feat not achieved by a visiting team for three years – to draw level on points with Liverpool, but overhaul them to the top spot on goal difference.

A tense opening 45 minutes ended 0-0 – just how manager George Graham envisaged it would – before Alan Smith headed in Paul Merson's free kick after 51 minutes to give Arsenal the lead.

The match ebbed and flowed, but Liverpool, whose players were famously seen congratulating each other late on despite trailing 1-0 at the time, seemed to have done just enough to scrape their 18th league title. However, with nearly two minutes of stoppage time played, young Arsenal midfielder Michael Thomas found himself through on goal and flicked the ball past Bruce Grobbelaar to spark almost unprecedented scenes among Arsenal's magnificent travelling supporters behind the goal at the Anfield Road end.

Arsenal chairman Peter Hill-Wood, puffing on a cigar in the directors' box, turned to vice-chairman David Dein and drolly commented, 'Never in any doubt'.

Despite Liverpool's place as the most successful club side in English football, Arsenal have enjoyed several notable successes in front of the famous Kop.

Cliff Bastin's double gave Arsenal a 3-2 win in October 1932 and Joe Hulme hit two the following season as Arsenal repeated the scoreline in the title run-in. A hat-trick of Anfield wins came the season after with Ted Drake and a rare Eddie Hapgood strike seeing off Liverpool 2-0 in front of 55,794. And to complete a super run of success for Arsenal, Christmas Day 1935 brought a 1-0 Gunners win courtesy of Joe Hulme's strike. All eyes had been on Ted Drake, who scored seven in his previous outing at Aston Villa, still a Club record. In November 1952 Cliff Holton scored a hat-trick and Ben Marden the other two as Arsenal earned a stunning 5-1 win on Merseyside – their biggest ever win at Anfield – on their way to their seventh league title success.

Another of Arsenal's great Anfield wins came in February 1973 when the two title challengers came head to head. Alan Ball – barracked incessantly by the home fans for his past Everton association – scored from the spot in front of the Kop and then John Radford ran half the length of the pitch to complete a 2-0 win and snatch top spot from Liverpool for the first time since 23 September. Liverpool, however, got their revenge by claiming the title by three points in May.

Ray Kennedy, later a Liverpool star, struck the only goal as Arsenal stole a 1-0 win the following April, the last Anfield win until 1989. Paul Merson hit a memorable 66th minute winner to earn his side a 1-0 win in March 1991 as Arsenal headed towards another title and two seasons later Anders Limpar and Ian Wright netted in a 2-0 win. Successive Robbie Fowler hat-tricks saw off Arsenal

Right High drama at Anfield on 26 May 1989 as Michael Thomas (second right) scores the second goal for Arsenal deep into injury time to earn a 2-0 win – and a first title for 18 long years.

in 1994 and 1995, and the next success did not come until 23 December 2001 when ten-man Arsenal – Giovanni van Bronckhorst had been shown a red card – managed a heroic 2-1 win with Kanu starring in an unlikely central midfield role.

In January 2007 Arsenal chalked up two stunning wins inside four days at the stadium. First they beat the hosts 3-1 in the third round of the FA Cup and returned just days later in the Carling Cup quarter-finals to record a fantastic 6-3 victory. Brazil international Julio Baptista, on-loan from Real Madrid, bagged four goals – and missed a penalty – on a humiliating night for the Merseysiders. It was Liverpool's biggest home defeat since the 1929/30 season.'

ANTHEM

If any one chant can be called Arsenal's anthem, it would have to be 'Good Old Arsenal'. Its origins, though, will surprise many.

The words were written by none other than football's self-styled 'elder

statesman' Jimmy Hill, former manager of Coventry City and, for the past 40 years, one of football's most famous media personalities.

Proud Jimmy – who penned the song in 1971 – takes up the story: 'Not a lot of people know I wrote the lyrics for the Arsenal club song, "Good old Arsenal". We had a competition on ITV for it and none of the entries were any good so I approached their manager Bertie Mee and asked him if he would let me have a stab. He did and within a few weeks they were singing it at Wembley on the way to the 1971 Double.'

ANTI-HEROES

However hard they tried, here are some players who never fulfilled their promise in a red and white shirt.

BRYN JONES
Touted as the man to fill the boots of the great Alex James, the little Wales star didn't stand a chance from day one and was often barracked by an unforgiving Highbury crowd which had never really got over James' retirement in 1936. Jones was even put in the reserves to take the pressure off him, but more than 30,000 showed up to see him humiliated. Ironically, his best form came at the start of the aborted 1939/40 season and even the crowd began to thaw – until the war ended his hopes of Arsenal stardom.

IAN URE
Bought for a world-record fee for a centre-half, here was another man who became a laughing stock for many fans. The size of the fee, the unique pressures of Arsenal and a clear problem with his temperament all conspired against him. Ure was sent off four times at Highbury, a remarkable record in the days when red cards were a rarity in Division One.

JEFF BLOCKLEY
Billed as a possible successor to Frank McLintock, the Leicester-born stopper proved anything but. Old school defending and little guile or flair was Blockley's game

and the crowd, along with several of his colleagues, were not impressed. Soon the boo-boys found their voice and after a mistake in the 1973 FA Cup semi-final, the crowd were long past giving him a chance. He stayed 18 more months before heading home to Filbert Street.

LEE CHAPMAN
The young, blonde forward from Stoke was, back in 1982, woefully out of his depth after a high-profile move. His commitment was rarely doubted, but his abilities frequently were, and he exhibited a lack of goals and an ungainly manner. After one season he was offloaded at a huge loss.

However, what makes Chapman even less popular, is that after leaving Highbury his career gradually improved – and he always had a knack of scoring against his former employers. He even, to the bemusement of many who had seen him ten years before, won a title medal at Leeds in 1992. It goes without saying he scored against Arsenal at Highbury during the title run-in.

GUS CAESAR
A man born in Tottenham never stood a chance at Highbury. Caesar was a promising defender capped by England Under-21s and widely tipped for a glittering Highbury future and full international honours. But a lapse in concentration in the 1988 Littlewoods Cup Final, when a bizarre stumble on the lush Wembley turf let in Luton for a goal, destroyed years of hard work.

The Highbury crowd never forgave him and his introduction to games was greeted with jeers and even laughter. The fact was that Caesar was an athletic defender with great qualities, but he never regained the fans' respect and is still remembered for all the wrong reasons.

APPEARANCES

MOST OVERALL
722 – David O'Leary
(debut v Burnley (a) 16 August 1975)

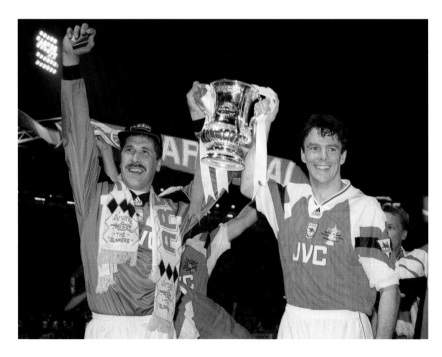
David Seaman (left) and David O'Leary, the two players with the most appearances for the Club, seen here celebrating with the FA Cup trophy in 1993.

George Armstrong (right) flicks the ball over West Bromwich Albion's Jim Cumbes (left) and John Talbut (centre) to score. Arsenal won 6-2 with Ray Kennedy and Charlie George scoring two each and an own goal on 19 September 1970, their fifth win in what was to be a championship winning season.

MOST LEAGUE
558 - David O'Leary

MOST PREMIERSHIP
344 - David Seaman

MOST EUROPEAN
78 - Thierry Henry

MOST FA CUP
70 - David O'Leary

**MOST CONSECUTIVE
(ALL COMPETITIONS)**
172 - Tom Parker
(3 April 1926/26 December 1929)

David O'Leary remains the player to have made the most appearances for the Club with a massive 772 games under his belt in all competitions. It's unlikely it will ever be beaten with squad rotation the norm these days. His first game, on the opening day of the 1975/76 season, saw Arsenal draw 0-0 with Burnley at Turf Moor. He broke George Armstrong's previous record of 621 appearances against Norwich City in November 1989, celebrating the occasion with a rare double strike in a 4-3 win. His 722nd and final game came in May 1993 when he came on as a substitute at Wembley in Arsenal's 2-1 FA Cup Final replay win over Sheffield Wednesday.

In the Premiership David Seaman remains the Club's appearance holder with 344 outings, with Ray Parlour having played just 12 games fewer in the top flight.

And former captain Tom Parker, the first Gunner to lift a major trophy, has the record for consecutive appearances, again unlikely ever to be beaten, with an astonishing unbroken run of 172 matches stretching from a 4-2 Highbury win over Blackburn Rovers on 3 April 1926 all the way through to a 2-1 home defeat to Portsmouth on Boxing Day 1929 – a remarkable 44 months. He had beaten Jimmy Ashcroft's previous record of 154 successive matches set 25 years earlier.

ARMSTRONG, George

Born **Hebburn, Co Durham, 9 August 1944**
Died **1 November 2000**
Arsenal appearances **621**
Arsenal goals **70**

Arsenal to the core, 'Geordie' spent 15 full seasons at Highbury and held the Club's all-time appearance record of 621 for nearly 15 years. A pure winger of the old school, the 5ft 6in Armstrong made his first-team bow at the age of 17 against Blackpool in February 1962 and before long became a valued member of the side. He could play on both the left and right side of the attack and was a regular provider of goals with his unerringly accurate crosses and corners.

The County Durham-born attacker, who had joined Arsenal straight from school, was never one for personal glory and didn't care who scored the goals needed to win games. He was an ever present in the 1971 Double side after helping the Gunners win the Inter-Cities Fairs Cup the year before, when he was named Arsenal's player of the season, a magnificent achievement in a side brimming with players at their peak.

Internationally he was in the wrong place at the wrong time, England manager Sir Alf Ramsey's insistence on not using wingers precluding him from the senior side after he was capped at youth and Under-21 level.

In 1977 he left for Leicester City before finishing his career at Stockport County. He then became a coach in the Middle East before returning to Highbury in 1990 after an invitation from former team-mate George Graham, who said, 'He was such a thorough professional and a great help to me at Arsenal. As soon as I knew he was available I jumped at the chance to bring him back.' He nurtured many young Gunners, but on 31 October 2000 he suddenly collapsed with a brain haemorrhage while at a training session at London Colney and died the next morning.

ARSENAL

WHERE DOES THE WORD COME FROM?
It is not entirely clear where the word derives from. It appears in various forms in Romanic languages (from which it has been adopted into Teutonic), i.e. Italian *arzenale* and Spanish *arsenal*. Italian also has the words *arzana* and *darsena*, and Spanish has a longer word of Arabic origin, *daras-sina'ah*, which means house of trade or manufacture (from *dar* meaning 'house' and *sina'ah* meaning 'trade' or 'manufacture').

The meaning is much more obvious: an arsenal is an establishment for the construction, repair, receipt, storage and issue of weapons and ammunition, and the Club was named after the Royal Arsenal in Woolwich, south London.

If you travel to any football-conscious country, most people instantly associate the word Arsenal with the Club, rather than with any military connotations.

ART DECO

Visitors to the old Highbury stadium can see fantastic examples of Art Deco design in the East Stand – a Grade II listed building – and the West Stand, both of which are currently being converted into one, two and three-bedroom flats. They were the inspiration of architects Claude Waterlow Ferrier and William Binnie and provided the Art Deco majesty that remained Highbury's defining characteristic since their construction in 1931 and 1936 and ensured the stadium was unique throughout world football.

Art Deco derived its name from the World's Fair held in Paris in 1925, formally titled the Exposition Internationale des Arts Décoratifs et Industriels Modernes,

This picture taken in 1967 displays the full majesty of Highbury's Art Deco East Stand facade on Avenell Road.

A combination of brilliant planning, superb design and astute financial management turned Ashburton Grove from on old dump into the site of one of the finest football stadiums in the country, and all within walking distance of the old Highbury Stadium.

which showcased French luxury goods. The term was coined during the exhibition, but did not receive wider usage until the 1960s.

ASHBURTON GROVE

Arsenal's impressive new 60,000-seater home used to be a right old dump – literally. Until 2002 it housed a major waste transfer station serving Islington and the surrounding area. The 17-acre site was also home to a number of businesses of varying sizes before it was identified as a potential new home for the Club.

Other sites had been explored, notably King's Cross, Alexandra Palace and Wembley, and King's Cross had seemed a likely prospect. However, the huge work being carried out in the area due to the cross-channel rail link and regeneration scheme meant the earliest Arsenal could expect to move into a new stadium there would have been 2009.

Plans to extend Highbury to a 50,000-seater had been scuppered back in 1997 so, with a heavy heart, the board reluctantly began the search away from Avenell Road. Little were they to know the answer was so close (see Home Help on page 109).

When Ashburton Grove had been identified and Islington Council had been sounded out, initial plans were made public in November 1999. A huge public consultation process was then put into action and when planning permission was granted preparatory work began on Ashburton Grove in January 2002. Construction on a new waste transfer station also commenced in nearby Lough Road between Caledonian Road and Holloway Road and businesses were eventually moved to brand new premises in the area.

Arsenal were handed the keys to their new home (see Emirates Stadium) shortly after the final home game at Highbury against Wigan Athletic on 7 May 2006.

ASHCROFT, Jimmy

Born **Liverpool, 12 September 1878**
Died **9 April 1943**
Arsenal appearances **303**
Arsenal goals **0**
International caps (England) **3**

Jimmy Ashcroft was the Club's first England international and a record-breaking goalkeeper who signed for Woolwich Arsenal in 1900 from Gravesend United.

In 1901/02 he kept 17 clean sheets in 34 matches, including a run of six on the trot, which remained a Club record until Alex Manninger equalled it during the latter part of the 1997/98 season. In 1904/05 he set a Club record of 154 successive appearances, which has only been beaten once since, by captain Tom Parker more than 25 years later. In 1906 he kept goal during the run to the FA Cup semi-finals and made his three appearances for England.

Ashcroft, who began his career as an amateur with hometown club Everton, later played for Blackburn Rovers and then moved back to his native Merseyside to turn out for Tranmere Rovers.

ATTENDANCES

The biggest ever 'home' crowd saw Arsenal slip to a 1-0 defeat to RC Lens of France in the Champions League in November 1998 as nearly 74,000 flocked to the national stadium at Wembley, which Arsenal used for two seasons for their Champions League matches. The attendance beat Arsenal's previous record set in March 1935 by just 412. On that day, 73,295 were at Highbury to see Arsenal draw with league challengers Sunderland. It still remains a record and is unlikely ever to be beaten, especially as Arsenal's new Emirates Stadium home has a capacity of 60,000 with no plans to increase that total.

The lowest ever gate at Highbury was just 4,554. It came at the end of Billy Wright's four-year tenure as manager when Leeds United easily beat Arsenal 3-0 in May 1966. The match coincided with the live television broadcast of the European Cup-Winners' Cup Final between Borussia Dortmund and Liverpool that same night, and the Club was quick to blame the TV coverage for such an abysmal turnout.

Since the Premier League was launched in 1992, the lowest Highbury gate was just over 18,000, for a match with Wimbledon in February 1993.

HIGHEST

Premiership (Highbury) - 38,419
v Leicester City, 15 May 2004

Premiership (Emirates) - 60,161
v Manchester United, 3 November 2007

League - 73,295
v Sunderland, 9 March 1935

Overall - 73,295
v Sunderland, 9 March 1935

Wembley Stadium - 73,707
v RC Lens, 25 November 1998

LOWEST

Premiership (Highbury) - 18,253
v Wimbledon, 10 February 1993

Fans at the Clock End applaud Arsène Wenger before the final match of the 2003/04 season against Leicester City. Highbury's biggest ever Premiership crowd saw the Gunners win 2-1 to complete the season undefeated and win the title.

Carling Cup (Emirates) – 53,136
v Tottenham Hotspur, 9 January 2008

League – 4,554
v Leeds United, 5 May 1966

Overall – 4,554
v Leeds United, 5 May 1966

Wembley Stadium – 71,227
v AIK Solna, 22 September 1999

AVERAGE LEAGUE ATTENDANCES AT HIGHBURY (POST-WAR)

1946/47	43,266	1977/78	35,446
1947/48	54,892	1978/79	36,371
1948/49	51,478	1979/80	33,596
1949/50	49,001	1980/81	32,480
1950/51	50,474	1981/82	35,589
1951/52	51,030	1982/83	24,153
1952/53	49,141	1983/84	28,116
1953/54	46,944	1984/85	31,205
1954/55	43,725	1985/86	23,824
1955/56	42,034	1986/87	29,022
1956/57	41,093	1987/88	29,910
1957/58	39,835	1988/89	35,593
1958/59	45,227	1989/90	33,672
1959/60	39,341	1990/91	37,012
1960/61	34,318	1991/92	31,886
1961/62	34,447	1992/93	24,403
1962/63	32,288	1993/94	30,492
1963/64	34,793	1994/95	35,220
1964/65	31,327	1995/96	37,568
1965/66	29,036	1996/97	37,821
1966/67	31,773	1997/98	38,053
1967/68	31,896	1998/99	38,024
1968/69	38,423	1999/00	38,033
1969/70	35,758	2000/01	37,975
1970/71	43,776	2001/02	38,044
1971/72	40,500	2002/03	38,042
1972/73	40,246	2003/04	38,079
1973/74	30,212	2004/05	37,979
1974/75	28,315	2004/05	37,979
1975/76	26,495	2005/06	38,184
1976/77	32,671		

AVERAGE LEAGUE ATTENDANCES AT EMIRATES STADIUM

2006/07	60,046
2007/08	60,070

AUSSIE GUNNERS

Few Antiopdeans have played for the Club, although the most successful was certainly left-back Jimmy Jackson, appointed Club captain when he signed at the turn of the 19th century. He became the first skipper to lead the Club to promotion when Woolwich Arsenal finished runners-up in the Second Division in 1903/04, thanks largely to a magnificent home record in which Arsenal scored 67 goals and conceded just five all season.

The last notable Australian to represent Arsenal was John Kosmina. A striker, who had played for Polonia FC in Melbourne, he briefly passed through the Club in the 1978/79 season, but failed to impress manager Terry Neill and was released after just one first-team start and three further appearances from the bench. He is currently head coach for the Australian A-League football club Adelaide United. He steered United to the inaugural Hyundai A-League championship title in 2005/06 and in August 2006 was appointed assistant manager to the Socceroos.

AUSTRIA

The Club has a number of ties with Austria. Since the summer of 2001 Arsenal have held a pre-season training camp in Styria, around 30 miles east of Graz near the borders with Hungary and Slovakia. Arsène Wenger's side normally travel to central Europe immediately after kicking off their pre-season campaign with a traditional trip to Barnet at the beginning of July.

The last time that Arsenal played a competitive fixture in Austria was on 2 October 1991 against FK Austria Memphis in Vienna. The Gunners lost 1-0,

but progressed to the second round of the European Cup after winning the first leg 6-1 at Highbury, Alan Smith scoring four on his European debut.

The legendary Austrian goalkeeper Rudi Hiden was a target of Arsenal manager Herbert Chapman in the 1930s, but work permit constraints meant the move fell through. However, another goalkeeper did become the first Austrian to represent Arsenal, although it took another 70 years to happen. Alex Manninger (born 4 June 1977 in Salzburg) was signed in June 1997 as cover for David Seaman.

The following season Manninger was drafted into the side due to an injury to the England goalkeeper and performed

Keeper Alex Manninger's performances during the 1997/98 season were so impressive that he was awarded a Championship medal despite the fact that he had not played the requisite number of games.

heroically, keeping six clean sheets in a row to equal the pre-First World War record set by Jimmy Ashcroft. His performance in a 1-0 win at Old Trafford during the title run-in was exemplary.

After 64 appearances, he was loaned out to Serie A side Fiorentina and made a permanent move to RCS Espanyol in Spain in the summer of 2002. He then went back to Italy and turned out for Torino, Brescia and Siena. In 2005 he spent a year at his first club Salzburg before re-signing for Siena in 2006.

AUTOBIOGRAPHIES

Addicted - Tony Adams
Allison Calling - George Allison
An Autobiography
    - Malcolm Macdonald
Arsenal from the Heart - Bob Wall
Cliff Bastin Remembers - Cliff Bastin
Football Ambassador - Eddie Hapgood
Footballeur - Robert Pires
Going Great Guns - Kenny Sansom
Mr Wright - Ian Wright
My 20 Years of Soccer - Tommy Lawton

My Autobiography - Patrick Vieira
My Story - Charlie George
My Story - David O'Leary
Playing Extra Time - Alan Ball
Revelations of a Football Manager
    - Terry Neill
Rock Bottom - Paul Merson
Safe Hands - David Seaman
So Far So Good - Liam Brady
Soccer - David Jack
Tappy - Derek Tapscott
The Glory and the Grief - George Graham
To Cap It All - Kenny Sansom
True Grit - Frank McLintock
We All Live in a Perry Groves World
    - Perry Groves
You've Got to be Crazy - Bob Wilson

AVENELL ROAD

Arsenal's address for 93 years, Avenell Road is home to the famous East Stand and its Art Deco frontage, which can still be admired by visitors to the old stadium. The road has also been the starting point for Arsenal's trophy-winning sides' journeys from Highbury to Islington's town hall in Upper Street where they would be received by the borough's mayor.

Like the current Gunners side, the street has strong French connections. Avenell is a name that first reached England during the flood of immigration from France after the Norman conquest of 1066 and originates from Normandy. The street's exact origins are not clear, but it is believed most likely to have been named after the Avenell family from Sir Walter Scott's Waverley novel, *The Monastery*.

In 1840 the street became famous as the home to the new Church of England metropolitan training institution. By 1867 the institution became St John's Church of Divinity, which eventually gave Woolwich

Centre-forward David Jack heads for goal in the 1932 FA Cup Final defeat to Newcastle United at Wembley. He later wrote a celebrated book on his long, illustrious career, entitled simply *Soccer* (see Autobiographies).

Arsenal chairman Sir Henry Norris a 21-year lease to build a football ground on the land south of its college.

AWAY GAMES

FEWEST DEFEATS

Arsenal are the only side in modern times to go through an entire Premiership season unbeaten away from home. And they achieved it not once, but twice.

The first time was in the 2001/02 Premiership-winning season when they opened their account with a 4-0 demolition of Middlesbrough at the Riverside and ended it with a momentous 1-0 win at Old Trafford to clinch the title, Sylvain Wiltord scoring a priceless winner. The final record: played 19, won 14, drew 5 and lost 0.

Two seasons later, Arsenal won the title again, and again they were invincible on their travels. The campaign began, as in 2001, at the Riverside with a 4-0 victory, and the final trip was the short journey across London to Loftus Road where the Gunners beat Fulham 1-0 at their temporary home. Arsenal had won 11 times on the road and drawn the other 8 games.

In recent times another away campaign of note came in the 1990/91 season. Arsenal lost 2-1 at Chelsea in February, with Dennis Wise among the scorers, in their only league defeat of the season.

RECORDS

In addition to completing two entire Premiership campaigns without tasting defeat on the road, Arsenal have a clutch of other impressive statistics earned on their travels.

In 2001/02 Arsenal set a new record of eight successive away league wins, culminating in a 1-0 win at Manchester United on 8 May 2002.

Arsenal also set a Premiership record of scoring in 27 consecutive away games spanning the 2001/02 and 2002/03 seasons. In 2001/02 Arsenal also set a new Premiership record of 47 points earned away from home. The Gunners also hold the longest unbeaten away

Tony Woodcock remains the last Arsenal player to score five goals in an away match, against Aston Villa in 1983.

record in English top-flight football. Starting with a 1-1 draw at Aston Villa in April 2003, they next lost away from Highbury in October 2004 at Manchester United after 27 unbeaten games. The previous record of 23 was also set by Arsène Wenger's side in 2001/02 and 2002/03, a record that had beaten the previous biggest total of 22 set by Brian Clough's Nottingham Forest in 1978.

Arsenal's biggest away win was a 7-0 thrashing of Standard Liege in the Cup Winners' Cup in November 1993. In league competition, the 7-1 win at Aston Villa in December 1935, in which Ted Drake scored all seven goals, remains a Club record. The

Gunners' biggest win at Tottenham came in March that year when they won 6-0. Tony Woodcock was the last Gunner to score five goals away from home in any competition in a 6-2 win at Aston Villa on 29 October 1983.

Other record wins in various competitions have come up at Burnley in the FA Cup in 1937 (7-1), Staevnet in the Fairs Cup (7-1) in 1963, Scunthorpe and Plymouth in the League Cup (both 6-1) in 1968 and 1989 respectively, and Middlesbrough (6-1) in the Premiership on 24 April 1999. The Gunners' biggest win on the road in the Champions League was 5-1 at Internazionale in November 2003.

Golden Boys: Arsenal celebrate winning the league at Old Trafford after a 1-0 win over Manchester United in May 2002. It was the 19th, and last, away league fixture of the season and meant the Gunners became the first side to go through an entire season away from home unbeaten in the Premiership. They matched this remarkable feat two seasons later (see Away Games on page 21).

BAKER, Joe

Born **Liverpool, 17 August 1940**
Died **6 October 2003**
Arsenal appearances **156**
Arsenal goals **100**
International caps (England) **8 (3 goals)**

The England striker with the Scottish accent spent four swashbuckling years at Highbury, spanning the Billy Wright period from 1962 to 1966. Born in Liverpool, but raised north of the border in the town of Wishaw in Lanarkshire, near Motherwell, Baker was bought for £70,000 from Italian side Torino. He scored on his Gunners debut in a 2-1 win in the league at Leyton Orient in August 1962 and the goals never dried up. Baker was the Club's leading scorer for all four seasons, plundering exactly 100 goals and averaging a little under two every three games.

Goalscoring was in his blood; at his first club Hibernian, Baker chalked up an amazing tally of 159 goals in four seasons. He still has legendary status in Edinburgh for his four-goal haul in a 4-3 Scottish Cup win over Hearts. There was also a further nine goals in one match against Peebles Rovers in the same competition.

While Arsenal struggled to find consistency, and with the success of Bill Nicholson's Tottenham Hotspur up the Seven Sisters Road further highlighting the Gunners' woes, Baker bought glamour and incident to Highbury, memorably going in goal during one match at Leicester and getting sent off against Liverpool in a cup tie after going toe-to-toe with the huge defender Ron Yeats. He was brave, deadly, committed and a true character, all 5ft 8ins of him giving 100 per cent every game. It's just a shame his talents could not have shone in a better team and he eventually departed in March 1966 for Nottingham Forest.

Sunderland, Hibernian and Raith Rovers were all future destinations as, was Albion Rovers, where he was manager twice. A career as a publican and hospitality host at Hibernian followed before the sad news that he had died suddenly of a heart attack while playing golf in 2003.

BAKER'S DOZEN

Derbyshire-born utility man Alf Baker (born 27 April 1898, died 1 April 1955) holds a truly unique position in Arsenal's history. Although a right-half by trade, Alf is the only player to have ever played in all 11 positions for the Club – and skippered the side too. He took the captain's armband in Arsenal's first FA Cup Final appearance against Cardiff City in 1927,

Arsenal's manager Billy Wright (right) stands in front of the Clock End with Joe Baker on 2 July 1962 as they wait for a telephone call from Baker's former club Torino to conclude his transfer to Highbury. Baker went on to score 100 goals for the Gunners.

although the Gunners lost 1-0. That year 'Doughy' also won his solitary England cap against Wales.

His loyalty to the red cause was rewarded in 1930 when he was a member of the side that beat Huddersfield Town 2-0 at Wembley in the FA Cup Final. It came in the twilight of his career and after just one more game – his 351st for the Club, – he retired and later scouted for the Gunners.

BALL, Alan

Born **Farnworth, Lancashire, 12 May 1945**
Died **25 April 2007**
Arsenal appearances **217**
Arsenal goals **52**
International caps (England) **72 (8 goals)**

Alan Ball's capture from Everton in December 1971 sent the British transfer record tumbling. It proved money well spent with the red-headed England midfielder averaging nearly a goal every four games during his spell at Highbury.

As northern as tripe, flat caps and whippets, Everton and England midfielder Alan Ball shocked the soccer world when he made the long journey south in December 1971 for a then British record transfer fee of £220,000. He had been a World Cup winner shortly after his 21st birthday and was the inspiration behind Everton's 1970 title triumph before Bertie Mee decided to freshen up the Gunners' squad with a player of true class.

Initially reluctant to leave his native north west, the story goes that the Arsenal secretary Ken Friar took the precaution of intercepting his train journey to London at Watford Junction in case other possible suitors – notably, Manchester United and Manchester City – were waiting at Euston to put him on the next train back north.

Ball often found his new club's more direct style frustrating, constantly persuading skipper Frank McLintock to get the side to play through the midfield – a Plan B he felt would bring rich dividends in European competition.

With the Double squad slowly disintegrating, Ball's leadership qualities dragged the side through a period of transition, including the 1972 FA Cup Final defeat to Leeds and a league runners-up spot the following year, Ball firing Arsenal top in February that year with the winner at Liverpool before their challenge fell away.

That summer he took over the captain's armband from the departing Frank McLintock and revelled in his new responsibility as his influence grew. But injuries curtailed his powers and with quality being replaced with mediocrity in the squad, two successive relegation battles followed.

He captained his country for the first time when West Germany visited Wembley in 1975, memorably celebrating later that night at London club Tramps with a galaxy of stars, including Mel Brooks, Anne

Bancroft and 'Kojak' Telly Savalas, a typically flamboyant night for the hard-living, hard-working Ball. His love of gambling saw him buy a horse called Go Go Gunner, along with Peter Marinello, Charlie George and Stan Flashman (later to become the notorious chairman of Barnet FC). But with mounting debts, and a clash of footballing ideals with new manager Terry Neill, the diminutive Ball was soon gone, heading to Southampton – despite Bolton Wanderers and Leeds United bidding to take him back north – and he later played in north America.

Management saw him go back to his first club Blackpool and then Portsmouth, Stoke City, Exeter City, Southampton and Manchester City with varying degrees of success, before he took on less stressful media work.

Ball died of a heart attack at his Hampshire home, aged 61. He was the second of the 1966 World Cup-winning side to die, following Bobby Moore in 1993.

BANK OF ENGLAND CLUB

This nickname has been given to several big-spending clubs through the years, but it was Arsenal who were first dubbed the Bank of England Club, due to their open chequebook policy in the late 1920s and most of the 1930s. The tag stuck after the signing of David Jack from Bolton in 1928. The fee was £10,890 – doubling the previous record – and that was after Herbert Chapman had negotiated with Bolton Wanderers representatives while covertly ensuring they unknowingly drank plenty of alcohol. Critics accused Arsenal of buying success, overlooking the tactical acumen and motivational powers of the great Herbert Chapman, and even after his death in 1934 the tag remained in place.

With Arsenal's powers waning by the end of the decade, and debts piling up after the reconstruction of the Highbury stadium, the Gunners' board still sanctioned one final big transfer when they signed Bryn Jones as Alex James' long-term replacement. War clouds were looming over Europe, but it did not stop MPs in the Houses of Parliament debating the morality of Arsenal paying Wolverhampton Wanderers a world record of £14,000 for his services.

BARGAIN BUYS

Arsenal may have once been known as the Bank of England Club, but they have been known to pick up the odd bargain along the way...

PAT JENNINGS

An absolute steal in the summer of 1977. At the age of 32, he was deemed surplus to requirements at Tottenham and allowed to leave. Terry Neill stepped in with a cheeky offer – and he played on for eight more years, racking up 326 Gunners appearances including four major cup finals.

NICOLAS ANELKA

Enticed from hometown club Paris Saint-Germain when he was 17, French football's *enfant terrible* banged in 23 goals in 65 games for Arsenal and netted vital strikes in the 1998 Double-winning season before leaving for Real Madrid.

PATRICK VIEIRA

The fee seemed a huge risk at the time for an unknown 20-year-old – in hindsight it was a snip. Nine years later the Frenchman departed Highbury as skipper with three Premiership titles and four FA Cup medals, and Arsenal made a reputed 200 per cent profit in the process.

STEVE BOULD, NIGEL WINTERBURN AND LEE DIXON

The three arrived at Highbury within months of each other between 1987 and 1988 for a combined fee of just over £1m and each stayed for more than a decade as key members of the 'Famous Back Four', with ten titles and 38 years of Gunners' service between them.

PERRY GROVES

George Graham's first buy was one of the unsung heroes of Highbury. Bought from Colchester in 1987, the red-headed winger inspired Arsenal to the Littlewoods Cup in 1987 and won title medals in 1989 and 1991 – as well as cementing his place as a fans' favourite – before leaving for Southampton in 1992 for ten times the fee Arsenal paid for him.

JOHN HOLLINS

Supposedly washed up at 33 in July 1979, Hollins was on his way to Norfolk to sign for Norwich after 14 years at his beloved Chelsea before he got the call from Highbury and turned back to London. His dedication was impressive and he made 164 starts and even took the captain's armband on occasion, as well as setting impeccable standards for youngsters to follow.

EDDIE HAPGOOD

The Bristolian was snatched from Kettering Town in 1927 for a three-figure sum – and went on to become the most decorated player in the Club's history at the time, with five league titles and two FA Cups alongside the Gunners' captaincy. His suave good looks also made him an early marketing man's dream.

GEORGE GRAHAM

The Chelsea midfielder was seen as little more than a makeweight in the deal that took Tommy Baldwin to Stamford Bridge in 1966 – but it began an important association with the Club that would be reprised in the mid-1980s to bring the Gunners out of their slumber. Graham found his spiritual home at Highbury and won the Fairs Cup and the Double before leaving for Manchester United. He returned as manager in 1986 and won two titles, two league cups and the European Cup-Winners' Cup. He was possibly the biggest bargain of them all.

KOLO TOURE

Arsène Wenger's reputation for plucking jewels from obscurity was further cemented with the acquisition of Kolo Toure from Ivory Coast side, ASEC Mimosas. He arrived at Highbury after a short trial and, after a

season in the reserves, has been a first-team regular ever since, winning a Premier League title and two FA Cups.

BARNES, Walley

Born **Brecon, Wales, 16 January 1920**
Died **4 September 1975**
Arsenal appearances **292**
Arsenal goals **12**
International caps (Wales) **22**

Another player who lost his best years to the Second World War, Barnes excelled as a boxer, but chose football and signed for Southampton. Arsenal spotted him and he made his professional league debut in November 1946 against Preston North End.

Moved from inside-forward to right-back, Barnes won a league title medal in 1948 and an FA Cup winner's medal in 1950. Two years later he was forced out of the Cup Final defeat to Newcastle United after twisting a knee and as a result missed the entire following season, when Arsenal won their seventh title.

He retired in 1956 and enjoyed a successful media career as one of the BBC's most respected pundits right up to his sudden death in 1975.

BARNET FC

Most Arsenal fans have adopted Barnet FC as their second team due to the special relationship that the two clubs enjoy. Situated on the borders of North London and Hertfordshire, at the end of the Northern Line, their Underhill home also hosts Arsenal reserve team's Premier League South fixtures. Traditionally Arsenal also kick off their pre-season campaign every July with a match against the Bees at Underhill.

Barnet have enjoyed a colourful recent history. In 1985 the late Stan Flashman took over as chairman and he drafted in the ebullient Barry Fry as manager and between them they helped the Bees gain promotion from the Vauxhall Conference to the Football League.

They currently play in League Division Two and many Gunners fans choose to watch them when Arsenal are playing away. Due to planning constraints they are unable to redevelop their 5,500 capacity ground and have been actively looking to move elsewhere in the area, but without success. Many Arsenal fans have joined them in their campaign for a new home.

Like Arsenal, their traditional rivals also play in white (and are not too far from Tottenham) - Enfield v Barnet is seen by many as the second north London derby and the passion between the fans is equally fierce.

Another ex-Gunner - 1991 title-winner David Hillier - also briefly appeared for them in 2002/03, while former Wales Under-21 striker Adam Birchall, who began his career at Highbury in 2003, moved to Underhill from Mansfield in 2006.

Arsenal reserve games are generally played in the evenings and admission is free.

BARNWELL, John

Born **Newcastle, 24 December 1938**
Arsenal appearances **151**
Arsenal goals **24**

A stylish inside-forward, Barnwell signed from Bishop Auckland as a schoolboy.

One of his earliest memories was playing for an Arsenal side against the full England team who used to train midweek at Highbury. 'I remember thinking Stanley Matthews looked older than my dad - and he was,' he recalls.

He later played for his country when he won England Under-23 honours and moved to Nottingham Forest in March 1964.

He had moderate success as manager at Wolves and at AEK Athens and is now a respected figure throughout football as chief executive of the League Managers' Association.

BASTIN, Cliff

Born **Heavitree, Devon, 14 March 1912**
Died **4 December 1991**
Arsenal appearances **392**
Arsenal goals **176**
International caps (England) **21 (12 goals)**

Nicknamed 'Boy Bastin' on the terraces, the Devonian winger's career at Highbury spanned three decades and his goalscoring record of 178 goals would remain a Club best until Ian Wright finally beat it in 1997.

Herbert Chapman signed him from his local club Exeter City as a raw 16-year-old, in 1928, after just 17 games, when he scored six times, including two on his home debut against Newport County. He was reluctant to leave his home comforts and, after a day being trailed around Exeter by a desperate Chapman,

Cliff Bastin attempts a flying shot against Bolton Wanderers at Highbury on May Day, 1937. The Devonian winger was one of Herbert Chapman's greatest signings, winning five titles and two FA Cups in the glorious thirties.

he finally decided to put pen to paper only after strict consultation with his mum while she cooked the evening dinner. Many years later he would tell respected journalist Brian Glanville – who penned his autobiography *Cliff Bastin Remembers* – that he was more interested in a tennis match he had to play that night.

Chapman threw him straight into the starting line-up on the left wing and he was an almost instant success. He played a part in all of the Gunners' success in the 1930s – five league titles and two FA Cups – and represented England on 21 occasions, a low figure perhaps, but one that highlights the strong competition for places in a golden era for the national side. In 1932/33 he and wing partner Joe Hulme scored an astonishing 53 goals between them – Bastin scoring 33 from the wing – as Chapman won what would be his final title before his untimely death the following January.

Bastin had exceptionally quick feet, as well as the sharpest of footballing brains and pace to burn. He also made his name as a speciality penalty taker, rarely missing from the spot when called upon. The legendary Hugo Meisel, the 'father' of Austrian football and the power behind the formation of the World Cup, once lamented that if Bastin had been Austrian *his* country, and not Italy, would have won the competition in 1934.

When war broke out in 1939 Bastin was in his prime, still three months short of his 28th birthday, but his career was effectively over. He was excused military service due to poor hearing – he was virtually deaf – but that did not stop Benito Mussolini's Fascist government claiming Bastin, who was famous across Europe, had been captured in the Battle of Crete. Bastin was, in fact, manning an air raid post at Highbury, where he was stationed with Arsenal trainer Tom Whittaker.

When peace broke out Bastin tried to resume his playing career, but after just six more games he retired from football at New Year 1947 due to a long-term leg injury picked up in 1939. On retirement Bastin courted controversy with his forthright views in his autobiography, which upset a number of former colleagues, including Alex James. He later moved back to Devon to run a pub where he was a local hero. Exeter City recently named their new 4,000-capacity terrace the Cliff Bastin Stand in his honour. He died in 1991 at the age of 79.

BATTLE OF HIGHBURY, The

One of the most bruising encounters ever to take place at Highbury involved an England side with no less than seven Arsenal players in the starting line-up against world champions Italy on 14 November 1934. Coming just five months after the second ever World Cup Final, in which Italy beat Czechoslavakia, it was seen by many, especially the English media, as the 'real' World Cup Final.

The 'Arsenal Seven' who represented the Three Lions that day were Frank Moss, George Male, Eddie Hapgood, Wilf Copping, Ray Bowden, Ted Drake and Cliff Bastin. The trainer was Arsenal's man with the sponge, Tom Whittaker, who later managed the Club in 1947. No club has ever provided so many players in the starting line, although Manchester United provided five and two substitutes against Albania in 2001. The four other players who took the field for England that day were Stanley Matthews – winning his third cap for his country – Eric Brook, Jack Barker and Cliff Britton.

Five of the 'Arsenal Seven' who lined up for England against Italy in November 1934 in the infamous Battle of Highbury. From left to right, on a snowy Highbury day two months later, are Cliff Bastin, goalscorer Ted Drake, George Male, Eddie Hapgood and Wilf Copping. Frank Moss and Ray Bowden made up the seven.

A crowd of 56,044 was present and it took only two minutes for the first moment of controversy, when Gunners striker Drake broke Luisito Monti's foot with a late tackle. The incensed Italians made it their priority to gain suitable retribution and what ensued, according to one witness, was a free-for-all. This had come after Eric Brook had missed a penalty in the opening 60 seconds.

England, though, swept into an astonishing 3-0 lead, when, with only a quarter of an hour played Brook made up for his spot-kick woes by scoring twice and Drake hit a third. The hosts were temporarily reduced to ten men when Arsenal full-back Hapgood, never one to shirk a scrap, was smashed in the face by a stray Italian elbow at a free-kick.

Many good judges still felt Austria were the best team in the world - their coach, the legendary Hugo Meisel, said they would have won the World Cup had Bastin been an Austrian - but the Azzuri showed all their better qualities after the break and came within a whisker of earning a point. Milanese legend Giuseppe Meazza - who gives his name to the stadium used by AC Milan and Internazionale - struck twice and then hit the bar with England pegged back in their half. Only a miraculous save from Arsenal custodian Frank Moss late on denied Meazza a deserved hat-trick - and the visitors an equaliser.

The England dressing room, revealed Whittaker years later, was like a war zone. Hapgood's nose was broken, two-goal Brook had fractured his arm, Drake needed stitches in a nasty leg wound and John Barker had a bruised hand inflicted by an Italian boot as he lay on the floor.

The media were incandescent at the Italian's rough-house tactics and there were even calls for the FA to suspend all internationals against non-UK countries. Back home, the Italians were hailed as heroes and are still remembered as the 'Lions of London'. Highbury had not seen anything quite like it.

BEARDS

A list of facially endorsed persons who've played in red and white:
Ian Allinson
George Armstrong
Brian Chambers
George Graham (had a moustache for a brief time in the early 1970s)
John Hawley
Caesar Llewellyn Jenkyns
John Jensen
Ray Kennedy
John Matthews
Robert Pires
Kevin Richardson
Kenny Sansom
David Seaman
Peter Storey
Alan Sunderland
Kolo Toure

Kolo Toure sports perhaps the most fashionable beard and moustache ever seen on a Gunners' face.

Right Dennis Bergkamp took the field one last time during his testimonial match - the first game ever staged at the Emirates Stadium - when Arsenal played host to his first club, Ajax, on 22 July 2006.

BERGKAMP, Dennis

Born **Amsterdam, The Netherlands, 10 May 1969**
Arsenal appearances **345 (78)**
Arsenal goals **120**
International caps (The Netherlands) **79 (37 goals)**

No signing has come close to offering the excitement and expectation that followed news of the arrival of Dennis Bergkamp in the summer of 1995. He had topped most fans' wish lists, but surely a player of his class was even out of Arsenal's league. Apparently not, as he was unveiled along with England captain David Platt as an unexpected double capture from Serie A.

Bergkamp had endured a nightmare two years at Internazionale, being played out of position, and was desperate for footballing freedom. He got it at Highbury. Inter's president Massimo Moratti snarled, 'Arsenal will be lucky if he scores ten goals for them.' It took eight Premiership games for Bergkamp to get off the mark, but once that majestic double strike came against Southampton he never looked back.

Blessed with the guile, cunning and technique associated with the very best players at the very top of their game, the former Ajax youth player fitted into Bruce Rioch's side like a glove and scored a thrilling winner against Bolton Wanderers in the final home game of his first season to secure UEFA Cup football for 1996/97.

Rioch was sacked shortly before the start of the following season, but new boss Arsène Wenger continued Bergkamp's rehabilitation. In August 1997 he scored a stunning hat-trick at Leicester City, described by BBC pundit Alan Hansen as the best treble he had ever seen. He was at his irresistible best as Arsenal won the league title and the FA Cup and he scored the goal of the tournament in France 98 with his late winner against Argentina for the Netherlands, instantly

controlling a 70-yard pass before firing home with ice-cool precision. That season he came third in the FIFA World Player of the Year awards and won the PFA Footballer of the Year and Football Writers' Player of the Year awards as Wenger asked, 'Is there a better player in the world? I don't think so.'

He had enjoyed a fruitful partnership with Ian Wright - the pair becoming firm friends on and off the field - but when the veteran striker left the Dutch schemer just carried on creating goals for his next strike partner, Nicolas Anelka.

He announced his retirement from international football in 2000, the travelling becoming too much for him as he made public his famous fear of flying. But on the pitch he was untouchable and won another Double in 2002, as well as scoring the goal of the season with a mind-boggling effort in a 2-0 win at Newcastle, flicking the ball goalwards and then spinning past his marker to coolly finish, displaying the skills and vision that separated him from mere mortals.

He was again in superb form the next season and joined the 100 Club in January 2003 in a 2-0 win over Oxford United at Highbury in the FA Cup. Bergkamp said, 'It was a very special moment for me to score my 100th goal for Arsenal. It was historical for both me and the Club... It doesn't matter who the goal came against, it's 100 goals in all competitions and it's a very proud moment for me in my career.' Later that same month Bergkamp reached 300 games for the Club and celebrated with a goal in a 2-2 draw with Liverpool at Anfield. Another title came in 2004 as Arsenal went unbeaten, sandwiching two more FA Cup triumphs.

It is a sign of Arsenal fans' obvious affections for the Dutchman that, in the latter stages of the 2005/06 season, the fans held a Dennis Bergkamp day when West Bromwich Albion visited Highbury. Fittingly Arsenal won 3-1 with Bergkamp netting the third goal. Arsenal fans, as the song goes, have been 'walking in a Bergkamp wonder-land' for 11 years. It was his last goal for the Club before retiring, although he did pull on the red and white one last time for his testimonial, when 54,000 fans flocked to the new Emirates Stadium on 22 July 2006 to see Arsenal beat his first love, Ajax Amsterdam, 2-1. Bergkamp returned to Ajax,

when he accepted an invitation from new coach Marco van Basten to take up a trainee coaching role in September 2008.

Van Basten said: 'It is important for Ajax to have as much quality as possible and it is obvious that Dennis has qualities.'

KSK BEVEREN

In 2001 Arsenal established a five-year deal with Belgian outfit Koninklijke Sportkring Beveren as a continental nursery club, on a much larger scale to the arrangement the Club had with Margate in the 1930s.

KSK are based in East Flanders. Their greatest achievement came in 1979 when they reached the semi-finals of the Cup-Winners' Cup, beating Internazionale on the way, before losing to Barcelona. Several prominent Belgium internationals have played for KSK, notably 1980s goalkeeper Jean-Marie Pfaff.

The partnership has seen some of the cream of Africa's young players - mainly from the Ivory Coast - head to Belgium for experience. In return for technical support and loan players from the Highbury reserve and youth ranks, Arsenal can allow the youngsters to develop in a competitive European league. Emmanuel Eboue was the first Beveren player to officially make the move to Arsenal while Yaya Toure, younger brother of Arsenal defender Kolo, has also spent time at Freethiel Stadion. Many young Gunners have gone the other way, notably players such as Liam Chilvers, while Graham Stack and John Halls both moved across the North Sea for successful loan spells in the Jupiler League.

BIRTHDAY

Arsenal Football Club was 'born' on 25 December 1886 when players from the unofficial Dial Square FC, founded two months before, met at the Royal Oak public house next to Woolwich Arsenal Station, in south east London. They were all workers

from the nearby munitions factories and almost certainly chose the name Royal Arsenal after their place of work, although it has been suggested it was an amalgam of their work and the name of the pub.

On that day the members also decided on the main colour of the kit - red - after Nottingham Forest kindly donated the new club's first set of jerseys, after a begging letter from co-founder Fred Beardsley, who had previously played for Forest. It was also decided to play their home games at nearby Plumstead Common and their first match as an 'Arsenal' side was against neighbours Erith on 8 January 1887, the game ending 6-1 to the hosts.

Arsenal held a series of celebrations on the Club's centenary in 1986, with George Graham's young side doing their bit by leading the First Division at Christmas. On 27 December the Gunners invited dozens of players from the past, notably Joe Mercer, Ted Drake and George Male, the only surviving player from the Chapman era, to watch the Young Guns beat Southampton 1-0, Niall Quinn scoring the only goal of the game.

In October 2005 a plinth was erected at the site of the old Woolwich Armament Factory to commemorate the birthplace of London's most successful football club.

BLACK PLAYERS

With the sons of West Indian and African post-war immigrants slowly making their names in football in the 1960s and 1970s, Arsenal were rightly in the forefront.

Brendan Batson, born in Grenada in the West Indies, was the first black player to play for the Arsenal first team in the season following the Double. But his chances were limited, with the full-back making only ten appearances before moving to West Bromwich Albion, via Cambridge United where he made his name

Right Paul Davis was one of the first black players to represent the Club. He won every domestic honour with Arsenal.

alongside other black trailblazers such as Cyrille Regis and Laurie Cunningham. However, his efforts helped inspire a new generation of young black British stars.

By the early 1980s, black players were making inroads into the Arsenal team. Islington-born **Raphael Meade**, a powerful striker, made himself a hero when he scored on his debut at Panathinaikos in the UEFA Cup and netted 16 goals in 32 Gunners starts before moving on. Another local boy, **Chris Whyte**, was cementing his place in the Gunners defence while graceful midfielder **Paul Davis** made an instant impression with his elegance in the middle of the park. By the late 1980s he would form a magnificent

midfield triumvirate with fellow south Londoners **Michael Thomas** and **David Rocastle**. They were joined in 1984 by **Viv Anderson** – the first black player to represent England – who became the Club's outstanding right-back before he broke fans' hearts with a move to Manchester United after three great years. With Rocastle the jewel in the midfield crown, it was his good friend Thomas who would score the greatest goal in the Club's history with the dramatic late effort at Anfield in May 1989 that brought the title back to Highbury for the first time in 18 years.

Then came the greatest entertainer of them all, the irrepressible **Ian Wright**. Black,

bold and brash with the talent to back it all up and a smile that would so often light up Highbury, his unique goalscoring style and ebullient nature made him a true hero of the 1990s. In just six years he managed to break Cliff Bastin's 60-year-old Club goalscoring record and he became the epitome of cool with his swaggering nature and outlandish dress sense. But most importantly, his deep affection for the Club shone through and he enjoyed a fantastic rapport with the Highbury crowd.

In 2005/06, Arsenal's two England internationals were black Londoners – **Ashley Cole** and **Sol Campbell** – while teenage prodigy and surprise England World Cup squad member **Theo Walcott** heads up the new generation. And a contender for the title of Club's greatest-ever skipper was a Frenchman born in Dakar, the capital of Senegal. **Patrick Vieira**'s authority, strength and skills made him one of the leading black sporting role models for nine glorious years at Highbury. Black players are now common-place in the Arsenal squad, with another striking hero, **Thierry Henry** – a Frenchman born to West Indian parents who broke Wright's record – the latest in a long line to help push the Club on to further glories. Arsenal's scouting network is also bringing the cream of African talent into Highbury with the likes of **Kolo Toure**, **Emmanuel Eboue** and **Emmanuel Adebayor** proving that the only colours that matter at Highbury are the red and white of the shirt.

Arsenal is a keen supporter of the Kick It Out organisation, formerly based in Islington, which campaigns to end racism in football.

BLOOMFIELD, Jimmy

Born **Kensington, London, 15 February 1934**
Died **3 April 1983**
Arsenal appearances **227**
Arsenal goals **56**

During the trophy drought of the late 1950s, the slim Londoner emerged as one of the Gunners' few stars. Signed from relegated Brentford for £8,000 in 1954, he made his debut that August against Everton, but didn't become a regular in the side until the following season when his insatiable attitude for hard work and superb passing skills proved the fulcrum of Arsenal's side. He won England Under-23 caps and also played in the London XI that lost the first Inter-Cities Fairs Cup Final against Barcelona in 1959.

He also turned in an inspirational performance against Manchester United in February 1958, which was the last time the Busby Babes played in England before Munich, when Bloomfield scored one himself and set up another in a barn-storming Highbury affair that ended in a 5-4 United win.

He left the Club in 1960 for Birmingham City and later forged a highly successful managerial career at Leyton Orient (twice) and Leicester City. He died suddenly of a heart attack in 1983, aged 49, while he was a member of David Pleat's coaching staff at Luton Town.

BOARD OF DIRECTORS, The

PETER HILL-WOOD - Chairman
Followed in the footsteps of his father Denis and his grandfather Samuel, when appointed chairman in 1981. The family's involvement with the Club stretches back to 1919.

DANIEL FISZMAN - Director
A successful diamond dealer and Arsenal fanatic who has worked almost ex-clusively on the move to Emirates Stadium since 1999.

KEN FRIAR OBE - Director
Joined the Club as an office messenger boy in 1950 when he was just 12 years old. He has held the positions of assistant club secretary, club secretary and managing director (1983/2001). He put his retirement on hold to oversee the Emirates Stadium project along with Daniel Fiszman.

SIR CHIPS KESWICK - Director
A former director of the Bank of England and ex-chairman of Hambros Bank, he was elevated to the board in November 2005.

LORD HARRIS OF PECKHAM - Director
Conservative member of the House of Lords and chairman of Carpetright PLC, he was appointed to the board in November 2005.

LADY NINA BRACEWELL-SMITH - Director
Appointed to the board in 2005. Her father-in-law Sir Guy Bracewell-Smith was Gunners chairman from 1949 until 1962, when he was replaced by Denis Hill-Wood.

SIR ROGER GIBBS - Director
Joined the Board in 1980 at the age of 46. He has enjoyed a successful career in banking and was knighted in recognition of his extensive charity work for the Wellcome Trust.

Peter Hill-Wood has been Arsenal chairman for 25 years. His family's long association with the Club stretches back far longer, with grandfather Samuel becoming a board member in 1919 - six years before Herbert Chapman's appointment.

RICHARD CARR - Director
A barrister who joined the board at the same time as his older brother life president Clive Carr. He is now heavily involved in the youth development side of the Club.

CLIVE CARR - Life vice president
Mr Carr also joined the Board in 1980 and is the grandson of former chairman Sir Robert Bracewell-Smith. He is a hotelier by profession and had an interest in London's famous Park Lane hotel.

BOARDROOM, The

The Arsenal board of directors bade goodbye to the famous oak-panelled boardroom at Highbury in 2006 - but those same oak panels were taken out and installed in the new boardoom at Emirates. Situated directly above the dressing rooms in the old East Stand, the Highbury room is Grade I listed and the huge oak table that dominated it had been host to some of the most important decisions in the Club's history since 1936.

Among the room's more unusual items was a five-legged chair which was purpoted to have been made to prevent its incumbent from nodding off and falling backwards during meetings! Since before the Second World War, flowers in the colour of the visiting team have been used to adorn it on matchday, while since 1945 a roast dinner consisting of chicken or beef has been served there before every Sunday fixture.

Outside the boardroom was a specially commissioned shield to commemorate the Gunners' three successive title triumphs, between 1933 and 1935.

BOREHAM WOOD FC

Boreham Wood FC, formed in 1948, play in the Southern Football League Division One East. Their Meadow Park is a neat, tidy stadium that hosts Arsenal Ladies' home games. Its capacity is 4,502, with 500 seats and cover for more than 1,500 fans. Meadow Park is generally recognised in ladies' football to be the hardest ground in the country to visit due to Arsenal's strong home record and overall superiority in the modern game. It has become a fortress for the Gunners, also hosting all the Club's games in the Women's UEFA Cup.

Under the arrangement, an Arsenal XI men's side visits Meadow Park as part of the pre-season programme. The last time the Gunners played there was on 4 August 2006 when two goals from Arturo Lupoli set up a 4-0 win for the visitors.

In April 2007 Arsenal Ladies finally sealed England's first ever Women's UEFA Cup success at the ground when they drew 0-0 with Swedish side Umea IK in the second leg of the Final, to win the tie 1-0 on aggregate and take the trophy.

BORING, BORING ARSENAL

Boring Arsenal, lucky Arsenal... we've heard it all before. But why the reputation and where did it start? You have to go back to the 1930s when Arsenal first earned the tag.

Under revolutionary manager Herbert Chapman the Gunners became the first side to play counter-attacking football, allowing tactically naive opponents to push forward and leave gaps at the back. Then, with the opposition playing such a high line, legendary schemer Alex James would produce pinpoint passes out of defence to release pacy wingers Cliff Bastin and Joe Hulme. They would then cross for the likes of clinical strikers Jack Lambert and, later, Ted Drake to ruthlessly score past woefully exposed goalkeepers. The better team, as Chapman and successor George Allison would constantly remind their players, was the one that scored the most goals.

Opposition fans, frustrated at watching their side attack for long spells but with no end product, concluded Arsenal were 'lucky' to withstand such an onslaught and then score a goal themselves. Arsenal, they claimed, were

Arsenal captain Tom Parker (third left) keeps a tight grip on the FA Cup as he and his team-mates parade the Club's first trophy around Wembley after their 2-0 victory over Huddersfield Town in April 1930; (left to right) Cliff Bastin, Charlie Preedy, Tom Parker, Bill Seddon, Joe Hulme and Jack Lambert.

'boring' as they sat back and invited pressure. But to say Arsenal were boring was wrong. In the first title-winning season of 1930/31, for example, Arsenal fired 127 goals and conceded 59 as they chalked up a record 66 points (under the two points for a win system). Incredibly, runners-up Aston Villa managed to score one more - but conceded 78!

By now, though, the reputation had stuck and, being the dominant side of the inter-war years, other fans - notably in the north - would accuse Arsenal of having all the luck. In 1948, media and opponents were quick to criticise Tom Whittaker's defensive-minded title-winners as the Arsenal manager made subtle changes to shore up a leaky defence.

This continued through the years as Arsenal were again dubbed lucky for their Double-winning season of 1971. Again, George Graham's sides of the late 1980s and early 1990s had that accusation levelled at them - and again could feel aggrieved to say the least, top scoring in 1989 and 1991 title triumphs.

Since Arsène Wenger's arrival the cries of 'lucky Arsenal' have all but died due to a series of magnificent, entertaining seasons, although lazy Fleet Street sub-editors will dust it off for a cheap headline on the odd occasion. In any case, as Graham said in 1994 after yet more cries of 'boring' from Arsenal's detractors, 'I really don't care if we're not liked - it's part of our history.'

BOULD, Steve

Born **Stoke on Trent, 16 November 1962**
Arsenal appearances **329**
Arsenal goals **8**
International caps (England) **2**

Recruited from his hometown club Stoke City in 1988, Bould became part of Arsenal's 'famous four' defensive line-up, with Tony Adams, Nigel Winterburn and his former team-mate at the old Victoria Ground, Lee Dixon.

An inelegant but effective stopper, the tall centre-half gradually worked his way into the starting line-up at the expense of David O'Leary. Once installed he also became an effective attacker with his ability to cause a nuisance of himself at the near post by flicking on Brian Marwood's corners to devastating effect. Cool and unflappable, his importance grew by the year. He won two titles in 1989 and 1991, and reached new heights with a man-of-the-match award in the Cup Winners' Cup Final in 1994 against Parma.

With the arrival of Arsène Wenger many thought his days at Highbury were numbered, but he benefitted from the techniques brought in by the Frenchman and although his appearances became rarer he still never let the side down. He was a member of the squad that won the Double in 1998 and famously set up Adams with a chipped through ball for the final goal in Arsenal's 4–0 win over Everton to clinch the title at Highbury.

He moved to Sunderland the following year but injury forced him to retire in 2001. Since then he has moved back to Arsenal as a valued coach at the club's Academy, guiding the Under-18s to the semi-final of the 2007 FA Youth Cup where they lost to Manchester United over two legs.

BOXERS AND JOCKEYS

Highbury hosted a series of bizarre matches between boxers and jockeys back in the 1950s. The friendlies, always keenly contested affairs, drew good crowds with all proceeds going to the Sportsman's Aid Society. So popular were the matches that they became an annual fixture in the

sporting calendar, with members of the Arsenal first-team squad normally refereeing. The jockeys played in Arsenal home shirts and the boxers in Spurs kit. Denis and Leslie Compton both took charge of games and racing luminary Sir Gordon Richards was usually one of the linesmen with a leading figure from the boxing fraternity running the other line.

On 2 April 1951 the fixture had the honour of being the first match to be played under floodlights at Highbury. In 1959 and 1960 – the last year of the fixture – the two sporting professions joined forces to take on a team of entertainers which included West End star Tommy Steele and future James Bond Sean Connery. Arsenal commemorated

those rich and colourful games when they designated the Champions League match against Ajax in December 2005 a 'Boxers and Jockeys' themed day.

BOXING

Highbury hosted one of the truly great boxing encounters on 21 May 1966 when Muhammad Ali visited the capital for his second bout against London's finest boxer of the time, Henry Cooper. The pair had first met in 1963 when the little-known Cassius Clay – as he was known before converting to Islam – shocked Wembley by

Left Steve Bould deals with another opposition attack during the 1997/98 season. A physical centre-back with a speciality for thundering, sliding tackles, he is now a coach at the Club's Academy.

Right Workmen prepare Highbury for the big fight between Henry Cooper and Muhammad Ali in May 1966. Over 45,000 people turned out for a memorable encounter, which Ali won in the sixth round.

claiming victory, even after Cooper had put him down in the fourth round with a thunderous left hook.

Three years on a crowd of 45,973 packed out Highbury for the much-anticipated re-match against Ali, by now a world-famous figure. Childhood Arsenal fan Cooper – whose devastating punch was dubbed 'Enry's 'Ammer' – had been brought up in the East End and even used the same physio as the Club.

Then Club secretary Ken Friar recounted in later years, 'We had to apply for a theatre licence from Islington Council to stage the event … The whole pitch was re-seeded and renovated before it was boarded over. We must have been working 18-hour days on something that was completely different to what we were all used to at Highbury. Having said that, when the fight got underway it was an unforgettable occasion.'

That it was, with 32-year-old Cooper challenging Ali for his world heavyweight crown. Hollywood's heavyweights were also in attendance: Lee Marvin, George Raft and Laurence Harvey enjoying north London's hospitality. The fight, unfortunately for English hopes, went to form, with a deep gash above Cooper's left eye forcing referee Tommy Little to stop the fight one minute and 38 seconds into the sixth round of an absorbing contest.

BRADSHAW, Harry

Manager **1899/1904**
Born **circa 1854**
Died **1924**

The former Burnley manager enjoyed a successful five-year reign at Woolwich Arsenal from 1899 to 1904 and finally put London on the footballing map after more than a decade of Lancastrian dominance.

He had taken over a Club with falling attendances and precarious finances, but led them to their first ever promotion and oversaw huge changes in the

structure of the Gunners. He bought in Gravesend goalkeeper Jimmy Ashcroft, who would become the Club's first ever England international and kept 17 clean sheets in 34 games in 1901/02 when Arsenal finished the season in fourth place in the Second Division, their best position to date. They finished one place higher the next season and a year later were runners-up, securing promotion for the first time in the Plumstead outfit's 17-year history.

Bradshaw, whose two sons Joseph and William also played for the Club, then shocked the fans when he accepted a financially lucrative offer from chairman Henry Norris to take over Fulham FC (a few years later Norris would be a key figure in Arsenal's history – see Norris, Henry on page 154). Bradshaw won back-to-back Southern League Division Two titles with the Cottagers in 1906 and 1907 before they were accepted into the Football League.

BRADY, Liam

Born **Dublin, Ireland, 13 February 1956**
Arsenal appearances **294 (12)**
Arsenal goals **59**
International caps (Republic of Ireland) **72 (9 goals)**

Liam Brady is one of the very few Gunners who, prior to the arrival of the likes of Dennis Bergkamp and Thierry Henry, could unquestionably be described as world class. What a mouth-watering prospect it would have been for the Dubliner to have played in Arsène Wenger's line-up, a perfect foil for Patrick Vieira in the midfield, linking deliciously with Bergkamp to send defenders into a panic, or simply dropping inch-perfect, 60-yard passes over a retreating defence for Thierry Henry to run on to.

While it is easy to get carried away with some of those sensational individuals who Arsenal fans have been fortunate to witness in red and white, there is still a compelling argument that Brady remains the greatest player ever to have re-

presented the Club. Spotted as a slightly built, floppy-haired, 13-year-old in his native Ireland, Arsenal snapped up his burgeoning talents before any other club – and many were reputedly sniffing around – could snare him.

An early report on a young Brady by the Arsenal coaching staff claimed, 'He has a left foot that practically talks.' In six seasons Brady's talent shone like a beacon in an Arsenal side by and large treading water. His performances in the midfield were both consistent and out-standing, showing a grace and balance rarely seen in the English game. On his day, his influence could be compared with that of George Best at Manchester United or Kenny Dalglish at Liverpool. He would have been too good for most sides on the planet and certainly was for an Arsenal team that flirted with relegation and too often settled for mediocrity. But as the 1971 Double side slowly disbanded, Brady led a new breed driving through the Highbury youth system and, along with fellow Irish lads Frank Stapleton and David O'Leary, forged a young generation of 'green Gunners'.

He could skip past several challenges with the minimum of fuss – and maximum grace – and would more often than not decide matches with a moment of genius. As Arsenal slowly improved under Terry Neill – another component of the Irish revolution at Highbury in those heady days of the late 1970s – a stunning, swirling exocet of a goal in a famous 5-0 win at Tottenham remains one of the truly iconic Arsenal images as Brady, so much better than anyone else on the field, raced towards the delirious Arsenal fans to celebrate. And then came the 1979 FA Cup final, when he failed to score but had a hand in all three Arsenal goals as they beat Manchester United 3-2 in the most exhilarating Final since a Stanley Matthews-inspired Blackpool illuminated the Empire Stadium in 1953. He would pick up the PFA Player of the Year award as well.

Right Liam Brady shows superb balance to skip past a challenge during the 1979 Charity Shield against Liverpool at Wembley. He is now in charge of Arsenal's future stars.

Jimmy Brain was the first player to score more than 100 times for the Club - and it all started with a goal on his debut against the old enemy, Tottenham.

Like his compatriot from the north of Ireland, Best, he was robbed of the opportunity of playing in a major competition at a time when his country was suffering from a dearth of talent. By now the ambitious 23-year-old had outgrown his team and needed new challenges. Serie A beckoned.

His final season at Highbury ended in heartbreak with two cup finals lost in the space of four days – Brady missing a penalty in the Cup-Winners' Cup shootout with Valencia – and he soon departed for Juventus. In seven years Brady became one of the most successful foreign players in Italy, scoring the goal that won Juve the 1982 Scudetto against Catanzaro, before turning out for Sampdoria, Internazionale and Ascoli. He briefly returned to England with West Ham – even scoring once against Arsenal – before managerial spells at Brighton and Hove Albion and Celtic. But his 'home' was always Highbury and he returned in the 1990s, where he remains head of the Club's youth development, in recent years credited for nurturing the talents of England left-back Ashley Cole and Spaniard Cesc Fabregas (see The Academy on page 7).

BRAIN, Jimmy

Born **Bristol, 11 September 1900**
Died **1971**
Arsenal appearances **231**
Arsenal goals **139**

The first player to score 100 goals for the Club, Jimmy Brain started his career in Wales with Ton Pentre before moving to north London in 1923. In his time at Highbury he comfortably averaged more than a goal every two games and ingratiated himself with the fans when he scored against Tottenham on his league debut in October 1924.

The following season he struck 34 goals and another 31 came during the next campaign as he forged a lethal strikeforce with the legendary Charlie Buchan. But after losing his place to Jack Lambert, the Bristolian made the short move to Spurs for £2,500 in 1931, scoring just ten times in 47 games over the next three years.

He later moved back to Wales with Swansea City and then to hometown club Bristol City. After retiring from playing in 1937 he managed Cheltenham Town.

BRIEF ENCOUNTERS

There have been a number of brief encounters between Arsenal and players over the years, but few were as unlucky as Sidney Pugh, a young half-back who had impressed at nursery club Margate. He made his Gunners debut on 8 April 1939 at Birmingham, but broke his leg shortly into the game and by the time he was fully fit again, war had broken out. He died on 15 April 1944 when the Wellington bomber he was travelling in crashed in Staffordshire. He was one of nine Arsenal staff to die during hostilities.

In October 1997, Arsenal were taken to extra-time in the League Cup by Birmingham City. On came J. Crowe, who was seen as one of the more promising youngsters at the Club, but just 33 seconds later he was shown a straight red card – off for a high tackle in his one and only appearance.

Another fleeting first-teamer was Andy Cole, a legend at Newcastle United and a Champions League winner at Manchester United. The Nottingham-born forward's sole contribution for the Gunners, however, was six minutes as a substitute, hitting the side netting against Spurs in a 0-0 draw in the 1991 Charity Shield, before moving to Bristol City.

An inexplicable cult figure is Siggi Jonsson, who made only two starts for Arsenal in 1989/90 – scoring in a 3-0 win over QPR – before injury put paid to a hugely anticipated Highbury career.

But none of these compare to Clive Allen, signed on 12 June 1980 by Arsenal manager Terry Neill, who told the press his new £1m teenage striker had signed for the Club 'for a very, very long time'. Still smiling, and putting a fatherly arm around the lad – with his real dad Les watching proudly from the sidelines – Neill added, 'Our supporters deserve the best and that is what, I believe, we have given them in signing Clive.' Two months later he was a Crystal Palace player, a suitable carrot for the Eagles as Neill effectively swapped him for England left-back Kenny Sansom. He never played a competitive game for Arsenal.

BROTHERS

Ten sets of brothers have represented Arsenal, the most famous being Denis and Leslie Compton, who both represented the Club either side of the Second World War (see The Compton Brothers on page 52). Their joint highlight was playing a part in the 1950 FA Cup Final. The Buists were the first brothers to play for the Gunners, Robert playing for Woolwich Arsenal between 1891 and 1894 and George then spending the 1896/97 season at the Manor Ground. William and Joe Bradshaw were with the Club until both left in 1904, while David and Andrew Neave were pre-First World War Gunners, along with Willis and Thomas Rippon and Charles and Joe Satherwaite, the former scoring Arsenal's first ever top-flight goal in September 1904. In the 1950s Danny and Denis Clapton both had stints with the Club, Danny making 233 appearances. The first foreign brothers were Icelandic: Valur and Stefan Gislason spending the 1996/97 season together at Highbury. Essex-born Tommy and Michael Black both spent a considerable amount of time at Arsenal in the 1990s, Michael playing in the Champions League in 1998, while there is currently one pair of brothers with the Club – England Under-21 right-back Justin Hoyte and his younger sibling Gavin, who has been making steady progress in the reserves.

BRUSSELS

Arsenal have played in two European finals in the Belgian capital. In 1970 they lost 3-1 to local side RSC Anderlecht at the Constant Vanden Stock Stadium in the first leg of the Inter-Cities Fairs Cup Final, although Ray Kennedy scored late on to give Arsenal a glimmer of hope for the second leg. The Gunners won 3-0 back in north London to take the trophy 4-3 on aggregate. Ten years later Arsenal were back in the city, this time to take on Valencia CF in the Cup-Winners' Cup Final at the Heysel Stadium. on this occasion the Gunners drew 0-0 before losing 5-4 on penalties to the Spaniards, Graham Rix missing the deciding penalty.

Five years later the Heysel Stadium disaster shook the football world when 39 people were killed during violent clashes between Liverpool and Juventus fans prior to the European Cup Final. In 1995 the stadium was rebuilt at a cost of approximately £30m and renamed the Boudewijnstadion (in Flemish) or Stade Roi Baudouin (in French). In English it is now known as the King Baudouin Stadium.

BUCHAN, Charlie

Born **Plumstead, London, 22 September 1891**
Died **25 June 1960**
Arsenal appearances **120**
Arsenal goals **56**
International caps (England) **6 (4 goals)**

Arsenal's first superstar spent two spells with Club and was one of the few players to have played in Woolwich and Highbury. Born in Plumstead, the tall, elegant centre-forward joined his local side Woolwich Arsenal at the age of 18 in December 1909, but he left without playing a first-team game after a spectacular fall out with manager George Morrell over expenses.

It was the Gunners' loss as he went on to become the outstanding player of his generation, moving to Clapton Orient before finding fame and fortune at Sunderland,

Charlie Buchan, the Arsenal skipper, leads his side out. Buchan was the Club's first true superstar and a player many good judges believe would have made it in any era. After retiring the south Londoner became a respected journalist.

where he became a Wearside legend. They would win the First Division title in 1913, inspired by Buchan, who would go on to be the club's leading scorer for seven successive seasons between 1913 and 1924, excluding the war years when competitive football was suspended. He netted 209 times – still a Sunderland record – before Arsenal finally re-signed him in 1925.

He was 34 at the time, but manager Herbert Chapman still paid £2,000 for the player, plus £100 per goal for his first season. He doubled his fee by scoring 20 times in that first season at Highbury. The visionary duo of Buchan and Chapman would invent Arsenal's famous 'WM' formation – still used by the Brazilians 45 years later in their 1970 World Cup success – to exploit the new offside rules that had been brought in. Buchan's finest hour in a Gunners shirt came in 1927 when he skippered his side to the FA Cup Final, although defeat to Cardiff City hurt hard as it was his last chance of a medal.

His 56 goals in 120 Arsenal games – coming in his mid-30s – fully justified Chapman's outlay and Buchan retired in 1928 a hero, his last game a 3-3 draw at Everton in which Dixie Dean hit a famous hat-trick for the Toffees to reach 60 goals for the season.

Buchan later became one of the most respected football journalists in the world, his magazine *Charlie Buchan's Football Monthly* a veritable bible for all young soccer-mad lads in the 1950s. He passed away while on holiday in Monte Carlo in 1960, at the age of 68.

BUSTS

A bust of the former Arsenal manager Herbert Chapman stood in the splendid marble hall entrance of Arsenal's stadium at Highbury for more than 70 years. The monument to one of football's greatest innovators was the work of the famous American-born sculptor Jacob Epstein and was commissioned shortly after Chapman's sudden death in January 1934. The old boardroom also housed a bust which was of the late Denis Hill-Wood, former chairman and father of the clubs current chairman Peter Hill-Wood.

CAMPBELL, Kevin

Born **Lambeth, London, 4 February 1970**
Arsenal appearances **164 (62)**
Arsenal goals **59**

Kevin Campbell netted 94 times in just 89 reserve games before being unleashed on the First Division in 1990/91 – scoring eight goals in a vital 10-game spell to help secure the title. He was expected to be the club's main striker of the 1990s, but soon found himself down the pecking order. He played his part in the 1993 League Cup and FA Cup Double success and the European Cup-Winners' Cup a year later, but never regained his early promise and moved to Nottingham Forest in 1995.

Campbell later played for Trabzonspor in Turkey and returned to England to plunder 45 goals for Everton before winding down his career at West Brom and Cardiff.

Since retiring he has set up his own record label, 2 Wikid.

CAMPBELL, Sol

Born **Newham, London, 18 September 1974**
Arsenal appearances **195 (2)**
Arsenal goals **11**
International caps (England) **73 (1 goal)**

A powerful defender who crossed the north London divide in 2001 to join Arsenal, Campbell had been skipper at Spurs after switching from centre-forward to centre-half early in his White Hart Lane career. He made his England debut against Hungary in 1996 and continued to develop into one of the country's outstanding defenders before moving to Highbury on a Bosman free transfer.

In his first season as a Gunner, he won both Premiership and FA Cup winners'

medals and became the senior defender at the Club when stalwart Tony Adams retired. In 2003 he suffered an injury towards the end of the season which scuppered the Gunners' title chances and he missed the FA Cup Final win over Southampton. He was back the next season as Arsenal went the entire campaign unbeaten to win another title and he starred for England in Euro 2004, having a goal disallowed in the semifinal against hosts Portugal. Campbell's performances were also recognised by UEFA, who named him in their tournament all-star team.

Former Tottenham Hotspur skipper Sol Campbell rocked the north London football world when he moved to Arsenal on a Bosman free transfer in 2001. Here Campbell (airborne) celebrates scoring a goal at Newcastle.

In 2005 an injury in a league match in February against Manchester United ended his season early and Philippe Senderos took his place for the FA Cup Final win over the Red Devils. Injuries continued to affect him in 2005/06 as Senderos and Kolo Toure cemented their defensive partnership and Wenger rebuilt his side.

Articulate, intelligent and thoughtful, Campbell goes against the grain of stereo-

typical footballer and has acting aspirations when he retires. After five years, Sol left the Club following the World Cup finals in July 2006 for a fresh challenge with Portsmouth, and the move paid off when he skippered the South Coast outfit - whose assistant manager is another former Gunners centre-half, Tony Adams - to success in the 2008 FA Cup final, beating Cardiff City 1-0 at Wembley.

Kenny Sansom (right) tussles with Spurs' Glenn Hoddle in a north London derby at Highbury in the early 1980s. Sansom remains Arsenal's most capped English player - and he skippered the Club until 1988.

CAPS – Most Capped Gunners

Patrick Vieira, who left the Club in the summer of 2005, won more caps while an Arsenal player than anybody else, with 79. The former Highbury skipper made his debut for France on 26 February 1997 in a 2-1 win over the Netherlands. He was also the second Arsenal player to appear in a World Cup Final, coming on as a substitute to join club-mate Emmanuel Petit in Les Bleus' 3-0 win over Brazil at the Stade de France on 12 July 1998. He set up the third French goal, scored by Petit.

Kenny Sansom remains the most capped Englishman with 77 appearances for the national side between 1980 and 1988. He was England's most capped full-back until Stuart Pearce's 78th appearance in 1999. Sansom scored just once for his country, in a World Cup qualifier against Finland in 1984. His last cap came in a 3-1 defeat against the Soviet Union at the European Championships in 1988.

CAPTAINS

The Club's first trophy-winning captain was right-back **Tom Parker**, who led the side to the 1930 FA Cup Final win and the first league title the next season. He left the Club in 1933 after 294 matches and 17 goals to be replaced by legendary schemer **Alex James** and, later, left-back **Eddie Hapgood**, who skippered the side for the rest of the 1930s, winning five titles and two FA Cups in total. Hapgood also skippered England to their famous 3-2 win over world champions Italy in the Battle of Highbury in 1934 (see Battle of Highbury) and then to a controversial 6-3 victory over Germany in Berlin four years later. Renowned for his never-say-die mentality, he was a tough man to replace.

After the Second World War came the legendary **Joe Mercer**, who many claim is the greatest skipper in Arsenal's history. Despite his advancing years he captained Arsenal to the 1950 FA Cup Final, an emotional win which he described as the greatest day of his life, and the 1953 title.

Inspirational Double-winning captain Frank McLintock (centre) is carried on the shoulders of Charlie George (left) and Pat Rice at the end of the 1971 FA Cup Final. For many, the Scot is the best skipper in the Club's history.

In 1952 he led Arsenal to the Cup Final, but his side lost to Newcastle United. Afterwards he famously said in the post-match interview, the greatest honour in sport was to captain the Arsenal. He put off his retirement on more than one occasion, but a broken leg against Liverpool in 1953/54 finally ended his remarkable career. As he was stretchered off he raised a hand to wave goodbye to Highbury and many a grown man reputedly shed a tear when he was carried down the tunnel.

George **Eastham** was one of Arsenal's most popular skippers in the 1960s, before **Frank McLintock** was given the captain's armband by manager Bertie Mee. The Scotsman was Mee's right-hand man on the pitch and commanded total respect. 'He was an amazing, inspirational leader,' says his former team-mate and coach, Don Howe. 'Frank never knew when he was beaten.' After winning the Fairs Cup he skippered the side to the Double by showing all of his leadership qualities to pick up his men after going a goal down in extra time of the FA Cup Final against Liverpool. He had lost the four previous Wembley finals he had played in, but put personal misery aside for the good of the team and he finally picked up his winner's medal thanks to goals from Eddie Kelly and Charlie George.

Full-backs **Pat Rice** and **Kenny Sansom** then led the team competently before **Tony Adams** became the Club's youngest captain in January 1988 at the age of just 21. He would remain in the role for the next 14 years, like McLintock laying himself on the line time after time for the red and white cause. Despite numerous personal problems and ridicule from opposing fans for his ungainly style, Adams became the most successful skipper in Arsenal history, winning four titles, two league cups, three FA Cups and a European Cup-Winners' Cup. He also holds the unique distinction of winning titles in three different decades, all with Arsenal, as he remained at Highbury proving himself to be a one-club man - a magnificent achievement in the current game. Since then three Frenchmen have worn the armband. **Patrick Vieira** led Arsenal to the Premiership in 2004 and the FA Cup in 2003 and 2005, although he did not play in the former due to injury but still lifted the trophy. After his departure to Juventus in the summer of 2005, **Thierry Henry** was handed the captaincy and in his first season skippered the Club to the UEFA Champions League Final. He also led the club into their inaugural campaign at the new Emirates Stadium. When Henry left for Barcelona in 2007, his friend and international colleague **William Gallas** was appointed the Club's new skipper.

CARDIFF

In recent years Arsenal may have enjoyed their trips to Cardiff - appearing in four FA Cup Finals in the city's magnificent Millennium Stadium and winning three of them - but the Welsh capital's only professional club gave Arsenal one of their most frustrating days.

On 23 April 1927 Cardiff City were the Gunners' opponents in the FA Cup Final and won 1-0, courtesy of Hughie Ferguson's goal 16 minutes from time. His weak shot somehow evaded Arsenal goalkeeper Dan Lewis - ironically a Welshman - who let the ball slip through his fingers and trickle over the line. Lewis was inconsolable and threw his loser's medal away in frustration at his costly error. It is the only time the Cup has left England.

The last occasion the two clubs met in the FA Cup was in January 2006, when Arsenal won 2-1 at Highbury. The game was watched by Derek Tapscott, a popular figure who played for both clubs in the 1950s. Sadly, Tapscott died in June 2008.

CARLING CUP – Losers 2007

Arsenal faced Chelsea in the first ever all-London Final of the League Cup, sponsored by Carling, on 25 February 2007. Arsenal had got to Cardiff in style, with no home draw until the penultimate game of their run but getting superb away results, winning at West Bromwich Albion (2-0), Everton (1-0) and then, most impressively of all, 6-3 at Liverpool, with Julio Baptista netting four.

The Gunners met arch-rivals Tottenham Hotspur in the semi-final - 20 years after the two sides had met in an epic Littlewoods Cup semi-final, which Arsenal had won after the two-legged tie had gone to a third game. This time Arsenal earned a 2-2 draw at White Hart Lane in the first leg before winning 3-1 after extra time in the second to set up a meeting with the west Londoners in the Final.

Throughout the Carling Cup campaign manager Arsène Wenger had adopted a policy of fielding mainly youth and reserve players and, despite calls to reinstate senior stars such as Thierry Henry for the big game, he stuck with those who had propelled the club to their first League Cup Final since 1993. The average age of Arsenal's outfield players was under 21.

One of those youngsters, 17-year-old Theo Walcott, gave Arsenal the lead after 12 minutes to reward the Gunners for an excellent start to the game during which their crisp passing style had the more experienced Chelsea chasing shadows for long periods. Didier Drogba levelled for the Blues eight minutes later but Arsenal continued to dominate with Abou Diaby, Cesc Fabregas and Jeremie Aliadiere all going close to restoring the lead.

The quality of Arsenal's play at Cardiff's Millennium Stadium enthralled much of the 70,073 crowd, but after an hour their young legs began to tire and Chelsea's older heads began to take control. Drogba scored the winner for Chelsea after 84 minutes with a powerful header, and the game ended in ugly fashion with red cards for Arsenal's Emmanuel Adebayor and Kolo Toure along with Chelsea's John Obi Mikel.

Wenger, though, was upbeat at the end of the game, 'I'm very proud of the performance of my team... For long periods we were the better team but the regrets we have are that we should have put this game beyond Chelsea.'

CELEBRITY FANS

SPORT

James Anderson (cricketer)
Stuart Barnes (ex-rugby player) – 'Thierry Henry would be a world star at rugby too'
Martin Brundle (ex-F1 driver) – 'My earliest sporting memory is watching Arsenal because my dad was from Islington'
Thomas Castaignède (rugby union player)
Frankie Dettori (jockey)
Audley Harrison (boxer)
Lennart Johannsson (President of UEFA)
Jan Molby (ex-footballer) – 'Arsenal have always been my team. I started supporting them for the 1971 FA Cup Final back home in Denmark'

Jacob Oram (cricketer)
Ian Poulter (golfer)
Ferenc Puskas (ex-footballer) – 'I remember as a boy growing up in Hungary that there was only one club for me – Arsenal'
Michael Watson (ex-boxer)
Frank Warren (boxing promoter)

TV/BROADCASTING

Clive Anderson (presenter and writer)
Kathy Burke (actress)
Alan Davies (actor and comedian)
Ainsley Harriot (TV chef)
Paul Kaye (comedian, writer and actor)
Matt Lucas (comedian)
Rory McGrath (comedian)
Dermot O'Leary (presenter)
Linda Robson (actress)
Bradley Walsh (actor)
Tom Watt (writer, actor and broadcaster)

MEDIA/LITERARY WORLD

Melvyn Bragg (broadcaster)
Maurice Gran (comedy writer)
Brian Glanville (sports journalist)
Nick Hornby (author)
Sir Nicholas Lloyd (journalist)
Laurence Marks (comedy writer)
Piers Morgan (journalist)
Andrew Motion (poet laureate)

POLITICS

Fidel Castro (president of Cuba)
Kate Hoey (MP)
Aleksander Kwasniewski (Polish president)
Brian Mawhinney (MP and chairman of the Football League)
Sir Trevor Phillips (chairman of the Campaign for Racial Equality)
Chris Smith (MP)

MUSIC

Roger Daltrey (The Who)
Ray Davies (The Kinks)
Dido
Steve Earle
Tony Hadley (Spandau Ballet)
Judge Jules (DJ)
Gary Kemp (Spandau Ballet)
Martin Kemp (Spandau Ballet)

John Lydon (ex-Sex Pistols)
Gilles Peterson (DJ)
Gavin Rossdale (Bush)
Pete Tong (DJ)
Shovell (ex-M People)

HOLLYWOOD STARS

Kevin Costner
Colin Firth
Spike Lee
Demi Moore
Freddie Prinz Jr
David Schwimmer
David Soul
Joanne Whalley-Kilmer

CELTA DE VIGO

Arsenal formed a 'technical partnership' with the Spanish club on 2 December 2005. The initial deal was set to run for three years and is similar to the relationship with Belgian club KSK Beveren. Former Arsenal left-back Silvinho, now at Barcelona, is a link between the two clubs after he moved from Highbury to the Estadio de Balaidos in 2001. Another more recent link is striker Quincy Owusu-Abeyie, a graduate of the Academy, who left Highbury for Spartak Moscow back in January 2006 and is currently on loan with Celta.

Arsène Wenger explained exactly what the link-up will do – and how it will benefit both clubs. 'There will be an exchange of coaches and scouting,' he said. 'It could also happen that some of their young players spend a little time with us and some of our young players spend a little time with them. We chose Celta because we have good relations with them – that goes back to the Silvinho transfer. Also they do serious work with the youth teams and have a great youth set up. They are well known in Spain for having an excellent scouting system, so we can take advantage of that too.'

The city of Vigo is in Galicia in the north west of Spain near the Portuguese border and their traditional rivals are close neighbours Deportivo La Coruña.

CENTENARY

Arsenal celebrated its 100th birthday on Christmas Day 1986. On Boxing Day the Gunners drew 1-1 at Leicester City wearing a special centenary shirt, the last to be manufactured by kit supplier Umbro, to mark the occasion. The following day the Club hosted a centenary party at Highbury with many past stars, including the likes of Ted Drake and Tom Parker, being presented to the fans. The celebrations continued that afternoon as Arsenal beat Southampton 1-0 to maintain the leadership of the Today League Division One.

CHAMPIONS

1931

W 28 D 10 L 4 F 127 A 59 Pts 66*
This was the first time the title went south of Birmingham. It was won at a canter with a record 66 points (in the days of two points for a win) and 127 goals scored, including 60 away from Highbury.

1933

W 25 D 8 L 9 F 118 A 61 Pts 58*
A 3-1 victory over Chelsea at Stamford Bridge on 22 April 1933 clinched Herbert Chapman his second championship, putting the Gunners out of reach of nearest rivals Aston Villa, who had been hammered 5-0 at Highbury earlier in the month. Cliff Bastin scored twice after David Jack hit the opener in front of the biggest English league crowd of the season – more than 74,000. It helped to exorcise the embarrassment of an FA Cup third round defeat at Walsall in January.

1934

W 25 D 9 L 8 F 75 A 47 Pts 59*
A second successive title was tinged with sadness. Herbert Chapman did not live to see Arsenal complete their third championship after he died of pneumonia in January. Arsenal lost three of their four matches immediately following his death, but rallied sufficiently on a tide of emotion to finish four points clear of Chapman's other great love, Huddersfield Town.

1935

W 23 D 12 L 7 F 115 A 46 Pts 58*
A hat-trick of titles – equalling Huddersfield's achievement under Chapman in the early 1920s – was sealed thanks largely to the goalscoring prowess of Ted Drake. The season started with an 8-1 win over Liverpool, Drake scoring three, at fortress Highbury with other notable home wins including 7-0 v Wolves (Drake 4), Leicester 8-0 (Drake 3) and Middlesbrough 8-0 (Drake 4). The former Southampton striker ended the season with a record 42 league goals.

1938

W 21 D 10 L 11 F 77 A 44 Pts 52*
The last championship of Arsenal's golden era saw the Gunners stumble over the line

Arsenal team group 1931: (back row, left to right) assistant manager J Shaw, H Cope, Ralph Robinson, W Allison, Jimmy Brain, Charles Preedy, A Haynes, Herbie Roberts, W Harper, W Seddon, Dan Lewis, George Male, R Parkin, assistant trainer W Milne (middle row, left to right) J Williams, L Thompson, W Maycock, Alf Baker, B Diaper, Cliff Bastin, Eddie Hapgood, H Lewis, Bob John, Jack Lambert (front row, left to right) Joe Hulme, Tom Parker, manager Herbert Chapman, trainer Tom Whittaker, David Jack, Charlie Jones. The trophies are (left to right) the Northampton Hospital Shield, the 'Evening News' Cricket Cup, the League Championship trophy, the Sheriff of London's Shield, the Charity Shield and the Combination Cup.

after Wolves, a point ahead on the final day of the season, surprisingly lost 1-0 at Sunderland. Arsenal had beaten Bolton 5-0 at Highbury on the same day to take the title by a point. It was Arsenal's last piece of silverware for ten years.

1948
W 23 D 13 L 6 F 81 A 32 Pts 59*
Tom Whittaker's first title as manager was won with almost a month to spare courtesy of a 1-1 draw at Huddersfield. The Gunners were tagged 'lucky' and 'boring' for their defensive tactics, but they dominated from start to finish - winning 11 of their opening 13 matches - despite a spirited late run by Matt Busby's Manchester United.

1953
W 21 D 12 L 9 F 97 A 64 Pts 54*
Arsenal's tightest title yet was won on the final day of the season when Burnley were beaten 3-2 at Highbury. Alec Forbes, Doug Lishman and Jimmy Logie gave Arsenal victory and the championship after they finished with an identical record as second-placed Preston North End - 21 wins, 12 draws and nine defeats. However, Whittaker's side just scraped over the line first on the perplexing goal average system used in those days. Arsenal's goal average was 1.51, compared to North End's 1.41.

1971
W 29 D 7 L 6 F 71 A 29 Pts 65*
The first stage of the Double was clinched at White Hart Lane on 3 May 1971 when Ray Kennedy's last-minute header gave Arsenal a 1-0 win - and the title. Five days later Charlie George's winner beat Liverpool 2-1 in the FA Cup Final to emulate the Spurs Double of 1961.

1989
W 22 D 10 L 6 F 73 A 36 Pts 76
The most dramatic climax to an English league season ever: Arsenal beat Liverpool 2-0 at Anfield with Michael Thomas scoring in the second minute of injury time on Friday 26 May to bring the title south for the first time in 18 years. George Graham's side had gone to Anfield

needing to win by two clear goals - winning the title with the same goal difference as Liverpool, but having scored more goals.

1991
W 24 D 13 L 1 F 74 A 18 Pts 83†
Arsenal lost just one league game all season - at Chelsea - to clinch a second title in three years. Liverpool's defeat to Nottingham Forest meant they could not catch the Gunners, who celebrated with an Alan Smith hat-trick to beat Manchester United 3-1 at Highbury later that day.

1998
W 23 D 9 L 6 F 68 A 33 Pts 78
Arsène Wenger's first title was earned in thrilling fashion after Marc Overmars put Arsenal in the driving seat with the winner at nearest rivals Manchester United in March. The title was won after Arsenal beat Everton 4-0 at Highbury, Tony Adams memorably scoring the fourth as Wenger's side produced a series of brilliant displays in the run-in. Wenger became the first foreign manager to win the English title.

2002
W 26 D 9 L 3 F 79 A 36 Pts 87
Arsenal continued their habit of winning the championship at the homes of their main rivals when Sylvain Wiltord scored the only goal to beat Manchester United at Old Trafford. Arsenal had been runners-up for the previous three years, but set a new Club record with an 87-point haul. The Double was clinched with a 2-0 win over Chelsea in the FA Cup Final.

2004
W 26 D 12 L 0 F 73 A 26 Pts 90
A remarkable season, as Arsenal went the entire league campaign unbeaten, the first club to do so since Preston North End in 1889. On a tense final day, with the title already wrapped up, ex-Gunner Paul Dickov gave relegated Leicester the lead at Highbury, but Arsenal went on to win 2-1 with skipper Patrick Vieira scoring a late winner.

* 2 points for a win.
† 2 points deducted for disciplinary reasons.

CHAMPIONS LEAGUE

Arsenal have qualified for every Champions League competition since 1998/99 and are one of only three English club sides to have reached the final, losing to Barcelona in Paris in May 2006. The Gunners also set a tournament record by keeping ten successive clean sheets in the 2005/06 season. Until then Arsenal's previous best performances had come in 2000/01 and 2003/04, when they reached the quarter-final stage.

Here is a rundown of the Gunners' complete record in the competition:

1998/99 - GROUP STAGES
Arsenal's first foray into the Champions League saw the club play home matches at Wembley in order to satisfy the huge demand for tickets. The first ever tie was on 16 September when they drew 1-1 at Racing Club Lens. The French side put the final nail in the coffin of Arsenal's hopes with a 1-0 win at Wembley in front of 73,707 people - the largest ever 'home' crowd in the Club's history.

In the interim Arsenal's first Champions League win came against Panathinaikos, Martin Keown scoring a late winner in a 2-1 victory. Arsenal's first away win in the competition came on Matchday Six, with a 3-1 at Panathinaikos, the only other win of their first Champions League campaign.

1999/2000 - 1ST GROUP STAGE
Wembley again hosted all Arsenal's home games during this campaign, and again an average in excess of 70,000 fans flocked to all three matches against Fiorentina, Barcelona and AIK Solna.

Fiorentina and Barcelona both beat the Gunners in north west London, 1-0 and 4-2 respectively, but the Swedes were beaten 3-1, a game notable for Thierry Henry's first ever European goal in a Gunners shirt. Arsenal drew in both Florence and Catalonia, while ending another disappointing campaign with a 3-2 win in Sweden. Arsenal finished third in the group and entered the UEFA Cup.

2000/01 - QUARTER-FINALS
Arsenal progressed comfortably from the First Group Stage after three wins and a

superb 1-1 draw at Lazio courtesy of Robert Pires' late leveller. The Second Group Stage started horrendously with a 4-1 loss at Spartak Moscow, but home wins over Lyon and Spartak, along with a Highbury draw against Bayern Munich and another point in France, saw them scrape through to the last eight. Thierry Henry and Ray Parlour earned Arsenal a 2-1 home win over Valencia before John Carew's lone goal put the Spaniards through to the semi-finals on away goals after the tie finished 2-2 on aggregate.

2001/02 - 2ND GROUP STAGE
Arsenal were as devastating at home as they were awful across the Channel. Highbury wins over Schalke 04, Panathinaikos and Malaga earned Arsenal nine points after defeats to all three on their travels. But it was enough to put the Gunners through to the Second Stage

where they went out - again due to abysmal displays on their travels - despite thumping home wins over Juventus (3-1) and eventual finalists Bayer Leverkusen (4-1). A 2-0 home reverse against Deportivo La Coruña ultimately proved Arsenal's downfall.

2002/03 - 2ND GROUP STAGE
A 2-0 home win over Borussia Dortmund followed by a 4-0 demolition of PSV in Eindhoven - Gilberto scoring the fastest goal in Champions League history - helped Arsenal finish top of a group also containing Auxerre, where Arsenal would win 1-0 to enhance an improving away record in Europe. But the Gunners came unstuck in the second group, despite opening with an astonishing 3-1 win at AS Roma courtesy of a Thierry Henry hat-trick. It would be their only win in the group, old European

nemesis Valencia and Ajax qualifying for the knockout stages.

2003/04 - QUARTER-FINALS
A late winner from Wayne Bridge at Highbury gave Chelsea a 2-1 win on the night - and a 3-2 aggregate victory - to knock Arsenal out at the quarter-final stage. The campaign had started poorly with a 3-0 home defeat to Internazionale, and after taking just one point from their next two away games at Lokomotiv Moscow and Dynamo Kiev they looked down and out. But a 1-0 home win over Kiev was followed by a fantastic 5-1 win at Inter and Arsenal finished top when they wrapped up the group stages with a 2-0 home win victory over Lokomotiv.

The Gunners overcame Celta de Vigo comfortably in the last 16 before Chelsea earned a famous victory after a 1-1 draw at Stamford Bridge to break red and white hearts in the big London derby.

Arsenal moved their Champions League games from Highbury to Wembley for two seasons during the late 1990s in a valiant attempt to satisfy the huge demand for tickets. The decision was vindicated as crowds averaged 70,000.

2004/05 - 1ST KNOCKOUT STAGE

Arsenal finished top of their group ahead of PSV, Panathinaikos and Rosenborg - thumping the Norwegians 5-1 in the final group game - and remained unbeaten going into the knockout stages where they met Bayern Munich.

On a shocking night in Bavaria, Arsenal performed poorly and limped to a 3-1 defeat, needing to win 2-0 in the return at Highbury. Thierry Henry gave Arsenal the lead with a brilliant opportunist effort, but it wasn't enough and the Germans went through.

2005/06 - RUNNERS-UP

This was a season to defy all expectations. While Arsenal's Premiership form was patchy, in Europe it was a different story with Arsène Wenger's side winning at Ajax, Sparta Prague and FC Thun to top the group unbeaten.

In the first knockout stage, an outstanding 1-0 win at Real Madrid - Thierry Henry scoring a fantastic winner at the Santiago Bernabeu - followed by a heart-stopping 0-0 draw at Highbury put Arsenal through to a quarter-final against Juventus, where Cesc Fabregas ruined Patrick Vieira's return to Highbury by

scoring one and setting up the other in a 2-0 win over a Juve side who ended the game with nine men on the pitch.

A 0-0 draw in Turin earned Arsenal a last-four showdown with the other surprise package of the tournament, Villarreal. Kolo Toure scored the only goal of a tense first leg in north London and a last-gasp save from Jens Lehmann - denying Juan Riquelme's spot kick in stoppage time - earned a goalless draw in Spain and a place in the final.

The Champions League Final

Barcelona were Arsenal's opponents at the magnificent Stade de France, but hero Lehmann's final was over after just 18 minutes when he was sent off for a professional foul on Samuel Eto'o, who was hauled down when through on goal.

It didn't deter the Gunners and Sol Campbell defied the odds by heading them into a half-time lead, while Thierry Henry and Fredrik Ljungberg both spurned chances to make it 2-0. Arsenal had kept ten successive clean sheets - a competition record - and were on the verge of an historic win before Eto'o finally hauled Barca level 14 minutes from time. Barca were in the ascendancy and reserve keeper Manuel

Almunia - who replaced Lehmann after coming on as a sub for Robert Pires - was beaten again four minutes later by Juliano Belletti to send the trophy to Catalonia.

Arsenal's magnificent run had ended in heart-breaking fashion.

2006/07 - 1ST KNOCKOUT ROUND

After the previous year's exploits hopes were high that Arsenal could go one stage further and win the trophy in 2007. After four straight victories - including a 2-1 home win over Dinamo Zagreb in the first-ever competitive match at Emirates Stadium - Arsenal qualified for the knockout stages with a 0-0 draw in Porto.

The Gunners were drawn against PSV Eindhoven and were beaten 1-0 in the first leg in the Netherlands. In the return match, Brazil defender Alex turned the ball into his own net to hand Arsenal the lead and square the tie, but he quickly made amends by heading the equaliser and putting PSV through 2-1 on aggregate.

To add to the disappointment, it also turned out to be Thierry Henry's final appearance in an Arsenal shirt as he picked up a stomach injury, which ended his season prematurely.

2007/08 - QUARTER FINALS

Arsenal cruised through the Group Stages after wins home and away against Sparta Prague in the Third qualifying round had ensured a tenth successive Champions League campaign. Group H began with a stirring 3-0 victory over Sevilla but the highlight was a stunning 7-0 home win over another Czech side, Slavia Prague. Theo Walcott netted twice at Emirates as the Gunners went top of the group but a 1-3 reverse in Seville, coupled with a 0-0 draw in Prague, meant Arsenal finished in second place behind the Spaniards despite ending with a 2-1 home win over Steaua Bucharest.

In the first knockout stage holders AC Milan earned a goalless draw in the first leg in north London but Arsenal were

Jens Lehmann beats out Villarreal midfielder Juan Riquelme's last-minute spot-kick in the Champions League semi-final second leg in April 2006 to send Arsenal through to their first final in the competition.

irresistible at the San Siro and won 2-0, courtesy of goals from Cesc Fabregas and Emmanuel Adebayor to set up an all-Premier League quarter-final against 2005 winners Liverpool.

The two sides drew 1-1 at Emirates but despite a stunning opening half-hour of football from Arsenal, in which Abou Diaby gave the visitors the lead at Anfield, Liverpool roared back to take a 2-1 lead after goals from Sami Hyypia and Fernando Torres. Substitute Theo Walcott's 80-yard run and cross set up Adebayor to make it 2-2 and put Arsenal into the lead on the away goals rule with six minutes to play. Incredibly Liverpool hit back again with two goals in the final four minutes - a Steven Gerrard penalty and a shot under the goalkeeper from the speedy Ryan Babel during a counter-attack - to win the game 4-2 and leave the Londoners heartbroken.

CHAPMAN, Herbert

MANAGER 1925/34
Born **Sheffield, Yorkshire,**
19 January 1878
Died **6 January 1934**

Herbert Chapman is quite simply the greatest visionary the English game has ever seen.

His managerial career began at Northampton Town in 1907, where he became the first notable player-manager – 80 years before it was fashionable. This innovation was the first of many for the no-nonsense Yorkshireman. He won three successive titles with Huddersfield Town before taking on the challenge at Highbury in 1925.

His first game in August ended in a 1-0 home defeat to Tottenham, but results would soon pick up with star signing Charlie Buchan finding the net regularly as Arsenal ended the season in second place. The following year they reached their first FA Cup Final, losing 1-0 to Cardiff City.

Chapman implemented the 'WM' formation in response to changes in

the offside law, which would become standard for most clubs for the next 40 years. Arsenal would, in time, become the most fearsome attacking side in English football because of his changes. He could also spot talent, drafting in teenage winger Cliff Bastin from Exeter who, in time, would become the Club's leading scorer for nearly 60 years. Goalkeeper Frank Moss was another who was plucked from obscurity to international stardom.

Chapman was not afraid to spend money too, and broke the transfer record for Alex James, who would become a Club legend. He then guided Arsenal to their first trophy with the FA Cup in 1930 and the title came the following year.

He was relentless in his pursuit of excellence to improve Arsenal and the game in general. Long before they were commonplace he proposed white footballs, floodlit matches, artificial surfaces and numbered shirts. He also erected a 45-minute clock so the crowd knew how long had been played. The FA were unimpressed and ordered it to be taken down. It said he was undermining the referee, but the suits had missed the point - the clock was changed to a 60-minute timepiece and was present at Highbury up until 2006. Chapman was simply trying to make the sport more user-friendly in an age when the fans were treated like cattle. However, they had no objections to him managing the England team for a 1-1 draw in Italy in 1933. He was the first professional manager to coach the national side.

He also insisted on improving facilities at Highbury and was instrumental in the redevelopment of the ground, which started in the 1930s, culminating in the East and West stands and a roof over the North Bank. Chapman then managed to persuade London Underground to change the name of Gillespie Road to Arsenal station to put the Club on the map - literally! It was a public relations coup of staggering proportions.

He was also an advocate of special diets, an almost alien concept to the 1930s footballer, and had a strict training regime that had to be adhered to.

In 1933 he secured a second title and added white sleeves to the red shirts to

Herbert Chapman - a true football legend. Young protégé Cliff Bastin once said he should have been prime minister.

make the Gunners' kit distinctive, another innovation that lasts to this day.

But on the morning of 6 January 1934 at the age of 55 pneumonia claimed him just 12 hours before a home game with Sheffield Wednesday. Dedicated to the end, he ignored doctor's orders by insisting on watching the third team play, despite nursing a heavy cold. His condition deteriorated rapidly and he never recovered.

By then, he had made Arsenal the best side in England, and the team went on to win a third title that year and another in 1935.

In 2003 Chapman was inducted into the English Football Hall of Fame and a blue plaque was unveiled in 2005, at 6 Haslemere Avenue, Hendon, where he lived from 1926 until his death. His bust sat in the marble halls at Highbury until 2006.

As Bastin said after his death, 'There was an aura of true greatness about him. He should have been prime minister.'

CHAPMAN'S STARS

While **Charlie Buchan** retired before the successful 1930s, his influence helped move the Club in the right direction. Chapman had the utmost respect for the Londoner and was grateful for both his goals on the pitch, and his input and wisdom off it.

Chapman's love of pacy wingers saw **Joe Hulme** arrive at Highbury in 1926, a man in the Marc Overmars mode, blessed with phenomenal speed he would be perfect for Arsenal's counter-attacking style away from Highbury. Along with **Cliff Bastin**, picked up on the cheap from Exeter after just 17 games at St James' Park, their blistering runs down both flanks would cause havoc among opposition defences.

Eddie Hapgood and **George Male** – both signed by Chapman – would be a considerable full-back partnership for Arsenal and England throughout the 1930s, while England goalkeeper **Frank Moss** could be excused his occasional eccentricities with his superb handling and incredibly bravery.

The heartbeat of the team, however, was **Alex James**, one of Scotland's famous Wembley Wizards. Chapman understood man management better than anyone and mindful of the little midfielder's importance to the side – and his fiery temperament – would give him a wide berth to get the best out of him.

Chapman's team then had the talented, wily forward **David Jack** at its sharp end to finish off the many chances that came his way. The former Bolton striker, who cost a world record £10,890 when he came to Highbury, was consistently the Club's leading scorer until he departed in 1934, winning three titles and an FA Cup while at Highbury.

By then Chapman was dead, but he had already laid the foundations for the glorious 1930s.

CHARITIES

Arsenal have raised millions of pounds for charity since forming the Arsenal Charitable Trust in 1992 with funds being distributed annually to local causes subject to the approval of the Trustees. In addition, the Club adopts a charity for the season. The first 'Arsenal charity', ChildLine, was adopted in the 2003/04 campaign, and proved such a success that the link was extended until the summer of 2005. Over the two-year period, Arsenal's fundraising activities raised nearly £200,000 for the children's charity and generated huge awareness for ChildLine's many initiatives.

Arsenal's charity of the season for 2005/06 – the final season at Highbury – was the David Rocastle Trust. The initiative remembered the Arsenal legend, affectionately known as 'Rocky', who lost his battle with cancer in 2001 at the age of just 33 (see Rocastle, David on page 170). Through consultation with David's family, his former agent and best friend Jerome Anderson and Arsenal supporters, the charity assisted community projects along with backing the efforts of registered charities closely linked to both David and the Trust.

In 2006/07 the Willow Foundation, which was set up by former Arsenal goalkeeper Bob Wilson and his wife Megs in memory of their daughter Anna who died of cancer aged 31, was nominated as the Club's charity for the inaugural season at Emirates Stadium. Two other former Arsenal goalkeepers and close friends of the family, David Seaman and Pat Jennings, remain patrons of the charity, which gets its name from Wilson's nickname during his Highbury playing days. Present-day Arsenal star Theo Walcott is an ambassador for the organisation, alongside Arsenal-supporting golfer Ian Poulter and celebrity chef Gary Rhodes.

Arsenal chose their last season at Highbury to adopt the David Rocastle Trust as its charity. Rocky died of cancer in 2001, aged just 33.

For the club's second season at their new home, north London-based autism education charity TreeHouse was appointed as the Club's new charitable organisation. TreeHouse was set up in 1997 by a number of parents, including Arsenal fan Nick Hornby, whose children had recently been diagnosed with the condition. At a spectacular finale ball the Club smashed its £250,000 target during the season-long partnership; the figure required to build much needed sports facilities at TreeHouse's new National Centre for Autism Education. Many of the players donated a day's wages to the charity as part of the highly successful, 'Be a Gooner, Be a Giver' initiative.

CHARITY/COMMUNITY SHIELD

Arsenal have made 19 appearances in the Charity and Community Shield, joint second in the list alongside Liverpool, behind record appearance holders Manchester United with 23. The Gunners have won the shield on 11 occasions and shared it once, with north London neighbours Spurs after a 0-0 draw at Wembley in 1991, notable for a rare appearance for Arsenal by Andy Cole.

The first appearance, in 1930, ended in a 2-1 win for Arsenal against Sheffield Wednesday at Stamford Bridge. Arsenal won the first four shields before Wednesday exacted some revenge in 1935 with a 1-0 win.

Since 1993 Arsenal have met Manchester United five times, winning three and drawing the other two, although losing both those games on penalties.

The Gunners appeared in the first four Community Shields from 2002, when debutant Gilberto Silva scored the winner against Liverpool, to 2005 as champions Chelsea beat the FA Cup holders 2-1.

FA CHARITY SHIELD
1930 Arsenal 2-1 Sheffield Wednesday
1931 Arsenal 1-0 West Bromwich Albion
1933 Arsenal 3-0 Everton
1934 Arsenal 4-0 Manchester City
1935 Sheffield Wednesday 1-0 Arsenal
1936 Sunderland 2-0 Arsenal
1938 Arsenal 2-1 Preston North End
1948 Arsenal 4-3 Manchester United
1953 Arsenal 3-1 Blackpool
1979 Liverpool 3-1 Arsenal
1989 Liverpool 1-0 Arsenal
1991* Arsenal 0-0 Tottenham Hotspur
1993 Manchester United 1-1 Arsenal
     (Man Utd won 5-4 on penalties)
1998 Arsenal 3-0 Manchester United
1999 Arsenal 2-1 Manchester United
shared, each team retained the shield for six months

FA COMMUNITY SHIELD
2002 Arsenal 1-0 Liverpool
2003 Manchester United 1-1 Arsenal
     (Man Utd won 4-3 on penalties)
2004 Arsenal 3-1 Manchester United
2005 Chelsea 2-1 Arsenal

CLOCK, The

The famous Highbury clock was originally placed at the back of the North Bank terrace, then known as the Laundry End, in August 1928. It was moved to the south terrace in 1935 when the north end of the stadium was redeveloped and roofed. Its new home was soon dubbed the 'Clock End' by its regulars – who loved their new landmark – and the name stuck.

Originally the clock provided supporters with a 45-minute countdown of each half on the orders of team manager Herbert Chapman, but the FA believed this undermined the match officials and the club was forced to change it to a conventional timepiece.

When executive boxes were installed above the terrace in 1988 the clock was temporarily removed before being integrated into the new structure. In July 2006, with the demolition of Highbury well underway, the original clock, which measures 2.6 metres in diameter, was finally taken down and later installed outside Emirates Stadium, facing the Clock End Bridge as a reminder of the club's time at its previous home.

Arsenal director Ken Friar said, 'The Club always felt that it was important to supporters and everyone involved with the Club that parts of Highbury and the Club's history, that are so intrinsic to Arsenal, were brought along to our new home... We hope that supporters will enjoy seeing the famous clock when they visit the stadium for many, many years to come.'

CLOCK END, The

The South Stand at Highbury – dubbed the 'Tick-tock' by regulars – was known through-out football as the famous Clock End after the erection of a 12ft-diameter clock in 1935. In the days before segregation the terrace was traditionally used by away supporters as well as Arsenal fans, but in the 1970s, when growing disturbances necessitated an allocated 'away end', the south west portion of the terrace was given over to visiting supporters. On some occasions, when large numbers were expected –

The famous old clock on the south terrace stares down as ground staff get to work repairing the pitch after a match. In 1988, when executive boxes and a roof were erected, the clock was incorporated into the new stand. It remained until Highbury closed in 2006 and can now be seen outside Emirates Stadium.

notably north London derbies – the entire stand would be allocated to Spurs fans.

The old training pitch was situated behind the terrace, later replaced by an artificial surface in an indoor training facility. The only significant visible change on the terrace for half a century was the erection of an electronic scoreboard in 1984, but the experiment was short-lived after objections from local residents and Islington Council.

In 1988 work began on a new stand to provide cover for many of the Clock End's patrons, along with 48 executive boxes, office space, restaurants and conference facilities. The south east corner of the terrace, linked to the East Stand, was also demolished to make way for a new First Aid facility.

In November 1993, following the Taylor Report, the Clock End's capacity was reduced to 5,795 seats, plus a further 432 in the executive suites, when it was converted into an all-seater stand.

CLUB CREST

Despite leaving Woolwich nearly 100 years ago, Arsenal's crest is a permanent reminder of its south-London origins. The Club was founded in 1886 by workers at an armaments factory in Woolwich – the Royal Arsenal – and was originally named Dial Square after the workshops at the heart of the factory. The crest, which has always featured the name 'Arsenal', has changed many times over the years, but the one feature that has remained is the cannon in various derivatives.

The original badge – based on Woolwich's coat of arms – comprised three upstanding cannons, closely resembling chimneys. A new design, first seen in the matchday programme in the summer of 1922, featured an east-facing cannon with the name 'The Gunners' next to it. By 1925 a sleeker cannon facing west was used and this design remained the same until the

beginning of the championship-winning 1949/50 season, when an additional crest with a prominent 'A' was also introduced and is still seen on Highbury's East Stand facade. By now the familiar cannon crest appeared on the players' jerseys for all matches and not just special occasions such as cup finals, as had been the case until the Chapman years.

The new design featured a new club motto – *Victoria Concorida Crescit* – Latin for 'Victory grows out of harmony'. Its origins dated back to the end of the 1947/48 title season when the matchday programme editor Harry Homer had used the motto to describe, in his own inimitable manner, his view on why the harmonious Gunners squad had succeeded. The gothic writing so familiar to fans today was also introduced, along with the borough of Islington's coat of arms.

The red and white crest had green added to it much later and it barely changed until 2001 when it was 'cleaned up' with smart yellow trim. But only a year later the Club made the decision to redesign the crest when the board decided on setting Arsenal on a modern course with an ambitious rebranding project. The new 21st-century crest had the cannon east-facing once more, while a snazzy design modernised the look.

After early criticism from fans, it seems most people now appear to have embraced the new design. Despite all the changes and redesigns down the years the cannon has remained one of the most recognisable symbols across the footballing world.

COCA-COLA CUP, The

In April 1993 Arsenal completed the first part of a unique domestic cup double with a 2-1 win over Sheffield Wednesday at Wembley.

David Seaman had set them on their way with three saves in a thrilling penalty shootout to dispose of Millwall in their final season at the old Den. This was in a second round replay after a 1-1 draw at Highbury and the same scoreline again in south London after extra time.

Goals from Ian Wright and Kevin Campbell saw off Derby County 2-1 at Highbury, again after a 1-1 away draw in the third round. A foggy Scarborough was the venue in the next round and Nigel Winterburn netted the only goal of a dour contest with a 20-yard piledriver, although few saw it through poor visibility on the Yorkshire coast. An Ian Wright double beat Nottingham Forest in the fifth round at Highbury and Crystal Palace were no match in the two-legged semi-final, going down 5-1 on aggregate.

Wednesday struck first through American John Harkes in front of 74,000 at Wembley, but Paul Merson curled in an equaliser after 20 minutes and Steve Morrow made himself a hero with a close range winner in the 68th minute. His afternoon ended in hospital though, when he broke his arm in the post-match celebrations after skipper Tony Adams dropped him. The Northern Ireland international left the stadium in an ambulance, but was later given his medal before the FA Cup Final a few weeks later.

COMPTON BROTHERS, The

Ten sets of brothers have played for Arsenal but none have made the same impact as these two remarkable men. Mainstays of the Arsenal side in the 1940s, Leslie was the regular centre-half from the war until 1951 while younger brother Denis made fewer appearances due to his cricketing obligations.

But both were exceptional with the bat and ball. They missed the first weeks of the 1947/48 title-winning season as they were helping Middlesex to win the County Championship and in 1950 they both won the County Championship and the FA Cup, the only two people to have done so in the same calendar year.

Leslie's late equaliser from a corner kick in the semi-final against Chelsea kept Arsenal's Wembley dream alive after he blatantly ignored the orders of his younger brother to stay back. For Arsenal he appeared in 273 matches and scored six goals. He also worked for the Club as a coach and scout after retiring as a player.

He is also the oldest ever England debutant, making his international bow aged 38 years and 64 days against Wales in 1950, a record that is unlikely to ever be beaten. Leslie played as wicketkeeper for Middlesex, from 1938 to 1956, making 272 appearances, scoring 5,814 runs (an average of 16.75), and taking 468 catches and 131 stumpings.

But it was his brother, Denis, who was the more famous cricketer (see Cricket Connections on page 54). Like Leslie, he was an inter-national at both sports and was awarded the CBE. At Highbury he was an occasional, whole-hearted winger, winning a title and an FA Cup while scoring 16 times in 59 appearances, before a recurring knee injury sustained against Charlton Athletic ended his football career.

Denis died in 1997, aged 79. Leslie passed away in December 1984, aged 72.

COURT, David

Born **Mitcham, Surrey,
1 March 1944**
Arsenal appearances **194 (10)**
Arsenal goals **18**

A hard-working utility man, David Court spent most of the 1960s at Highbury, mainly operating in midfield, but also occasionally helping out the forward line where he had started his career in the Gunners' youth and reserve sides.

A mainstay of both Billy Wright and Bertie Mee's sides, he continued to be a regular, and ended up playing in virtually every outfield position and picking up loser's medals in the 1968 and 1969 League Cup Finals.

He moved to Luton Town in 1970 for £30,000 and later played for Brentford. In 1996 the popular Court returned to Highbury as Liam Brady's number two at the Club's Academy.

CRAYSTON, Jack

MANAGER 1956/58
Born **Grange-over-Sands, Lancashire,
9 October 1910**
Died **December 1992**
Arsenal appearances **207**
Arsenal goals **17**
International caps (England) **8 (1 goal)**

A Lancastrian by birth, Jack Crayston served the Club well as player and manager for nearly a quarter of a century after transferring from Bradford Park Avenue. He made a dream start to his

(Right to left) Sunderland's Cecil Irwin looks on as his goalkeeper Alex McLaughlin, assisted by Len Ashurst, clears the ball from Arsenal's David Court and George Armstrong.

Highbury career when he scored on his debut in an 8-1 thrashing of Liverpool on 1 September 1934.

A powerful right-half, Crayston won two league titles (1935 and 1938) and was a member of the 1936 FA Cup-winning side, before retiring at the age of 33 after picking up a knee injury in a war-time game with West Ham.

He moved into coaching and was appointed manager Tom Whittaker's deputy in 1947, after George Allison's retirement. A further two titles and one FA Cup came to Highbury and when Whittaker passed away suddenly in 1956, Crayston was elevated to the top job.

He steered the Club to fifth place in his first full season, but his stewardship was ultimately unsuccessful and after a 12th-place finish in 1957/58 - their worst position for 38 years - and a humiliating 3-1 FA Cup defeat at Northampton Town, he resigned to take up the reins at Doncaster Rovers, retiring from the game three years later.

CRICKET CONNECTIONS

Arsenal have a cricketing tradition dating back to the turn of the last century. Before the Great War the Club could boast two dual internationals who had represented England at both cricket and soccer. Kent legend Wally Hardinge played for Woolwich Arsenal shortly after the move to Highbury and scored 14 goals in 55 games before retiring in 1921 to dedicate his time to cricket. In his first-class career - spanning 31 seasons - he scored 33,519 runs and 75 centuries and was named *Wisden* Cricketer of the Year in 1915, while still at Highbury. He was also a member of Kent's first four championship-winning teams and played for them for 31 seasons.

Andy Ducat was a teenage prodigy at both sports who, like fellow south Londoner Hardinge, represented his country in both sports. He was a star player for Woolwich Arsenal before the First World War, while also excelling for Surrey CCC. He only played once for England at cricket and was victim to a bizarre dismissal in 1921. Facing Australian fast bowler Ted McDonald, Ducat failed to add to his overnight three when he broke the shoulder of his bat as he attempted a steer through the covers. His tame lob went straight to slip and the bails were dislodged by a shard of his broken bat.

Ducat managed just two more runs in his international career as Australia secured a 219-run victory. He died at the age of 56 while playing in a wartime match at Lord's in July 1942, when he collapsed with a heart attack shortly after lunch. Despite strenuous efforts he could not be revived.

Ted Drake, prior to his move from Southampton to Arsenal in 1934, turned out for his home county Hampshire, and was forced to decide between the two sports before choosing soccer. And winger Joe Hulme also played 223 times for Middlesex between 1929 and 1939. Later in the 1950s, another winger, Don Roper, would also occasionally turn out for Hampshire, as well as playing for Arsenal and Southampton.

It was that post-war period that represented a golden era for Arsenal in cricketing circles. The legendary Compton brothers, Leslie and Dennis, are the Gunners' most famous examples. Leslie, the elder brother, served Arsenal for 23 years from 1930 and also played cricket for Middlesex, as wicketkeeper from 1938 to 1956. He appeared 272 times for his county, scoring 5,814 runs at an average of 16.75, taking 468 catches and 131 stumpings.

His younger brother Denis, the 'Brylcreem Boy', thrilled Lord's - where he started on the groundstaff - as a right-hand batsman and slow left-arm bowler for Middlesex and England. As a 19-year-old he scored 102 against Don Bradman's Australians in the first Test in 1938 and the following season he hit 120 against the West Indies at Lord's, scoring 2,468 runs in a glorious summer.

Jack Crayston came to Arsenal as a player in 1934 from Bradford Park Avenue. An elegant creative wing-half, he made 184 appearances and was one of the earliest long throw experts. He joined the coaching staff as assistant manager in June 1947, when Tom Whittaker took over the reins.

The war robbed him of his prime years, but in 1947 records tumbled when he scored 3,816 runs and 18 centuries, while smashing 753 runs against the touring South Africans. He jointly captained Middlesex with WJ Edrich before retiring in 1957, finishing with 123 first-class tons, including 17 centuries in 78 Tests at an average of 50.06. This was an impressive haul along with a league title and an FA Cup-winner's medal with Arsenal, before a knee injury ended his footballing ambitions. A Lord's stand is named after him.

The Comptons' Arsenal team-mate Arthur Milton is the last person to play both football and cricket for England. Milton, a right-sided midfielder, picked up his solitary cap in a 2-2 draw against Austria in November 1951 and a title medal in 1953, before departing for Bristol City two years later. While he was at Ashton Gate he excelled for Gloucestershire and played six Tests for England in 1958 and 1959. In 620 first-class cricket matches he hit 32,150 runs, averaging 33.73. His record for England was solid, averaging 25.50.

Another player from that era, Cliff Holton, also played for four years with Essex second XI. Yorkshire and England legend Brian Close also represented Arsenal, playing at centre-forward for the reserves while breaking cricketing records as the youngest player to play for England and Yorkshire's first XI, as well as being the youngest all-rounder to take 100 wickets and score 1,000 runs in a season.

Steve Gatting – brother of England captain Mike – briefly played for the Gunners in the late 1970s. Current Surrey star Mark Ramprakash also turns out for the Arsenal celebrity side, while England pace bowler James Anderson is a big Gunners fan, as are former spinner Phil Tufnell and current New Zealand all-rounder Jacob Oram, who confessed to getting on the Tube and heading straight to Highbury in the summer of 2004 after his side touched down in London for their Test series with England.

That same year Steve Waugh also visited Highbury. Many fans were rubbing their eyes when they saw the Aussie cricket legend by the side of the pitch. He was there pursuing his hobby of photography and quipped, 'I'd love to have a bat on that surface!'

And that isn't such a crazy notion. The sound of leather on willow has echoed around the old stadium on several occasions in the past. In August 1949 an Arsenal XI played Middlesex in a benefit match for Denis Compton and three years later a similar match was played under floodlights for Jack Young. A third game took place, again with Middlesex the visitors, for Leslie Compton on 9 August 1955.

Even in the boardroom there has been cricketing excellence. Former chairman Samuel Hill-Wood, grandfather of current incumbent Peter, was an opening batsman for his native Derbyshire and once scored ten runs off one ball against the MCC.

CROSSING THE DIVIDE

Pat Jennings is the only player in north London's football history to move from Spurs to Arsenal – and back again. The Northern Ireland goalkeeper joined Arsenal in 1977 for £45,000, replacing Jimmy Rimmer and making four appearances in major cup finals, before heading back to White Hart Lane in 1985. He is also in the almost unique position of enjoying a favourable reputation with both sets of fans. Big Pat is currently goalkeeping coach at Tottenham Hotspur, a position he has held since 1993.

Steve Walford, Kevin Stead and Willie Young followed Jennings to Highbury in 1977, with the latter admitting it took a while to convince the Arsenal faithful he was now a true Gunner. 'They basically thought I was a Spurs man,' Young recalls. 'Then when we played Spurs at Easter, our keeper Jimmy Rimmer's knee connected with my head. I went off, had stitches and came back on with a bloodied bandage. Then the fans realised I was committed to Arsenal – Spurs meant nothing to me.'

Striker Freddie Cox had earlier moved from Spurs in September 1949 and returned to the Lane later that season to score twice: once direct from a corner in a 2-2 draw in the FA Cup semi-final against Chelsea and then the winner in the replay. While wing-half Vic Groves made his name at Highbury,

Pat Jennings dominates his area in a match against Luton at Highbury in the early 1980s. The Ulsterman represented both Spurs and Arsenal with distinction and remains a north London legend.

he also turned out for Spurs in the early 1950s as an amateur, before moving to Leyton Orient and then Arsenal. Scottish winger Jimmy Robertson also made the move from white to red in October 1968 in a straight swap for striker David Jenkins.

Four years previously Geordie striker Laurie Brown was bought by Spurs for £40,000 after failing to impress at Highbury, despite starring for Britain in the 1960 Rome Olympics. The only major pre-war switch saw Jimmy Brain - the first Gunner to score 100 goals for the Club - make the short trip up the Seven Sisters Road for £2,500 in 1931, although he only scored ten times for Spurs in 47 appearances in three years.

Only two players have gone in either direction in the new Millennium. Spurs captain Sol Campbell was involved in the most controversial cross-town move in 2001 when he arrived at Highbury on a Bosman free. Shrugging off the controversy, Campbell was unveiled at London Colney and told the media, 'My decision was based on football - I felt this was the place to be.' The latest player to swap the two north London clubs was Rohan Ricketts, an England Under-21 midfielder, who was snapped up by Spurs boss Glenn Hoddle. He has since followed Hoddle to Wolves.

There are also managerial links between the two clubs. The great Herbert Chapman was, in fact, a former Spurs player, turning out for the Lilywhites for two years until 1907, although his time at White Hart Lane was spent mostly in the reserves. Despite his lack of success there, his two years constituted the longest period he stayed with any club as a player. It was Tottenham captain Walter Bull, in the spring of 1907, who persuaded Chapman to become a manager. Bull had been offered the Northampton Town post, but instead turned to his team-mate in the post-match bath and said, 'You take it, Herbert'.

Arsenal's 1930s wing legend Joe Hulme was Spurs' first post-war manager, before leaving in 1949, although he was credited with laying the foundations for their 1951 title success. Terry Neill, an Arsenal player for nine years, shocked Gunners fans when he took the Tottenham job in 1974 before moving back to Highbury for the big job two

years later. And more recently George Graham - a Gunners stalwart both as player and manager - was tempted back to north London after a spell at Leeds United in 1997 to become the manager of Tottenham, leading them to European competition via a League Cup Final success in 1999, their only trophy since 1991.

CULT HEROES

Arsenal fans have had many cult heroes down the years and the reasons for their special status on the terraces are many and varied.

The likes of Eddie Hapgood, Joe Mercer, Frank McLintock, Willie Young and Tony Adams, for example, have all been known as 'Mr Arsenal' for their enormous influence and single-minded will to win at all costs. They were men who put their body on the line for the cause.

Then there are those who hold a special place in fans' hearts for reasons other than pure talent. Perry Groves - the 'Ginger Genius' - made up in effort what he lacked in ability. As did Johnny Jensen, whose mix

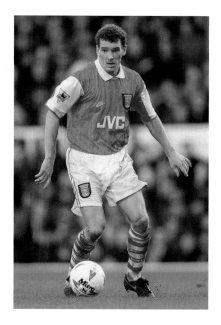

John Jensen - Arsenal fans have huge affection for the Great Dane.

of odd appearance, 100 per cent effort and lack of success in front of goal combined to make him a fans' favourite. Alan Sunderland remains an Arsenal icon for his bubble perm and moustache as much as his goalscoring prowess.

And there are those who just had the word 'class' stamped through them like a stick of rock. David Rocastle, tragically lost at such an early age, was the outstanding star in the George Graham era and was adored by the Highbury faithful. Liam Brady - bedraggled in appearance but a Rolls Royce of a player - was a teenage hero and Alex James' eccentricities struck a chord with fans who loved his oversized shorts, slick centre parting and ability to make any opponent in the land look foolish.

Goalscoring rebels also made their mark to become cult heroes, with the swash-buckling figures of Joe Baker and Malcolm Macdonald and the aggressive, streetwise goalgetters Charlie George and Ian Wright all names that are talked about and revered long after they departed the Club.

So who is the ultimate Arsenal cult hero? The answer, according to a BBC poll in 2004, is Tony Adams, whose two decades of service tipped the balance for supporters.

CUP KINGS

In 1993 Arsenal became the first club to win both domestic knockout competitions in the same season. In the Coca-Cola Cup Final in April of that year, goals from Paul Merson and Steven Morrow gave Arsenal a 2-1 win over Sheffield Wednesday. A month later Arsenal again faced the Owls in the FA Cup Final. Ian Wright's neat header gave Arsenal the lead, but Wednesday levelled to take the tie to a replay on a wet Thursday night. Only 62,000 were at the replay to see Wright score again, only for Chris Waddle to equalise. With extra time almost over, Andy Linighan headed the winner for Arsenal to seal a unique double.

DARLINGS OF THE NORTH BANK

Since the 1930s the North Bank has been seduced by a succession of strikers who scored goals for fun and had a neverending supply of confidence. But it isn't just goals that have won over the fans...

TED DRAKE

The first hero of the then Laundry End? The Hampshire-born goal machine's arrival in 1934 coincided with the erection of the famous dark roof above the terrace. A goal on his debut at home to Wolves instantly endeared him to the fans and for the rest of the decade he didn't stop - 136 goals later he was a Gunners legend.

JOE MERCER

The North Bank held their inspirational skipper in the highest esteem as he won two titles and a cup. The old terrace was a sea of tears when Mercer waved goodbye for the last time as he was stretchered off with a broken leg in 1954.

JOE BAKER

There is nothing like a swashbuckling striker to melt the hearts. And in Joe the Goal the North Bank had one of the very best. Feisty and hungry for goals, Baker knew no fear and they loved his commitment, netting 100 goals in 156 games.

CHARLIE GEORGE

Maybe the greatest North Bank darling of them all. He had grown up on the terrace and his long hair and rebellious style made him Islington's No.1 pin up in the early 1970s.

When he scored he would always acknowledge his old mates under the roof. 'A player who just runs back to the centre circle may as well be dead,' he once said. 'Born is the king of Highbury,' the fans sang back.

LIAM BRADY

Long hair, socks rolled down around his ankles, shirt hanging out and the kind of talent you see once in a generation, Brady was the epitome of cool in the late 1970s. The scorer of classic goals, he was a shining light in Terry Neill's Irish generation.

Ted Drake endeared himself to the demanding Highbury crowd with a feast of goals after becoming George Allison's first signing in 1934.

MALCOLM MACDONALD

On his arrival in 1976 Supermac vowed to beat Cliff Bastin's record, but unfortunately injury cut short his career after 57 goals in 108 games. Like Joe Baker, he was fearless and exciting and, despite his brief stay at Highbury, remains a North Bank icon.

DAVID O'LEARY

While others left for greater riches, O'Leary turned down far more lucrative offers to stay at Highbury and break the Club's all-time appearance record. The North Bank loved his loyalty and, through thick and thin, always backed him. On his last visit to Highbury, as a manager in April 2006, his Aston Villa side lost 5–0, but the North Bank still chanted 'Spider's' name throughout.

CHARLIE NICHOLAS

In the pop-obsessed 1980s, the flash clothes, wedge haircut and sexy flair of the Scot proved irresistible. He was never prolific, but seemed to always score against Spurs – including a brilliant individual effort in a 3–2 win in April 1984. And, like all good players, he always showed his appreciation to the loyal fans behind the goal.

IAN WRIGHT

That toothy grin flashed after yet another goal would light up Highbury for seven years. Like Charlie George, he was a working-class lad with world-class talent. His thirst for goals and the outrageous celebrations were such an infectious combination.

THIERRY HENRY

The last great hero of the North Bank. The fans have gorged on his goals and talents since 1999. The Frenchman is arguably the greatest talent the famous old end has ever seen.

Ian Wright is one of the greatest stars ever to grace the Highbury turf. Theatrical he may have been, but his appetite for goals and ability to score them endeared him to the North Bank throughout his seven years with the Club.

DAVIS, Paul

Born **London, 9 December 1961**
Arsenal appearances **414 (31)**
Arsenal goals **37**

A graceful midfielder, Paul Davis gave the Club 15 years' fine service and earned a clutch of medals. He debuted in a 2–1 win at Tottenham in April 1980 and won many plaudits for his classy play, displaying a range of passing with his prized left foot that even drew distant comparisons with the departed Liam Brady.

He wasn't that good – who is? – but he matured into a super addition for Arsenal's young midfield, excelling on George Graham's arrival as manager and playing a key role in the Littlewoods Cup triumph in 1987.

In the title year of 1988/89 he blotted his copybook with an eight-match ban after an uncharacteristic altercation with Southampton's Glenn Cockerill, a mysterious incident which he has barely talked about in public since.

An occasional skipper, at times Davis was leaned on heavily by Graham, and on other occasions he was discarded, but he would always come back to show that he could offer something no other Gunner could; an almost ballet-like poise in the rough and tumble of the red and white engine room.

FA and Coca-Cola Cups followed and then he was a steadying influence as Arsenal won the Cup-Winners' Cup, before he left on a free transfer to Brentford.

He returned to London Colney as an Academy coach and also had a brief stint as Kettering player-coach alongside Paul Gascoigne in 2005.

DEBUTS – TO DIE FOR

JACK CRAYSTON

v Liverpool, Highbury, September 1934
Crayston couldn't have asked for a better start to his career. He scored one, set up another and was cheered off the pitch as Arsenal thrashed Liverpool 8–1.

ALF KIRCHEN

v Tottenham, White Hart Lane, March 1935
Kirchen hit the ground running after his move from Norwich with two goals – and setting up Ted Drake for the fourth – as Arsenal smashed six without reply past their neighbours. This remains Arsenal's record win at White Hart Lane.

PETER MARINELLO

v Manchester United, Old Trafford, January 1970
The 'Scottish George Best' scored a stunning debut goal at the real George Best's home. He turned in the centre circle and ran half the length of the pitch before taking the ball past Alex Stepney and slotting home to silence the Stretford End. It didn't get any better than that for Marinello. When Arsenal signed another teenage prodigy, Theo Walcott, he joked, 'Just don't score on your debut, Theo.'

IAN WRIGHT

v Southampton, The Dell, September 1991
He had already netted on his first start in a Gunners shirt when he scored in a 1–1 draw at Leicester in the League Cup – and did even better on his league bow with a hat-trick at Southampton in the pouring rain. It rained goals for seven more years...

FREDDIE LJUNGBERG

v Manchester United, Highbury, September 1998
The little known Swede instantly endeared himself to Gunners fans when he scored just four minutes and 42 seconds after coming on as a substitute in his first appearance for the Club – a 3–0 home win over arch rivals Manchester United – when he brilliantly lobbed Peter Schmeichel.

JERMAINE PENNANT

v Southampton, Highbury, May 2003
The winger announced his full Premiership debut in devastating fashion – smashing a hat-trick past Southampton in a 6–1 win. The following week Pennant was dropped as Arsenal beat Saints 1–0 in the FA Cup Final.

DEBUTS – FROM HELL

SIDNEY PUGH
v Birmingham, St Andrew's, April 1939
It was Good Friday and young left-half Sidney Pugh seemed to have a promising career ahead of him. However, minutes into the game he broke his leg and never played for the Club again. He died in a plane crash five years later – one of nine Gunners to lose their lives in the Second World War.

JACK KELSEY
v Charlton, Highbury, February 1952
The Welsh goalkeeper had been chomping at the bit for his first-team debut. George Allison threw him in against Charlton – and the Gunners lost 5-2. It was the first time Arsenal had conceded five since a 5-2 defeat to Manchester United six years earlier.

PETER SIMPSON
v Chelsea, Highbury, March 1964
Simpson spent 14 great years at Highbury, but got off to a dreadful start when his direct opponent, Bobby Tambling, scored all four of Chelsea's goals in a 4-2 win at Highbury, the last opposition player to do so at the old stadium.

WILLIE YOUNG
v Ipswich, Highbury, March 1977
The Scotsman became a cult figure at Highbury, but he had to take the rough before the smooth, making his debut after a controversial move from Tottenham in a devastating 4-1 home defeat. He had a stinker and had the indignity of being booed by his own supporters. After the game he had to be physically restrained by his father as angry fans told him to go back to Spurs.

TONY ADAMS
v Sunderland, Highbury, November 1983
Character-building stuff for the nervous young defender who put his shorts on back to front in the changing room, gave the ball away for Sunderland's opener with virtually his first touch and later had a goal of his own disallowed! He didn't do too badly in the end, though...

JASON CROWE
v Birmingham, Highbury, October 1997
The teenager came on as a substitute in extra time at Arsenal's League Cup clash against Birmingham City. But 33 seconds later he was shown a red card by referee Uriah Rennie for a high tackle. It was his first and last appearance for the Club.

DEFEATS

Arsenal's record defeat remains an 8-0 loss at Loughborough Town in Division Two on 12 December 1896. It was a poor period for the Club and just over two years later Derby County inflicted a 6-0 home defeat on Arsenal in the FA Cup, which is still a record.

The biggest defeat at Highbury in the top-flight was 0-5 on Valentine's Day 1925 by Huddersfield – a scoreline repeated by Chelsea in the League Cup in 1999.

Arsenal have lost by three goals at home in the Premiership three times, Mick Quinn memorably scoring a hat-trick on the first occasion as Coventry won 3-0 on the opening day of the 1993/94 season in front of the new North Bank stand, and when Middlesbrough left Highbury with a 3-0 win on 14 April 2001.

Biggest home defeat overall
0-6 v Derby County, 28 Jan 1899,
FA Cup, Rd 1

Biggest away defeat overall
0-8 v Loughborough Town, 12 Dec 1896,
Lge Div 2

Biggest home defeat in the League
0-5 v Liverpool, 28 Oct 1893, Div 2

Biggest home defeat in Top Division
0-5 v Huddersfield Town, 14 Feb 1925, Div 1

Peter Simpson (right) chases after Jimmy Greaves in a north London derby. Simpson's first London derby - against Chelsea - was a debut to forget.

Biggest away defeats in the League
0-7 v Blackburn Rovers, 2 Oct 1909, Div 1

0-7 v West Brom Alb, 14 Oct 1922, Div 1

0-7 v Newcastle United, 3 Oct 1925, Div 1

0-7 v West Ham United, 7 March 1927, Div 1

Biggest home defeats in the Premiership
0-3 v Coventry City, 14 Aug 1993

0-3 v Middlesbrough, 14 April 2001

2-4 v Charlton Athletic, 4 Nov 2001

Biggest away defeat in the Premiership
1-6 v Manchester United, 25 Feb 2001

Biggest home defeat in all European competitions
2-5 v Spartak Moscow, 29 Sept 1982, UEFA Cup, Rd 1

Biggest away defeats in all European competitions
0-3 v Shakhtar Donetsk, 7 Nov 2000, CL, Gp St 1

1-4 v Spartak Moscow, 22 Nov 2000, CL Gp St 2

Biggest home defeat in UEFA Champions League
0-3 v Inter Milan, 17 September 2003, Gp St 1

Biggest away defeats in UEFA Champions League
0-3 v Shakhtar Donetsk, 7 Nov 2000, Gp St 1

1-4 v Spartak Moscow, 22 Nov 2000, Gp St 2

Biggest Wembley defeat in UEFA Champions League
2-4 v Barcelona, 19 Oct 1999, Gp St 1

Biggest home defeat in the FA Cup
0-6 v Derby County, 28 Jan 1899, Rd 1

Biggest away defeat in the FA Cup
1-6 v Burnley, 1 Feb 1896, Rd 1

Biggest home defeat in the League Cup
0-5 v Chelsea, 11 Nov 1999, Rd 4

Biggest away defeat in the League Cup
0-4 v Blackburn, 11 Dec 2001, Rd 5

Biggest home defeat under Arsène Wenger
0-5 v Chelsea, 11 Nov 1999, Lge Cup, Rd 4

Biggest away defeat under Arsène Wenger
1-6 v Manchester Utd, 25 Feb 2001, Prem

DENMARK

Arsenal's connections with Denmark go back to their first ever European tie in September 1963, when the team travelled to Copenhagen and won their Inter Cities' Fairs Cup first leg tie with Staevnet Kobenhavn 7-1. The second leg at Highbury, though, ended 3-2 to the Danish amateurs.

Denmark also hosted Arsenal twice in their successful 1993/94 Cup-Winners' Cup campaign. In the first round, first leg, Arsenal beat OB in Odense 2-1 courtesy of goals from Ian Wright and Paul Merson, before a 1-1 draw at Highbury saw them through. The Gunners then returned to the magnificent Parken Stadium in Copenhagen, home to the Danish national side, to beat AS Parma 1-0 in the Final. Arsenal's popularity in Scandinavia ensured the majority of the 33,000 crowd – swelled by Arsenal-supporting locals – roared the Gunners to victory when Alan Smith volleyed the only goal of the game. Cult hero John Jensen, returning to his home country, was forced on to the sidelines for the big game through injury.

Copenhagen was again the host city for the 2000 UEFA Cup Final against Turkish side Galatasaray. The Turks held on for a 0-0 draw before winning the penalty shootout, former Spurs defender Gica Poescu scoring the winning penalty.

As a results of these connections, Arsenal's support in Denmark is extensive. The official Danish supporters club is one of the most active overseas fans' groups with chairman Thomas Ballegaard arranging regular club trips to north London. Membership stands at approximately 1,300.

DERBY DAYS

A BRIEF HISTORY OF THE NORTH LONDON DERBY

The first recorded match between the two sides was played on Tottenham marshes on 19 November 1887. The match was abandoned due to failing light with Spurs leading Royal Arsenal 2-1. Woolwich Arsenal took the honours in the first league match between the two sides, winning 1-0 at the Manor Ground in Plumstead in December 1909. But it was not until 1913 when Arsenal moved to north London – just four miles from Tottenham – that the game took on added signifcance.

Spurs won their first ever match at Highbury, 2-0 in 1922, and proved party poopers again when they won 1-0 in August 1925 for Herbert Chapman's first game in charge. But in the glorious 1930s Arsenal finally won bragging rights with their biggest ever win at White Hart Lane courtesy of a 6-0 thrashing in March 1935. Earlier that season Ted Drake had scored a hat-trick in a 5-1 home win over the old enemy too, as Arsenal chalked up their best ever aggregate score in a league season against Spurs.

Both sides had equal success in the early 1950s, but Arsenal's good away form in derbies continued with 2-1 and 3-1 wins in February and September 1952 respectively. In October 1953 Jimmy Logie struck twice as Arsenal won 4-1 at the Lane, but later that season Spurs left Highbury 3-0 victors.

The early 1960s saw some titanic battles, including two 4-4 draws in successive seasons, but Spurs ruled the roost until a 4-0 home win for Arsenal in September 1967, all the more memorable as George Graham got married in the morning and scored in the afternoon. His best man? Spurs opponent Terry Venables.

Arsenal won the league at Spurs thanks to Ray Kennedy's late header in the 1-0 win in May 1971 – one of the greatest victories at the home of the arch rivals – and they came close to emulating the record win of 1935 when Alan Sunderland scored a hat-trick in a 5-0 win at the Lane in 1978. Spurs gained revenge five years later with a 5-0 win of their own. The next season Arsenal achieved a treble over Spurs (including a 2-1 away win in the League Cup) before the titanic Littlewoods Cup classics of 1987. Spurs won the first leg of the semi-final 1-0 at Highbury, but in the second leg Arsenal forced a replay through Viv Anderson and Niall Quinn goals. Clive Allen scored for the third time in the tie and Spurs appeared to be heading to Wembley, but substitute Ian Allinson made it 1-1 and David Rocastle scrambled a 90th-minute winner for the Gunners.

In 1991 Spurs were on top after a 3-1 in the FA Cup semi-final at Wembley, thanks to two goals from Gary Lineker and a free-kick by Paul Gascogine, but two years later Arsenal beat them in the same stage of the competition at Wembley 1-0 with a Tony Adams header.

Since then Arsenal have had the upper hand. Tony Adams scored a brilliant volley in a 3-1 home win in 1996, capped by a stunning third from Dennis Bergkamp, and Kanu scored a brilliant goal in a 3-1 win at the Lane in May 1999. In Spring 2001 Arsenal beat Spurs 2-0 at Highbury on the day David Rocastle's death was announced at an emotional Highbury, both sets of fans impeccably observing a minute's silence before the game. Eight days later Robert Pires scored the winner in a 2-1 FA Cup

semi-final win at Old Trafford in Sol Campbell's last appearance for Spurs before heading to Highbury. Thierry Henry scored after a mazy 70-yard run in a comprehensive 3-0 home win in November 2002, and in April 2004 Arsenal won the title at Tottenham for the second time in their history courtesy of a 2-2 draw.

The following season Arsenal enjoyed another memorable day up the Seven Sisters Road – winning a see-saw battle 5-4 in one of the most thrilling derbies in north London's footballing history. The last north London derby at Highbury, in April 2006, ended in a 1-1 draw – and, as ever, it wasn't short of controversy with Spurs scoring while two Arsenal players lay in the centre circle injured.

But then again when was N5 v N17 ever friendly?

Robert Pires proved a constant thorn in the side of neighbours Spurs. Here he nets Arsenal's fifth past Paul Robinson in a 5-4 win at White Hart Lane on 13 November 2004.

DIAL SQUARE

Dial Square, situated in the middle of the workshops of the Royal Arsenal in Woolwich, south east London, was constructed around 1717. It was given its name in 1764 when a sundial was built over the entrance. On 11 December 1886 a football team made up of staff from one of the workshops played a football match against Eastern Wanderers. They called themselves Dial Square. In the event they won the match 6-0 – although the scoreline was disputed due to the lack of pitch markings and crossbars – on a quagmire of a surface on the Isle of Dogs. Two weeks later, on Christmas Day 1886, they officially founded a football club, Royal Arsenal, and the rest, as they say, is history...

DIRE STRAITS

CASH CRISIS NO.1

In 1913, the Club had just £19 in the bank and was on the verge of folding. Woolwich Arsenal made the brave move to Highbury that summer, but costs were astronomical. Chairman Sir Henry Norris had managed to secure £125,000 funding – much of it coming from crippling bank loans – to pay for the move and to build a new stadium next to Avenell Road at the site of St John's College of Divinity, N5. Builders were even willing to take a cut of gate receipts when cash ran out.

By the end of the 1914/15 season, the last full campaign before football was abandoned due to the growing conflict in Europe, manager George Morrell was sacked to save money as Arsenal ended the season with a 7-0 win over Nottingham Forest at Highbury to finish fifth in Division Two.

The Club was £60,000 overdrawn, not including Norris' huge investment.

It is still unclear how he managed it, but Norris persuaded the Football League to promote Arsenal to the First Division, a move that, with the regular 30,000-plus crowds it brought with it saved the Club from financial ruin.

Arsenal have not played a game outside the top-flight since.

CASH CRISIS NO.2

The cash tills had been ringing regularly at Highbury in the trophy-laden 1930s. In the six years up to the Second World War Arsenal had recorded monster profits of £136,000. Turnstiles were clicking with huge crowds watching the best side in the land, so the decision was taken to rebuild the stadium.

The West Stand was built at a cost of £40,000 in 1932, but the East Stand would cost far more due to the extensive public frontage and office space incorporated into the structure. It would also house the boardroom, bars and a host of other facilities. This pushed the price up to a staggering £130,000.

It opened in 1936, but within a year Arsenal were £200,000 in debt due to huge loans taken out by the Club to complete the rebuilding. Crowds of 40,000 were needed to break even and a world record £14,000 for Wolves schemer Bryn Jones in August 1938 was deemed foolish by many fans.

By the time Hitler invaded Poland, the Club was £150,000 in the red.

The debts were frozen during hostilities, and the post-war boom in attendances meant Arsenal, rather fortunately, managed to pay off their creditors.

DISABLED FANS

In November 2004 Arsenal appointed Alan Francis as its disability liaison officer. 'My job,' he explains, 'is to help with ticketing for our disabled fans and to ensure the Club's activities are compliant with the Disability Discrimination Act. I'm disabled myself so I know first hand the needs of fans with disabilities.'

Emirates Stadium has 250 wheelchair places across the lower, upper and club levels with fans paying half-price for their tickets. Carers' entrance is free. In addition, the Club has been providing a full matchday audio service for visually impaired fans since 1992 and a special audio subscription service for every home programme. Emirates also had dedicated parking spaces for disabled badge holders and extensive toilet facilities after the Club set up an advisory group of disabled fans called 'Arsenal on the Move' to advise on the new stadium.

Disabled fans have also had a voice on the fans' forums. For more information contact disability@arsenal.co.uk or call Alan on 020 7704 4000.

DISMISSALS

Some notable red cards...

JASON CROWE

The Sidcup-born full-back can lay claim to the shortest Arsenal first-team debut in the Club's history after an evening to forget on 14 October 1997. It was during a League Cup tie with Birmingham City when manager Arsène Wenger sent him on as a substitute in extra time. Just 33 seconds had elapsed when referee Uriah Rennie adjudged that Crowe had committed a high challenge and he was shown a straight red. It remains the fastest sending off in English football history.

JOSE ANTONIO REYES

The Spaniard became only the second player to be sent off in FA Cup final history when the Gunners faced Manchester United in May 2005. Just seconds remained in extra time when he earned a second booking for a lunge on Cristiano Ronaldo, but it didn't matter as the Gunners beat Manchester United 5-4 on penalties after the game had ended 0-0 after 120 minutes of football.

JENS LEHMANN

German goalkeeper Jens Lehmann, who had played a huge part in getting the Gunners to the 2006 Champions League final by keeping ten successive clean sheets in the run-up to their Paris showdown with Barcelona, played just 18 minutes of the biggest match in the Club's history before being sent off. Lehmann was shown a straight red card for fouling Samuel Eto'o as he raced through on goal. Although Ludovic Giuly actually put the ball into the net, the goal was ruled out as Norwegian referee Terje Hauge awarding a free-kick. It was a decision which infuriated both sides as Arsenal were reduced to ten men for the remaining 72 minutes and Barcelona were denied a goal.

'I would have liked to have taken a few more seconds before I made a decision,' Hauge said later. 'If I'd done that, I could have given a goal and given a yellow card as well.' Despite the setback, Arsenal, miraculously, took the lead later in the first half before Barca beat substitute keeper Manuel Almunia twice late on to snatch the trophy.

EMMANUEL ADEBAYOR AND KOLO TOURE

Arsenal ended the 2007 Carling Cup final with only nine men after the two African stars were sent off. The Gunners were pushing for an equalizer with Chelsea leading 2-1 when tempers boiled over between the two sides. When the dust had settled referee Howard Webb produced a red card for the two Gunnners along with one for Chelsea's Jon Obi Mikel. It was a disappointing end to a fantastic game – and Arsenal's last appearance in a final at Cardiff's Millennium Stadium before the major English finals moved to the new Wembley Stadium.

DIXON, Lee

Born **Manchester, 17 March 1964**
Arsenal appearances **602 (21)**
Arsenal goals **27**
International caps (England) **22 (1 goal)**

Signed in Janaury 1988 from Stoke City, the popular Mancunian became the first choice right-back by the summer and held that position for more than a decade as a member of the legendary and famous back four.

A tenacious defender who could provide an attacking threat when given the freedom to cross the halfway line, Dixon epitomised the steely deter-mination and strong work ethic driven into the players by George Graham. Supremely fit, he appeared to get stronger as games progressed and thrived on physical battles.

Lee Dixon spent 14 years at Highbury and is one of the most decorated players in the Club's history. He formed a formidable full-back partnership with Nigel Winterburn and was a constant attacking threat.

In the Graham years he won two titles, was a valuable member of the team that won the 1989 championship at Anfield, and earned the bulk of his 22 England caps. He missed out on the 1993 Coca-Cola Cup Final through injury, but won the FA Cup that year after being sent off in the semi-final win over Tottenham. Along with the rest of his defensive colleagues, Dixon reached new peaks to earn European glory in 1994.

On Arsène Wenger's arrival, Dixon, now 32, benefitted from the new man's fitness regime and maintained his place in the 1998 Double side and, despite growing competition, won another title in 2002 before calling it a day to concentrate on media work and his businesses.

DOCHERTY, Tommy

Born **Glasgow, 24 August 1928**
Arsenal appearances **90**
Arsenal goals **1**
International caps (Scotland) **25**

Arriving in 1958 from Preston North End for £27,000, the hard-working Scottish midfielder was one of the shining lights in the bleak late 1950s and early 1960s. Arsenal would be the last club he seriously played for, leaving in September 1961 to replace former Arsenal striker Ted Drake as Chelsea's coach, where he made a handful of appearances before hanging up his boots.

He later managed Manchester United and Scotland among others and was Terry Neill's assistant at Hull City, as well as attracting newspapers headlines for his outspoken behaviour and colourful private life.

DOUBLES

Arsenal have achieved a record-equalling three Doubles.

The first – and most famous – came in 1971, when Bertie Mee's side clinched the league title for the first time in 18 years courtesy of a 1-0 victory at

Spurs. Ray Kennedy headed the winner in the final minute of the game. They completed the second part of the Double five days later when Charlie George struck an extra-time decider to beat Liverpool 2-1 in the FA Cup Final at Wembley. Arsenal had matched Spurs' achievement of 1960/61.

The second Double 27 years later was not quite so dramatic, a 4-0 victory over Everton at Highbury securing Arsène Wenger's first Premiership trophy. Newcastle were beaten 2-0 in the FA Cup Final – Marc Overmars and Nicolas Anelka scoring – to bring the trophy back to north London for a seventh time.

Arsenal then became the first team to achieve the Double in two different centuries when they won in 2001/02. The league title was sealed with a 1-0 win at Old Trafford when Sylvain Wiltord scored late in the game. Chelsea were the opponents in the FA Cup Final at Cardiff's Millennium Stadium, but were no match for an Arsenal side featuring skipper Tony Adams for the last time. Long-range drives from Ray Parlour and Freddie Ljungberg in the second half gave Adams a dream send off after 20 years with the Club.

Manchester United are the only other club to win the Double on three occasions – 1994, 1996 and 1999. Apart from Spurs, only two other clubs have achieved the Double: Preston North End in 1888/89 and Liverpool in 1985/86.

DRAKE, Ted

Born **Southampton, 16 August 1912**
Died **30 May 1995**
Arsenal appearances **184**
Arsenal goals **139**
International caps (England) **5 (6 goals)**

Ted Drake was quite simply a goal machine. A remarkable athlete who could have excelled at several sports, Drake was a very competent cricketer who turned out for Hampshire CCC, but chose football as a long-term career. Like Alan Shearer nearly 60 years later, Drake scored a hat-trick on his

when Arsenal drew 6-6 at Leicester City. Reserve striker David Halliday scored four goals that day - and he was still dropped for the Final. To reach that Final Arsenal had to battle back from 2-0 down to scrape a draw with Huddersfield, mirroring an almost identical scenario to that of the 1971 semi-final against Stoke City - both games going down as two of the most important in the Club's history.

Another memorable draw occurred in October 1963 when Spurs were cruising to a 4-2 win before two late goals - the equaliser coming from the head of Geoff Strong - pegged the old rivals back. It came almost a year to the day after the two sides achieved the same scoreline at White Hart Lane.

And one of Highbury's last nights was also one of the Club's greatest, when a pulsating 0-0 draw with Real Madrid gave Arsenal a fantastic 1-0 aggregate win in the Champions League first knockout round.

In the Wenger era, a draw that also stands out came in 1997 when Dennis Bergkamp scored a hat-trick at Leicester in a pulsating Premiership clash which ended 3-3, with two of the goals coming in injury time.

Highest scoring home draw overall
4-4 on six occasions - most recently
v Tottenham, 15 Oct 1963, Div 1

Highest scoring away draw overall
6-6 v Leicester City, 21 April 1930, Div 1

Highest scoring home draws in the Premiership
3-3 v Chelsea, 4 Sept 1996

3-3 v Sheffield Wednesday,
9 May 2000

---

debut as a teenager for Southampton in 1931 and after 48 goals in 72 appearances became George Allison's first signing as Arsenal manager for £6,500 in March 1934.

He scored on his Gunners debut in a 3-2 win over Wolves and won a title medal the following season after firing 42 goals in just 41 league games, and 44 in total - a Club record. That season he had also been one of seven Arsenal players to feature for England in a 3-2 win over world champions Italy at Highbury. Naturally, he scored the opener.

His finest hour came at Villa Park in December 1935 when he set a record with all seven goals in a 7-1 victory, but he missed large chunks of that season due to a serious knee injury. However, he returned to score the winner against Sheffield

United in the FA Cup Final and earned another title medal in 1938, putting in an heroic performance at Brentford in the run-in which saw him sustain a broken wrist and several stitches in his head before he was eventually carried off unconscious.

After the war he became the first Chelsea manager to win the title, in 1955, with an exciting young team dubbed 'Drake's Ducklings'.

DRAWS

The greatest draw in the history of English top-flight football involved the Gunners just a few days before the 1930 FA Cup Final,

3-3 v Blackburn Rovers,
20 Oct 2001

Highest scoring away draw in the Premiership
3-3 v Leicester City, 27 Aug 1997

Highest scoring home draws in all European competitions
2-2 v Brondby (Den), 3 Nov 1994, ECWC, Rd 2

2-2 v Bayern Munich (Ger), 5 Dec 2000, CL, Gp St 2

Highest scoring away draws in all European competitions
3-3 v Nantes (Fra), 9 Dec 1999, UEFA Cup, Rd 3

2-2 v Magdeburg (Ger), 7 Nov 1979, ECWC, Rd 2

Highest scoring home draw in UEFA Champions League
2-2 v Bayern Munich (Ger), 5 Dec 2000, GpSt 2

Highest scoring away draw in UEFA Champions League
1-1 v Chelsea, 24 March 2004, QF, 1 lg

DUCAT, Andy

Born **Brixton, London, 16 February 1886**
Died **23 July 1942**
Arsenal appearances **175**
Arsenal goals **19**

Andy Ducat was the Brixton-born prodigy who excelled for Woolwich Arsenal as the Club's premier player before the First World War as well as starring with bat and ball for Surrey CCC and England. He made his debut as an 18-year-old against Blackburn Rovers in February 1905. Three years later he joined Surrey, and he ran two careers side by side until his retirement from football in 1924. In July 1942, while batting at Lord's for the Army,

he collapsed after lunch and died – the last person to die while playing at the home of cricket. He was 56.

DUTCH GUNNERS

The first foreigner to play for Arsenal was a Dutchman, **Gerard Keyser** (see Foreign Players on page 86).

The Ajax goalkeeper arrived at Highbury in the summer of 1930 and made 12 appearances for the Club. He later moved back to Ajax and, because of his links with the two clubs, Arsenal provided the Amsterdammers with a set of kit after the war as Holland was in the grip of huge shortages.

Rudi Krol – the Netherlands' skipper in the 1978 World Cup – came within a whisker of becoming the second Dutchman to play for Arsenal. Manager Terry Neill bid £225,000 for the Ajax midfielder in 1979, but despite Krol's willingness to move, the deal broke down at the last minute.

One of George Graham's last acts as manager was to sign winger **Glenn Helder** from Vitesse Arnhem in February 1995. The Lieden-born flankman could perform an array of bewildering stepovers and darting runs, but he was dogged by inconsistency.

His former Ajax youth team-mate, however, would become an Arsenal legend. The Club's most celebrated Dutch signing came in the summer of 1995 when **Dennis Bergkamp** arrived from Internazionale. After a few meek performances for Arsenal, Bergkamp hit form spectacularly with a double against Southampton and never looked back, illuminating Highbury for more than a decade until his retirement in the summer of 2006. Blessed with skill, vision and a sublime first touch, the Dutch Master comfortably joined the Arsenal Hundred Club (see The Hundred Club on page 112) and was outstanding for many seasons, notably the Double year of 1997/98 when he hit unparalleled form in the run-in.

He was joined at the beginning of that season by another Ajax old boy – **Marc Overmars.** The little winger had been ignored by many clubs due to a persistent

knee injury, but Arsène Wenger had no such fears and he was rewarded as Overmars' lightning pace and scoring touch gave Arsenal new attacking options. His goal in a 1-0 win at Manchester United in March 1998, which put Arsenal in the driving seat on the run-in, epitomised his qualities, his little legs scampering away from trailing defenders before scoring with a crisp finish. He also scored in the FA Cup Final win over Newcastle United as Arsenal clinched the Double that year.

Giovanni van Bronckhorst was a left-sided utility man equally comfortable in defence or midfield signed from Glasgow Rangers in 2001, but he failed to make an impact and picked up his career at Barcelona after playing just enough games to earn a title medal in 2001/02.

Quincy Owusu-Abeyie, bought up in Amsterdam but of Ghanaian ancestry, was another former student of the Ajax school of excellence. He joined Arsenal in September 2002, but despite immense promise failed to make an impact and after just 23 appearances and two goals he departed for Spartak Moscow in January 2006 and is currently on loan with Celta de Vigo.

Robin van Persie was voted Dutch Young Player of the Year while at local club Feyenoord, where he starred in their UEFA Cup win of 2002. Strong, athletic and with an eye for the unexpected, comparisons have already been made with another Dutch Arsenal legend, Dennis Bergkamp. Jaap de Groot, chief football writer of *De Telegraaf,* says, 'It's in a lot of people's minds that he is the perfect replacement.' Injuries have hampered van Persie's Gunners career so far, but he remains a key component of Arsène Wenger's squad.

Vincent van den Berg played for SC Heerenveen as a youngster before moving to Arsenal in the summer of 2006. The striker represented the Netherlands when they reached third place in the FIFA Under-17 World Cup in Peru that year. He came on as a substitute in the first ever game at Emirates Stadium, Bergkamp's testimonial, just weeks after joining the club. He played the second half of the 2007/08 season in his native country on loan at Go Ahead Eagles of Deventer.

EAST STAND

One of the most recognisable structures in world football, the famous Art Deco East Stand was constructed in 1936 at a cost of £130,000 and opened in October of that year as an identical twin for the West Stand.

Until the summer of 2006 and the move to Emirates Stadium, the stand accommodated much of Arsenal's administrative offices, the media and press and publications department, the boardroom and the trophy room. It also housed the dressing rooms and famous marble halls inside its grand entrance on Avenell Road.

Designed by William Binnie, it originally had 8,000 seats – 4,000 in the upper tier and 4,000 in the lower – along with a paddock for standing spectators. It remained as it had been built for most of its life, the only noticeable changes to the naked eye were that its original green seats were replaced by red and white ones in 1988 and an electric scoreboard was added shortly afterwards. The paddock was also made all-seater in the early 1990s. The stand's listed status means it cannot be demolished, and, after its conversion, will include more than 100 homes as part of the new Highbury Square development.

EASTENDERS

Here's a list of Gunners, past and present, born within – or not far from – the sound of Bow Bells:

Tony Adams (Romford)
Sol Campbell (Newham)
Danny Clapton (Stepney)
Dennis Clapton (Hackney)
Ashley Cole (Stepney)
Perry Groves (Bow)
Vic Groves (Stepney)
George Male (West Ham)
David O'Leary (Stoke Newington)
Ray Parlour (Romford)
Richie Powling (Barking)
Gerry Ward (Stepney)
Len Wills (Hackney)

EASTHAM, George

Born **Blackpool, 23 September 1936**
Arsenal appearances **223**
Arsenal goals **41**
International caps (England) **19 (2 goals)**

The Jean-Marc Bosman of his day, George Eastham's dogged determination to earn a decent wage now allows the modern player to earn fabulous wealth from simply playing the beautiful game.

When, in December 1959, Eastham wanted to move to Highbury from Newcastle United, his employers dug their heels in and refused, retaining his playing licence. Clubs had been doing this to their players for as long as anyone could remember under the 'retain and transfer' system and Eastham decided enough was

George Eastham (with ball) and John Barnwell take to the field at Highbury. Eastham's battle to join Arsenal helped change the face of football.

E

enough. He took his case to the High Court, claiming it was unfair restraint of trade, and eventually won his battle for freedom of contract. Newcastle were forced to accept a £47,500 fee and, after a year out of the game, he made his debut for the Gunners in a 5-1 win over Bolton Wanderers, scoring twice.

Eastham went on to captain the Club and made 19 appearances for England. When he was on form, his deft touches, eye for a defence-splitting ball and adroit technique made him a delight to watch for Highbury crowds in the early 1960s.

He was an unused member of England's 1966 World Cup-winning squad.

ELCOAT, George

MANAGER 1898/99
Born Stockton-on-Tees, circa 1864
Died Unknown

Woolwich Arsenal's second professional manager only stayed with the Club for one season - 1898/99 - resigning after he became fed up with the financial constraints being imposed on his teambuilding.

Elcoat played mainly Scottish players - eight of his regular side were from north of the border - but his pro-Caledonian policy didn't pay in the FA Cup, the Gunners being soundly beaten 6-0 at home by Derby County in the first round. However, in the newly expanded 18-team Second Division, the Club finished a creditable seventh behind champions Manchester City. He signed off his tenure with a 3-0 home win over Barnsley on 22 April 1899.

EMIRATES STADIUM

Arsenal's brand new stadium has breathed new life into the centre of Islington - and propelled the club into Europe's elite. The

skyline has changed dramatically in north London with the new arena rising just a few hundred yards from Highbury.

The Gunners finally moved to their plush new home in the summer of 2006 – nearly seven years after first making public their commitment to leaving Highbury. The stadium is the focal point of a huge £357m project that has so far created nearly 1,800 new jobs and is well on the way to building 2,000 extra homes in an area in desperate need of new accommodation. The former stadium is also set to become one of north London's premier housing developments. Meanwhile, the new state-of-the-art arena – named Emirates after the airline secured a £100m sponsorship deal with the Club – is now established as one of the finest sporting venues in the world.

Arsenal first announced their intention to move in November 1999 and construction work - carried out by Robert McAlpine Ltd - commenced early in 2004 after the Club had secured planning permission, with approximately 2,500 separate legal documents needing to be signed in order for the site to be cleared and ready. At the project's peak 1,000 construction workers were employed at the stadium, which dominates a 17-acre site between Drayton Park and Holloway Road.

Designed by HOK Sport - the same company behind the new Wembley and the revamped Centre Court at Wimbledon - the stadium is a far cry from the 1930s Art Deco opulence of Highbury. The huge roof is 42 metres high and underneath its massive span has 150 executive boxes - compared to less than a third of that number at Highbury - and 41 TV camera positions to home in on all the action on the new pitch, which measures 113 x 76 metres, compared to 105 x 70 metres at the old stadium. To improve the quality of the new playing surface, extensive computer modelling was carried out to study the

Well in excess of 1.1 million fans have clicked through the custom-made, automated turnstiles at the Emirates Stadium during Arsenal's first two seasons at their magnificent, state-of-the-art home.

sunlight and ventilation at pitch level, in full consultation with Arsenal's multi-award winning groundsman Paul Burgess (see Groundsman on page 101). It obviously worked: Burgess and his dedicated team picked up yet another gong in 2007/08 – the Premier League best pitch award.

Outside the stadium two new bridges have been constructed to ease congestion, while the pride of Arsenal's retail arm - the 10,000 square feet Club shop 'The Armoury' - dominates the stadium's west flank. Inside, the stadium boasts more legroom than any other arena in the UK while there are also 500 television screens dotted around to ensure spectators don't miss any of the action. This is in addition to two massive screens at either end of the ground.

More importantly, the increased number of seats means an extra 22,000

supporters have been able to watch every home game, helping create a huge leap in revenue. In Arsenal's first two seasons at the Emirates, well in excess of 1.1m fans clicked through the turnstiles - nearly 400,000 more than visited Highbury in its final season. Average attendances since the move have been in excess of 60,000 - the highest in the Club's history. The official stadium capacity stands at 60,432. This is divided up into the following: Lower Tier 24,435, Upper Tier 26,646, Club Level 7,139 and Box Level 2,222.

In May 2008 the stadium also hosted its first rock concert when American legend Bruce Springsteen played in front of 60,000 fans. 'Let's christen the Emirates Stadium,' he roared.

ENGLAND CAPTAINS

Eight Arsenal players have captained the national side. Striker David Jack was the first Gunner afforded the honour when he wore the captain's armband on four occasions between 1930 and 1932. He was followed by Eddie Hapgood, who skippered England more times than any other Gunner - on 21 occasions between 1934 and 1939, including the infamous 3-2 win over world champions Italy at Highbury (see Battle of Highbury on page 27). His full-back partner George Male was also skipper six times in 1936 and 1937. The last Arsenal player to captain England was Martin Keown in 2000.

The full list of Arsenal's England captains:
David Jack (4) - 1930/32
Eddie Hapgood (21) - 1934/39
George Male (6) - 1936/37
Alan Ball (6) - 1975
David Platt (2) - 1996
Tony Adams (15) - 1994/2000
David Seaman (1) - 1997
Martin Keown (1) - 2000

In addition, in 1933 Herbert Chapman became the first professional manager to take charge of England for a 1-1 draw with Italy in Rome, although he was not allowed

---

Left Home sweet home: Emirates Stadium looks resplendent for its first ever match - Dennis Bergkamp's testimonial between Arsenal and Ajax Amsterdam on 22 July 2006. Completed within budget and on time, it is one of the premier footballing arenas in Europe.

any input into the selection process, the team being determined by the FA's International Selection Committee. One Arsenal player was in the England 1966 World Cup-winning squad - George Eastham - but he failed to get a game during the tournament.

ENGLISH XI

These days we are used to seeing Arsenal manager Arsène Wenger field a team with maybe only one or two Englishmen in the starting line-up. 'I don't look at their passport, only their ability,' he says.

It has been a long time since an exclusive English XI was fielded. You have to go all the way back to 19 April 1994, when the following players were chosen to play in the 1-1 home draw with Wimbledon, Steve Bould scoring Arsenal's goal.

David Seaman
Lee Dixon
Martin Keown
Tony Adams (captain)
Steve Bould
Paul Davis
Ray Parlour
Ian Selley
Ian Wright
Alan Smith
Kevin Campbell
Sub:
Mark Flatts

The all-English side was broken up in the next match - a 2-1 win at Aston Villa courtesy of a Ian Wright double - when Northern Ireland midfielder Steve Morrow replaced Ray Parlour in the starting line-up.

EPIC CUP REPLAYS

We got there in the end... here are a few cup ties that needed more than one game.

v Hull City,
FA Cup semi-final, 1930
David Jack and Cliff Bastin clawed Arsenal back after they were 2-0 down in the first match and Jack did the rest in the replay with the only goal in a tense affair.

v Newcastle United,
FA Cup 5th round, 1936
Ray Bowden (2) and Joe Hulme had salvaged a 3-3 draw in front of 65,484 at St James' Park before two Cliff Bastin penalties and a Pat Beasley strike earned a 3-0 win in the Highbury replay.

v Chelsea, FA Cup semi-final, 1950
Leslie Compton's last-gasp header earned a replay after Chelsea had led 2-0 at White Hart Lane and Freddie Cox's solitary strike in the second game - at the same ground - put Arsenal through, despite ferocious Chelsea pressure.

v Bedford, FA Cup 3rd round, 1956
Southern League Bedford were four minutes from a replay win before Vic Groves equalised and Derek Tapscott scored an extra-time winner at the Eyrie to hand Arsenal a 2-1 victory. Bedford had earned a 2-2 Highbury draw to take the tie to a second game.

v Stoke City,
FA Cup semi-final, 1971
Arsenal were dead and buried at half-time at Hillsborough as they trailed 2-0. But Peter Storey pulled one back and then held his nerve to score an injury-time penalty. More than 62,000 were at the Villa Park replay - won 2-0 thanks to goals from George Graham and Ray Kennedy.

Martin Keown on international duty. The Oxford-born defender was in the last Gunners side to field 11 Englishmen - in April 1994.

v Sheffield Wednesday, FA Cup 3rd Round, 1979

A true epic against the Third Division pace-setters who took the tie to five matches, including a thrilling 3-3 draw in the third replay, before goals from Frank Stapleton and Steve Gatting finally put Arsenal through.

v Liverpool, FA Cup semi-final, 1980

This was another titanic struggle as champions-elect Liverpool proved stubborn opponents with three games drawn before Brian Talbot settled the fourth with a firm header to put Arsenal through to their third successive FA Cup Final.

v Tottenham, Littlewoods Cup semi-final, 1987

Niall Quinn and Viv Anderson both scored in the second leg to make the tie 2-2 on aggregate, but the replay brought new drama. Clive Allen fired Spurs into the lead, but substitute Ian Allison levelled at the near post with less than ten minutes to go. David Rocastle fired a 90th-minute winner through the legs of Ray Clemence to earn a first Wembley final in seven years.

v Leeds United, FA Cup 4th round, 1993

The first game had ended 2-2 and it was back to Fortess Elland Road where Leeds led 2-1 before Alan Smith levelled and Ian Wright scored a dramatic extra-time winner to win it 3-2 for the Gunners.

EUROPEAN CUP

Arsenal played in two European Cup campaigns before the switch to the Champions League format in 1992. On both occasions the Gunners limped out of the competition after devastating home defeats, despite being strongly fancied by the bookies to go all the way.

Arsenal's 1971 title gave them their first stab at the world's premier club competition. Norwegian part-timers Strømgodset were easily beaten 7-1 on aggregate in the first round: John Radford (2), George Armstrong and Ray Kennedy netting in a 4-0 home win

after Peter Simpson, Eddie Kelly and Peter Marinello's goals earned Arsenal a 3-1 win in Norway in the Club's first ever European Cup tie. The second round saw Grasshopper Zurich beaten 2-0 in Switzerland, courtesy of goals from Kennedy and George Graham, before Kennedy, Charlie George and Radford wrapped up a 3-0 home win.

Then came the glamour tie everyone had been waiting for against reigning European Cup holders Ajax in March 1972. Arsenal came away from the Netherlands with a narrow 2-1 defeat after a Gerrit Muhren double gave Ajax a 2-1 win in the Olympic Stadium, Kennedy replying for Arsenal with a header. It set up a stirring return in north London. The maths were simple – a 1-0 win would put Arsenal through. There was only one goal at Highbury and unfortunately it went to the Dutch masters after poor communication between Bob Wilson and George Graham saw Graham head the ball over the keeper and into his own net.

UEFA's ban on English clubs meant Arsenal could not contest the 1989/90 European Cup, but the 1991/92 competition finally saw them make a long overdue return to continental competition. However, just 24,124 turned out for the visit of Vienna outfit Austria Memphis, with many preferring to watch the game on television, but those who stayed away missed out as Alan Smith marked his European bow with four goals in a 6-1 win, Andy Linighan netting the first and Anders Limpar the last. A 1-0 defeat in the second leg in central Europe proved merely academic and Arsenal progressed to meet Portuguese giants Benfica, managed by Sven-Goran Eriksson.

Kevin Campbell silenced the 84,000 crowd at Lisbon's Stadium of Light in the first leg when he equalised late on in a 1-1 draw. Arsenal went for the jugular in the return leg at Highbury with a barnstorming opening and their endeavours paid off when Colin Pates, recently signed from Chelsea, gave them the lead until a sensational curling strike from Brazilian Isaias beat David Seaman and levelled matters just before the break.

After 90 minutes the scoreline was still 1-1, with Arsenal enjoying far more of the play and feeling a touch aggrieved not to have won the tie after Paul Merson's strike was ruled out and Campbell hit the woodwork.

But European know-how counted in extra time with tiring limbs and minds affecting George Graham's side. Benfica pulled away to take advantage of gaps at the back with Russian Kulkov, and the impressive Isaias with his second, giving the Eagles of Lisbon a 3-1 win.

EUROPEAN CUP-WINNERS' CUP

WINNERS

Arsenal's first European trophy for 24 years was secured when Alan Smith scored the only goal of the game to defeat favourites AS Parma 1-0 at Copenhagen's Parken Stadium in 1994.

The campaign had started a short way from the Danish capital in Odense when Arsenal beat local side OB 2-1, late goals from Ian Wright and Paul Merson proving decisive. Kevin Campbell scored in a 1-1 draw in the second leg at Highbury. It had been a shaky start to the competition, but Arsenal improved to beat Standard Liege 3-0 in the next round, Ian Wright plundering two more. He was dropped for the return, but it didn't matter as Arsenal won 7-0 in Belgium – their biggest ever European win.

Next up was a real war of attrition against Torino. Lee Dixon came closest to breaking the deadlock, but his late effort skidded wide of the Torino goal in a defensive stalemate in Italy. That set up a tense Highbury affair with Torino knowing a 1-1 draw would put them through. But their strikeforce of Benito Carbone and Andrea Silenzi were snuffed out in a masterful defensive performance by captain Tony Adams. And it was the skipper who was on hand to score the only goal of the game with a firm header from a set piece that put Arsenal through to the last four.

Paris Saint-Germain were next, spearheaded by the mercurial talents of David Ginola and unbeaten in 35 matches. But Ian Wright soon gave them food for thought when he brilliantly headed in Paul Davis' cross. PSG levelled five minutes after the break, but Arsenal – roared on by a fantastic support – had got that vital away goal. Kevin Campbell headed the only goal of the second leg to put Arsenal through to the Final.

The only black mark was a second yellow card for Wright, earning the striker a one-match European ban – from the Final. He sat out the match along with Dane John Jensen who had picked up an injury a few days before the match.

In the event Arsenal packed the midfield and relied on Smith, with his ability to hold the ball up, to cause Parma problems. Parma looked to get an early goal with the attacking triumvirate of Gianfranco Zola, Tomas Brolin and Tino Asprilla. Brolin struck a post and Zola saw his effort magnificently turned over by David Seaman, who had been given injections minutes before kick-off to dull the pain of bruised ribs. The keeper would later say it was the best save of his career to date.

Parma had flair in abundance, but Arsenal's red wall of shirts stood firm and then, with 21 minutes played, they took a shock lead when Smith pounced on a poor header from Lorenzo Minotti to send an excellent volley past Luca Bucci. Try as they might Parma could not trouble Seaman and Arsenal held on to take the trophy. Ecstatic Gunners boss George Graham said, 'We're a Club with marvellous spirit.'

Graham – a player when the Fairs Cup was won in 1970 – holds a unique position in Arsenal history, having been involved in both of the Club's first two European successes.

LOSERS

Arsenal lost two finals in this competition, and both times it was in heart-breaking circumstances against Spanish opposition.

1980

Arsenal's energy-sapping 70-game season was coming to its conclusion. Terry Neill's side had already lost the FA Cup Final to West Ham on the Saturday, before heading to Brussels to take on Valencia. Fenerbahce, Magdeburg and IFK Gothenburg had all been beaten, before Paul Vaessen's last-minute header at Juventus in the second leg of the semi-final had secured a dramatic 2–1 aggregate win. By the time they reached Belgium, Arsenal were exhausted.

Liam Brady was playing his last game for the Club before moving to Juve, whose coach Giovanni Trapattoni had been suitably impressed with his two performances in the semi-finals, and he wanted to go out on a high. Despite his best efforts, Arsenal could not make the breakthrough and with

Wonderful, Wonderful Copenhagen. Alan Smith volleys the only goal of the 1994 European Cup-Winners'-Cup final against Parma at the Parken Stadium.

Valencia also failing to trouble Pat Jennings, the tie went to a penalty shootout.

The two outstanding players on the pitch – Brady and Argentina World Cup-winner Mario Kempes, superbly shacked by David O'Leary over the 120 minutes – missed the first two penalties. The next eight were all converted, before Ricardo Arias put Valencia 5-4 up in sudden death. Graham Rix needed to score to keep Arsenal in the match, but saw his effort saved by Carlos Perreira to send the cup to Spain. 'I'll never forget the Arsenal fans singing my name afterwards. They were incredible. It still makes me emotional even now to think of their support,' Rix said 25 years later.

1995

It had been a season of turmoil for Arsenal with George Graham departing in controversial circumstances and a huge underperformance in the league seeing the side even briefly flirt with relegation. But caretaker Stewart Houston had managed to guide the holders to a second successive final, thanks largely to Ian Wright, who had set a new European club record of scoring in every match en route to the Final at the Parc de Prince in Paris.

Omonia Nicosia, Brondby and Auxerre had been overcome before an enthralling two-legged semi-final against Italians Sampdoria ended 6-6 on aggregate. The second leg, in Genoa, had eventually gone to penalties with David Seaman the hero as he saved Attilio Lombardo's spot-kick to put the Gunners through.

Arsenal faced Real Zaragoza in the Final and the Spaniards took the lead through Juan Esnaider. But Wales striker John Hartson stabbed home a second-half equaliser and the match went to extra time.

Penalties looked to be on the cards again, but Arsenal were undone by a moment of true genius. With Seaman off his line playing as a sweeper to intercept Zaragoza's penatrating through balls, former Spurs midfielder Nayim looked up and fired a majestic 50-yard shot over his head. Seaman scuttled back to his goal and did well to get a touch of the ball, but he could only help it over the line. It was the 120th minute of the game and there was no way back for a devastated Arsenal.

EUROPEAN NIGHTS

GREAT GAMES ON THE CONTINENT

Arsenal have consistently achieved remarkable results on their European travels.

The Gunners' first ever tie produced eight goals – with seven going to the Gunners. Geoff Strong and Joe Baker both hit trebles in a 7-1 victory at Staevnet from Copenhagen in September 1963.

Arsenal took several trips behind the Iron Curtain in the late 1970s, but none gave them more satisfaction than a powerful 4-1 UEFA Cup win over Lokomotiv Leipzig in September 1978, Frank Stapleton silencing a partisan 22,000 crowd in East Germany with two goals.

The greatest European night during Terry Neill's rein undoubtedly came in Turin's Stadio Communale in the second leg of the 1980 Cup-Winners' Cup semi-final against mighty Juventus. The sides drew 1-1 at Highbury and Juve only needed to keep a clean sheet to reach the final. Just two minutes remained when substitute Paul Vaessen, who had promised coach Don Howe he would score if given the chance, headed Graham Rix's deep cross past Dino Zoff for the only goal of the game. It was the first time a British side had beaten the 'Old Lady' in her own backyard. Arsenal would enjoy another glory night at Juve in April 2006 when they drew 0-0 to reach the Champions League semi-final for the first in their history. In fact, Italy has been a happy stomping ground for the Gunners in the Champions League. In November 2002 Thierry Henry hit a brilliant hat-trick to beat Roma 3-1 at the Stadio Olimpico and 12 months later he scored twice as Arsenal romped to a stunning 5-1 win at Internazionale. Fredrik Ljungberg, Edu and Robert Pires completed the scoring in a game voted the second greatest in the Club's history in a recent fans' poll.

The biggest ever win away from home came at Standard Liege in November 1993 when George Graham's side hit seven without reply in a Cup-Winners' Cup second round tie. The following season the same competition provided two great nights. Guy Roux's Auxerre had drawn 1-1 at Highbury in the first leg of the quarter-final, but Arsenal displayed all their famous spirit to shut them

out in France and Ian Wright snatched a goal at the other end with a stunning 30-yard strike to win the tie. In the semi-final, Arsenal beat Sampdoria 3-2 at Highbury, but looked to be going out as they trailed 3-1 late in the second leg until a fabulous Stefan Schwarz free-kick made it 6-6 on aggregate. David Seaman then produced a fine display in the penalty shootout to brilliantly save Attilio Lombardo's kick and send Arsenal through.

Seaman was injured in 2000 when Ray Parlour scored an unlikely hat-trick in Germany as Arsenal chalked up an excellent 4-2 win at Werder Bremen in a UEFA Cup quarter-final, second leg, despite having Thierry Henry – scorer of the other goal – being sent off.

And Gilberto memorably scored the fastest goal in Champions League history – in just 20.07 seconds – to set up a thrilling 4-0 win at Eredivisie leaders PSV Eindhoven. Ajax were also beaten 2-1 in Amsterdam in the same competition in 2005/06, and later that season Henry scored the only goal as Arsenal became the first British side to beat Real Madrid in the Spanish capital.

GREAT GAMES AT HIGHBURY

Highbury at night was a magical – and intimidating – setting when the continent's finest came to north London. Remember these games?

Arsenal 3-0 Ajax, April 1970, European Fairs Cup semi-final, first leg

The Gunners announced their arrival on the European stage with a devastating show against the previous season's European Cup finalists containing Dutch masters Rudi Krol and Johan Cruyff. Charlie George hit two and Jon Sammels the other that night... all the more impressive when you consider the Dutch side went on to win three European Cups in a row shortly afterwards.

Arsenal 3-0 Anderlecht 0, April 1970, European Fairs Cup Final, second leg

Arsenal fought back from a 3-1 first-leg deficit to win their first trophy for 17 years amid unprecedented scenes at Highbury. Eddie Kelly fired an early goal to make it 2-3 on aggregate and John Radford made it 2-0 on the night to pull the sides level. Jon Sammels drilled home a late third to clinch the trophy.

EUROPEAN SUPER CUP

Arsenal have only contested the European Super Cup on one occasion. As European-Cup-Winners' Cup holders, the Gunners were pitted against crack Italian opposition in European Cup holders AC Milan. The first leg was played at Highbury on 1 February 1995 and an entertaining game ended all square at 0-0. Arsenal then travelled to Italy, but were comfortably beaten 2-0 at the San Siro.

EXILED THEN ELECTED

Arsenal 6-1 Austria Memphis, Sept 1991, European Cup, Rd 1, first leg

Alan Smith made a dream European debut as the Gunners fired some heavy artillery in their first European Cup tie for nearly 20 years. The centre-forward scored four against a shell-shocked Austrian side who had fallen behind in the first half to Andy Linighan's close-range strike. Anders Limpar capped a fine display late on with Arsenal's sixth.

Arsenal 5-1 Deportivo La Coruña, March 2000, UEFA Cup, Rd 4, first leg

Arsenal were back at Highbury after two Champions League campaigns at Wembley and it was a case of home sweet home as the La Liga champions-elect were blown away. This was thanks to two goals from Thierry Henry, and other goals from Dennis Bergkamp, Lee Dixon and Kanu, the latter scoring a brilliant solo effort after an outrageous dummy on the Coruña goalkeeper.

Arsenal 3-1 Juventus, December 2001, Champions League, Gp St

Stuart Taylor played the game of his life in goal on a rare first-team start and Fredrik

Ljungberg was sensational at the other end with a two-goal show to see off the Old Lady. Thierry Henry hit the other in the best Champions League showing to date.

Arsenal 0-0 Real Madrid, April 2006, Champions League, first knockout rd

0-0 to the Arsenal! The Gunners, with the comfort of a one-goal advantage, locked horns with the Galacticos in a truly titanic night of football. The game ebbed and flowed with missed chances, great saves and derring-do on both sides. If ever a game deserved a goal it was this, but, for pure aesthetics, this still must go down as the most entertaining European match ever played at Highbury.

Arsenal 2-0 Juventus, April 2006, Champions League, quarter-final

Patrick Vieira's return to Highbury was dominated by his replacement, young Cesc Fabregas. The Spanish teenager was outstanding against the Serie A leaders and scored the opener with a well-placed shot past Gianluigi Buffon. Arsenal's superiority was confirmed in the second half when Thierry Henry hit a second as the Bianconeri finished the game with nine men.

In 1891 members of Woolwich Arsenal voted to make the Club professional, the first football club south of Birmingham to do so. The London FA – which opposed all forms of professionalism – was furious its leading side had 'sold out' and immediately ostracised the Club, banning it from all local competitions. The only competition open to them that year was the FA Cup – they lost 5-1 to Small Heath (later Birmingham) in the first round. Arsenal had to resort to playing friendlies against sides from the Midlands and north of England. When the Club proposed the formation of a Southern League the London FA threatened to ban any club that joined it, leaving the Gunners isolated.

Woolwich Arsenal had been in the wilderness for two years by 1893 and, after failing in their proposal to set up a southern professional league, were desperate for competitive football. But the Club's exile from the London FA would be a blessing in disguise when it decided to apply for election to the new expanded Second Division. Along with Newcastle and Liverpool, Woolwich Arsenal were elected to become the first side south of Birmingham to join the new professional ranks.

WINNERS (TEN TIMES)

1930 - Arsenal 2-0 Huddersfield Town

Herbert Chapman's side were fortunate to reach their second FA Cup Final in four years after they came back from 2-0 down to force a replay against Hull in the semi-final. David Jack, who had scored the opener for Bolton against West Ham in the first ever Wembley final in 1923, netted the only goal of the replay to hand Chapman a place at Wembley against his former club Huddersfield.

Out of respect for football's most charismatic – and successful – manager, the two sides entered the playing arena side-by-side, establishing a cup tradition. The German *Graf Zeppelin* airship flew over the stadium, much to the 100,000 crowd's bemusement, but down on the ground Arsenal were flying and took an early lead when Alex James took a quick free-kick, collected the return from Cliff Bastin and fired home. Jack Lambert sealed it late on when he raced on to James' long ball.

1936 - Arsenal 1-0 Sheffield United

The run up to Wembley had been an exhilarating one after Arsenal opened with a 5-1 win at Bristol Rovers. A 2-0 victory at Liverpool followed – described by the Arsenal programme as 'one of the most glorious performances' in the Club's history – and then a 3-3 draw at Newcastle in front of nearly 66,000 fans. A 3-0 home win in the replay – the first Highbury FA Cup game for two years – gave Arsenal a home tie with Barnsley, the Gunners in unfamiliar striped shirts winning 4-1, before Cliff Bastin hit the only goal of the semi-final against Grimsby at Leeds Road.

Ted Drake returned from injury for the Final to save the Gunners' season with a late winner against Second Division Sheffield United, a match from which newsreels were banned after a dispute with the FA.

1950 - Arsenal 2-0 Liverpool

Arsenal wore gold for their first post-war FA Cup win. Reg Lewis struck either side of the interval in a 2-0 victory, but the star of the show was veteran skipper Joe Mercer, the affable scouser who commuted to north London for home games from his native Merseyside, where he ran a grocery store in Wallasey. 'This is the greatest moment of my life,' he said afterwards, clutching his one and only FA Cup winner's medal, 'but I would like to say how wonderful the Liverpool boys have been.'

Arsenal had not left north London in their cup run. Highbury wins against Sheffield Wednesday, Swansea, Burnley and Leeds, watched by an average of more than 57,000, set up a semi-final with Chelsea at White Hart Lane. Chelsea led 2-0, but goals from Freddie Cox and Leslie Compton earned a replay. Cox scored the only goal in the second game to take the Gunners to Wembley.

1971 - Arsenal 2-1 Liverpool (aet)

While the 1950 Final was the story of a hero in the twilight of his career, 1971 was all about a youthful Charlie George. His 20-yard scorcher in extra time whistled past a helpless Ray Clemence for one of Wembley's greatest winners.

It had come after Liverpool had taken the lead in the early stages of extra time when Ireland international winger Steve Heighway beat Bob Wilson at his near post.

Joe Mercer holding the FA Cup Trophy is chaired off the pitch by his team-mates after Arsenal beat Liverpool 2-0 in the Final at Wembley on 29 April 1950. It was Arsenal's third cup win and the Gunners wore an unusual gold strip for the occasion.

But Arsenal, shattered after winning the title at Spurs the Monday before, defied the heat to level through Eddie Kelly before George – a former Holloway schoolboy – became the hero of the hour for his boyhood favourites.

Arsenal, incidentally, nearly didn't make it to Wembley – 2-0 down to Stoke at Hillsborough, Peter Storey pulled one back early in the second half and then showed true courage to score a last-minute penalty past England goalkeeper Gordon Banks. Arsenal won the replay 2-0, thanks to goals from Ray Kennedy and George Graham.

1979 – Arsenal 3-2 Manchester United
The 1979 Final was a classic thanks to a late flurry of activity that earned it the nickname the 'Five-minute Final'. Brian Talbot and Frank Stapleton had given Arsenal a seemingly invincible 2-0 lead by half-time. But Gordon McQueen and Sammy McIlroy looked to have taken the game into extra time with two goals in as many minutes. With a minute left of normal time, Arsenal broke United hearts from the restart when Alan Sunderland converted Graham Rix's deep cross to leave the watching fans exhausted. Liam Brady admitted afterwards, 'I was dreading extra time – we were shattered!'

1993 – Arsenal 2-1 Sheffield Wednesday (aet)
There were more last-minute heroics for Arsenal when they won their sixth FA Cup in 1993. But this time the winner came in the final throes of extra time in a replay. Ian Wright had given Arsenal the lead, but American John Harkes levelled for Sheffield Wednesday to force a second game the following Thursday. Just 62,267 – the lowest post-war FA Cup Final attendance at the national stadium – were present to see Wright fire Arsenal ahead again, but Chris Waddle equalised to take the tie to extra time. Penalties looked on the cards until Paul Merson swung over a corner and defender Andy Linighan headed the decider after another 120 minutes of football.

1998 – Arsenal 2-0 Newcastle United
Goals from Marc Overmars and Nicolas Anelka saw off Newcastle United 2-0 and earned a second Double for the Club. Overmars raced past Alessandro Pistone

to poke the ball under goalkeeper Shay Given for the opener and, despite a spirited Newcastle fightback in which Alan Shearer hit the post and was then denied with a brilliant goal-saving tackle by Nigel Winterburn, Anelka wrapped it up by springing the offside trap to run through and score after the break.

2002 – Arsenal 2-0 Chelsea
The first stage of a record-equalling third Double was secured in 2002 when Ray Parlour and Freddie Ljungberg scored second-half goals in a 2-0 win against Chelsea. Parlour hit the opener from 25 yards and Ljungberg scored for a second successive Final (he scored Arsenal's consolation goal against Liverpool in 2001) to confirm the win, in Tony Adams' last match for the Club.

Watford, Liverpool, Gillingham and, after a replay, Newcastle had been disposed of before an own goal was enough to see off Steve McClaren's Middlesbrough in the semi-final at Old Trafford.

2003 – Arsenal 1-0 Southampton
Southampton had reached their first FA Cup Final since 1976 and their raucous fans made for a stunning atmosphere in the Millennium Stadium. The game, however, was an uninspired affair, which Arsenal won 1-0.

David Seaman was playing his last game for the Club after a heroic performance in the semi-final which earned Arsenal their third successive appearance in the FA Cup Final. Freddie Ljungberg scored the winner against Sheffield United at Old Trafford, but it was Seaman – in his 1,000th senior appearance – that earned the accolades, somehow beating out Paul Peschisolido's point-blank header and prompting the great Gordon Banks to comment, 'It was in the same category as my save against Brazil in 1970.'

There was no such drama in Cardiff where one goal was enough to beat the Saints, Robert Pires breaking their hearts with a close-range winner late in the first half.

2005 – Arsenal 0-0 Manchester United (aet, Arsenal won 5-4 on pens)
Jens Lehmann saved Paul Scholes' penalty in a thrilling shootout – and, in his final competitive game in a Gunners jersey,

skipper Patrick Vieira scored the decisive spot-kick to hand Arsenal a tenth FA Cup.

It was rotten luck on United who had dominated the game from start to finish and had missed a host of chances, Ruud van Nistelrooy the main culprit, squandering a hat-trick of opportunities.

Lehmann had played his part with a sparkling performance between the sticks to save well from Paul Scholes, Cristiano Ronaldo and Wayne Rooney, the latter in his first major domestic final. But the game ended 0-0 after extra time – with Jose Antonio Reyes seeing red at the end – leaving Vieira to make his mark in the Welsh capital and ensure his place in Arsenal folklore forever.

RUNNERS-UP (SEVEN TIMES)
1927 – Arsenal 0-1 Cardiff City
Arsenal had reached the semis in 1906 and 1907, but went a step further in 1927. It was also the first occasion that the FA Cup Final was broadcast live on BBC radio. Scottish forward Hugh Ferguson scored the winner for Cardiff in a 1-0 win when his weak effort just had enough on it to beat Arsenal goalkeeper Dan Lewis, who let the ball slip through his fingers before it trickled over the line. Lewis was so distraught he threw away his loser's medal – and always blamed the shiny new jersey for the goal. It is the only occasion the cup has left England.

1932 – Arsenal 1-2 Newcastle United
Aiming for a second FA Cup Final success after their 1930 victory over Huddersfield Town, Arsenal lost to Newcastle United in controversial fashion in the infamous 'Over the Line Final'. Bob John's header gave the Gunners an early lead before Newcastle levelled when Jack Allen scored from Jimmy Richardson's centre. Arsenal's defenders had all stopped as the ball had appeared to cross the byline before Richardson crossed. When Allen stuck the ball into the net referee Bill Harper was expected to signal a goal kick. Instead, much to Arsenal's anger, he gave the goal. Nearly everyone in the stadium had seen the ball cross the line – with one exception. Arsenal players bit their lips but were now on the back foot and Allen scored again to take the cup north.

The infamous 1927 FA Cup Final's deciding moment: Arsenal goalkeeper Dan Lewis lets the ball slip through his fingers and over the line. A distraught Lewis later blamed his shiny new jersey for the error that sent the cup to his native Wales.

1980 – Arsenal 0-1 West Ham United
The third of three successive finals was an all-London affair and Arsenal were expected to overcome Second Division opponents West Ham with ease.

The Gunners had reached Wembley after a four-game semi-final marathon against Liverpool. But a tired Arsenal team – in the middle of an exhausting run of games – went down to a rare Trevor Brooking header. It could have been worse as Willie Young later infamously hauled down the Hammers' 17-year-old midfielder Paul Allen as he bore down on Pat Jennings' goal, but no penalty was given.

2001 – Arsenal 1-2 Liverpool
Arsenal's first visit to Cardiff's Millennium Stadium ended in a heartbreaking defeat after they looked set for a 1-0 victory. Freddie Ljungberg gave his side the lead against Liverpool as the Londoners dominated Gerard Houllier's side. Thierry Henry twice went close to adding to that goal – Stephane Henchoz appearing to handle the ball on the line – before Michael Owen took over.

First the England striker expertly dispatched the loose ball past David Seaman as Arsenal's defence went to sleep and then, with seconds remaining, he raced past the tired legs of Lee Dixon and placed the ball just inside Seaman's far post to leave Arsenal stunned and the cup on its way to Merseyside.

1952 – Arsenal 0-1 Newcastle United
Chilean George Robledo squeezed in his shot off the post for the only goal of the game against an injury-ravaged Gunners side who had to play the final 55 minutes with ten men when the inspirational Walley Barnes was carried off with a twisted knee. In the days before substitutes, Arsenal just had to make do and nearly levelled when Alex Forbes struck the woodwork, but it was not meant to be.

Captain Joe Mercer made an emotional speech at the cup final banquet later that evening. He famously told the diners, 'I thought football's greatest honour was to captain England. I was wrong. It was to captain Arsenal today.'

1972 – Arsenal 0-1 Leeds United
Arsenal's road to Wembley's Twin Towers in the FA Cup's centenary year was tough with away wins at Stoke and Reading before Derby were finally beaten after three games, with Charlie George scoring the winner. Leyton Orient were then overcome before Stoke provided the opposition in a semi-final in which keeper Bob Wilson was carried off with a cartilage injury and John Radford took the green jersey as Arsenal heroically held out for a draw.

They won the Goodison Park replay with Geoff Barnett in goal, but old enemy Leeds United denied Arsenal a second successive cup win when Allan Clarke headed Mick Jones' centre past goalkeeper Barnett for a 1-0 win.

1978 – Arsenal 0-1 Ipswich Town
Two FA Cup Final defeats sandwiched the 1979 success over Manchester United. In 1978 Bobby Robson's Ipswich side dominated from start to finish as a second-half Roger Osbourne goal proved enough to take the cup to East Anglia for the first time. Arsenal had played poorly with the barely fit Liam Brady substituted and Malcolm Macdonald again failing to shine at Wembley as he picked up another loser's medal.

FA YOUTH CUP

Arsenal made their first FA Youth Cup Final appearance in 1965, but were beaten 3-2 on aggregate by Everton. Since then they have reached five more finals – and won them all.

Charlie George (1966), David Hillier (1988) and Ashley Cole (2000) are three young guns who played in FA Youth Cup-winning sides and later went on to play for the first team.

1965 – Arsenal v Everton (lost 2-3 on agg)

1966 – Arsenal v Sunderland (won 5-3 on agg)

1971 – Arsenal v Cardiff City (won 2-0 on agg)

1988 – Arsenal v Doncaster Rovers (won 6-1 on agg)

2000 – Arsenal v Coventry City (won 5-1 on agg)

2001 – Arsenal v Blackburn Rovers (won 6-3 on agg)

FAB FREDDIE

Born **Halmstads, Sweden, 16 April 1977**
Arsenal appearances **285 (43)**
Arsenal goals **72**
International caps (Sweden) **71 (14 goals)**

An attacking midfielder and terrace favourite, Freddie Ljungberg announced his arrival from Halmstads in September 1998 with a debut goal against arch-rivals Manchester United in a 3-0 win, making himself an instant hero with the Highbury faithful. Since then a long series of eye-catching displays – and goals from midfield where he can excel at latching onto passes to arrive late in the opposition box to score – have ensured his status among fans. He impressed, in particular, in the 2001/02 Double-winning campaign and netted a superb second in the 2-0 FA Cup Final win over Chelsea. His overall scoring record for the Club is roughly one goal every four games.

Since signing for the Gunners in 2003 Cesc Fabregas has shown maturity beyond his years – it's no wonder that Arsène Wenger put so much faith in the youngster when he brought him into the side to replace Patrick Vieira.

His weird and wonderful fashion style has made him a regular in newspapers and magazines and his now famous dyed red hair caused a huge stir and inspired a fans' anthem sung to the tune of 'Can't Take My Eyes Off You' by Frankie Valli and the Four Seasons. He has also become one of the faces of Calvin Klein underwear.

Back on the pitch 'Freddie' has been a regular for the Swedish national side since Euro 2000, appearing over 50 times for his country. Injuries have hampered his progress at times, but with three Premiership title medals under his belt, the Swede's impact on English football was cemented when he was voted into the Premier League Overseas Team of the Decade in the Ten Seasons Award poll in 2002. With two titles and three FA Cups under his belt, he left Arsenal in July 2007, moving to West Ham United.

FABREGAS, Cesc

Born **Vilessoc de Mar, Spain, 4 May 1987**
Arsenal appearances **169 (29)**
Arsenal goals **26**
International caps (Spain) **24**

With Cesc Fabregas barely out of his teens, he had already become the fulcrum of Arsène Wenger's developing Arsenal team. A prodigious talent, the Catalan has had plaudits raining down on him since making his debut aged 16 and 177 days in September 2003, becoming Arsenal's youngest ever first-team player in the process. He also became Arsenal's youngest ever goalscorer when he netted in a 5-1 win over Wolves in December that year.

Club legend and Academy boss Liam Brady says of him, 'Fabregas is fast becoming the brain of this Arsenal team. It's already apparent he's on his way to becoming a giant of the game. He's one of those rare players who can pass a ball that, up in the stands, you won't have seen. Like Dennis Bergkamp, he can make that totally original pass.'

Fabregas made a huge impact during the 2004/05 season and won an FA Cup-

winner's medal at the end of the campaign. The following season he established himself as the side's playmaker, taking the No.4 shirt from the departing Patrick Vieira and producing a series of eye-catching performances in both the league and Champions League.

Criticized for his lack of goals, he answered his few critics in 2007/08 by reaching double figures and playing his part in Spain's Euro 2008 triumph. Fabregas has also shown his commitment to Arsenal, despite repeated speculation that Real Madrid and Barcelona want to buy him, by signing an eight-year contract at Emirates – the longest ever offered in the Club's history.

His eye for a pass and ability to play the game on his terms – perfectly illustrated by his match-winning performance during the 2-0 Champions League win at holders AC Milan in March 2008 – has already made the articulate Spaniard one of the world's leading midfielders.

FAMOUS BACK FOUR

The legendary backline that defied the odds – and its advancing years – provided a rock solid base for more than a decade. Built by manager George Graham, he worked meticulously with the four key components – full-backs **Lee Dixon** and **Nigel Winterburn**, stopper centre-half **Steve Bould** and inspirational skipper **Tony Adams** – to turn them into a disciplined unit. Their first full season together was 1988/89, although **David O'Leary** would occasionally deputise or play as a third centre-back when Graham varied the formation near the latter stages of the campaign.

Over the next few years the unit developed a reputation for unflinching resistance, with just 18 goals conceded in the 1991 title-winning campaign, despite Adams missing two months because of a jail sentence. Their finest hour was in Copenhagen in 1994 when the four, Bould in particular, gave career-best performances to repel concerted pressure from AS Parma to win the European Cup-Winners' Cup. By then the fan's favourite song was 'One-Nil to the Arsenal', a respectful nod to the defence's magnificence against supposedly better opponents.

Other defenders came along and provided ample cover, notably **Andy Linighan**, **Colin Pates** and **Martin Keown**, the latter eventually breaking up the 'old faithful' four when he won a regular place in the backline in the 1998 Premiership-winning campaign.

Arsène Wenger's arrival had helped the defenders' creaking joints eke out a few more seasons, but when Bould departed for Sunderland in 1999, the dismantling of the old guard began. The following year, Winterburn ended his 13-year spell at Highbury by moving to West Ham and in 2002 Dixon and Adams called it a day.

Between them, Arsenal's famous back four boasted more than 2,000 Gunners appearances.

FANFARES

Long gone are the days Arsenal took the pitch to the strains of the Metropolitan Police Band led by Constable Alex Morgan, which was a regular occurrence at Highbury during the 1970s. Now, matchday DJ Paul Burrell and his assistant, David Duncan, take control of the music at Emirates Stadium although it still has an old-fashioned feel with Elvis Presley's 1970 UK No.1 hit 'The Wonder of You' the chosen song played as the team entered the pitch during the 2007/08 season.

'That record was chosen by the Club in consultation with the fans and it has proved really popular,' explains David. 'Some songs work, some songs don't – you really don't know until you try them.'

In recent years various styles of music have been used prior to kick-off for sporting, inspirational and commercial reasons. They are as follows:

'*Theme from the A-Team*', Mike Post & Pete Carpenter
'*Hot Stuff*', Arsenal FC squad 1998
'*Right Here, Right Now*', Fatboy Slim
'*Release the Pressure*', Leftfield (O2 sponsorship)

'*Good Old Arsenal*' version 1, Arsenal FC squad 1971
'*Good Old Arsenal*' version 2, Dial Square – Shovell & Charlie George
Premier League '*handshake music*'
UEFA Champions League '*handshake music*'
'*The Wonder of You*', Elvis Presley

FANS' FORUM

Since 2001 the Club has hosted regular meetings with fans' representatives in a bid to foster stronger relations between the two and ensure supporters have a better say in the running of the Club. Held on a matchday four times a season, the fans' forum is a place to discuss anything from half-time meat pies to better access for wheelchair users.

The fans are represented by a group of more than a dozen people drawn from a cross section of the crowd, usually including disabled fans, under 18s, season ticket holders, pensioners and executive box members. While no members of the senior playing or coaching staff attend meetings, most departments have been represented with managing director Keith Edelman regularly answering questions and listening to views.

The group made visits to Emirates Stadium during its construction to check on its progress and also travelled to the Club's Hale End Academy.

Every two seasons potential new members are invited to apply to join the forum, details of which can be found in the matchday programme or on the Club's official website, www.arsenal.com

FANZINES

Arsenal has spawned a number of fanzines of varying success, but the most prominent is *The Gooner*, which was launched in 1987 and passed the 150 issue mark in 2004. It was the first Arsenal fanzine and saw off the opposition, such as the popular but short-

lived *Arsenal Echo Echo*, *An Imperfect Match* and *One-Nil Down, Two-One Up*.

The Gooner currently has two established rivals in *Highbury High* and *Up The Arse!*

FASTEST GOALS

DOMESTIC
The fastest goal scored by Arsenal in any domestic competition came on 28 April 1980 when Alan Sunderland scored the opener against Liverpool in the FA Cup semi-final second replay. His goal came just 13 seconds after kick-off. However, Liverpool equalised later to make it 1–1 and take the tie to a third replay.

EUROPEAN
Brazilian Gilberto holds the record for the fastest Arsenal goal scored in European competition. He finished off a sweeping move in just 20 seconds against PSV Eindhoven in the Netherlands on 25 September 2002 to set up a 4–0 win for the Gunners. It remains the fastest goal scored in Champions League history.

FEVER PITCH

This bestselling novel illustrates why football plays such an important part in people's lives. It centres around author Nick Hornby – now a celebrated chronicler of male insecurities – and his love of Arsenal. Hornby laid himself bare in the book, admitting that Arsenal would often take precedence in his personal life over more pressing matters. It culminates with Michael Thomas' title-winning goal at Liverpool in May 1989.

First published in 1992, at the inception of the FA Premier League, it is now credited by many as helping change the public perception of the national game among the chattering classes. The book has sold in excess of a million copies in the UK alone, was successfully transferred to the big

Gilberto Silva lifts the ball over PSV Eindhoven goalkeeper Ronald Wattereus to score the fastest goal in UEFA Champions League history in 2002 at the Philips Stadion in the First Group Stage of the competition.

year, the Famous Back Four were referred to in a memorable scene where a dance move is explained to a group of unemployed men in Sheffield.

FILMS WITH ARSENAL REFERENCES:
Sabotage (1936)
A Hitchcock movie in which one man asks another if he supports Arsenal – and advises him to do so if he doesn't.

The Arsenal Stadium Mystery (1939)
(see below, left)

Frenzy (1972)
A Hitchcock thriller which features a pub that has an Arsenal stained-glass window.

Rising Damp (1980)
In the film version of the ITV comedy series, Rigsby's local pub has an Arsenal scarf and rosette hanging behind the bar.

Corrupt (1983)
Ex-Sex Pistol John Lydon – in real life an Islingtonian and an Arsenal supporter – carried an Arsenal holdall when starring alongside Harvey Keitel.

Lamb (1985)
Liam Neeson stars as a priest who takes an epileptic boy to Arsenal. Some scenes were filmed on the North Bank.

The Young Americans (1993)
Harvey Keitel stars in a gangster flick with scenes from an Arsenal game.

When Saturday Comes (1996)
Sean Bean plays a substitute for Sheffield United against Arsenal at Bramall Lane.

Fever Pitch (1997) (see left)

The Full Monty (1997) (see left)

Plunkett And Macleane (1999)
Robert Carlyle and Jonny Lee Miller star as

screen in 1997 with Colin Firth playing Paul Ashworth, the north London teacher based on Hornby, who himself makes a cameo appearance in the film.

FILM – ARSENAL AT THE MOVIES

Few clubs have had a film named after them but the 1939 classic *The Arsenal Stadium Mystery* is a murder-mystery whodunnit about a footballer who dies playing for fictional side Trojans against Arsenal at Highbury. The film used action scenes from a 2-0 home win over Brentford filmed on 6 May 1938. Brentford wore white shirts for the game – not their normal away strip – to provide contrast for the black and white film. Much of the side also feature in some revealing shots taken inside the dressing room with manager George Allison giving a team talk and later commentating on the game for the radio.

Arsenal also featured in two of the biggest Brit flicks of the 1990s – *Fever Pitch* (see *Fever Pitch*) and *The Full Monty*. *Fever Pitch* is the big-screen version of Nick Hornby's best-selling autobiographical book of the same name, made in 1997 and starring Colin Firth and Ruth Gemmell. In *The Full Monty*, the shock hit of the same

Highbury's floodlights in use for the first time for a friendly between Arsenal and Hapoel Tel Aviv in September 1951.

First league match away 9 Sept 1893 v Notts County (a), League (Second Division) - lost 2-3 (Elliott, Shaw)

First Premiership match 15 Aug 1992 v Norwich City (h) - lost 2-4 (Bould, Campbell)

First FA Cup match 14 Oct 1893 v Ashford United (h), (Manor Ground, Plumstead), - won 12-0 (Elliott 3, Henderson 3, Booth 2, Heath 2, Crawford, Powell)

First League Cup match 13 Sept 1966 v Gillingham (h), (Rd 2) - drew 1-1 (Baldwin)

First match in European competition 25 Sept 1963 v Staevnet (Denmark) (a), Inter-Cities Fairs Cup, (Rd 1, 1st leg) - won 7-1 (Strong 3, Baker 3, MacLeod)

First home match in European competition 22 Oct 1963 v Staevnet (Denmark), Inter-Cities Fairs Cup, (Rd 1, 2nd leg) - lost 2-3 (Skirton, Barnwell)

First match in UEFA Champions League 16 Sept 1998 v RC Lens (a) - drew 1-1 (Overmars)

First appearance in Charity/Community Shield 8 Oct 1930 v Sheffield Wednesday (at Stamford Bridge) - won 2-1 (Hulme, Jack)

18th-century highwaymen. Two other characters are called Winterburn and Dixon.

Muggers (2000)
An indpendent film made by a company called Clock End Films. An Arsenal scarf can be seen in one shot and Arsenal FC is thanked in the credits.

The Baby Juice Express (2001)
A film in which David Seaman and Ray Parlour both make cameo appearances.

Ocean's 12 (2004)
George Clooney and Brad Pitt wear Arsenal tracksuits in this crime thriller.

There was also a film called *Arsenal* made in 1928. It centres around the hardships of Ukrainian workers at the Kiev Arsenal - and has nothing to do with the Gunners.

FIRSTS

First competitive match (as Woolwich Arsenal) 2 Sept 1893 v Newcastle Utd (h), (Manor Ground, Plumstead), League (Second Divison) - drew 2-2 (Shaw, Elliott)

First competitive match at Highbury (as Woolwich Arsenal) 6 Sept 1913 v Leicester Fosse, League (Second Division) - won 2-1 (Jobey, Devine [pen])

First competitive match as Arsenal 4 April 1914 v Bristol City (h) - League (Second Division) - drew 1-1 (Winship)

First league match at home 2 Sept 1893 v Newcastle Utd (h), (Manor Ground, Plumstead), League (Second Divison) - drew 2-2 (Shaw, Elliott)

FLAIR

Boring Arsenal? Not a chance of it with these entertaining players, whose ample flair and imagination would enhance any Gunners side in any era:
Charlie Buchan
Alex James
Jimmy Logie
George Eastham
Charlie George
Liam Brady
Malcolm Macdonald
Charlie Nicholas
David Rocastle
Paul Merson
Ian Wright
Dennis Bergkamp
Thierry Henry

The placement of the light fittings around Emirates Stadium ensure a smooth, bright illumination of the entire pitch with virtually no shadow. It was designed to provide a lighting level five times brighter than that of the average office.

FLOODLIGHTS

Herbert Chapman had advocated the use of floodlights back in the 1920s and the new East and West stands were both built, in the early 1930s, with provision for floodlight use at a later date. Chapman had used artificial lighting at the training ground for occasional night-time training sessions and had a set of lights fitted on to the West Stand, but he was not alive to see the Club's first official match under artificial light on 19 September 1951, when Israeli side Hapoel Tel Aviv visited Highbury for a friendly. More than 51,000 turned out for the match, which Arsenal won 6-1.

Later the Club programme said, 'It was interesting to hear a remark from the terraces that a considerably better view was enjoyed than on a number of poor Saturdays when strained eyes were peering into the falling gloom just before the final whistle.'

Glasgow Rangers also played under the lights a few days later.

The last game to be played under Highbury's floodlights was the UEFA Champions League semi-final against Villarreal CF in April 2006.

The floodlight system installed at Emirates Stadium is considered to be among the best in the world. Mounted on a gantry that runs around the entire circumference of the roof 188 two-kilowatt Philips Arenavision bulbs bathe the stadium in stunning light. Each floodlight has around 5,000 hours of life – approximately ten years – but Arsenal are expected to replace them in under half that period. For the record, including internal lighting, the new arena has approximately 12,500 bulbs lit during an evening match.

FOOTBALL WRITERS' ASSOCIATION PLAYER OF THE YEAR

Since it's launch in 1948, the Football Writers' Footballer of the Year award has gone to Arsenal players on five occasions. Joe Mercer was the first Highbury recipient in 1950, the year of the emotional FA Cup win over his native Liverpool. Inspirational skipper, Frank McLintock, got the award in 1971 for leading his side to the Double. Another 27 years would pass before the next Arsenal player – Dennis Bergkamp – was given the award. More recently, Thierry Henry was chosen for two years in succession, in 2003 and 2004.

Arsenal winners:
1950   Joe Mercer
1971   Frank McLintock
1998   Dennis Bergkamp
2003 & 2004 Thierry Henry

FOREIGN PLAYERS

FIRST EVER

The first ever non-UK player to represent the Club came from across the North Sea. Amsterdam-born Gerard Keyser (born 8 August 1910 – died 5 December 1980) – also known as Gerard Pieter Keizer – was a goalkeeper who had been No.2 at Ajax to Jan de Boer before moving to Margate. In Kent he caught the attentions of Herbert Chapman, who took him to Highbury after failing in his bid to land Austria's Rudi Hiden, and he was thrown straight into the first team for the first 12 matches of the 1930/31 title-winning campaign. He made his debut in a 4-1 win at Blackpool and picked up a Charity Shield winner's medal against Sheffield Wednesday.

He remained on the books at Ajax during his time at Highbury and regularly flew to Amsterdam straight after a Saturday match to play in the Dutch league on Sundays, where he was nicknamed *Vliegende Keep* – the Flying Keeper. He finally returned to the Netherlands in 1933 and became Ajax's No.1 for 15 years, representing his country twice.

After the war, he was sent to prison when he was found guilty of smuggling money, but he later joined the board of directors at Ajax, where he is considered a club legend.

FIRST MAJOR FOREIGN SIGNING
Petrovic, Vladimir
Born Belgrade, Yugoslavia, 1 July 1955
Arsenal appearances **22**
Arsenal goals **3**
International caps (Yugoslavia) **34 (11 goals)**

Petrovic lasted just six months at Highbury following his arrival from Red Star Belgrade in 1982. The Yugoslav international was lauded as the playmaker to replace Liam Brady – he had been his country's player of the year in 1981 and 1982 – but after making his debut on New Year's Day 1983 Petrovic made only 22 appearances before the player,

Manuel Almunia, a substitute in Arsenal's first-ever all-foreign line-up, was used primarily for cup games during his first two seasons at Highbury. However, his good form and patience were rewarded in 2007/08 when he took over as the Gunners top keeper.

nicknamed 'The Pigeon', flew off to pastures new in the less taxing French league.

Recently a coach for his country's Under-21s side, Petrovic was also an international team-mate of current Arsenal first-team coach Boro Primorac.

ALL FOREIGN LINE-UP

On Valentine's Day 2005 Arsenal became the first team in English football history to name an entire squad with no UK players.

The Gunners beat Crystal Palace 5-1 at Highbury with two goals from Thierry Henry – making his 200th league appearance for Arsenal – and one each for Dennis Bergkamp, Jose Antonio Reyes and Patrick Vieira.

The team that day was:

Jens Lehmann (Germany)
Gael Clichy (France)
Pascal Cygan (France)
Kolo Toure (Ivory Coast)
Lauren (Cameroon)
Patrick Vieira (France)
Edu (Brazil)
Robert Pires (France)
Jose Antonio Reyes (Spain)
Dennis Bergkamp (Netherlands)
Thierry Henry (France)

Subs:

Mathieu Flamini (France)
Robin van Persie (Netherlands)
Cesc Fabregas (Spain)
Manuel Almunia (Spain)
Philippe Senderos (Switzerland)

One Briton did make an impact in the game. Bedford-born England international Andrew Johnson – ironically an Arsenal fan as a youth – scored the Eagles' consolation goal from the penalty spot.

FOUNDING FATHER – DAVID DANSKIN

A mechanical engineer and football enthusiast at the Royal Arsenal, David Danskin was the principal founding member of Dial Square.

Born in Burntisland, Fife, in January 1863, he grew up in Kirkcaldy before moving to London in his early 20s and taking a job at the Dial Square workshop, where he set the ball rolling by forming a works football side for the many Scots working there. Together with work colleagues Jack Humble, Morris Bates and Fred Beardsley. He enthusastically worked hard to get the club off the ground and is credited with purchasing Dial Square FC's first football.

Danskin captained the team in their very first match against Eastern Wanderers on 11 December 1886, which they won 6-0. He played for the Club for the next three seasons, but his interest waned and he set up his own bicycle manufacturing business in Plumstead, before moving to Coventry.

He was one of the few founders to live to see the Club's rise and cheered the side's 1936 FA Cup win from his sickbed, while listening to the radio commentary. He died in 1948, aged 85.

In July 2007 the Arsenal Scotland Supporters' Club and Burntisland Heritage Trust commemorated Danskin when a plaque was unveiled jointly by his grandson Richard Wyatt and former Arsenal goalkeeper Bob Wilson. The plaque is located in the Kirkgate, Burntisland (at the corner with Somerville Street).

FREE KICKS

Here are a few deadball moments of magic worth remembering:

Alex James v Huddersfield Town at Wembley, FA Cup Final, 1930

The little Scotsman put Arsenal ahead midway in the first half with a characteristic moment of genius. Hacked to the floor in the Huddersfield half, he jumped to his feet and instantly played a free kick to Cliff Bastin who quickly returned it. Before the Huddersfield players had a chance to react James had drilled the ball home. The Yorkshire side were angry, fuming at James' so-called unsporting behaviour. But the goal stood and James trotted back to the halfway line with a chuckle.

Brian Talbot v Liverpool at Highbury League Division One, Sept 1984

The midfielder curled a stunning free kick, replayed on TV for years after, past Bruce Grobbelaar to give Arsenal a sensational lead, the ball sailing majestically into the top corner for a carbon copy of his free kick just days before against Newcastle. Arsenal went top of Division One for the first time in 11 years.

Paul Merson v Spurs at Wembley, FA Cup semi-final, 1993

Merson is one of the finest deadball players of modern times and his free kick unlocked Spurs to set up Tony Adams for the winner. The game was heading for extra time when Merson floated over a magnificent ball to the far post and Adams stole in to head past Erik Thorsvedt and gain revenge for defeat in the same competition two years before.

Stefan Schwartz v Sampdoria at the Stadio Luigi Ferraris, European Cup-Winners-Cup semi-final, 2nd leg, 1995

The Swede only stayed for one season at Highbury, but made his mark late on in Genoa. Arsenal were trailing 3-1 (6-5 on aggregate) and heading for the exit when he drilled an unstoppable 30-yard free kick past Gianluca Pagliuca to take the tie to extra time. It was the cue for wild celebrations among the travelling fans.

Thierry Henry v AS Roma at the Olympic Stadium, UEFA Champions League, Second Group Stage, November 2002

Henry's finest hour in Europe – the Gallic star completed a brilliant hat-trick in the Italian capital when Sylvain Wiltord was felled on the edge of the box and Henry curled home a superb free kick to make it 3-1.

Thierry Henry v Aston Villa at Villa Park, Premiership, January 2004

Olof Mellberg upended Patrick Vieira and Henry placed the ball 25 yards out. Referee Mark Halsey gave the all-clear and Henry curled the ball past Thomas Sorensen before he could even react. Villa complained, but the goal stood.

Thierry Henry v Chelsea at Highbury, Premiership, December 2004

The Frenchman did it again 11 months later; by rolling the ball into an empty Chelsea net while goalkeeper Petr Cech was still aligning his defensive wall in the correct position. Chelsea were furious, but referee Graham Poll, like Halsey, had given the players the all-clear and the goal, as at Villa Park, was legitimate.

FRENCH CONNECTION

Maybe 'La Marseillaise' should be played on matchdays in honour of the many Frenchman that have shaped the Club's recent history. Since Arsène Wenger arrived in September 1996, there has been a flow of talent from across the Channel.

The first French player to arrive was **Remi Garde**, on a free transfer, just weeks before Wenger's official arrival. But it was the second Gallic star to join the Club who would become the heartbeat of the side for much of the next decade: **Patrick Vieira**. Along with compatriot **Emmanuel Petit**, he would form a steely midfield partnership for the 1998 title win and go on to skipper the side when Tony Adams retired. Vieira chalked up three titles and three FA Cups with the Club, scoring the final penalty in the 2005 penalty shootout win over Manchester United before leaving for Juventus.

Nicolas Anelka was a rising young star when he signed from Paris Saint-Germain in February 1997 and by the end of following season he was a hero, scoring in the 1998 FA Cup final to clinch the Double.

Utility man **Gilles Grimandi** was an unsung hero, providing ample cover across the defence and midfield as Wenger changed the Arsenal style from attrition to a virtual copy of Holland's Total Football of the 1970s.

Wenger's knowledge of his country's footballing set up gave him a head start when he beat Real Madrid CF to the signature of Marseille's **Robert Pires** in 2000. Pires was an integral component of the 2002 title win, achieving the Premiership record number of assists and picking up the Football Writers' Assocation Player of the Year award, despite missing the last few weeks of the season through injury. He also scored the winner in the 2003 FA Cup Final against Southampton.

Sylvain Wiltord arrived at the same time as Pires and proved a selfless hard worker, playing in midfield rather than his favoured attacking role, but still popping up with important goals, including the 2002 title-clinching winner at Manchester United.

But no Frenchman provided as much excitement as **Thierry Henry**, rescued from Juventus in 1999. Wenger had worked with the Parisian at AS Monaco, but admits he did not anticipate the impact he would make at Highbury. Henry was sensational. He is the first Premiership player to hit 20 goals in five successive seasons and surpassed Ian Wright's goalscoring club record in October 2005. He won two titles, three FA Cups and was within a whisker of the World Footballer of the Year award on three occasions.

The French influence remained as strong as ever by the end of the 2007/08 campaign. **Gael Clichy** had firmly established himself as the club's first choice left-back, with compatriot **Armand Traore** his deputy, while on the other flank France international **Bacary Sagna**, signed from Auxerre, enjoyed an outstanding debut season at right-back.

In midfield former Marseille star **Mathieu Flamini** had also displaced **Gilberto Silva** as the main defensive midfielder in the side. Flamini, along with Clichy, had both broken into the French national squad before the former moved on to pastures new in May 2008, signing a four-year deal with AC Milan.

FRIAR, Ken

In 1950 a 12-year-old Ken Friar was playing football in Avenell Road when he accidentally kicked the ball against a car. The car belonged to manager George Allison. After reprimanding the terrified boy Mr Allison took pity on him and gave him a job as a matchday messenger. Four years later he joined the accounts department and steadily worked his way up through the offices to be made assistant club secretary in 1965, and then club secretary seven years later. His unswerving loyalty and hard work was rewarded in 1983 when he was appointed managing director.

In 2000, by then on the board of directors, he was awarded an OBE for his services to football. He later stepped down as MD – replaced by Keith Edelman – so he could take charge of the Emirates Stadium project alongside fellow director Daniel Fiszman. The new home, opened in August 2006, is the fitting legacy of a truly unique footballing man.

In May 2008 Edelman resigned his position and Friar took over as acting MD.

FULL-BACKS

Arsenal have built a reputation for a rock solid defence, although the full-back's importance can often be forgotten and there have been many fine purveyors of the trade in red and white over the years.

Joe Shaw was one of the first great Arsenal defenders, who joined in 1907 and ended his association with the Club almost half a century later. Shaw was made captain after the First World War and made more than 300 appearances. The giant **Bob Benson** also promised much on the other flank, but played only 52 league games before he died tragically during a wartime match.

The first captain to pick up major silverware was right-back **Tom Parker**, who played a record 172 successive matches for the Club and won the FA Cup and a league title until he was replaced by **George Male** who, along with **Eddie Hapgood**, provided a formidable full-back partnership in the 1930s. Both Male and Hapgood, who won a Club record five title medals along with Cliff Bastin, captained England during the 1930s, winning more than 60 caps between them. Wales captain **Walley**

Without doubt the leading light of the Club's French connection has been Thierry Henry. The team built around him won two Championships and three FA Cups during eight years during which time he was regarded by many as the best player in the world. He moved on to Barcelona in 2007.

89

Nigel Winterburn in action in 1995. He formed a hugely successful full-back partnership with Lee Dixon which spanned a decade.

Barnes was the outstanding full-back in the post-war years, playing on either flank and winning a title and an FA Cup medal, although he missed the entire 1952/53 title-wining campaign after a serious knee injury in the 1952 FA Cup Final.

Bob McNab became the world's most expensive full-back when Arsenal paid Huddersfield £50,000 for his services in 1966. The Yorkshireman was a tenacious defender and stayed for nine years, forming a superb Double-winning partnership with **Pat Rice**. Rice was a homegrown starlet who became the Mr Reliable of a team with many Irishman, which included **Sammy Nelson** across the back four in the left-back berth.

Nelson was eventually replaced by the most capped player in Arsenal's history, Crystal Palace and England left-back **Kenny Sansom**. The Camberwell-born defender was the outstanding player in his position in the 1980s. A model of consistency, he was equally comfortable defending against a winger and providing a potent attacking threat down the flank with Graham Rix. With England's **Viv Anderson** spending three fine years at Highbury on the right side of the defence, Arsenal again provided the national team with both full-backs.

But with both leaving at the end of the 1980s, **Nigel Winterburn** and **Lee Dixon** – signed by George Graham for less than £800,000 for the pair – soon became the two flank defenders and regulars in the Famous Back Four. Dixon was a lower league journeyman signed from Stoke, while Winterburn had been Wimbledon's player of the year prior to his move north of the river. But as a partnership they were a sensation, spending the best part of ten seasons with little or no competition for their places, winning three titles each, along with the FA Cup, League Cup and Cup-Winners' Cup.

Ashley Cole cemented his place as one of Europe's outstanding left-backs – also becoming an England regular – during his six years of first-team football at Highbury. His replacement at Arsenal, **Gael Clichy**, is now a France international as is his right-sided partner, **Bacary Sagna**, continuing a long line of out-standing full-backs in red and white. Both Clichy and Sagna were named in the 2008 PFA Team of the Year.

G

GENIUSES

There is an elite band of Arsenal players clearly above the common herd.

While there had been many stars before his arrival, **Charlie Buchan** was the first Gunner to possess that extra something that separated him from his peers. His technique was comparable to players 70 years ahead of him, but it was his tactical nous that was really impressive. It was Buchan who had the insight to insist Herbert Chapman employ the unheard of 'WM' formation in a bid to stay one step ahead of the new 1925 offside laws (see WM Formation on page 203) after a 7-0 defeat at Newcastle. Arsenal won their next game 4-0 at West Ham and the foundations were set for total dominance.

Chapman was fortunate to employ another such star just a year after Buchan's retirement in 1928. **Alex James** is generally considered the finest player of the 1930s side. His mastery of a football and ability to see passes nobody else in the stadium had spotted were the sparks that ignited Arsenal's superiority in the inter-war years. Tom Whittaker claimed he was the best player in the world.

Liam Brady ran the Arsenal midfield in the late 1970s with a grace and intelligence hitherto unseen in the modern game at Highbury. Renowned for his supremely elegant technical skills – notably his famous left foot – play appeared to slow down when he was on the ball, as he picked out the best option every time. Many believe he is the greatest, most natural talent, to have ever played in red and white.

In recent history, **Dennis Bergkamp**'s excellence sparked the foreign revolution at Highbury and took the Club on to a higher level. The Dutch master is the supreme footballer; like a great chess player working out moves three or four passes ahead and executing many a breathtaking goal. In 1997 his hat-trick at Leicester was described by respected TV pundit Alan Hansen as the greatest treble he had ever seen and Thierry Henry admits to being in awe of the Amsterdammer's ability. He is also considered a hero at hometown club Ajax and was, briefly, the leading all-time scorer for the Netherlands.

GEORGE, Charlie

Born **Islington, London, 10 October 1950**
Arsenal appearances **157 (22)**
Arsenal goals **49**
International caps (England) **1**

Brash, cocky, forthright... Charlie George was rebellion personified, and, allied with total mastery of a football and supreme confidence, it was an irresistible cocktail for an adoring North Bank. 'I've never felt in awe of anybody, never ever in my life. There was nothing that any footballer could do that I felt I couldn't do. Whether that was right or wrong it's a good attitude to have,' he claimed in later years.

Born and bred in Holloway, in his formative years George idolised the likes of Jimmy Logie and Joe Baker from the terraces and fulfilled a dream by signing for his boyhood heroes in May 1966.

He made his debut for the Gunners three years later and won the 1970 Fairs Cup after playing both legs of the Final against Belgian club Anderlecht.

The following season started badly when he broke his leg in the act of scoring in the opening game at Everton. Ray Kennedy took his place, but George, with his long flowing hair and cocksure swagger, returned from injury in the early weeks of 1971 to give Bertie Mee's title-chasing side a lift – and an exciting Plan B. The season would end in glory with him completing his journey from North Bank to Wembley hero when he struck the extra-time winner against Liverpool in the FA Cup Final to complete the Double.

His ability shone sporadically over the next four seasons, but as the Double side broke up, his brushes with officialdom and inconsistency drew criticism. In 1975 – aged just 24 – he had one too many run-ins with Mee and left his spiritual home for a fresh start at Derby County.

It seems unthinkable that George was on the verge of signing for Tottenham before

Islington's own: Charlie George dreamed of playing for Arsenal when he was a lad on the North Bank. By 19 he had scored a Cup Final winner – and won the Double.

Rams boss Dave Mackay took him to the Baseball Ground, where he scored a hat-trick against mighty Real Madrid in a European Cup semi-final and won his one and only England cap against Ireland in 1976.

Southampton and Nottingham Forest were later destinations and he could boast of playing club football in no less than four continents after spells in Australia, USA and Hong Kong. But despite his many moves, Charlie was always an Arsenal man. 'I have never met anyone who loves this Club more than Charlie. There's all this stuff written about him, but you could never question his commitment to the Arsenal,' says his former coach Don Howe.

He now lives back in Islington and was a regular visitor at Highbury, working as a corporate matchday host, and now at Emirates where he is one of the former Arsenal stars who accompany visitors on the Legends Tour of the stadium, as well as pursuing other business interests. As he always says, 'I've been a supporter and then I played and now I'm a supporter again. I'll only watch Arsenal.'

GERMAN GUNNERS

It's surprising that in Arsène Wenger's ten years at Highbury he has only signed four Germans. The Arsenal manager was brought up on the French-German border and has a slight German accent, as many do in the bi-lingual Alsace region of France. He also regularly crossed the border to watch Borussia Mönchengladbach as a youth, ironically Arsenal's first opponents of the new Wenger era (although he did not officially take charge until a league match at Blackburn two weeks later).

His first German signing in 1998 was the very un-Teutonic sounding **Alberto Mendez**, raised in Germany to Spanish parents, although the midfielder failed to make an impact and he soon left for Racing Ferrol. Midfielder **Stefan Malz** signed from TSV 1860 Munich in 1999, but after just two Premiership starts and one goal he moved back to Bundesliga outfit Kaiserslautern two years later. Full-back **Moritz Volz** also

signed that year after impressing in Schalke 04's junior sides and showed huge promise. However, he could not break into the first team at Highbury and, after a six-month loan spell at Fulham, he signed permanently for the Cottagers in January 2004.

The most successful German Gunner, however, has been **Jens Lehmann**. The big goalkeeper had an astonishing first year, winning a Premiership medal to go with a Bundesliga title he won with Dortmund and the UEFA Cup he won while at Schalke.

Lehmann's experience and athleticism has made him an excellent replacement for David Seaman and, despite criticism from some quarters, in 2005 he continued to impress, saving Paul Scholes' penalty as Arsenal won the FA Cup.

Lehmann has courted controversy in his homeland because of his outspoken views, especially regarding the German national goalkeeping position, but at Highbury he has established himself as a true fans' favourite.

GIANT-KILLINGS

Arsenal have been on the wrong end of some rather unfortunate cup upsets to lower division sides during their history, the last notable occasion in January 1992 when the league champions were humbled 2-1 at Fourth Division's bottom club Wrexham at the Racecourse Ground. But as far back as 1921, Third Division QPR beat struggling Arsenal 2-0 in the third round of the FA Cup at Shepherd's Bush. And probably the most famous giant-killing feat of all-time occurred at Walsall's Fellows Park on 14 January 1933, when Herbert Chapman's Arsenal travelled to the West Midlands in the third round.

The league leaders drafted in reserves Charlie Walsh, Tommy Black, Norman Sidey and Billy Warnes, but still had enough stars to beat a Saddlers side that cost just £69. However, goals from Gilbert

Left Exhausted but happy, Charlie George waits for his team-mates on the Wembley turf after scoring the winner in the 111th minute of the 1971 FA Cup Final.

Alsop and Billy Shephard sealed a famous Walsall win. Chapman was furious and he sold Walsh and Black within a fortnight.

Another Third Division side, Norwich, would humble Arsenal 31 years later when they adapted themselves better to a rock-hard Highbury surface to win 2-1 with two second-half goals in front of a crowd of 55,767. Southern League Bedford were beaten 2-1 in a replay after pegging the Gunners back to 2-2 at Highbury in 1956, but their near neighbours Northampton humiliated the Gunners two years later, winning 3-1 at the County Ground.

The League Cup Final of 1969 saw another defeat at the hands of opponents from Division Three, when Swindon Town won 3-1 on a bog of a Wembley pitch. Walsall cropped up again when they beat Arsenal 2-1 at Highbury in the Milk Cup in November 1983, a result that cost manager Terry Neill his job. And two years before Keith Houchen scored a diving header for Coventry to win the FA Cup against Spurs in 1987, he netted a last-minute penalty for York City after he was upended by Steve Williams to beat Arsenal 1-0 at Bootham Crescent.

In December 2005 Doncaster Rovers came close to becoming the first lower division club to beat the Gunners for nearly 14 years, when they led 2-1 with minutes to go before Gilberto Silva struck a late face-saving equaliser at the Earth Stadium.

GOAL CELEBRATIONS

CHARLIE GEORGE
v Liverpool

From North Bank to Wembley hero, Charlie George's stunning winner in the 1971 FA Cup Final was matched by an equally fitting celebration. The Islington-born striker, who was exhausted after 90 minutes of energy-sapping heat, lashed a brilliant 20-yard strike past Reds goalkeeper Ray Clemence in extra time to seal the Double and fell to the ground, lying on his back in the sun waiting for his team-mates to mob him. After four decades, the image of him lying alone on the Wembley turf, peering up to see his colleagues running towards him, remains the most iconic of all Arsenal goal celebrations.

SAMMY NELSON
v Coventry City

The award for the most controversial celebration would belong to Northern Ireland defender Sammy Nelson. The full-back had a rush of blood to the head after scoring a rare goal in front of the North Bank in a 1-1 draw with Coventry in April 1979 – and promptly dropped his shorts. Nelson had earlier put through his own net and was obviously relieved to have made up for it. But with the FA Cup Final on the horizon, there was a real possibility he would be banned for his indiscretion. The Club fined him and, after appearing at a disciplinary hearing at Lancaster Gate, the FA handed him a lenient two-week ban – meaning he could still play in the forthcoming Wembley Final.

BRIAN KIDD
v Manchester City

The cheekiest award would surely go to Brian Kidd. The striker netted twice in a 4-0 win over hometown club Manchester City in August 1974 and after netting in front of the North Bank he grabbed the nearest policeman's hat and promptly placed it on the top of his head with the fans roaring their approval. Fortunately, the Islington constabulary saw the funny side of it.

Brian Kidd dons a policeman's helmet while celebrating one of his two goals in a 4-0 win against Manchester City at Highbury in August 1974.

He's 'almost' done it; Ian Wright and Lee Dixon celebrate the fact that Wrighty had just equalled Cliff Bastin's Club goalscoring record. However, he was still one goal short.

DENNIS BERGKAMP
v Tottenham Hotspur

Dennis Bergkamp showed he wasn't made of ice on a rain-sodden afternoon in November 1996. The Dutchman sealed a 3-1 win over Tottenham Hotspur in the final seconds of a pulsating encounter with a brilliant piece of skill ending in a sublime finish for the third goal. Bergkamp turned to the North Bank and slid to his knees in celebration before he was submerged under his adoring team-mates.

IAN WRIGHT
v Bolton Wanderers

Ian Wright seemed to have a different celebration for every one of his many goals, but the one that remains in fans' minds was a mistake. The ebullient striker wheeled away in delight after scoring against Bolton in September 1997 to make it 178 goals for the Club to equal Cliff Bastin's 50-year-old record. Wright peeled off his red shirt to reveal a Nike-sponsored vest emblazoned with the words 'Just Done It' and the number 179. Unfortunately, he was still one goal away from that figure – and beating Bastin's record. Not to worry; Wright netted twice more in a 4-1 win and revealed the vest again for any of the 38,000-strong crowd who hadn't seen it the first time.

THIERRY HENRY
v Tottenham Hotspur

Thierry Henry further ingratiated himself to the Arsenal followers with a stunning 70-yard run and goal against Tottenham Hotspur in a 3-0 Highbury win in November 2002. That goal, in itself, was one of the finest seen in a north London derby for many years, but the French striker found one last burst of energy to run virtually the entire length of the pitch again, whooping with delight at the West Stand, and then sliding to his knees nonchalantly in front of the shell-shocked Spurs fans in the Clock End.

GOALKEEPERS

Arsenal have always been known for the excellence of their goalkeepers. The green jersey – more recently orange, grey or yellow – has always been hard to claim, with a succession of top-class custodians, going back to Edwardian times.

Arsenal's first England international was keeper **Jimmy Ashcroft**, a record breaker who held a 97-year-old Club record of six successive clean sheets and also played 154 games on the trot – another record which lasted a quarter of a century.

Herbert Chapman's era saw the likes of **Gerard Keyser** – a Dutch legend and Arsenal's first ever foreigner – enjoy a brief spell battling for the jersey, along with the likes of **Charlie Preedy** and **George Swindin**. But the outstanding 1930s custodian was the undisputed No.1 for five years, **Frank Moss**, who won three title medals and showed remarkable bravery, highlighted when he played outside-right in a match at Everton after sustaining a dislocated shoulder. Not only did he last 90 minutes, he also scored in a 2-0 win. The injury, though, ended his career.

Jack Kelsey's rein as Arsenal first choice throughout the 1950s coincided with the Club's worst run for 30 years. However, his bravery and agility gave him hero status with the crowd and his pinnacle was serving his beloved Wales with distinction at the 1958 World Cup – the national side's only major tournament appearance.

The late 1960s and early 1970s were dominated by **Bob Wilson**, the Chesterfield-born stopper who took bravery to a new level. His commanding performances and thirst for clean sheets proved the backbone for the Bertie Mee glory years. **Jimmy Rimmer** heroically replaced him and worked wonders to help maintain Arsenal's First Division status in the mid-1970s, deservedly winning a title and European Cup with Aston Villa in the twilight of his career.

Jack Kelsey leaps to claim the ball in a match against
Manchester City at Highbury in 1961. The Wales international
was the undisputed No.1 for a decade.

from QPR in 1990 for a then world record goalkeeping fee of £1.3m. Comparisons to Jennings are obvious: both were softly-spoken, unassuming men, dedicated to their trade, with massive frames and the ability to make the hard saves look simple. Neither went to ground easily and both filled the goal to dishearten opposition strikers and reassure their own defences. The giant Yorkshireman was the undisputed No.1 for 13 years and became the most decorated Arsenal goalkeeper ever, with a haul of three titles, one Cup-Winners' Cup, one League Cup and four FA Cups.

The English No. 1 was replaced in 2003 by former Schalke 04, Borussia Dortmund and AC Milan goalkeeper **Jens Lehmann**. The Germany international showed his credentials in his first season as the team went through the entire league campaign unbeaten, having to wait more than a full calendar year before tasting defeat in England.

Despite criticism from outside the Club Lehmann's form was outstanding again in 2005/06, but the following season **Manuel Almunia**, who was signed from Spanish club Albacete in 2003, began to challenge his position and the Spaniard finally took his place in August 2007. Almunia was soon recognised as the club's new No. 1 after an outstanding run of form and was rewarded with an improved four-year contract in April 2008.

GOALSCORING RECORDS, overall

Up to and including May 2008

MOST GOALS OVERALL
226 Thierry Henry

MOST PREMIERSHIP GOALS
174 Thierry Henry

By then **Pat Jennings** was between the sticks at Highbury and his consistency was a constant reminder to Spurs they had made a huge mistake allowing him to cross the north London divide in 1977. Few players have shown such composure and presence in any position for the Club – nor commanded such respect. He played in four finals for the Club before moving back to White Hart Lane eight years later.

John Lukic was the dependable man in green for the rest of the 1980s, winning a League Cup and a title medal – but he was displaced by **David Seaman**, who signed

MOST LEAGUE GOALS
174 Thierry Henry

MOST FA CUP GOALS
26 Cliff Bastin

MOST LEAGUE CUP GOALS
29 Ian Wright

MOST EUROPEAN GOALS OVERALL
42 Thierry Henry

MOST UEFA CHAMPIONS LEAGUE GOALS
35 Thierry Henry

MOST GOALS IN A SEASON
44 Ted Drake 1934/35 (42 Lge, 1 FAC, 1 CS)

MOST LEAGUE GOALS IN A SEASON
42 Ted Drake 1934/35

MOST PREMIERSHIP GOALS IN A SEASON
30 Thierry Henry 2003/04
(previously 23 Ian Wright 1993/94 & 1996/97)

MOST GOALS BY AN ARSENAL PLAYER IN ANY MATCH
7 Ted Drake (v Aston Villa (a)
14 Dec 1935, won 7-1, Lge)

MOST GOALS BY AN ARSENAL PLAYER IN ANY MATCH AT HIGHBURY
5 Jack Lambert (v Sheffield Utd
24 Dec 1932, won 9-2, Lge)

MOST GOALS BY AN ARSENAL PLAYER IN A LEAGUE MATCH AT HIGHBURY
5 Jack Lambert (v Sheffield Utd
24 Dec 1932, won 9-2)

MOST GOALS BY AN ARSENAL PLAYER IN A LEAGUE MATCH AWAY
7 Ted Drake (v Aston Villa 14 Dec 1935, won 7-1)

MOST GOALS BY AN ARSENAL PLAYER IN A FA CUP MATCH AT HIGHBURY
4 Cliff Bastin (v Darwen 9 Jan 1932, won 11-1, 3rd rd)

Young Gunner: Francesc Fabregas deflects the ball past a number of Blackburn players into the net during the Premiership match in August 2004 to become the club's youngest ever goalscorer at 17 years and 113 days old.

MOST GOALS BY AN ARSENAL PLAYER IN AN FA CUP MATCH AWAY

4 Ted Drake (v Burnley 20 Feb 1937, won 7-1, 5th rd)

MOST GOALS BY AN ARSENAL PLAYER IN A EUROPEAN MATCH

4 Alan Smith (v FK Austria (h) 18 Sep 1991, won 6-1, EC, 1st rd)

MOST GOALS BY AN ARSENAL PLAYER IN A LEAGUE CUP MATCH

No Arsenal player has scored over three goals in a League Cup match

LAST ARSENAL PLAYERS TO SCORE A HAT-TRICK AWAY

Thierry Henry (v AS Roma 27 Nov 2002, won 3-1, CL, Gp St 2)

Ray Parlour (v Werder Bremen 23 Mar 2000, won 4-2, UEFA, QF)

Kanu (v Chelsea 23 Oct 1999, won 3-2, Lge)

LAST ARSENAL PLAYERS TO SCORE MORE THAN THREE GOALS AT HIGHBURY

4 Thierry Henry (v Leeds United 16 April 2004, won 5-0, Lge)

4 Ian Wright (v Everton 21 Dec 1991, won 4-2, Lge)

4 Alan Smith (v FK Austria 18 Sep 1991, won 6-1, EC, 1st rd)

4 Cliff Holton (v Manchester City 6 Oct 1956, won 7-3, Lge)

LAST TIME AN ARSENAL PLAYER SCORED MORE THAN THREE GOALS AWAY

5 Tony Woodcock (v Aston Villa 29 Oct 1983, won 6-2, Lge)

4 David Herd (v Everton 6 Sep 1958, won 6-1, Lge)

YOUNGEST ARSENAL GOALSCORER EVER

Francesc Fabregas (16 years 212 days v Wolverhampton Wanderers (h) 2 Dec 2003, won 5-1, LC)

YOUNGEST ARSENAL GOALSCORER IN LEAGUE

Francesc Fabregas (17 years 113 days v Blackburn Rovers (h) 25 Aug 2004, won 3-0, Lge)

YOUNGEST ARSENAL GOALSCORER IN PREMIERSHIP

Francesc Fabregas (17 years 113 days v Blackburn Rovers (h) 25 Aug 2004, won 3-0, Lge)

YOUNGEST ARSENAL GOALSCORER IN EUROPE

Francesc Fabregas (17 years 217 days v Rosenborg (h) 7 Dec 2004, won 5-1, CL)

YOUNGEST ARSENAL GOALSCORER IN FA CUP

Cliff Bastin (17 years 303 days v Chelsea (h) 11 Jan 1930, won 2-0, 3rd rd)

YOUNGEST ARSENAL SCORER OF HAT-TRICK

John Radford (17 years 315 days v Wolverhampton Wanderers (h) 2 Jan 1965, won 4-1, Lge)

GOALSCORING RECORDS, players

John Radford hit a treble for the Gunners against Wolves on 2 January 1965 - 50 days before his 18th birthday.

THIERRY HENRY 226

The French striker broke Ian Wright's eight-year Club record of 185 goals on 18 October 2005 when Arsenal beat Sparta Prague 2-0 in the Czech Republic in the UEFA Champions League.

His first goal for the Club came in September 1999 when he scored the only goal in 1-0 win against Southampton at The Dell. It was the first of 26 goals he scored in his first season. His best year came during the Premiership-winning season of 2004 when the side when unbeaten for the entire league campaign and Henry scored an astonishing 32 goals in all competitions, just three short of Ted Drake's Club record of 42 in one season set in 1935.

During his time at Highbury his favourite opponents were Middlesbrough - in total he netted 13 times against the Teesiders. He also reached double figures against old adversaries Chelsea (10) while scoring nine times each against Manchester United and Liverpool. Henry

eventually scored an incredible 226 goals in just 364 appearances for the Gunners.

Below is a comprehensive list of all Henry's goals for Arsenal. Numbers in parentheses show Henry goals in that game or season.

Key:
P - Premiership
FAC - FA Cup
LC - League Cup
CL - Champions League
UEFA - UEFA Cup

1999/2000 [26]

18 Sep 1999	P	v Southampton	1-0	(1)
22 Sep 1999	CL	v AIK Solna	3-1	(1)
28 Nov 1999	P	v Derby County	2-1	(2)
30 Nov 1999	LC	v Middlesbrough	2-2	(1)
9 Dec 1999	UEFA	v Nantes	3-3	(1)
18 Dec 1999	P	v Wimbledon	1-1	(1)
28 Dec 1999	P	v Leeds United	2-0	(1)
15 Jan 2000	P	v Sunderland	4-1	(2)
5 Feb 2000	P	v Bradford City	1-2	(1)
2 Mar 2000	UEFA	v Deportivo La Coruña	5-1	(2)
9 Mar 2000	UEFA	v Deportivo La Coruña	1-2	(1)
16 Mar 2000	UEFA	v Werder Bremen	2-0	(1)
19 Mar 2000	P	v Tottenham Hotspur	2-1	(1)
23 Mar 2000	UEFA	v Werder Bremen	4-2	(1)
26 Mar 2000	P	v Coventry City	3-0	(1)
1 Apr 2000	P	v Wimbledon	3-1	(1)
16 Apr 2000	P	v Leeds United	4-0	(1)
20 Apr 2000	UEFA	v RC Lens	2-1	(1)
23 Apr 2000	P	v Watford	3-2	(2)
6 May 2000	P	v Chelsea	2-1	(2)
9 May 2000	P	v Sheffield Wednesday	3-3	(1)

2000/01 [22]

21 Aug 2000	P	v Liverpool	2-0	(1)
26 Aug 2000	P	v Charlton Athletic	5-3	(2)
6 Sep 2000	P	v Chelsea	2-2	(1)
1 Oct 2000	P	v Manchester United	1-0	(1)
14 Oct 2000	P	v Aston Villa	1-0	(1)
28 Oct 2000	P	v Manchester City	5-0	(2)
4 Nov 2000	P	v Middlesbrough	1-0	(1)
5 Dec 2000	CL	v Bayern Munich	2-2	(1)

9 Dec 2000	P	v Newcastle United	5-0	(1)
26 Dec 2000	P	v Leicester City	6-1	(3)
10 Feb 2001	P	v Ipswich Town	1-0	(1)
13 Feb 2001	CL	v Lyon	1-0	(1)
18 Feb 2001	FAC	v Chelsea	3-1	(1)
25 Feb 2001	P	v Manchester United	1-6	(1)
6 Mar 2001	CL	v Spartak Moscow	1-0	(1)
31 Mar 2001	P	v Tottenham Hotspur	2-0	(1)
4 Apr 2001	CL	v Valencia	2-1	(1)
21 Apr 2001	P	v Everton	4-1	(1)

2001/02 [32]

18 Aug 2001	P	v Middlesbrough	4-0	(1)
25 Aug 2001	P	v Leicester City	4-0	(1)
8 Sep 2001	P	v Chelsea	1-1	(1)
15 Sep 2001	P	v Fulham	3-1	(1)
19 Sep 2001	CL	v FC Schalke	3-2	(2)
29 Sep 2001	P	v Derby County	2-0	(2)
13 Oct 2001	P	v Southampton	2-0	(1)
16 Oct 2001	CL	v Panathinaikos	2-1	(2)
20 Oct 2001	P	v Blackburn Rovers	3-3	(1)
24 Oct 2001	CL	v Mallorca	3-1	(1)
4 Nov 2001	P	v Charlton Athletic	2-4	(2)
25 Nov 2001	P	v Manchester United	3-1	(2)
1 Dec 2001	P	v Ipswich Town	2-0	(1)
4 Dec 2001	CL	v Juventus	3-1	(1)
9 Dec 2001	P	v Aston Villa	3-2	(2)
23 Dec 2001	P	v Liverpool	2-1	(1)
5 Jan 2002	FAC	v Watford	4-2	(1)
23 Jan 2002	P	v Leicester City	3-1	(1)
30 Jan 2002	P	v Blackburn Rovers	3-2	(1)
23 Feb 2002	P	v Fulham	4-1	(2)
27 Feb 2002	CL	v Bayer Leverkusen	4-1	(1)
1 Apr 2002	P	v Charlton Athletic	3-0	(2)
11 May 2002	P	v Everton	4-3	(2)

2002/03 [32]

18 Aug 2002	P	v Birmingham City	2-0	(1)
24 Aug 2002	P	v West Ham United	2-2	(1)
10 Sep 2002	P	v Manchester City	2-1	(1)
14 Sep 2002	P	v Charlton Athletic	3-0	(1)
21 Sep 2002	P	v Bolton Wanderers	2-1	(1)
25 Sep 2002	CL	v PSV Eindhoven	4-0	(2)
28 Sep 2002	P	v Leeds United	4-1	(1)
30 Oct 2002	CL	v Borussia Dortmund	1-2	(1)
16 Nov 2002	P	v Tottenham Hotspur	3-0	(1)
27 Nov 2002	CL	v AS Roma	3-1	(3)
30 Nov 2002	P	v Aston Villa	3-1	(2)
26 Dec 2002	P	v West Brom	2-1	(1)
29 Dec 2002	P	v Liverpool	1-1	(1)
1 Jan 2003	P	v Chelsea	3-2	(1)
12 Jan 2003	P	v Birmingham City	4-0	(2)
19 Jan 2003	P	v West Ham United	3-1	(3)
9 Feb 2003	P	v Newcastle United	1-1	(1)

22 Feb 2003	P	v Manchester City	5-1	(1)
8 Mar 2003	FAC	v Chelsea	2-2	(1)
19 Mar 2003	CL	v Valencia	1-2	(1)
16 Apr 2003	P	v Manchester United	2-2	(2)
19 Apr 2003	P	v Middlesbrough	2-0	(1)
4 May 2003	P	v Leeds United	2-3	(1)
11 May 2003	P	v Sunderland	4-0	(1)

2003/04 [39]

10 Aug 2003	CS	v Manchester United	1-1	(1)
16 Aug 2003	P	v Everton	2-1	(1)
24 Aug 2003	P	v Middlesbrough	4-0	(1)
27 Aug 2003	P	v Aston Villa	2-0	(1)
13 Sep 2003	P	v Portsmouth	1-1	(1)
26 Sep 2003	P	v Newcastle United	3-2	(2)
18 Oct 2003	P	v Chelsea	2-1	(1)
21 Oct 2003	CL	v Dynamo Kiev	1-2	(1)
26 Oct 2003	P	v Charlton Athletic	1-1	(1)
1 Nov 2003	P	v Leeds United	4-1	(2)
25 Nov 2003	CL	v Inter Milan	5-1	(2)
26 Dec 2003	P	v Wolves	3-0	(1)
4 Jan 2004	FAC	v Leeds United	4-1	(1)
10 Jan 2004	P	v Middlesbrough	4-1	(1)
18 Jan 2004	P	v Aston Villa	2-0	(2)
1 Feb 2004	P	v Manchester City	2-1	(1)
7 Feb 2004	P	v Wolves	3-1	(1)
10 Feb 2004	P	v Southampton	2-0	(1)
28 Feb 2004	P	v Charlton Athletic	2-1	(1)
6 Mar 2004	FAC	v Portsmouth	5-1	(1)
10 Mar 2004	CL	v Celta Vigo	2-0	(2)
13 Mar 2004	P	v Blackburn Rovers	2-0	(1)
28 Mar 2004	P	v Manchester United	1-1	(1)
9 Apr 2004	P	v Liverpool	4-2	(3)
16 Apr 2004	P	v Leeds United	5-0	(4)
15 May 2004	P	v Leicester City	2-1	(1)

2004/05 [30]

22 Aug 2004	P	v Middlesbrough	5-3	(2)
25 Aug 2004	P	v Blackburn Rovers	3-0	(1)
28 Aug 2004	P	v Norwich City	4-1	(1)
18 Sep 2004	P	v Bolton Wanderers	2-2	(1)
2 Oct 2004	P	v Charlton Athletic	4-0	(2)
16 Oct 2004	P	v Aston Villa	3-1	(1)
20 Oct 2004	CL	v Panathinaikos	2-2	(1)
30 Oct 2004	P	v Southampton	2-2	(1)
2 Nov 2004	CL	v Panathinaikos	1-1	(1)
6 Nov 2004	P	v Crystal Palace	1-1	(1)
13 Nov 2004	P	v Tottenham Hotspur	5-4	(1)
24 Nov 2004	CL	v PSV Eindhoven	1-1	(1)
4 Dec 2004	P	v Birmingham City	3-0	(1)
7 Dec 2004	CL	v Rosenborg	5-1	(1)
12 Dec 2004	P	v Chelsea	2-2	(2)
26 Dec 2004	P	v Fulham	2-0	(1)
7 Feb 2005	P	v Aston Villa	3-1	(1)

14 Feb 2005	P	v Crystal Palace	5-1	(2)
5 Mar 2005	P	v Portsmouth	3-0	(3)
9 Mar 2005	CL	v Bayern Munich	1-0	(1)
2 Apr 2005	P	v Norwich City	4-1	(3)

2005/06 [33]

14 Aug 2005	P	v Newcastle	2-0	(1)
24 Aug 2005	P	v Fulham	4-1	(2)
18 Oct 2005	CL	v Sparta Prague	2-0	(2)
(surpassed Ian Wright's all-time scoring record)				
2 Nov 2005	CL	v Sparta Prague	3-0	(1)
5 Nov 2005	P	v Sunderland	3-1	(2)
19 Nov 2005	P	v Wigan Athletic	3-2	(2)
26 Nov 2005	P	v Blackburn Rovers	3-0	(1)
28 Dec 2005	P	v Portsmouth	4-0	(2)
14 Jan 2006	P	v Middlesbrough	7-0	(3)
24 Jan 2006	CC	v Wigan Athletic	2-1	(1)
1 Feb 2006	P	v West Ham Utd	2-3	(1)
4 Feb 2006	P	v Birmingham	2-0	(1)
21 Feb 2006	CL	v Real Madrid	1-0	(1)
4 Mar 2006	P	v Fulham	4-0	(2)
12 Mar 2006	P	v Liverpool	2-1	(2)
28 Mar 2006	CL	v Juventus	2-0	(1)
1 Apr 2006	P	v Aston Villa	5-0	(2)
12 Apr 2006	P	v Portsmouth	1-1	(1)
22 Apr 2006	P	v Tottenham Hotspur	1-1	(1)
1 May 2006	P	v Sunderland	3-0	(1)
7 May 2006	P	v Wigan Athletic	4-2	(3)

2006/07 [12]

9 Sep 2006	P	v Middlesbrough	1-1	(1)
23 Sep 2006	P	v Sheffield United	3-0	(1)
26 Sep 2006	CL	v Porto	2-0	(1)
14 Oct 2006	P	v Watford	3-0	(1)
22 Oct 2006	P	v Reading	4-0	(2)
18 Nov 2006	P	v Newcastle United	1-1	(1)
2 Jan 2007	P	v Charlton Athletic	4-0	(1)
6 Jan 2007	FAC	v Liverpool	3-1	(1)
13 Jan 2007	P	v Blackburn Rovers	2-0	(1)
21 Jan 2007	P	v Manchester United	2-1	(1)
3 Feb 2007	P	v Middlesbrough	1-1	(1)

GOALSCORING RECORDS, team

Between 19 May 2001 and 30 November 2002 Arsenal scored in 55 consecutive league matches – an English record. That sequence began in a 3-2 defeat to Southampton in the last ever competitive match to be played at The Dell, and

ended on 7 December 2002 when the Gunners lost 2-0 at Manchester United, a result which also ended a 49-game unbeaten run.

The previous English record was held by Chesterfield (46 matches) achieved in Division Three North between 1929 and 1930.

GOLDEN BOOT, The

The leading scorer in European football has been awarded the Golden Boot since 1968. Thierry Henry is the only Arsenal player to receive the prestigious gong, winning it in 2003 after scoring 30 goals, and he retained the title the following season after scoring another 25 goals, sharing the award with Villarreal forward Diego Forlan.

Ted Drake is the only other Arsenal striker to have finished as the leading scorer in Europe, when he hit 42 goals in 1934/35, though Arsenal legend Charlie Buchan topped the European scoring charts in 1922/23 with 30 goals while playing for Sunderland - two years before he returned south.

GOONERS

'Gooners' is the collective name for Arsenal fans, although the origins of the name are uncertain and strongly debated in the pubs of north London. What is clear is that it is an obvious deviation of the Club's nickname, 'The Gunners'. Although initially thought to be a name used by some of the Club's more rowdy followers, by the late 1980s it was generally used by all. In 1987 it even lent its name to Arsenal's first independently produced fanzine, *The Gooner*, which is now the biggest selling publication of its type. In 2006, the name 'Gooners' is so ingrained in footballing culture it has all but replaced the word 'Gunners' to describe the fans, Club and players.

GRAHAM, George

MANAGER 1986/95
Born Bargeddie, Scotland,
30 November 1944
Arsenal appearances **296 (12)**
Arsenal goals **77**
International caps (Scotland) **12**

A stylish centre-forward who Bertie Mee converted into a goalscoring midfielder, Graham was an integral member of the Fairs Cup and Double-winning side of the late 1960s and early 70s. Signed from Chelsea in 1966, he finished leading scorer for two successive seasons before his lack of pace necessitated a move into the middle of the field, where his style and elegance earned him the nickname 'Stroller'. An outstanding header of the ball, Graham possessed a lethal shot into the bargain and was a prolific scorer, netting on average once every four games.

He was sold to Manchester United and later drifted towards a career in the pub trade before best pal Terry Venables convinced him to take up coaching. A spell at Millwall, where he nurtured a young Teddy Sheringham, impressed Arsenal's board and he returned to Highbury in May 1986. Graham revitalised a club treading water, jettisoning many of the older, high-earning members of the squad and promoting several youngsters from the talent-rich youth sides. 'He just did the basics brilliantly. He could see that half of the young reserves were better than most of the first team,' recalls midfielder Steve Williams.

Graham became a master at fostering a 'them against us' mentality and the new steely determination brought the Littlewoods Cup and a fourth-place finish in his first season. He also built the greatest defence in the Club's history for little money - Lee Dixon, Nigel Winterburn and Steve Bould arriving for less than £1m combined - and promoting 20-year-old Tony Adams to the captaincy.

Nicknamed 'Gaddafi' by the players for his uncompromising style, his strong work ethic and belief rubbed off on young players like David Rocastle, Niall Quinn, Paul Merson and Michael Thomas. The title was won in 1989 and another followed in

George Graham (right) with his assistant Stewart Houston in 1994/95. The former Gunners midfielder returned to Highbury in 1986 as manager and immediately revived the Club's fortunes.

another Londoner with the skills and ingenuity to unlock the tightest defence. Winger **Anders Limpar** oozed class and cunning and provided an extra exciting dimension in the 1991 title-winning side.

Graham also paid Leicester £750,000 for **Alan Smith**, who would in turn earn two golden shoes and join that select band of Arsenal players to have scored 100 goals for the Club, as did another striker signed by the Scotsman. At £2.5m **Ian Wright** was deemed an expensive luxury on arrival, but soon won the fans over with a series of match-winning displays and, six years after his September 1991 arrival, would overtake Cliff Bastin's Club goals record.

GROUNDS

Plumstead Common – 1886
Sportsman Ground, Plumstead – 1887/88
Manor Ground, Plumstead – 1888/90
Invicta Ground, Plumstead – 1890/93
Manor Ground, Plumstead – 1893/1913
Arsenal Stadium, Highbury – 1913/2006*
Wembley Stadium – 1998 and 1999**
Emirates Stadium, Islington – 2006-

*Arsenal were forced to play home games at White Hart Lane during the Second World War due to bomb damage at Highbury. Arsenal's home also was used as an air raid post during hostilities.
**Arsenal used Wembley for home games in the UEFA Champions League for the 1998/99 and 1999/2000 seasons, playing six games in front of an average crowd of nearly 70,000 fans.

GROUNDSMAN

Steve Braddock was the outstanding groundsman in English football throughout the 1990s until present incumbent Paul

1991, but his sides were often criticised for a lack of flair, which was an unfair accusation about a team possessing players of the ability of Merson, Rocastle and Anders Limpar. The two domestic cups were won in 1993 and then came his finest hour, winning the Cup-Winners' Cup with a scratch team the next year.

Graham readily admitted he relished the opportunity to pit his tactical skills against the continent's finest. One banner regularly seen on Highbury matchdays said it all: 'George Knows'.

He left under a cloud in 1995, amid the now infamous bung allegations, but after a year away had further success with Leeds and Spurs. Now a media pundit, it is a mystery to many why he is not back in management. Despite his much-publicised misdemeanour, Graham still remains firmly

in the hearts of Arsenal fans as the only man to have won the title as player and manager at Highbury.

GRAHAM'S STARS

George Graham may have cultivated the image of a dour, defensive mastermind, but despite the criticisms his sides were packed with flair and style. With **Tony Adams** acting as his eyes and ears on the pitch, and a solid defensive wall built to withstand the best strikers of the day, it gave his attacking players the chance to express themselves at the other end of the field.

The exciting **David Rocastle** blossomed under Graham, as did **Paul Merson**,

Burgess took over the maintenance of the celebrated Highbury playing surface in September 1999.

Born and bred in Blackpool, Burgess originally worked on his hometown club's Bloomfield Park surface before moving to north London to continue his education under Braddock, who now maintains the Hertfordshire training pitches. Burgess and his assistant Paul Ashcroft have since continued Braddock's impeccable standards at both Highbury and Emirates Stadium.

Burgess' hard work has been recognised at the highest level and he has even been flown over to Reykjavik on several occasions to offer his expert advice on maintaining the Iceland FA's national stadium surface – a tough task in the harsh freezing cold north Atlantic environment. In 2005 he won the prestigious Institute of Groundsmanship Professional Football Groundsman of the Year award – the youngest ever winner at the age of just 27. Burgess and his dedicated team picked up another gong in 2007/08 – the Premier League best pitch award.

GROVES, Vic and Perry

Three decades separated Vic and nephew Perry's time at Highbury, but both left their mark at the Club.

Cockney Vic was a larger-than-life character and Arsenal fan who started as a centre-forward after signing in November 1955 from Leyton Orient, endearing himself to the North Bank with a debut goal against Sheffield United. Injuries slowed his progress, but he was soon made captain and, in 1959, converted to wing-half where he remained for the rest of his time at Highbury, playing 203 games and netting 37 times.

Perry may not have had the natural footballing talents of his uncle, but George Graham's first signing, a cut-price acquisition from Colchester, spent six productive seasons at Highbury, although he saw his chances confined mainly to the final 20 minutes of games, his speedy legs thrown into the fray to test tiring opposition

defences. He made 120 appearances in red and white, with 83 of those as a substitute.

His best remembered cameo came in his first season when, on as a replacement for Niall Quinn, it was his burst down the left-hand side that set up the winner for Charlie Nicholas in the 1987 Littlewoods Cup Final.

He never grumbled about his role as the perennial supersub and, allied to a tireless energy and a monster throw-in, it made him a cult figure amongst fans on the North Bank, who affectionately dubbed him the 'Ginger Genius'.

He played peripheral roles in the 1989 and 1991 title triumphs – scoring 28 goals – before moving to Southampton for £750,000 in the summer of 1992.

He still dons the red and white for Arsenal in the popular Masters events and he is one of the former Arsenal stars who accompany visitors on the Legends Tour around Emirates stadium.

GUEST PLAYERS

The Second World War turned football on its head and, although players went off to fight in the four corners of the globe, the authorities soon realised the masses needed their weekly fix of the beautiful game and set up wartime competitions.

Many players 'guested' for the Gunners due to their postings in the south of England, but the most famous stars to have pulled on the red and white jersey were Preston's Bill Shankly, who went on to manage Liverpool to great success, Stoke City's legendary winger Stanley Matthews and Blackpool's Stan Mortensen, who would score a hat-trick in the 1953 FA Cup Final.

West Ham's Len Goulden – later to make an impact at Chelsea – and Manchester United's Bill Wrigglesworth were also prominent guests at White Hart Lane, where Arsenal were based until 1946 after Highbury was requisitioned for the war effort.

In total more than three dozen guest players represented Arsenal – including four from Spurs – while several Arsenal players also helped other clubs. Club captain Eddie Hapgood, for example,

would occasionally travel across London to turn out for West Ham United.

GUNFLASH

The Arsenal Supporters Club's official magazine claims to be the oldest publication of its kind in the world, pre-dating the fanzine boom of the mid-1980s by more than 35 years. Supporters Club founder members Richard 'Dick' Jones and JE Overed are believed to have jointly edited the first issue in September 1949, which was in the form of a seven-page newsletter. By the time of its fourth issue it took the form of a magazine and by issue five it was officially christened *Gunflash*. Mr Jones held the position of editor for 30 years and 296 issues before he stepped down in 1979. *Gunflash* reached an impressive milestone in March 2005 with its 500th issue. Its current editor is Barry Hatch, who took over from previous incumbent Paul Lindsell in 1997. The magazine currently has a print-run of 1,000 copies per issue.

GUNNERSAURUS

In the summer of 1993 the Club asked members of the Junior Gunners to come up with ideas for a new mascot in celebration of their tenth anniversary. Two members – who did not know each other and came from different parts of the country – came up with virtually identical designs for a prehistoric character – and Gunnersaurus was created. He is now the official Club mascot.

The 'official' Club history records that an egg was discovered when demolition work began on the old North Bank terrace and hatched in time for the new season.

JGs' membership manager Sue Campbell says, 'Gunnersaurus has been hugely popular since arriving.' He has even made visits to many away grounds and has travelled to Europe where he visited RC Lens in France. The furthest he has travelled is the Ukraine.

HAIL CAESAR!

Born **Builth Wells, Wales, 24 August 1866**
Died **23 July 1941**
Arsenal appearances **27**
Arsenal goals **6**
International caps (Wales) **8**

Caesar Llewellyn Jenkyns started his career at Small Heath (later to become Birmingham City) but moved to Second Division Woolwich Arsenal in April 1895 where he was given the captain's armband as a centre-half. Significantly he became the Club's first-ever international player when he was capped for Wales against Scotland on 21 March 1896 – less than ten years after the Club was formed. However, his stay at the Gunners did not last long and that summer he moved to Newton Heath, later to become Manchester United. A police officer in later life, he died aged 74 in 1941.

HAIRCUTS

From the slicked down centre partings of 1930s stars Ted Drake and Alex James, to the Hoxton fin-style mullet of Cesc Fabregas, Arsenal players have had some interesting hairstyles through the years, reflecting the times in which they played.

Denis Compton was the original Brylcreem Boy when he became a national celebrity and one of the first footballers to have an endorsement deal after the Second World War. The 1950s saw the likes of Vic Groves and Alan Skirton perfect the quiff and ducktail look, Joe Baker and Dave Bacuzzi just opting for the Elvis quiff as the swinging 1960s kicked off.

The rebellious Charlie George – famed for his long locks – actually made his debut with a 'suedehead' and ended his career at the Club with a strange bubble perm ready for his move to Derby County. Terry Mancini stood out too for his bald head circled by thick curly dark hair, while fellow

1970s defender Willie Young had an unmanageable ginger mop which would cause mass confusion in the opposition area at a corner. Striker Alan Sunderland favoured a bubble perm similar to Charlie George's – and later seen by such luminaries as Tommy Caton and Graham Rix – while Charlie Nicholas arrived in 1983 with a Spandau Ballet-esque short-at-the-sides long-at-the-back mullet that added to his playboy image.

Winger Perry Groves lived up to his Tintin nickname with a short-back-and-sides ginger crop complete with pointed-up tuft at the front, while Paul Merson, the epitome of cool on the North Bank in the late 1980s, wore his hair long, shaggy and unkempt in line with the new Acid House and Indie fashions, until shearing half off to create a not-so-fetching curly 'mini-bob', as seen at the 1993 Coca-Cola Cup Final. Anfield hero Michael Thomas went for a flat top in the style of Grace Jones, but Dutch winger Glenn Helder went several stages further with a Lionel Ritchie-style, wet-look perm.

Ian Wright was never one to slink into the corner and for a period of the 1995/96 season dyed his hair blond, before wisely shaving it all off. David Seaman had one of the most talked about footballer's hairstyles when his hair grew and grew and grew until he had a ten-inch ponytail, while Emmanuel Petit also favoured his blond locks tied back tightly.

In recent years there has been no let-up in the weird and wonderful hairstyles adopted by some of the Club's younger players. Cesc Fabregas favoured an ultra-fashionable mullet when he first broke into the team while Emmanuel Adebayor opted to straighten his afro with interesting results – before sensibly going for a short back and sides. And Bacary Sagna's distinctive blond dreadlocks have also caused a stir – particularly when they disappeared for one game and miraculously returned a week later. Not only was it revealed they were, in fact, hair extensions, but the France defender also disclosed that his mother is the inspiration behind them and regularly replaces and re-attaches them herself.

Perry Groves had many nicknames... and one was Tintin due to his short-back-and-sides ginger crop.

HAPGOOD, Eddie

Born **Bristol, 24 September 1908**
Died **20 April 1973**
Arsenal appearances **440**
Arsenal goals **2**
International caps (England) **30**

This Bristol milkman became one of the most successful players in Arsenal's history and is in an elite band of players who have won five title medals. His first big break came when Kettering Town gave him a contract and,

after a short spell with the Poppies, Herbert Chapman offered £950 for his services. It would be one of the shrewdest moves Chapman ever made as Hapgood went on to skipper both Club and country in the trophy-laden 1930s. Arguably the finest left-back in world football during the decade, he barely missed a game right up to the outbreak of the Second World War, as he formed an excellent full-back pairing with George Male for both Arsenal and England.

He made his England debut in Rome against Italy in May 1933 and legend has it one of his mighty clearances landed in the lap

of a Benito Mussolini. It would not be his only brush with fascist regimes. He captained his country for the first time against Italy in the infamous Battle of Highbury in November 1934 when England beat the reigning World champions 3–2. It was a bad-tempered affair and Hapgood didn't get off lightly, sustaining a broken nose due to a flailing Italian elbow (see Battle of Highbury on page 27).

Another moment of controversy came when he skippered his country in a 6–3 win over Germany in May 1938, just days after he picked up his fifth title medal. The game is remembered as the England players were reluctant to give a Nazi salute prior to kick-off in the Olympic Stadium. An outraged Hapgood led a players' revolt in the dressing room when they were asked to make the salute as a gesture of goodwill. Despite the bravado, the diplomats – backed up by FA officials – won and the team famously made the hated salute.

After the war he managed Blackburn Rovers and Watford before turning his back on the game to run a YMCA hostel in Berkshire. He moved to Leamington in 1971 when he retired, but just two years later he collapsed and died suddenly while attending a sports forum in the town.

HARD MEN, The

WILF COPPING (1934/38)

The 'enforcer' in George Allison's great side – a boxer's nose and unshaven appearance just added to Copping's menace. The former miner was snapped up from Leeds in 1934 by Allison after predecessor Herbert Chapman had tried and failed to attract him south. Drafted in to replace the ageing Bob John, he slotted straight into the side and added steel with his usual war cry of, 'Get stuck in!'

He dispensed a few bone-jarring tackles when he was one of seven Gunners to play

Full-back Eddie Hapgood warms up before a game. The Bristol-born defender was signed from non-league Kettering and played a key role in all five inter-war championships.

Hard man Peter Storey shows typical aggression and determination as he battles for possession in the 1972 FA Cup Final defeat to Leeds.

Taylor – after an FA Cup defeat in 1987. And he further endeared himself to the fans with a clear dislike for the 'fancy dans' at Spurs. 'They always thought they were better than us,' he says, 'but I don't remember them beating us too many times though, do you?'

MARTIN KEOWN (1984/86 & 1993/2004)
Like Steve Williams, 'The Rash', as he was known, was first and foremost a fan lucky enough to pull on the red and white. Reputations went out of the window, as Keown would stick methodically to the task of shackling the opposition's playmaker by any means possible. Hated by opposition fans but revered by Gooners, his un-compromising style looked clumsy to the untrained eye, but won him respect from fellow professionals. His long-running feud with Ruud van Nistelrooy provided much entertainment and further stoked the flames of rivalry between Arsenal and Manchester United. Even Thierry Henry admitted he hated being marked by Keown in training.

against Italy in 1934 in his finest hour for England. His captain Eddie Hapgood, said, 'Wilf enjoyed himself that afternoon. For the first time in their lives, the Italians were given a sample of real honest shoulder charging, and Wilf's famous double-footed tackle was causing them furiously to think.' Copping also played through the pain barrier in a 2-0 win at Everton in 1935 – before fainting on the final whistle due to the excruciating pain.

PETER STOREY (1965/77)
Hugely disliked outside of Highbury, Storey provided spadefuls of aggression in the centre of the park. The Surrey-born defender appeared to have a genuine disregard for danger and relished his reputation as one of the toughest characters in the game, along with the likes of Ron Harris, Tommy Smith and Billy Bremner. In an era where every side had a 'hard man', Leeds and Ireland legend Johnny Giles has freely admitted that the one man he didn't relish facing was Storey.

After leaving Highbury Storey had several brushes with the law before becoming a taxi driver in south London.

WILLIE YOUNG (1977/1981)
A fearless, single-minded giant of a defender, Young could lift the crowd with a crunching tackle or clenched fist. He showed great character after arriving from Tottenham and making his debut in a 4-1 home defeat to Ipswich. The fans clearly disliked this 'Spurs' man until the north London derby in Easter 1977 when he played on with concussion and blood pouring from a head wound. Then, a new North Bank hero was born.

STEVE WILLIAMS (1984/88)
He could start an argument in an empty room and nobody was exempt from a tongue-lashing if he saw fit. A graceful midfielder with a wild streak, Williams' passion was also fuelled from a childhood watching the Gunners from the North Bank. 'I just love Arsenal, they're the greatest club in the world,' he says.

He could play an inch-perfect 60-yard ball one minute, and the next fly in late and wild on an opponent to 'liven things up'. Williams once tried to take on the entire Watford bench – and manager Graham

HARTSON, John

Born **Swansea, 5 April 1975**
Arsenal appearances **55 (16)**
Arsenal goals **17**
International caps (Wales) **51 (14 goals)**

In January 1995, Welsh international centre-forward, John Hartson became the most expensive teenager in British football history when George Graham paid Luton Town £2.5m for his services. His size and aerial strength disguised a clinical goal-scoring talent and excellent technique. But when Arsène Wenger arrived he was soon on his way to West Ham. He later turned out for Wimbledon and Coventry before he found his spiritual home with Glasgow giants Celtic and spent five seasons north of the border. In the summer of 2006 he signed for West Bromwich Albion, scoring twice on his debut, but weight and fitness problems were always an issue and he went to Norwich for a short loan spell before announcing his retirement in early 2008.

HAT-TRICK HEROES

Ted Drake, Jimmy Brain and Jack Lambert are the Club's leading hat-trick scorers with 12 apiece – although one of Drake's was a double hat-trick – while Ian Wright netted 11 trebles in his seven years at Highbury.

Doug Lishman still remains the only Gunner to score hat-tricks in three successive home matches: netting against Fulham in a 4-3 win on 27 October 1951 and repeating his feat in 6-3 and 4-2 wins over West Brom and Bolton respectively. Thierry Henry went close to equalling the record when he scored successive hat-tricks at home in April 2004, hitting three in a 4-2 win over Liverpool and then smashing four past Leeds in a 5-0 win, before drawing a blank against Birmingham.

Alan Smith is the only Gunner to score a hat-trick on his European debut, netting four times against Austria Vienna in the European Cup in 1991.

In total 90 players have scored hat-tricks for Arsenal with Andy Ducat and Ian Wright doing so on their league debuts for the Club. Ducat was only 19 when he hit three against Newcastle in a 4-3 home win in 1905 and Wright scored three on his First Division bow at Southampton 86 years later.

And Henrys scored the first and last hat-tricks at Highbury: Henry King struck three in a 6-0 win over Grimsby Town on 14 November 1914, and King Henry – aka Thierry Henry – also saw off the old stadium with a thrilling treble to see off Wigan in a 4-2 win in the last ever Highbury match on 6 May 2006.

HAYES, Martin

Born **Walthamstow, London, 21 March 1966**
Arsenal appearances **92 (40)**
Arsenal goals **34**

Left-winger Martin Hayes came through the ranks to score 24 goals in the 1986/87 season and earned a reputation for being deadly from the penalty spot (12 of his 34 goals were from spot-kicks). He almost moved to Huddersfield Town in the autumn of 1986 but

injuries propelled him into the Arsenal starting line-up, where he cemented his place with a string of eye-catching displays. His first-team opportunities were limited, but he picked up a Littlewoods League Cup winner's medal that season and in the next year's Final he came off the bench to score, although Arsenal lost 2-3 to Luton Town. He also won a title medal in 1988/89, racing through to score the winner at Ayresome Park against Middlesbrough in the run-in.

Hayes moved to Celtic for £650,000 in 1990 and later played for Wimbledon and Swansea City. He was appointed player-manager of Bishop's Stortford FC in 1999.

HELDER, Glenn

Born **Leiden, Netherlands, 28 October 1968**
Arsenal appearances **33 (16)**
Arsenal goals **1**

George Graham's last signing, in February 1995, was a precocious talent from Vitesse Arnhem who failed to shine at Highbury. His sublime skills and occasional flashes of preposterous brilliance were too often overshadowed by frustrating inconsistency, and he was offloaded to Benfica on loan and then moved back to his homeland with NAC Breda. Whether he was a genius or not is a subject still debated among Arsenal fans.

He returned to Arsenal for a guest appearance in Bergkamp's Testimonial.

HENRY, Thierry

Born **Paris, 17 August 1977**
Arsenal appearances **337 (33)**
Arsenal goals **226**
International caps (France) **100 (44 goals)**

Thierry Henry is a truly world-class talent who many good judges believe is the greatest player on the planet. His professional career began at AS Monaco under Arsène Wenger and he teamed up with his

old mentor again in 1999 after Wenger rescued his compatriot from a nightmare spell at Juventus, who were on the verge of farming him out on loan to Udinese.

Henry arrived at Highbury as a left-winger, but Wenger could see more potential with him leading the line. Already a World Cup-winner, Henry also won Euro 2000 with Les Bleus after ending his first season at Highbury with 26 goals in 48 appearances. In 2001/02 he netted 32 times as Arsenal won the Double and the next season he won an FA Cup medal after hitting another 32 goals. His personal best haul came in the unbeaten 2003/04 season when he finished just one short of the magic 40, with 30 of his goals coming in just 37 Premiership appearances.

Though only runner-up in the 2003 and 2004 FIFA World Player of the Year awards, he won the Football Writers' Association Footballer of the Year, the PFA Players' Player of the Year twice and the French Player of the Year on four occasions – an all-time record. In 2004/5, despite Arsenal being the runners-up in the Premiership, Henry emerged with the European Golden Boot – the award for the top goalscorer in Europe – for the second consecutive year.

He was promoted to Club captain in 2005 when Patrick Vieira left for Juventus – and celebrated by securing his place in Highbury history on 18 October when his second goal at Sparta Prague took him past Ian Wright's Club record of 185 goals. The new skipper reached 200 goals for Arsenal on 4 February, during a 2-0 victory against Birmingham at St Andrews, a little over three years after he completed his first century at the same ground. In March 2006 his two goals against Aston Villa ensured he was the first player in Premiership history to score 20 goals in five successive seasons.

His French team-mate Lillian Thuram says of Henry, 'He's a wizard... and is blessed with a gift for scoring goals. His best quality is his speed while the ball is at his feet. He may be the fastest man ever to lace up a football boot. No defender in the world can keep up with him.'

After much soul-searching, Henry accepted a new challenge in June 2007 when he moved to long-term suitors Barcelona. But while he may have moved to Spain, his love affair with the Gunners will continue unabated: "Beating the record of Wrighty, putting it at 226, playing for Arsenal, loving the club. It was and will remain the most difficult decision of my life. I will always love the club."

HIGHBURY

Highbury, N5 – home to Arsenal from 1913 to 2006 – is in the east of Islington and has a population of 21,959, according to the 2001 census. The area lies between Finsbury Park in the north, Holloway in the west, Canonbury in the south and Stoke Newington in the east. It has a chequered history: during the famous peasants' revolt of the 14th century, protest leader Jack Straw led a mob of 20,000 rioters, who, 'so offended by the wealth and haughtiness' of Highbury, destroyed the area's large manor house. Straw and some of his followers used the site as a temporary headquarters – consequently the derelict manor became known for the next 500 years as Jack Straw's Castle.

In the 19th century the entire Highbury area was earmarked as a huge royal park, but the idea was eventually shelved. In recent years gentrification has seen a great deal of development, although the area still retains pockets of working-class housing, while newly-arrived immigrants have further added to the eclectic mix.

Although the old stadium was often referred to as Highbury, its official title was in fact Arsenal Stadium. Arsenal spent 93 years at Highbury, playing their first game there on 6 September 1913 against Leicester Fosse. The new arena had been designed by the celebrated football stadium architect Archibald Leitch (see Leitch, Archibald on page 132) and was one of the grandest grounds in the country.

When success came to the Club in the 1930s the stadium took on the shape still recognisable to this day. The distinctive Art Deco East and West stands were built and the stadium recorded its official record attendance of 73,295 for a 0-0 draw with Sunderland in March 1935. During the Second World War the stadium was used as

Highbury was Arsenal's home for 93 years, from 1913/2006, before the Club moved less than a mile to Emirates Stadium. This is the view from the North Bank towards the Clock End.

an air raid centre and was bombed several times. Apart from repairs following the conflict very few changes were made to the stadium – except for the addition of more seats in place of terracing – until the 1990s when the Taylor Report necessitated the construction of all-seater stands at the North Bank and Clock End terraces. Because of the safety improvements, the capacity dropped steeply from 60,000 in the mid-1980s, to 38,500 by 1993.

But throughout its life, the old ground retained its unique character, which made it one of the last true footballing landmarks of the 20th century. Its grandeur was famed, as was its confined space with the fans so close to the action, making it a tough place to visit for opponents. The final European match – and the last game to be played under floodlights – was the visit of Villarreal CF in the Champions League semi-final on 19 April 2006. Arsenal's last

competitive fixture at the stadium was against Wigan Athletic on 6 May 2006 in the FA Premiership.

P	W	D	L	F	A
2010	1196	475	339	4038	1959

Win rate (all competitions) 59%
Win rate (League) 59%
Win rate (FA Cup) 65%
Win rate (League Cup) 70%
Win rate (Europe) 66%
Win rate (Charity/Community Shield) 80%

HIGHBURY SQUARE

When Arsenal vacated Highbury in 2006, work began immediately on turning the stadium into a housing complex comprising

711 high-specification studio, one-, two-, three-bedroom and penthouse apartments. Renamed Highbury Square, residents will have access to a full range of amenities including a fitness centre, 24-hour concierge service and underground car parking. All apartments will face inwards and have access to the two-acre pitch which will be converted into the largest private garden square in the area.

The Art Deco façades of the existing Grade II-Listed East Stand – with its famous Marble Hall – and the locally-listed West Stand will be preserved, in order to retain the iconic status of the site. The North and South Stands will be replaced by new-built apartments designed in a contemporary style to harmonise with the remaining buildings.

HILL-WOOD FAMILY, The

The link goes right back to 1919, when businessman Sir Samuel Hill-Wood moved south after several business dealings in his native Derbyshire went wrong. He had quite a sporting pedigree himself, once scoring ten runs off one ball while playing for Derbyshire against the MCC in May 1900 – unsurprisingly, this record still stands – and he was also a talented rugby league player. Football was another passion and the family had owned local club Glossop North End, still the smallest town in England to stage professional league football. When he moved south, according to his grandson, current Arsenal chairman Peter, he got involved with the Gunners because, simply 'he just thought they were the best team in the south'. He succeeded Sir Henry Norris as chairman in 1929 and served for seven years, steering the Club through the trauma of Herbert Chapman's death in 1934, before stepping down two years later. He returned to the post in 1946 and remained until his death in January 1949.

Sir Robert Bracewell-Smith (chairman 1949/69) took over but, when he passed away 14 years later, Samuel's son Denis

Hill-Wood was appointed chairman – his bust sat next to the trophy cabinet in the old East Stand – and immediately appointed *his* son Peter to the board.

Peter recalls how his father – affectionately known as 'the Old Man' around the Club – at times found the ever-changing world of football hard to understand. 'I remember my father being absolutely horrified at the thought of having perimeter advertising,' he recalls. 'It was a case of "over my dead body".'

Peter, who has worked for Hambros merchant bank for most of his professional life, was appointed chairman in 1981 and, like his father and grandfather before him, has made every effort to ensure he is very much in the background, preferring dynamic vice-chairman David Dein to be the public face of the Arsenal boardroom. Former centre-forward Alan Smith said he was rarely seen: 'As players we always knew something special was afoot if the chairman popped his head around the dressing room door. There he stood – brown pinstriped suit, lucky red socks poking out underneath, with the obligatory cigar in tow. The reason for his visit? One of two, normally: we were either about to win something and he had come to wish us luck, or we'd done the deed and he wanted to congratulate us.'

HILLIER, David

Born **Blackheath, London,
18 December 1969**
Arsenal appearances **142**
Arsenal goals **2**

Captain of the 1988 FA Youth Cup-winning side, which beat Doncaster Rovers in the Final, big things were predicted for the confident south Londoner who made his first-team debut in a League Cup-tie with Chester City in September 1990. He made an instant impact and played enough games in the midfield to earn him a title medal at the end of that first season.

Hard-working with good technique and a willingness to chase lost causes – a

perfect George Graham-type midfielder – he edged his way into the starting line-up, but injuries saw him miss out on the Cup Finals of 1993 and 1994 until he appeared in the Cup-Winners' Cup Final defeat to Real Zaragoza in 1995.

His opportunties became limited under Bruce Rioch and Arsène Wenger, and he moved to Portsmouth for £250,000 in late 1996. He later turned out for Bristol Rovers and Barnet.

HILLSBOROUGH

Sheffield Wednesday's famous old ground is one of the most used FA Cup semi-final venues in football history and in the 1970s Arsenal played there three times.

One of the most important goals in the Gunners' history was scored at the ground on 27 March 1971. Trailing 2-1 to Stoke City with just seconds remaining of the FA Cup semi-final, Peter Storey kept his head to score a vital penalty past England goalkeeper Gordon Banks and send the tie to a replay, won 2-0 at Villa Park four days later.

Arsenal also played at Hillsborough in the third round of the Cup in 1979, drawing 1-1 with Third Division Wednesday at the start of a mammoth five-game battle. Arsenal finally won the fourth replay 2-0 and went on to lift the trophy.

The next season another Cup epic began at the ground, when Arsenal drew 0-0 with Liverpool in the semi-final. The Gunners finally won the third replay to go on to Wembley, where they lost 1-0 to West Ham.

HOLLINS, John

Born **Guildford, Surrey, 16 July 1946**
Arsenal appearances **164 (8)**
Arsenal goals **13**
International caps (England) **1**

A hard-working midfielder and Chelsea legend, John Hollins' career appeared to be winding down with an imminent

John Hollins in Arsenal's short-lived green and blue away strip during the 1982/83 season. The former Chelsea man's career caught a second wind at Highbury.

His son Chris, a successful sports correspondent seen regularly on BBC breakfast news, is a keen Arsenal fan and was the Club's first ever mascot.

HOME HELP

Arsenal's search for a new stadium was leading up cul-de-sacs until Anthony Spencer came along. A friend of David Dein, a surveyor with a West End retail estate consultancy, one day he was scouring a map of Islington on a CD-Rom. When he saw the 17-acre Ashburton Grove site, earmarked for redevelopment for years, housing a few businesses and a waste transfer station, and wedged between two railway lines, he realised he had found the answer. 'I got my *A to Z*, cut out Wembley Stadium and plonked it on Ashburton Grove – it fitted,' he explains. He soon convinced the board the answer to their frustrating search was just 500 yards from Highbury and the ball was rolling. Nearly eight years later, Emirates Stadium became the centrepiece of Arsenal's £357m project which regenerated Holloway and kept the Gunners in Islington.

HONOURS

DIVISION ONE CHAMPIONS
1930/31, 1932/33, 1933/34, 1934/35, 1937/38, 1947/48, 1952/53, 1970/71, 1988/89, 1990/91

PREMIERSHIP CHAMPIONS
1997/98, 2001/02, 2003/04

CHARITY/COMMUNITY SHIELD
Winners
1930, 1931, 1933, 1934, 1938, 1948, 1953, 1998, 1999, 2002, 2004

move to Norwich City before Arsenal stepped in at the 11th hour to take him to Highbury in July 1979. It was the day before his 33rd birthday, but, a dedicated athlete, he responded to his unexpected move in typical fashion, grafting hard to muscle his way into the starting line-up and even being voted supporters' Player of the Year in 1982. Impossibly polite and keen to help the younger players, his influence was felt very strongly throughout the whole of the Club before his decision to return to Stamford Bridge, where he had spent more than a decade previously, as player-manager.

FA CUP

Winners

1930   Beat Huddersfield Town 2-0
1936   Beat Sheffield Utd 1-0
1950   Beat Liverpool 2-0
1971   Beat Liverpool 2-1
1979   Beat Manchester Utd 3-2
1993   Beat Sheffield Wednesday 2-1
1998   Beat Newcastle United 2-0
2002   Beat Chelsea 2-0
2003   Beat Southampton 1-0
2005   Beat Manchester United 0-0
        (aet, Arsenal won 5-4 on pens)

Runners-up

1927   Lost to Cardiff City 1-0
1932   Lost to Newcastle United 2-1
1952   Lost to Newcastle United 1-0
1972   Lost to Leeds United 1-0
1978   Lost to Ipswich Town 1-0
1980   Lost to West Ham United 1-0
2001   Lost to Liverpool 2-1

LEAGUE CUP

Winners

1987   Beat Liverpool 2-1
1993   Beat Sheffield Wednesday 2-1

Runners-up

1968   Lost 3-1 to Swindon Town (aet)
1969   Lost 1-0 to Leeds United
1988   Lost 3-2 to Luton Town

FAIRS CUP

Winners

1970   Beat Anderlecht 4-3 on agg. (1-3, 3-0)

UEFA CUP

Runners-up

2000   Lost to Galatasaray 0-0
        (aet, Arsenal lost 1-4 on pens)

EUROPEAN CUP-WINNERS' CUP

Winners

1994   Beat AS Parma 1-0

Runners-up

1980   Lost to Valencia CF 0-0
        (aet, Arsenal lost 4-5 on pens)
1995   Lost 2-1 to Real Zaragoza (aet)

EUROPEAN CHAMPIONS LEAGUE

Runners-up

2006   Lost to Barcelona 2-1

HOOF IT!

According to Highbury legend, a horse was buried under the North Bank when it was being redeveloped in the mid-1930s. Local residents were encouraged to dump rubbish into a hole in the terrace and one contractor got too close to the edge and his horse and cart toppled in. It proved impossible to save the injured horse and it was destroyed where it lay – buried in the middle of the terracing. Some fans claimed they could even hear the noise of a distressed horse in later years – although no ghostly sightings ever materialised.

HOUSTON, Stewart

CARETAKER MANAGER 1995 & 1996

The Scotsman, who arrived at Highbury as reserve manager in 1987, spent two short spells as caretaker manager in the mid-1990s after five years as George Graham's No.2. He first took the reins after Graham's departure in February 1995, working well to guide the Club to the European Cup-Winners' Cup Final in May. He also spent most of August 1996 filling in after Bruce Rioch was sacked, before he left to take the top job at QPR, where Rioch would, in turn, become his assistant.

Opposite Graham Rix (left), Pat Rice (yellow) and Liam Brady lead their team-mates on a lap of honour around the pitch proudly holding on to the FA Cup, after the Gunners' 1979 dramatic 3-2 win over Manchester United at Wembley. Arsenal have won the trophy ten times in total.

Right Don Howe (right) looks tense during the 1978 FA Cup Final, with Ipswich manager Bobby Robson chatting over his right shoulder. Howe has played for, coached and managed the Gunners since first arriving at Highbury in 1964, and he still occasionally scouts for the Club.

HOWE, Don

MANAGER 1983/86
Born **Wolverhampton, 12 October 1935**
Arsenal appearances **74**
Arsenal goals **1**
International caps (England) **23**

Respected throughout world football for his playing achievements, innovative coaching skills and encyclopaedic knowledge of the game, Don Howe spent most of his playing career at West Bromwich Albion before Arsenal manager Billy Wright paid £35,000 to bring him south in 1964 at the age of 29. A silky full-back who earned 23 England caps, he soon took the captain's armband before his playing career came to a premature end in 1966 after he sustained a broken leg playing against Blackpool.

He remained at Highbury as chief scout and soon became Bertie Mee's right-hand man – helping mastermind the Fairs Cup and Double successes of the early 1970s – before he went back to first love West Brom in 1971 as manager. But Mee desperately wanted him to continue his footballing education in north London and he soon returned under new manager Terry Neill, replacing him as manager in 1983 before leaving the Club in 1986. 'The thing with my time at Arsenal is, I maybe should have stayed when I should have gone and gone when I should have stayed,' he says.

His influence was immense when he and Bobby Gould later guided little Wimbledon to an FA Cup in 1988 and he later managed QPR and Coventry to varying success before returning to Arsenal again as an Academy coach, finally retiring in 2003. In between he was a key member of England's coaching set up, working with managers Ron Greenwood, Bobby Robson and Terry Venables. Now he occasionally scouts for Arsenal and is still a passionate coach, setting up schemes for youngsters across the UK.

HUGHES, Stephen

Born **Wokingham, Surrey, 18 September 1976**
Arsenal appearances **36 (40)**
Arsenal goals **7**

A highly promising left-sided England Under-21 midfielder, Hughes looked set for a long and successful Highbury career after starring in the 1994 FA Youth Cup-winning side. But, after initially impressing new manager Arsène Wenger, he was loaned to Fulham and then sold to Everton during the 1999/2000 season.

HULME, Joe

Born **Stafford, 26 August 1904**
Died **26 September 1991**
Arsenal appearances **374**
Arsenal goals **125**
International caps (England) **9 (4 goals)**

Herbert Chapman loved Hulme's blinding pace and ball control after snapping him up from Blackburn in 1926. Hulme become part of the great Arsenal side of the 1930s, winning the Football League four times and the FA Cup twice as Cliff Bastin's fellow winger. After nearly 12 years at Arsenal, he left for Huddersfield in January 1938. He also played cricket for Middlesex regularly in the 1930s and later managed Spurs, before becoming a journalist.

HUNDRED CLUB, The

Up to the end of the 2007/08 season, 16 players have scored more than 100 goals for Arsenal. Legendary 1930s striker Ted Drake got there quickest, completing his ton in just his 108th match. He finished with 139 goals in total, the same number as Jimmy Brain who was the first Gunner to hit the magic century. Joe Hulme was the slowest, scoring his 100th goal in his 307th appearance for the Club, though his record was superb for a winger.

The list nearly included 17, but Paul Merson moved to Middlesbrough in the summer of 1997... while marooned on 99 goals.

The Hundred Club includes the following:

Player	Total goals	Total games	100th-game goal
Thierry Henry	226	370	181st
Ian Wright	185	288	143rd
Cliff Bastin	178	396	174th
John Radford	149	481	306th
Jimmy Brain	139	232	144th
Ted Drake	139	184	108th
Doug Lishman	137	244	163rd
Joe Hulme	125	374	307th
David Jack	124	208	156th
Reg Lewis	118	176	152nd
Dennis Bergkamp	118	401	296th
Alan Smith	115	347	251st
Jack Lambert	109	161	149th
Frank Stapleton	108	300	276th
David Herd	107	180	165th
Joe Baker	100	156	152nd

Reg Lewis is one of only 16 players in Arsenal's history to score 100 goals. His ton came in his 152nd appearance.

ICELAND

First an astonishing statistic – nearly one per cent of the entire population of Iceland is a member of the island's Arsenal supporters club. That's around 2,000 people. One of the most colourful fans is Johann Freyr Ragnusson, a car mechanic from Reykjavik and a regular on matchdays with his dyed red hair and moustache. He celebrated the 2004 title win by climbing the highest mountain in Iceland – at 7,000 feet – and hoisting a Gunners flag at the summit. A tour of the island by Arsenal in 1969 cemented their place in the nation's hearts, and inspired such devotion, when they beat a Reykjavik XI 3-1.

But Arsenal's Icelandic connection dates back to 1946, when the Club signed Albert Gudmundsson. Manager Tom Whittaker snapped up the powerful inside-forward after he had been spotted playing for Glasgow Rangers. He later played for AC Milan, Racing Club de Paris and Nancy, before returning to Highbury to play in the Club's 1951 Brazil tour. After retiring he became one of the country's leading politicians and president of the Icelandic FA.

Siggi Jonsson was another high-profile Icelandic Gunner, but he only managed a handful of appearances before injury ended his career at Highbury in 1992. However, despite his brief stay, he remains very much a cult figure among 30-something fans. Brothers Valur and Stefan Gislason were briefly Arsenal youth-team players in the mid-1990s and Olafur-Ingi Skulason was a regular in the reserves before he left the Club in the summer of 2005.

But Arsenal's Icelandic roots on the pitch don't end there – literally. Arsenal's award-winning groundsman Paul Burgess and his assistant Paul Ashcroft have travelled to Reykjavik on several occasions, passing on their expertise to the Icelandic FA – even preparing their pitch for a Euro 2004 qualifier with Germany.

Innovation: Arsenal and Leeds take to the Wembley pitch side by side for the 1972 FA Cup Final. This was a tradition first started by the Gunners and Huddersfield in honour of Herbert Chapman 42 years before.

INNOVATIONS

Arsenal's reputation as a leading Club in world football undoubtedly stems from Herbert Chapman's nine-year tenure as manager. Until his death in January 1934, Chapman was a constant source of new ideas to improve the game as a spectacle and to offer supporters maximum comfort and value for money. The most obvious example of this was the construction of the East and West stands at Highbury, structures of class and quality built in an era when fans were treated as second-class citizens by most clubs.

But Chapman was full of ideas, many of them ahead of their time. He was a great believer in floodlit football and even had lights installed at Highbury before the FA ordered them to be taken down. Many years later, in 1951, Highbury hosted the first major game under lights when they beat Hapoel of Tel Aviv 6-1 to kick-start a new era of English

football. Arsenal was also the first Club to install a clock for the spectators' benefit, although it was altered from a 45-minute clock to a standard timepiece, again after objections from the FA. Chapman was also keen to use white footballs to help players and fans follow the game more easily - they were introduced 20 years after his death. And Arsenal were the first side to play in numbered shirts, losing 3-2 at Sheffield Wednesday on 25 August 1928. The Football League management committee refused to give officially sanction the wearing of numbered shirts for many years, but Arsenal did so in reserve fixtures and again at Highbury on 4 December 1933 as an experiment during a 4-2 friendly win against FC Vienna. It was five more years before numbered shirts were made compulsory.

Chapman also gave his players boots with rubber studs to enable them to keep their balance on hard pitches and, to further help his side, he was the first manager to employ physiotherapists to aid their recovery from injuries.

And while Arsenal fans were also the first in England to enjoy big screens, when the Jumbotrons were erected in 1993, some things didn't quite come off. Holes drilled under the seats in the East and West stands were originally to allow warm air to blow out and heat up cold fans on winter nights. However, despite the fact that heaters are now commonplace in European stadiums, the idea was put on hold and never completed.

It seems appropriate then that one of football's most enduring traditions began in 1930 before the start of the FA Cup Final when the players and managers of Arsenal and Huddersfield Town walked out side by side in honour of the great Herbert Chapman, who had managed both teams with distinction.

The remarkable goalkeeper Frank Moss (right) makes a save in the 1932 FA Cup Final. In a match at Everton three years later he would play - and even score - while nursing a serious shoulder injury, which would end his career.

INSPIRATIONAL PERFORMANCES

Over the years certain Arsenal players have singled themselves out with displays of courage, skill and commitment that have separated them from their team-mates.

Legendary Arsenal and England goalkeeper **Frank Moss**, for example, left his goal after sustaining a serious shoulder injury at Everton in 1935 to play on the wing. He lasted the full 90 minutes and even scored the opening goal in a 2-0 win. The injury later ended his career. The following year **Ted Drake** defied a serious knee injury to play through the pain barrier at Aston Villa - hitting all seven goals in a 7-1 win, which remains a league record. He had been the long-term replacement in attack for **Jack Lambert**, who himself scored five goals at Highbury - a record for a Gunner at home - in a 9-2 win over Sheffield United on Christmas Eve 1932, also a record league win at the old stadium.

David Herd and **Tony Woodcock** also both inspired huge post-war away wins. Herd scored four goals in a 6-1 win at Everton in 1958, which was Arsenal's biggest away league win until Woodcock went one better in a 6-2 victory at Villa 25 years later. But, for pure heart, **Frank McLintock** provided inspiration through toil and sweat. His finest hour came in the 1971 FA Cup Final when he refused to accept a fifth successive personal Wembley defeat as his side trailed 1-0 to Liverpool. The tired Scot drew on his reserves to drag his side through extra time to turn the game around and complete the Double.

More recently **David Seaman**'s display at Sampdoria in the Cup-Winners' Cup semi-final in 1995 saw him reach new heights. He repelled three penalties in the shootout, including a brilliant one-handed save from Attilio Lombardo, to put Arsenal through to the Final and earn the plaudits of even the Italian media. Nigerian striker **Nwankwo Kanu** became a Club legend in 20 mad minutes at Chelsea in 1999 when, with his side trailing 2-0 late on, he responded with a magnificent hat-trick, and a brilliant winner from the byline, to beat the Blues 3-2. And **Thierry Henry** single-handedly overcame Liverpool, despite nursing a hamstring injury, to score a hat-trick and inspire Arsenal to a 4-2 Highbury win in the 2003/04 run-in, after two devastating defeats against Chelsea and Manchester United which had threatened to derail their season.

INTER-CITIES FAIRS CUP

WINNERS

Arsenal won the 1970 Fairs Cup to end 17 years without a trophy after a stirring 4-3 aggregate win against Anderlecht.

A 3-0 home win over Ajax in the semifinal put the Gunners through to their first major final since 1952 and gave them the belief that their long search for silverware was about to end.

But Bertie Mee's side looked down and out against Anderlecht after a 3-1 first leg defeat in Belgium. Netherlands star Jan Mulder had scored two of the goals, but Ray Kennedy gave the Gunners hope with a vital away goal late on and captain Frank McLintock seized on it before the flight back to London, telling his players they would overcome the deficit and win the trophy.

'You could say that the second leg was won at that point,' says goalkeeper Bob Wilson, remembering his fellow Scotsman's rallying cry. Eddie Kelly struck an early goal to give the 51,000 Highbury fans further hope in the second leg on 28 April 1970 and Bertie Mee's men piled on the pressure. Arsenal pushed forward and their bravery reaped dividends when John Radford levelled it up on aggregate with a second-half header. Mulder hit the post as Arsenal piled forward for more, but Jon Sammels sealed an incredible comeback to make it 3-0 on the night and 4-3 overall and spark the wildest scenes of celebration ever seen at Highbury.

McLintock's never-say-die attitude had proved decisive. He said, 'I believed we could do it and I made sure the lads felt it too.'

INVICTA GROUND

Royal Arsenal's third home for three years between 1890 and 1893 was situated near their other ground at Manor Field, in Plumstead. The Invicta was deemed much more suitable for the Club's needs as it possessed a stand housing 1,500 spectators, terracing for a further 3,000 and the luxury of changing rooms, on the south side of Plumstead High Street. The Club stayed there for three years (in the meantime changing their name to Woolwich Arsenal and becoming the first southern side to turn professional), before leaving after the ground's landlord, George Weaver of the Weaver Mineral Water Company, raised the rent on the ground from £200 a year to an extortionate £350 a year plus tax. Arsenal opted to move back to the north side of Plumstead High Street and buy the Manor Ground outright.

INVINCIBLES

'The Invincibles' was the name given to the Arsenal title-winning side of 2003/04, who became the first top-flight side since Preston North End in 1888/89 side to remain unbeaten throughout the entire campaign. Though Preston had only played 22 games to reach their target, Arsenal played 38.

The Gunners won 26 and drew 12 games, beginning on 16 August 2003 when Thierry Henry and Robert Pires scored in a 2-1 win against Everton, and ending 37 games later on 15 May 2004 when Henry and Patrick Vieira scored against Leicester City to seal a 2-1 victory and an incredible achievement.

During the historic campaign Arsenal scored 73 goals and conceded just 26 as they picked up 90 points to win their 13th title.

Irish Gunners: Sammy Nelson was one of a number of Arsenal players from Northern Ireland in the 1970s.

IRISH GUNNERS

Ireland legend **David O'Leary** holds the Arsenal all-time appearances record. The Dubliner, who was actually born near Highbury, in Stoke Newington, before moving back to Eire with his family as a small child, made 722 appearances for the first team in an 18-year first-team career. He broke into the side in 1975 when the Emerald Isle was beginning to dominate the side.

Northern Ireland's **Pat Rice** and **Sammy Nelson** formed a fine full-back partnership, and they were soon followed by compatriot **Pat Jennings** from Tottenham, when Terry Neill – another Ulsterman – was appointed Arsenal manager.

And there were others from the Republic of Ireland. **Liam Brady** was the jewel in the Gunners' crown after being brought over from Dublin as a teenager, and **Frank Stapleton**, another from the Irish capital, was one of the gifted centreforwards of his generation, later playing for Manchester United and Ajax. **John Devine** also spent a decade with the Club before leaving in 1983, earning 30 caps for the Republic at right-back.

But until Neill's tenure, few Irishmen had worn red and white. Dr **Kevin O'Flanagan** – an Irish international at soccer and rugby – was a popular figure in the post-war years and winger **Joe Haverty** played more than 120 games between 1954 and 1961, breaking into the Ireland squad along the way.

Since the 1980s **Niall Quinn** (1985/90) spent five years with the Club, scoring on his debut in a 2-0 win against Liverpool in December 1985 and winning a title medal in 1989. Kilclenny-born midfielder **Steve Morrow** scored the winning goal in the 1993 Coca-Cola Cup Final and a year later played a key role in the 1-0 win over AS Parma in the European-Cup-Winners' Cup Final. **Eddie McGoldrick**, who was born in Islington but capped by the Republic, came on as an 86th-minute substitute against Parma and spent three years at Highbury in the mid-1990s.

Dublin-born **Anthony Stokes** made his first-team debut in October 2005 as a substitute in a 3-0 win over Sunderland in the League Cup. The following year he netted 16 times in 18 appearances on loan at Falkirk before earning a permanent £2 million move to Sunderland.

ISLINGTON

Arsenal's home since 1913 is one of the smallest districts in the entire Greater London area. In its current guise Islington is only just over 40 years old after the former Metropolitan boroughs of Islington and Finsbury merged in 1965. However, its origins go back more than a thousand years. Its first mention was in the 11th-century *Domesday Book* and was described at the time as a 'forest full of the lairs of wild beasts'.

In the Middle Ages the land belonged to religious institutions and later on was given to aristocratic families, while Henry VIII used to hunt in the area. Islington became famous for its dairy herds, providing much of the milk and cheese for the entire city, along with breweries and clock-making in Finsbury (not to be confused with Finsbury Park on the edge of the north-east of the borough).

By the 1800s Islington was enjoying a reputation as a great place for a day out, whether it be in the rolling fields behind Holloway Road or to its many theatres, most notably Sadlers Wells in Finsbury. But with it came some of London's worst slum areas, right up until the 1960s when gentrification took over and money poured into the borough. It also houses two of the most famous prisons in the UK – Pentonville and Holloway.

The area has remained at the heart of political change, local residents Tony Blair and Gordon Brown reputedly deciding over lunch at the Upper Street restaurant Granita who would lead New Labour after the sudden death of leader John Smith in 1994.

Other famous Islington residents of the past include adventurer Sir Walter Raleigh, writer Charles Dickens, Hollywood legend Charlie Chaplin, actor Peter Sellers, former PM Benjamin Disraeli and even Vladimir Lenin during his exile from Russia. In more recent years notable Islington residents have included punk rocker Johnny Rotten (also known as Lydon) – brought up near Finsbury Park – Martin and Gary Kemp of 1980s pop band Spandau Ballet, Essex Road born and bred singer Dido, broadcaster Clive Anderson and writer Nick Hornby, all fanatical Arsenal fans (see Celebrity Fans on page 44).

Since the 1980s the district has become synonymous with a new class of left-leaning fashionable professionals – and with it cutting-edge restaurants, bars and night-clubs – but it still retains its working-class roots, making it one of the most interesting and eclectic boroughs in Britain.

IVORY COAST

The West African nation and former French colony is the homeland of **Kolo Toure** and **Emmanuel Eboue**, both former graduates of the country's most successful

Ivory Coast: Emmanuel Eboue is a regular for both Club and country.

football club, ASEC Abidjan. ASEC's most gifted players are sent to KSK Beveren in Belgium, which has a 'feeder' arrangement with Arsenal.

While Toure was signed from ASEC in February 2002, Eboue turned out for the Flemish club before moving to Highbury in January 2005. Toure (born in Sokoura Bouake on 19 March 1981) started his Arsenal career as a right-back, but later replaced the ageing Martin Keown at centre-back and has established himself as first choice in the Gunners defence. Eboue (born in Abidjan on 4 June 1983) also arrived as a right-back and replaced the injured Lauren in the Arsenal line-up in 2006.

Swiss defender **Johan Djourou** was also born in the Ivory Coast before moving to Switzerland as a youngster and opting to represent his adopted homeland.

JACK, David

Born **Bolton, Lancashire, 3 April 1899**
Died **10 September 1958**
Arsenal appearances **208**
Arsenal goals **124**
International caps (England) **9 (3 goals)**

Herbert Chapman nearly doubled the previous transfer record when he paid a colossal £10,890 to take this cunning inside-forward from Bolton Wanderers. Jack had made history with the first ever goal at Wembley in the 1923 Final against West Ham before moving to Highbury five years later, Chapman memorably negotiating the transfer at Euston, ordering the waiter to bring him tonic waters while delivering large gin and tonics to the increasingly inebriated Bolton representatives. It was money well spent though and Chapman's gamble paid off with Jack winning three titles and an FA Cup winner's medal in 1930, while scoring more than a goal every other game for Arsenal.

JAMES, Alex

Born **Mossend, Lanarkshire,
14 September 1901**
Died **1 June 1953**
Arsenal appearances **259**
Arsenal goals **27**
International caps (Scotland) **8**

The little Scotsman with the huge personality lit up Highbury and helped turn the Gunners into the biggest club in world football in the 1930s. A cunning inside-forward, crowds all around the country would swell when James came to town, thousands clamouring to see what all the fuss was about. His slight figure - just 5 ft 6 in tall and 11 stone - and his outrageously baggy shorts were famed throughout the land.

James' career began at Raith Rovers, but he soon left for Preston where he became one of the Scottish 'Wembley Wizards' who destroyed England 5-1 at Wembley in 1928. Herbert Chapman paid a surprisingly small fee of just £8,750 for his services in 1929 and he made his debut in August against Leeds United.

His Highbury career started at a slow pace, one fan sending him a pair of battered old boots with a note attached saying, 'It doesn't matter what you wear anyhow.' But his talents could not be restrained and soon that lad must have rued his sarcastic missive.

If he had been playing these days there would be no doubt his eccentric behaviour

Herbert Chapman's greatest star... the irrepressible Alex James.

would have been both back and front page news. The stories are legendary: he was the only player allowed to skip the pre-match meeting and stay in bed until noon on matchdays and on one occasion Chapman, fed up with James' stalling tactics when thrashing out a new deal, lost patience and sent him on a cruise. Once on board he realised he had been duped and the 'cruise' was in fact a working cargo boat. James finally managed to disembark at Bordeaux, returning to London with his tail between his legs. But on the pitch he was solid gold and was made Club captain, an appointment he relished despite the odd brush with the Highbury hierarchy.

The hub of the side, Arsenal's much-criticised counter-attacking style was tailor-made for James' mercurial talents. A super passer of the ball, he would receive it and drop inch-perfect passes for wingers Cliff Bastin and Joe Hulme to race on to with devastating effect. George Allison, who succeeded Chapman as manager in 1934, gave James this glowing assessment: 'No one like him ever kicked a ball... He had a most uncanny and wonderful control.'

But getting goals was not his forte. His return of 27 in nearly 260 games was simply too few for his talents. However, he won four league titles, scored in the 1930 FA Cup Final – one of two winner's medals he received in that competition – and was skipper for the 1936 Final, which would be his last major honour before retiring a year later, aged 36.

James re-joined Arsenal in 1949 as part of the coaching set up but died suddenly in the summer of 1953 shortly after seeing his beloved Gunners clinch yet another title.

The current mayor of Islington, Councillor Steve Hitchins, is his godson.

JAPAN AND THE FAR EAST

Junichi Inamoto became the first Japanese footballer to play for the Club when he signed in 2001. Although he never started a Premiership match, Inamoto played in the Carling Cup and broke into

Japan international Junichi Inamoto found his first-team opportunities were limited.

his national side, scoring two goals in the 2002 World Cup finals in his home country. He later moved to Fulham, but his short time at Highbury raised the profile of the Club in Japan, which now has a large and active supporters club.

Elsewhere, the Far East is home to a significant number of Arsenal's estimated 27 million worldwide fans, thanks mainly to increased television coverage. The Club has even printed copies of its official magazine in Cantonese in recent years and now Arsenal.com is translated and available in Chinese, Korean, Japanese and Thai.

JENKYNS, Caesar Llewellyn

See **Hail Caesar!** on page 103

JENNINGS, Pat

Born **Newry, Northern Ireland, 12 June 1945**
Arsenal appearances **326**
International caps (Northern Ireland) **119**

Big Pat, a giant even among goalkeepers, was surprisingly released by Tottenham Hotspur in August 1977 at the age of 32 for just £45,000. Even stranger was Spurs' decision to allow him to join their biggest rivals, who were looking for an experienced pair of hands to take over from the superb Jimmy Rimmer. Spurs fans were furious with the sale, many of them feeling that the Ulsterman still had his best years in front of him. Luckily for Arsenal fans they were right.

His giant frame filled the goal, his calm authority spread confidence through the back four, and his magnificent athleticism kept fans and players enthralled. During his time at Highbury he played a major part in Arsenal's run of four Cup Finals in three years between 1978 and 1980, while he was still out in front as Northern Ireland's undisputed No.1, earning a then world record 119 caps, which would be beaten by another member of the goalkeeping union, Peter Shilton, in 1990.

He relished a seesaw battle for the Gunners green jersey with Scottish goalkeeper George Wood for two seasons before making 38 league appearances in the 1983/84 season. The following campaign was his last after eight fantastic years at Highbury, John Lukic taking over in goal with Jennings' last league appearance coming in a 2-1 defeat at Sheffield Wednesday in November 1984.

He moved back to Spurs – his undeniable first love – the next summer as goalkeeping cover for Ray Clemence and even managed to represent his country for one last time at the Mexico World Cup in 1986. He later became goalkeeping coach at Spurs Lodge.

No man has managed to transcend the great rivalry of north London's rich footballing history quite like Big Pat, a legend at both ends of the Seven Sisters Road.

JENSEN, John

Born **Copenhagen, Denmark, 3 May 1965**
Arsenal appearances **129 (8)**
Arsenal goals **1**
International caps (Denmark) **69 (4 goals)**

A Danish international, John Jensen became a cult figure at Highbury for his hard-working but limited style and his lack off success in front of goal.

He had caught the eye in Denmark's shock Euro 92 success and scored one of the goals of the tournament along the way. Ironically, he only scored one goal for Arsenal, but that was an event in itself, memorably arriving on New Year's Eve 1994 – a fine curling effort the consolation in a 3-1 home loss to QPR.

Nicknamed 'Faxe' by former team-mates after a popular Danish beer, his biggest regret had come earlier that year when an injury forced him to miss the Final of the Cup-Winners' Cup in Copenhagen, his hometown, Jensen was an overexcited spectator on the touchline.

A popular figure among fans and players alike, he returned to Denmark in 1996. After a spell as player-manager with Herfolge he became assistant manager at Brondby under Michael Laudrup in 2002. In 2007 Jensen followed Laudrup to Spanish side Getafe as his assistant, though Laudrup resigned his post after one season.

JOHN, Bob

Born **Barry, Wales, 3 February 1899**
Died **July 1982**
Arsenal appearances **467**
Arsenal goals **13**
International caps (Wales) **15**

A Wales-born left-half, John held the all-time Arsenal appearance record until the mid-1970s when he was overtaken by George Armstrong. The Club fought off stiff competition to sign John from Caerphilly in January 1921 and he made his first-team debut in October the next year against Newcastle, eventually taking the place of Tom Whittaker on the left flank. He won an FA Cup medal in 1930, followed by three First Division titles until his retirement in 1937, playing nearly 470 times for the Club, the most of any of Arsenal's pre-war players.

JONES, Bryn

Born **Penyard, near Merthyr Tydfil, Wales, 14 February 1912**
Died **1985**
Arsenal appearances **71**
Arsenal goals **7**

Despite the looming war clouds over Europe, MPs in the House of Commons found

Long-serving Bob John played more games than any other Gunner until the 1970s.

themselves preoccupied and venting their disgust at champions Arsenal's then world record transfer fee of £14,000 for Wolves' crowd favourite Bryn Jones. It had beaten the previous record of £10,890 – set by Arsenal a decade before when they bought David Jack.

The scheming inside-left arrived in August 1938, but failed to shine in his first season – 'He is clearly suffering from too much publicity,' mused one hack – and by the start of his second season Hitler had invaded Poland, robbing Jones of his best footballing years. He left Arsenal in 1948, a costly failure. One unimpressed team-mate was Cliff Bastin, who in his forthright autobiography, *Cliff Bastin Remembers*, said, 'He'd have been much happier if he'd stayed at Wolves.'

Jones, whose four brothers were also footballers, as was his nephew Cliff who starred in the Spurs Double-winning side of 1961, retired to run a newsagents in Stoke Newington until his death in 1985, aged 73.

JONSSON, Siggi

Born **Akranes, Iceland, 27 September 1966**
Arsenal appearances **3 (6)**
Arsenal goals **1**

A cult figure among Arsenal fans, despite starting just three times for the Gunners following a high profile move from Sheffield Wednesday during the summer of 1989, scoring his only goal in November against QPR. A tall athletic midfielder, injury cut short his Highbury career and he moved to hometown club Akranes. He later came back to Britain and turned out for Dundee United.

JOY, Bernard

Born **Fulham, London, 29 October 1911**
Died **18 July 1984**
Arsenal appearances **95**
Arsenal goals **0**
International caps (England) **1**

Joining Arsenal in May 1935, while still captain of London amateurs the Casuals (later the Corinthian Casuals), Joy was a formidable centre-half, but played mainly for the reserves until an injury to Herbie Roberts propelled him into the first team, playing enough games to earn a title medal in 1938. He earned his one and only international cap in a 3-2 defeat in Belgium in May 1936 – the last amateur to play for England – and that summer skippered the Great Britain side at the Berlin Olympics. He also won ten caps for the England amateur side. During the war he played more than 200 unofficial matches for Arsenal before he stopped playing and moved into journalism. He became football correspondent for the *Evening Standard* and the *Sunday Express* until he retired in 1976. He also wrote the celebrated *Forward Arsenal*, a history of the Club, in 1952.

JUMBOTRONS

Arsenal broke new ground in the early 1990s when they took delivery of two state-of-the-art Jumbotron screens, manufactured by Sony. The Gunners were the first English club to use the screens, which were installed in the south east and north west corners of the stadium, and provided pre-match entertainment for more than a decade. On several occasions they were hired out for use at pop concerts and other large events across the UK.

In March 2006 the Club signed another groundbreaking deal – this time with Mitsubishi Electric – for two new Diamond Vision screens for Emirates Stadium. The new screens weigh five tonnes each and at 72 square metres each are nearly double the size of the old screens at Highbury.

JUNIOR GUNNERS

Formed in the summer of 1983, the Junior Gunners has been the most successful junior membership scheme of its type in English football. It was launched in the matchday programme for the visit of Luton Town on 27 August of that year and has had a dedicated section ever since. The Junior Gunners mascot that day was seven-year-old Daniel Quy from Stoke Newington, who is now the JG's assistant manager.

Arsenal set up the JGs membership to encourage its younger supporters to keep in touch with the Club and make them feel more involved. By the end of the 2005/06 season it boasted seven dedicated full-time staff and 20,000 members, with the number expected to grow. Children up to 16 years of age can join and there is a dedicated Family Enclosure section in the stadium where members can sit with their parents or guardians. At Highbury this was first situated in the East Stand paddock and latterly in the West Stand before the move to Emirates.

Members receive packs with a host of goodies and also a regular newsletter, birthday card and special offers. And the JGs hold many events, with the Christmas Party now an established 'fixture', with most of the first-team squad turning out for the festivities. Every member is also put in a free draw to become a matchday mascot.

Bernard Joy leaps to head the ball clear with Brentford's Jack Gibbons in close attendance in a match at Griffin Park in 1938. He was Arsenal's and England's last great amateur player.

KANU, Nwankwo

Born **Owerri, Nigeria, 1 August 1976**
Arsenal appearances **105 (92)**
Arsenal goals **44**
International caps (Nigeria) **46 (8 goals)**

The fans' favourite with rubber-like legs and fantastic ability, complete with his unique lackadaisical style, will be remembered for a rainy day at Stamford Bridge in October 1999. Arsenal were losing 2-0 with the time ticking down when the Nigerian produced a magical finale. First he pulled a goal back and then splashed through the puddles for an unlikely equaliser. And it got better. With a minute remaining his long legs chased down a clearance, he slipped past Chelsea goal-keeper Ed de Goey by the corner flag with insulting ease, and then curled the ball from an impossible angle past the despairing lunge of Frank Leboeuf and over the line.

He also showed an ability to work like a Trojan in more unglamorous roles when needed; his performance in the centre of midfield took the breath away and earned him yet more fans as he inspired ten-man Arsenal to a 2-1 Premiership win at Liverpool in 2001.

But he was mainly used from the bench to try and force the game in the last 20 minutes, punctuating his substitute appearances with some memorable starts. His outrageous backheeled goal capped another stupendous performance in a 6-1 win at Middlesbrough in April 1999.

But, dogged by inconsistency, he moved further down the pecking order and, after two titles and an FA Cup winner's medal in his time at Highbury, Bryan Robson took him to West Bromwich Albion in 2004.

Kanu left the Hawthorns in August 2006 to join former Gunners Tony Adams and Sol Campbell at Portsmouth and went on to collect another FA Cup winners medal in May 2008, scoring the only goal of the game to beat Cardiff City.

Kanu holds off Chelsea defender Graeme Le Saux. The Nigerian arrived from Internazionale in 1999 after making his name at Ajax Amsterdam, where he won the Champions League in 1995.

KELLY, Eddie

Born **Glasgow, Scotland, 7 February 1951**
Arsenal appearances **211 (11)**
Arsenal goals **19**

This pocket dynamo midfielder was another of Bertie Mee's young starlets, as Arsenal swept to the 1971 Double. His name is firmly embedded in Highbury folklore for two important Cup Final goals. The first was a 25-yard beauty in the 1970 Fairs Cup Final at Highbury, the opening goal of the night, as

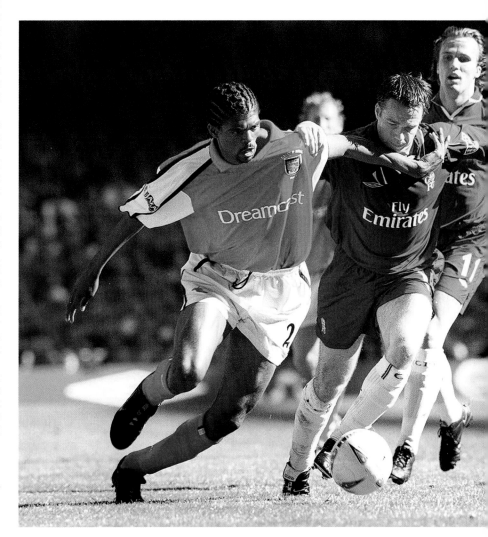

Arsenal tasted glory for the first time in 17 years. His other was not so spectacular, but equally crucial, when he stabbed the ball home from close range to equalise in extra time against Liverpool in the 1971 FA Cup Final. He was later made Club captain for a brief spell before moving to QPR in 1976.

Kelly is now one of the former Arsenal stars who accompany visitors on the Legends Tour of Emirates Stadium.

KELSEY, Jack

Born **Wales, 19 November 1929**
Died **19 March 1992**
Arsenal appearances **352**
International caps (Wales) **41**

Ask many a fan fortunate enough to watch this Welsh colossus and they will tell you that in the pantheon of Arsenal goalkeepers, he stands alone. Signed from Welsh outfit Winch Wen in 1949, it was two years before he made his debut and that was a nightmare 2–5 home reverse to Charlton. But here was a man of tremendous character and he bounced back to play in over half the league games in the title-winning side of 1952/53, including a memorable 6–4 win at Bolton on Christmas Day 1952 in which he saved a penalty to halt a late rally by the home side.

The Welshman became a regular feature between the sticks throughout the austere 1950s and was also recognised on the international stage. He was at his peak when Wales made their only appearance in a major finals in the 1958 World Cup in Sweden. Though they were knocked out in the quarter-finals by eventual winners Brazil, Kelsey had impressed the watching world.

In a cruel twist of fate he sustained an injury in a friendly against the world champions Brazil in May 1962 and was forced to retire, making way for Jim Furnell in the Gunners line-up. However, his association with the Club did not end until well into the 1980s, when he was manager of the Gunners Shop, an immensely popular figure around Highbury, who sadly passed away in 1992.

KELSO, Phil

MANAGER 1904/08
Born **Largs, Scotland, 1871**
Died **February 1935**

Woolwich Arsenal's fourth professional manager was the second to come from north of the border. The Scot made his name at Edinburgh side Hibernian and was brought into the Manor Ground to consolidate the Gunners' recently acquired Division One status.

In 1906 he guided the Club to the FA Cup semi-final before Newcastle ended their dream with a 2–0 win. The following season was the Club's best to date: FA Cup semi-finalists again until losing to Sheffield Wednesday, and a seventh-place finish in the top-flight, pushing Woolwich Arsenal's name into the limelight.

But with little money to spend he could not sustain the momentum and left the Club to go and run a hotel in Scotland, before heading back south in 1909 to manage Fulham.

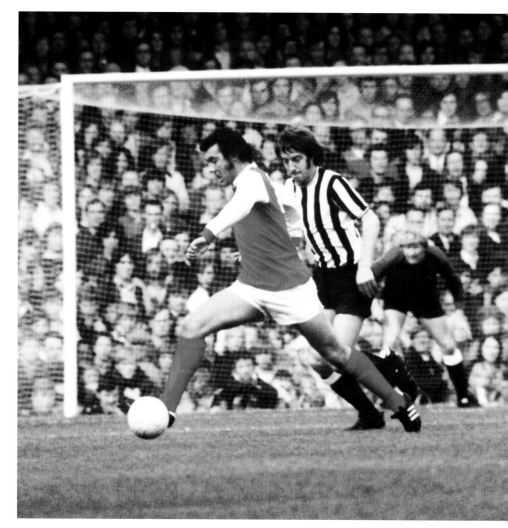

KENNEDY, Ray

Born **Seaton Delaval, Northumberland, 28 July 1951**
Arsenal appearances **206 (6)**
Arsenal goals **71**
International caps (England) **17 (3 goals)**

Young striker Kennedy starred in the 1971 Double side, up front with John Radford, before moving to Liverpool and back into midfield, where he became one of European football's most outstanding performers for the remainder of the 1970s.

He looked to have missed the boat after failing to impress Port Vale as a youngster until Bertie Mee handed him an apprenticeship at Highbury. Kennedy made his name when he came off the bench to head a late consolation for Arsenal in their 3-1 defeat at Anderlecht in the first leg of the 1970 Fairs Cup Final. Arsenal barely deserved it on the night, but the goal offered a lifeline and a 3-0 win at Highbury gave them their first trophy for 17 years. The next season he was promoted to the starting 11 and responded with 26 goals, including the winner at Spurs to clinch the title. But he moved in and out of the side for the next three seasons as Mee's team slowly broke up.

By then Bill Shankly had seen enough and made him his last signing for Liverpool in the summer of 1974 for £180,000, where he went on to realise his huge potential in spectacular fashion with ten more medals.

After retiring he was diagnosed with Parkinson's disease and later admitted signs of the condition appeared as far back as his early Arsenal days. In 1991 Arsenal and Liverpool played a benefit game for the Northumbrian at Highbury, providing him with welcome funds to live more comfortably.

Left Ray Kennedy made a superb start to his Arsenal career, winning the Fairs Cup, League Championship and FA Cup before his 20th birthday. He later moved to Liverpool where even greater success followed.

KENT

In its early years, Woolwich Arsenal was the premier club in Kent as its home in Plumstead sat right on the county border. One of the Club's early homes was the Invicta Ground – the Latin word for 'invincible' or 'unconquered' – and the county's motto.

Nearly all opposition for the first few years after the Club's official formation in 1886 came from the county, including Royal Arsenal's first ever opponents, Erith. In 1890 the first big trophies the Reds won were the Kent Senior and Junior Cups, to go with the London Charity Cup.

KEOWN, Martin

Born **Oxford, 24 July 1966**
Arsenal appearances **449**
Arsenal goals **8**
International caps (England) **43 (2 goals)**

Nicknamed 'The Rash' for his peerless, uncompromising man-marking skills, the Oxford-born defender had two spells with the Club. He first joined as a schoolboy in 1980 and signed professional forms in 1984. But after just 22 appearances George Graham sold him to Aston Villa and he later moved to Everton, where he earned the first of his 43 England caps, before coming home to Highbury in February 1993.

Much maligned outside north London, his professionalism was well respected within the Marble Halls and he was seen as a more than adequate backup to first choice centre-backs Steve Bould and his old youth team colleague Tony Adams. His speciality was snuffing out the threat of the opposition's danger man. The likes of Matthew Le Tissier and Gianfranco Zola can testify to that, both being relentlessly shadowed by the scuttling, stooped figure of Keown.

He was a substitute in the 1994 Cup Winners' Cup Final win over Parma and picked up a loser's medal against Real Zaragoza in Paris a year later. But when Arsène Wenger arrived in 1996 his career really took off and he was an integral member of the 1998 and 2002 Double-winning sides. In the meantime he was in the England squads for the World Cups in 1998 and 2002 and Euro 2000, adding to his involvement in the disastrous Euro 92 campaign in Sweden while he was an Evertonian.

He played a role in the 2003 FA Cup win, but with his advancing years his first-team opportunities were limited, although he just scraped a third title medal in 2004, memorably cajoling Wenger to put him on for the final few minutes of the last game of the season against Leicester so he could qualify for a medal. His manager duly obliged, roared on by the crowd.

He was rewarded with a much-deserved testimonial a few days later when an Arsenal XI beat an England XI 6-0 at a sold-out Highbury with stars like Ian Wright, David Beckham and Paul Gascoigne all playing for their old pal. A free transfer to Leicester City followed and after a brief stint with Reading, near to his Oxfordshire home, he hung up his boots, although in 2006 he returned to Highbury in a coaching capacity.

KICK IT OUT

This organisation, originally based in Islington's Business Design Centre and now near Old Street, was born out of an initiative launched in the 1993/94 season called 'Let's Kick Racism Out of Football'. It has worked closely with its local club, Arsenal, and held many press launches at Highbury. The organisation was founded by members of the Professional Footballers Association (PFA) and the Commission For Racial Equality (CRE). The chairman of the CRE, Sir Trevor Phillips, has supported Arsenal since the 1960s when he was brought up in nearby Aubert Park and regularly watched the team from the old Schoolboys' Enclosure at Highbury. He has often praised the Club's crowd for its intolerance towards racists.

Arsenal's work in tackling racism and promoting equality was given prominence in March 2006 when the Club was awarded the preliminary level of the Racial Equality Standard for Professional Clubs by Kick It Out chairman Lord Herman Ouseley. The Racial Equality Standard, which has been developed by Kick It Out, sets out a series of measures for professional clubs. Lord Ouseley said, 'Arsenal is to be commended on the strides they have made to tackle racism and ensure that equality is at the heart of what they do. In achieving the preliminary level of the Racial Equality Standard the club are signalling their commitment to working towards a game free of any form of discrimination or exclusion.' Chairman Peter Hill-Wood accepted the award on behalf of the Club.

KIDD, Brian

Born **Manchester, 29 May 1949**
Arsenal appearances **90**
Arsenal goals **34**
International caps (England) **2 (1 goal)**

A man in the wrong place at the wrong time, the former Manchester United prodigy was a rare success in an otherwise bleak period for the Club, averaging more than a goal every three games. Signed from United for £110,000 in 1974, the former England striker replaced Liverpool-bound Ray Kennedy, but after a prolific first season he began to struggle in a side low in confidence. In 1976 he moved back to Manchester, to play for

City. Later he was a successful assistant to Sir Alex Ferguson at Old Trafford and briefly managed Blackburn Rovers. He now works as a coach at Leeds United.

KIRCHEN, Alf

Born **Shouldham, Norfolk, 26 August 1913**
Died **18 August 1999**
Arsenal appearances **99**
Arsenal goals **44**
International caps (England) **3 (2 goals)**

The right-winger from Norfolk made an immediate impact on arriving at Arsenal in

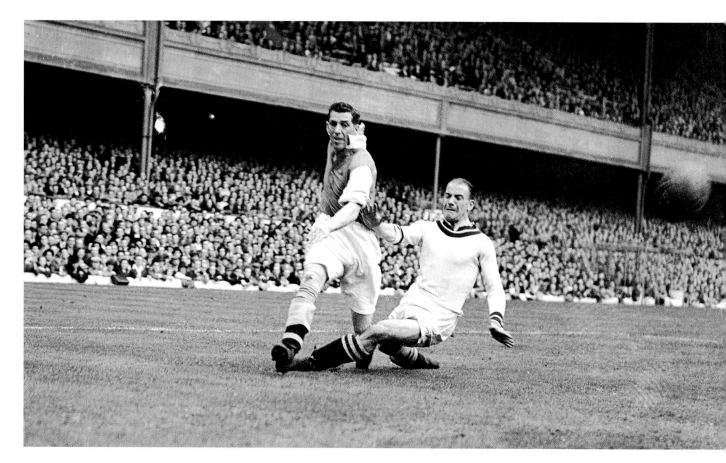

Alf Kirchen (left) beats Aston Villa's George Cummings and whips in a cross in a match at Highbury in 1938.

March 1935, scoring twice in a record 6-0 win at Spurs on his debut. He had been spotted by former Gunners skipper Tom Parker, who was then manager at Norwich, and after a brief spell at Carrow Road Arsenal paid £6,000 for his services.

He had muscled his way into the starting line-up at the expense of the legendary Joe Hulme by the start of the 1936/37 season and, like his predecessor, was renowned for a fierce shot and blistering pace, scoring regularly from the wings. His talents were recognised by his country in 1937 and a year later he won a title medal.

When the war came, like many footballers he became an army physical instructor and continued to represent Arsenal in unofficial matches, playing a further 116 times and scoring 81 goals during hostilities.

On retiring he returned to Norwich as a trainer and worked in the local agricultural industry before becoming a director at Carrow Road. He was also Honorary President of the Norfolk Arsenal Supporters Club before his death in 1999.

KITS

Arsenal wear red shirts thanks to Nottingham Forest. The first strip Arsenal played in was an all-red affair given to the fledgling Gunners - then called Dial Square - by goalkeeper Fred Beardsley, who had previously turned out for the East Midlands side. When the London club was formed he travelled back to Nottingham and managed to procure a set of second-hand strip - and a much-prized match ball - from his former team.

In 1895, the team briefly wore a new strip of red and light blue vertical stripes - needless to say it proved unpopular and all red soon returned. The 'red' in those early days at the beginning of the 20th century is believed to have resembled a much darker, aubergine shade.

In 1906 the president of Czech side Sparta Prague travelled to London and watched the Gunners. He was so impressed with the playing kit he took a set back to Prague and immediately replaced their old

black and white kit. They play in the same colour to this day and their shirts proved the inspiration for Arsenal's 'redcurrant' home jersey for the final season at Highbury in 2005/06.

Arsenal's shirt first sported a crest for the 1927 FA Cup Final against Cardiff - although the game will always be remembered for another kit story. The Gunners lost 1-0 after goalkeeper Dan Lewis let a shot squirm through his hands. Distraught, he blamed the shiny new jersey he wore for making him lose his grip on the ball.

The famous white sleeves were first added in March 1933 for the 1-0 home defeat to Liverpool. Herbert Chapman, as Highbury legend has it, spotted a member of the groundstaff wearing a red sleeveless jumper with a white shirt underneath - and instantly liked the look. Mindful that so many other leading English clubs had adopted all-red shirts, he ordered the kit change and, one season in the early 1960s aside when the club reverted to red sleeves, it has remained the Club's main colours. Arsenal also sported blue and white hooped socks, although that would later to change to all red and all white.

There have also been occasions when Arsenal have worn unusual shirts due to a clash of kits. A 4-1 FA Cup Highbury win over Barnsley - who also wore red - in February 1936 saw Alex James and co wear unusual horizontal striped jerseys with black shorts. Black and white stripes were also worn on at least one occasion in the days before clubs had a standard second strip. In the 1950 FA Cup Final Arsenal wore a gold shirt as they beat Liverpool 2-0 - and it prove an early inspiration for the famous yellow away jersey which would become standard later in the decade.

The early 1960s saw most kits, including Arsenal's, change from a rugby style shirt to a round neck cotton affair. For the 1967/68 season the cannon motif finally became a permanent fixture on the players' shirts and by the late 1970s manufacturer Umbro had added its logo to the shirt. Arsenal's first major sponsor, Japanese firm JVC, had its logo stamped on the centre of the shirts at the end of the 1981/82 season as football entered the media age. The next season the

controversial green away shirts with blue sleeves - dubbed the Bluebottle kit - made a brief appearance before yellow returned.

Umbro's final kit for Arsenal marked the Club's centenary season 1985/86 before Adidas took over for George Graham's first campaign in charge in August 1986. The German company produced the strip many fans consider Arsenal's finest - the yellow away jersey with blue sleeves in which Arsenal won the league at Anfield in 1989.

In 1990 Adidas used the entire club crest - and not just the cannon - on the home jersey and by 1993 it moved the crest to the centre of the chest. It was the shirt Arsenal wore when they won the 1994 Cup-Winners' Cup.

Nike, who manufactures the present strip, became the Club's new kit supplier that summer and immediately courted controversy with a two-tone blue away kit. The yellow would return and a third kit would also be introduced by 1997. JVC finally ended its long relationship with Arsenal in 1999 with SEGA Europe becoming the new main sponsor, with Dreamcast on the home jersey and SEGA on the away strip. The popular gold jersey became a fan's favourite in 2001 and by 2003 telecommunications giant O2 were the new Club sponsor.

In May 2005 Arsenal appeared in red and white at Highbury for the final time when they played Everton. Fittingly, the old kit said goodbye to the old stadium with a thumping 7-0 win. Redcurrant was then introduced for the final season after consultation with fans' groups. Red and white, however, returned in August 2006 when Arsenal moved into their state-of-the-art new home - Emirates Stadium.

Arsenal, a club proud of its tradition, released a white away strip in July 2007 celebrating the pioneering spirit of former manager Herbert Chapman.

The jersey - white had been used as an away strip before the Second World War - contained a horizontal stripe listing many of Chapman's achievements and innovations while the poster campaign to accompany its launch featured many of the present day squad on the platform at Arsenal Tube station, whose name was changed from Gillespie Road in 1932 after pressure from Chapman.

KNIGHTON, Leslie

MANAGER 1919/25
Born **Unknown**
Died **1959**

Handed the tough task of keeping a financially strapped Arsenal in the First Division, Knighton faced an uphill struggle from day one following his appointment in May 1919. His chairman, Sir Henry Norris, had controversially earned Arsenal their top-flight status and the Gunners had few friends in that first season after the First World War. It is to Knighton's huge credit that he steadied the ship – while remaining thrifty in the transfer market – and steered the Club for six years up to the dawn of the great Chapman era.

Knighton was a managerial prodigy after being appointed boss of Castleford Town at the tender age of 20. His playing career had been cut short by injury, but he was desperate to prove himself as a manager. Impressive spells at Huddersfield Town and Manchester City followed before his move to Highbury.

His fractious relationship with Norris, who he claimed constantly meddled in managerial affairs, blew up in early 1925 when he demanded money to invest in the playing squad, and an advertisement was placed in *Athletic News* for a new boss.

Knighton, whose best league position was a respectable but unspectacular ninth place, moved to Bournemouth and then Birmingham, who he guided to the 1931 FA Cup Final.

A six-year spell as Chelsea manager followed and then time with lowly Shrewsbury Town, before he moved back to the south coast, where he died in 1959, aged 75.

(Left to right) Arsenal manager Leslie Knighton, captain Bill Blyth and goalkeeper Steve Dunn make their way to the FA enquiry into the controversial match between Arsenal and Tottenham Hotspur in September 1922, when two players were sent off during a particularly vicious and bitter game. Knighton oversaw a turbulent spell for the Club in the immediate years before Herbert Chapman's arrival.

LADIES

Arsenal Ladies FC are the dominant side of the modern women's game, having won 29 major trophies since their formation in 1987 by men's kit manager Vic Akers. In that period they have won no less than ten Premier League titles and by the summer of 2008, after winning the four previous titles and remaining unbeaten, they boasted nine full English internationals – including Kelly Smith, who is generally recognised as one of the best players in world football – as well as the captain of Wales, Jayne Ludlow, Scotland's No.1 striker, Julie Fleeting and

Ireland's No.1 Emma Byrne, who is the Club's first-choice goalkeeper.

Their finest achievement came in 2007 when they won the clean sweep of all four major trophies; the Premier League, the FA Cup, the League Cup and, most notably, the Women's UEFA Cup. The trophy, the first time the competition has ever been won by an English women's team, came after a hard-earned 1-0 aggregate victory over crack Swedish outfit Umea IK, one of the most successful sides in the world game.

'This is the greatest moment in our history,' said an emotional Akers afterwards. 'It's a massive boost for the game in Great Britain that the trophy has been taken out of Scandinavia and Germany. We

In an era where Arsenal have dominated the women's game, 2006/07 was a landmark campaign. The team won the Premier League, both domestic cups and the women's UEFA Cup – it was a staggering achievement even for a side that has won 29 major trophies since 1987.

should see more kids playing now and an improvement higher up.'

Arsenal Ladies play their home games at Boreham Wood (see Boreham Wood FC on page 32) but won their tenth title in 15 years in 2008 at Emirates Stadium when they beat Chelsea 4-1 in front of a sell-out crowd (only one section of the stadium was opened) of 5,000 fans. They clinched the Double a week later with a 4-1 win over Leeds United at Nottingham's City Ground in front of a record Women's FA Cup Final crowd of over 24,000 - their ninth win in nine finals.

ARSENAL LADIES' HONOURS

UEFA Cup

Winners
2006/07

Semi-finalists
2002/03, 2004/05

Quarter-finalists
2001/02, 2004/05, 2005/06, 2007/08

National Premier League

Champions
1992/93, 1994/95, 1996/97, 2000/01,
2001/02, 2003/04, 2004/05,
2005/06, 2006/07, 2007/08

Runners-up
1997/98, 1998/99

Women's FA Cup

Winners
1992/93, 1994/95, 1997/98,
1998/99, 2000/01, 2003/04,
2005/06, 2006/07, 2007/08

Semi-finalists
1990/91, 1995/96, 1996/97,
1999/2000, 2002/03, 2004/05

National League Cup

Winners
1991/92, 1992/93, 1993/94,
1997/98, 1998/99, 1999/2000,
2000/01, 2004/05, 2006/07

Runners-up
2002/03, 2005/06, 2007/08

Semi-finalists
1995/96, 2001/02, 2003/04

FA Women's Community Shield

Winners
1999/2000 (shared with Charlton),
2001/02, 2005/06, 2006/07

London Senior County Cup

Winners
1994/95, 1995/96, 1996/97, 1999/2000,
2003/04, 2006/07, 2007/08

AXA Challenge Cup

Winners
1998/99

National League South

Champions
1998/99

Middlesex Senior Cup

Winners
1994/95

Highfield Cup

Winners
1990/91

Reebok Cup

Winners
1991/92, 1995/96

Runners-up
1998/99

LADIES' COACH – VIC AKERS

Vic Akers has been manager of the Ladies' side since 1987 when he helped set up the club. He has been a huge champion of the women's game in general, while still combining his demanding role as the men's first-team kit manager.

During his time as boss the Ladies' team has won every major domestic honour. In 2007 his side made history when they finally won the Women's UEFA Cup having twice made it to the semi-finals.

In his playing days Vic, a stylish full-back, played for Slough Town before making 150 appearances for Cambridge United in the early 1970s and ending his career at Watford.

LAMBERT, Jack

Born **Greasborough, Yorkshire, 2 May 1902**
Died **December 1940**
Arsenal appearances **161**
Arsenal goals **109**

One of the most prolific goalscorers in Arsenal's history, Lambert hit the opener in the 2-0 FA Cup Final win over Huddersfield in 1930 to secure Arsenal's first ever trophy. He also hit a then Club record 38 league goals the following season as the Gunners won the title for the first time. He still holds the record for the most goals scored by an Arsenal player at Highbury after his five-goal haul in a 9-2 battering of Sheffield United on Christmas Eve 1932. Sold to Fulham in 1933, he returned to Highbury in a coaching capacity when he hung up his boots, but died tragically young in a car accident in 1940.

LAUNDRY END

Until the early 1960s, the North Bank terrace was known as the Laundry End. That had been its nickname ever since Highbury was built, in honour of the steam laundry behind the ground in Gillespie Road.

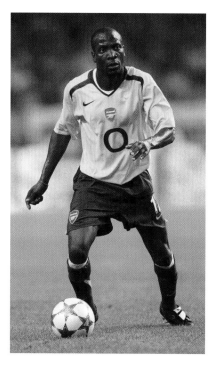

Lauren in possession during a Champions League fixture in 2005/06. The Cameroon international was raised in the Spanish city of Seville with his 20 siblings after his father fled a brutal regime in Equatorial Guinea.

LAUREN'S REMARKABLE LIFE

Born **Londi Kribi, Cameroon, 19 January 1977**
Arsenal appearances **227**
Arsenal goals **9**
International caps (Cameroon) **80**
(8 goals)

The youngest of 16 brothers and five sisters, the defender's early years were spent in Cameroon after his family had fled Equatorial Guinea, where his father was a politician who had been imprisoned by President Francisco Macias Nguema's regime. After his father had escaped from prison the family moved and settled in Montequinto on the outskirts of Seville in southern Spain when Lauren was three years old. 'You could say I had a very tough upbringing,' he admits with huge understatement. But his footballing talents, learned in the tough streets of Seville, offered him the chance of a better life.

He made his name at Real Mallorca where he won the Spanish Cup and the European Cup-Winners' Cup before Arsène Wenger brought him to Highbury in May 2000. Originally a midfielder, the Arsenal manager converted him to right-back where he soon displaced Lee Dixon. Lauren has since won two Premiership titles and three FA Cups, as well as Olympic gold and African Nations Cup medals with Cameroon, although he admits that after living in Spain since he was a child he feels more like a Spaniard.

A superstitious man, Lauren keeps an old peseta coin in his sock at all times, heads up, and refuses to take a saltcellar at the dinner table when it is handed to him. 'It must be put on the table first,' he says seriously.

In January 2007 – after 227 appearances and 9 goals – he left Arsenal for Portsmouth.

LAWTON, Tommy

Born **Bolton, Lancashire, 6 October 1919**
Died **6 November 1996**
Arsenal appearances **37**
Arsenal goals **14**
International caps (England) **23**
(16 goals)

The former England centre-forward looked to be winding down his career at Brentford but shocked the soccer world in November 1953 when he moved to Arsenal. Lawton had always claimed his biggest regret was turning down a move to Highbury before the war and he wanted to make up for lost time. But his tiring limbs and strong competition at the Club limited his appearances, with his highlight coming shortly after moving to north London when he scored in a Charity Shield win over Stanley Matthews' Blackpool. After two years he retired, but was always grateful for his late opportunity to pull on the famous and red and white shirt.

LEAGUE CUP – LOSERS

Bertie Mee's side were closing in on glory towards the end of the 1960s, but first they had to experience the bitter pill of Wembley defeat – twice in two years.

In 1968 Huddersfield were beaten 6–3 on aggregate in the two-legged semi-final to set up a date with Don Revie's Leeds United. It was Arsenal's first final for 16 years. Terry Cooper scored the only goal of the game to hand Leeds their first major trophy and spark the best period in the club's history – and a bitter rivalry with the Gunners which would last for five years.

The next season Arsenal were back after winning a titanic semi-final with Spurs thanks to two John Radford goals in a 2–1 aggregate win. Arsenal's long hunt for a trophy looked to be over as only Third Division Swindon Town stood in their way. But in one of the biggest cup upsets of all time, the Wiltshire side won 3–1 on a bog of a pitch that had hosted the Horse of the Year show just days before. Swindon led 1–0 until four minutes from time when Bobby Gould equalised, but a tired and weary Arsenal – with eight players still affected by a flu virus – capitulated in extra time and Don Rogers scored twice to become a Swindon legend and humble the mighty Gunners.

LEAGUE OF NATIONS

Jack Butler's name may be as English as rain and cream teas, but his Sri Lankan birth made him the first overseas-born player to represent Arsenal. He joined the Club in January 1914 and made 267 appearances. Other 'foreign' Brits included Reg Tricker and Charlie Preedy – who were both born in India. 'Aussie' James Jackson, who came in 1899 from Newcastle United, was actually born in Cambuslang in Scotland, but emigrated Down Under with his family when two years old.

However, the first non-British overseas player was Dutch goalkeeper Gerry Keyser (see Foreign Players on page 86). Up to March 2008, 92 non-UK born players had pulled on a Gunners shirt, but only nine had played for the first team before summer 1989. Patrick Vieira has made more appearances for Arsenal than any other foreigner – 406 – including ten from the subs' bench.

Below is a list of all the foreigners who have been on the books at Highbury:

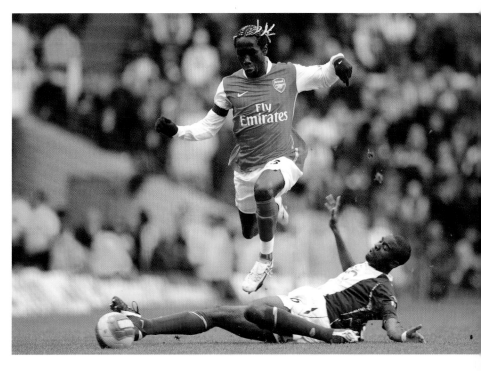

Right-back Bacary Sagna, born in France of Senegalese descent, joined Arsenal from Auxerre in July 2007. He made his international debut for France in a friendly against Slovakia the following month.

Name (nationality, if significant)	Birthplace
Jack Butler (English)	Sri Lanka
Reg Tricker (British)	India
Charlie Preedy (British)	India
Gerry Keizer	Holland
Albert Gudmundsson	Iceland
Daniel Le Roux	South Africa
Brendon Batson (English)	Grenada
John Kosmina	Australia
Vladimir Petrovic	Yugoslavia
Siggi Jonsson	Iceland
Anders Limpar	Sweden
Pal Lydersen (Norwegian)	Denmark
John Jensen	Denmark
Stefan Schwarz	Sweden
Glenn Helder	Holland
Dennis Bergkamp	Holland
Remi Garde	France
Patrick Vieira (French)	Senegal
Nicolas Anelka	France
Alex Manninger	Austria
Luis Boa Morte	Portugal
Gilles Grimandi	France
Emmanuel Petit	France
Jehad Muntasser	Libya
Marc Overmars	Holland
Alberto Mendez (Spanish)	Germany
Christopher Wreh	Liberia
David Grondin	France
Nelson Vivas	Argentina
Freddie Ljungberg	Sweden
Fabian Caballero	Argentina
Kaba Diawara	France
Nwankwo Kanu	Nigeria
Oleg Luzhny	Ukraine
Stefan Malz	Germany
Silvinho	Brazil
Thierry Henry	France
Davor Suker	Croatia
Moritz Volz	Germany
Jeremie Aliadiere	France
Lauren	Cameroon
Robert Pires	France
Sebastian Svard	Denmark
Sylvain Wiltord	France
Igors Stepanovs	Latvia

Tomas Danilevicius (Lithuanian)	Russia
Edu	Brazil
Giovanni Van Bronckhorst	Holland
Junichi Inamoto	Japan
Juan	Brazil
Carlin Itonga	DR Congo
Stathis Tavlaridis	Greece
Gilberto	Brazil
Kolo Toure	Ivory Coast
Pascal Cygan	France
Rami Shaaban	Sweden
Jose Antonio Reyes	Spain
Gael Clichy	France
Cesc Fabregas	Spain
Quincy (Dutch)	Ghana
Franki Simek	USA
Michal Papadopulos	Czech Republic
Olafur-Ingi Skulason	Iceland
Manuel Almunia	Spain
Mathieu Flamini	France
Emmanuel Eboue	Ivory Coast
Arturo Lupoli	Italy

Johan Djourou (Swiss)	Ivory Coast
Sebastian Larsson	Sweden
Danny Karbassiyoon	USA
Abou Diaby	France
Alexander Hleb	Belarus
Alexandre Song	Cameroon
Philippe Senderos	Switzerland
Mart Poom	Estonia
Emmanuel Adebayor	Togo
Nicklas Bendtner	Denmark
Fabrice Muamba (English)	DR Congo
Jens Lehmann	Germany
Tomas Rosicky	Czech Republic
Julio Baptista	Brazil
Lassana Diarra	France
Bacary Sagna	France
Eduardo	Croatia
Denilson	Brazil
Lukasz Fabianski	Poland
Armand Traore	France
Fran Merida	Spain
Nacer Barazite	Holland

LEICESTER FOSSE

The Midlands' team were Arsenal's first opponents at Highbury on 6 September 1913. The Gunners won the match 2-1, a result they replicated at the same ground against the same opponents (since renamed Leicester City) in May 2004 as Arsenal achieved an unbeaten league season.

LEITCH, Archibald

Scottish architect, Archibald Leitch designed many football grounds, including Ibrox and Hampden Park, in his native Glasgow, Old Trafford in Manchester, Molineux and Villa Park in Birmingham, and Highbury, Stamford Bridge and White Hart Lane in London.

He designed the original Highbury Stadium in 1913. It had one main two-tier stand on the east side (on Avenell Road), which held 9,000 spectators, and a multi-span roof. A similar roof was also built at Wolves while one can still be seen at Carlisle's Blundell Park. As other grounds designed by Leitch, there was terracing on the other three sides of the stadium.

The facade of the main stand at Ibrox, and the main stand and pavilion at Fulham's Craven Cottage, are some of the last remaining examples of his work. Both are listed buildings. Plymouth Argyle's main stand at Home Park is also a Leitch design, but is due to be demolished and replaced.

LEWIN, Gary (Sponging for a Living)

A well-known face around the Club, the East Ender joined Arsenal as a teenage goalkeeper and moved across north London to Barnet before injury put paid to his career at an early age. He decided to stay in the game and trained in physiotherapy at London's Guy's Hospital and returned to Highbury to take up the post of reserve team physio at the age of 19. Just three years later, in September 1986, he was appointed Arsenal's head physio-

therapist for the trip to Nottingham Forest and has held the position ever since.

After precisely 1,205 matches as first-team physio, ending at the Stadium of Light in Sunderland in May 2008, Gary, who had also been part-time physio for England for more than a decade, was appointed as the first full-time head of physiotherapy to the FA, taking up his post on 1 August 2008.

In his time at Arsenal, he worked under three managers - George Graham, Bruce Rioch and Arsène Wenger - and has been part of Arsenal teams that have won five League Championships, five FA Cups, two League Cups and one European Cup-Winners' Cup.

LEWIS, Reg

Born **Bilston, Staffordshire, 7 March 1920**
Died **1997**
Arsenal appearances **176**
Arsenal goals **118**

Lewis is in an elite band of Arsenal strikers who have scored more than 100 goals, his finest hour coming in the 1950 FA Cup Final when he scored twice in a 2-0 win. He netted on his Gunners debut 12 years earlier - New Year's Day 1938 - against Everton after he had impressed at nursery side Margate. The war disrupted his progress, but he did score four goals in a 7-1 War Cup Final win over Charlton Athletic at Wembley in May 1943. He was the Club's top scorer in the first full season after hostilities ended, and won a Championship medal the following year. He retired from the game aged 33 after one injury too many.

LIFE AFTER ARSENAL

For most people, leaving Arsenal means only one thing: a downward spiral. Here are a few men who broke the mould and enjoyed further success after saying goodbye:

CHARLIE BUCHAN
The tall, elegant striker left Woolwich Arsenal in 1909 after a row over expenses and made an unglamorous move to Leyton FC in east

London. Sunderland spotted his talents two years later and took him north. He became a Wearside legend, leading their scoring charts in seven out of eight seasons and winning the league title in 1913, as well as earning plaudits throughout the land for his talents. He remains Sunderland's all-time leading scorer with 209 goals. In 1925, aged 34, he returned to Arsenal, who were now in north London, and netted 56 times in 120 games.

TED DRAKE
As a hot-shot striker in the 1930s, Drake's goals helped the Gunners to two titles and an FA Cup. Two decades later he earned legendary status as manager of Chelsea, guiding the Blues to their first ever league title in 1955. He is also credited with discarding the pre-war Pensioners nickname and introducing the Lions badge. In later years he became Life President of Blues' neighbours Fulham.

JOE MERCER
The legendary Arsenal skipper, who led the club to two league titles and an FA Cup after the Second World War ended, forged a fine managerial career after leaving Highbury, but never took the reins as boss of his beloved Gunners. He led Aston Villa to the inaugural League Cup in 1961 before excelling at Manchester City alongside his young coaching protégé Malcolm Allison, winning the Division Two title in 1966 before leading them to the league title two years later. City won the FA Cup in 1969 and two more trophies - the League Cup and Cup-Winners' Cup - followed in 1970 before Mercer left. He later led England for seven matches too.

RAY KENNEDY
No player has left Arsenal and achieved so much. The Northumberland-born striker - discarded by Port Vale as a trainee - had won the Fairs Cup, FA Cup and League title, also finishing the 1970/71 Double season as top scorer with 27 goals, two months before his 20th birthday. But when he made a shock move to Liverpool in 1974 as Bill Shankly's last signing before he retired, Kennedy's pursuit of silverware went into overdrive, winning five more league titles with the Reds, three European cups, one UEFA Cup, one European Super Cup and a League Cup.

FRANK STAPLETON

The Ireland international broke Gunners fans' hearts when he moved to Manchester United in 1981. After appearing in four cup finals in three seasons – scoring in the 1979 FA Cup final win over his future employers – he went on to pick up two further winner's medals with the Red Devils in 1983 and, again, in 1985. He also became his country's all-time leading goalscorer with 20 goals before that record was broken by another Arsenal striker, Niall Quinn.

LIAM BRADY

Few fans begrudged the Irish hero his big move to Italy in 1980. The transfer proved a massive success for Brady, winning two Scudettos with Juventus in his first two years and earning a reputation as one of the finest players in Serie A with successful spells at Sampdoria, Internazionale, Milan and Ascoli. He ended his playing career back in London with West Ham.

ANDY COLE

It's often forgotten the prolific Premier League striker began his career as a Gunner, making just two substitute appearances in the league at Sheffield United in December 1990 and the Charity Shield against Tottenham in August 1991 before departing for Bristol City. He then became a Newcastle goalscoring hero before moving to Manchester United, winning 12 major honours including five league titles and a Champions League. He is also second in the all-time Premier League scoring chart with 187 goals.

PATRICK VIEIRA

Many people believed the Frenchman was washed up when he left Arsenal in the summer of 2005 after nine glorious years at Highbury. Instead, he went from strength to strength, earning a Scudetto in his first season at Juventus, although the club were later stripped of the title for their involvement in a match-fixing scandal. However, Vieira was comfortable in Serie A, he moved to Internazionale after just a year in Turin – and promptly starred for the Nerazzurri winning two titles in as many years, and scoring twice as Inter won the 2006 Italian Super Cup.

LIMPAR, Anders

Born **Solna, Sweden, 24 September 1965**
Arsenal appearances **95 (20)**
Arsenal goals **20**
International caps (Sweden) **58 (6 goals)**

The impish winger was the first major foreign player to succeed at Highbury after bewitching fans and bewildering opponents following his arrival in summer 1990 from Italian club Cremonese. His silky skills and goalscoring touch made him the star of the 1991 title win, his talents at times being the difference against tough opponents. Despite his slight frame, he had a hammer of a shot, while also possessing the guile to play in others, setting up many of Ian Wright's early goals for the Club. In the spring of 1992 he also scored one of the best goals ever seen at Highbury when he lobbed Liverpool keeper Mike Hooper from 50 yards in a 4-0 win.

After three seasons at the Club manager George Graham grew tired of the Swede's inconsistency, and Limpar found himself more out of the team than in it, before Everton rescued him during the 1993/94 season. But his strong bond with Arsenal fans continued and he later admitted he hankered for a move back to Highbury, but was left disappointed and later returned to Sweden where he won a title with AIK in 1998.

LINIGHAN, Andy

Born **Hartlepool, County Durham, 1962**
Arsenal appearances **134 (21)**
Arsenal goals **8**

The giant centre-half wrote his name in Arsenal folklore when his thumping header in injury time of extra time won the 1993 FA Cup Final against Sheffield Wednesday. Signed from Norwich in 1990, he won a title medal in his first season after making 10 league appearances and that set the tone for his six-and-a-half year stay at Highbury, where he was used mainly as a back up for

Andy Linighan, the scorer of the winning goal, celebrates with Ian Wright and the FA Cup Trophy after the Arsenal v Sheffield Wednesday FA Cup Final Replay at Wembley in 1993.

Steve Bould and Tony Adams. His moment of glory against Wednesday gave him cult hero status among fans, all the more so as he bravely headed the winner shortly after sustaining a broken nose. After sporadic appearances he moved to Crystal Palace in January 1997 where he was voted Player of the Year in 2000.

LISHMAN, Doug

Born **Birmingham, 14 September 1923**
Died **1994**
Arsenal appearances **243**
Arsenal goals **135**

Another of the select band of players who have scored more than 100 goals for the Club, Lishman signed from Walsall in the summer of 1948 for £10,500. He scored 13 goals in 25 appearances in his first season. He returned from a series of injuries to be top scorer in 1950/51, and the next season he hit a further 30 goals including hat-tricks in three successive home matches, a feat not matched since then. He top-scored again with 26 goals when Arsenal won the title in 1953, and finished top of the goalscoring pile for another two seasons after that, making it five successive seasons in total.

In March 1956 he was sold to Nottingham Forest and continued to score goals before announcing his retirement shortly after registering a hat-trick in a 4-0 win over Sheffield United, a victory that confirmed Forest's promotion to the top-flight.

LITTLEWOODS CUP

LOSERS
Holders Arsenal were expected to see off Luton Town and retain the trophy when the two sides met at Wembley on 24 April 1988. Optimism was sky high on that hot spring day, but it all went horribly wrong in the dying seconds of a pulsating game.

Brian Stein gave Luton an early lead and he was only denied a second moments

Doug Lishman (right) and Ronnie Rooke jog around the perimeter track during training.

after the start of the second half when John Lukic brilliantly kept out his point-blank header. Arsenal substitute Martin Hayes levelled almost immediately after a goalmouth scramble and Alan Smith turned the match on its head when he ran through to power home a second.

Smith then headed against the bar while Hayes, somehow, managed to hit the post from a yard out. When David Rocastle was felled in the area Nigel Winterburn stepped up to take the spot-kick but his effort was tipped around the post by Andy Dibble and the Hatters clung on.

It got worse for Arsenal - who had one hand on the trophy - when Gus Caesar

stumbled in the box and conceded possession allowing Danny Wilson to make it 2-2 with just five minutes left. Now Arsenal appeared punch drunk and with extra-time looming Luton stalwart Stein netted the fifth of a dramatic game to hand his side their major trophy in their 103-year history and leave Arsenal asking the question: how the hell did that happen?

WINNERS
A Charlie Nicholas double gave Arsenal their first major trophy for eight years as the Gunners came from behind against the mighty Liverpool to win the Littlewoods Cup in 1987.

Arsenal had reached the Final after a dramatic 2-1 win at Spurs in a semi-final replay, but champions Liverpool were overwhelming favourites for Wembley. And when Ian Rush scored midway through the first half it looked all over; no club had ever beaten Liverpool after Rush had scored first, a statistic spanning more than six years.

But Scottish striker Nicholas gave the Gunners hope when he levelled from close range after a goalmouth scramble just before the interval. And substitute Perry Groves set up a second-half winner when he skipped down the left wing and pulled the ball back for Nicholas whose deflected effort wrongfooted Liverpool goalkeeper Bruce Grobbelaar for the winner.

Kenny Sansom finally lifted his first trophy as Arsenal skipper and George Graham was a Wembley winner in his first full season as manager.

LIVERPOOL

Arsenal have enjoyed some titanic battles with the most successful club side in England, more often than not holding the upper hand in their personal duels.

The Gunners clinched their first title in 1931 with a 3-1 win over the Reds at Highbury and Liverpool were also Arsenal's opponents for their first ever game in the now famous red shirts and white sleeves in March in 1933, the Merseysiders winning that encounter 1-0 at Highbury. Arsenal, though, gained sweet revenge the following September with an 8-1 Highbury hammering – the biggest ever win against Liverpool – and one that surpassed a 6-0 home win in November 1931.

Arsenal also played Liverpool in the first game to be shown on *Match of the Day*, when Liverpool won 3-2 at Anfield on the opening day of the 1964/65 season.

In more recent history, Anders Limpar scored possibly the longest shot seen at Highbury when he lobbed goalkeeper Mike Hooper from just inside the Liverpool half in a 4-0 win in April 1992. While young striker Robbie Fowler scored hat-tricks in successive seasons against Arsenal in the mid-1990s, the last treble scored in this fixture came

from Thierry Henry, who hit three in a 4-2 win at Highbury in April 2004 to all but seal Arsène Wenger's third Premiership title.

Until 2001, Arsenal also enjoyed a 100 per cent winning record against Liverpool in cup finals. The 1950 and 1971 FA Cup Finals saw Arsenal win 2-0 and 2-1 respectively, and in 1987 the Club won the Littlewoods Cup 2-1 at Wembley in front of 96,000 fans – its first major trophy in eight years. The game was all the more remarkable as it was the first time Liverpool lost a competitive game in which their lethal marksman Ian Rush had scored first. Two Charlie Nicholas goals finally ended that amazing 145-game run. Arsenal also beat the Reds after a mammoth four-game epic in the 1980 FA Cup semi-final to avenge a 2-1 aggregate League Cup semi-final defeat two years previously.

The tables were turned in the 2001 FA Cup Final, the first to be held away from Wembley since 1922 (not counting replays). Freddie Ljungberg gave Arsenal a second-half lead in a match they had dominated from the start, but with the game virtually won, England striker Michael Owen showed his predatory instincts to pop up with two goals in the final minutes and earn Liverpool the win. However, the match voted the greatest in Arsenal's history by the Club's fans was at Anfield on 26 May 1989, when goals from Alan Smith and Michael Thomas earned Arsenal a 2-0 win – the first time Liverpool had lost by two goals at home for nearly three years – to earn the Gunners their first title in 18 years.

LJUNGBERG, Fredrik

See **Fab Freddie** on page 81

LONDON SENIOR CUP

The London Senior Cup was first played in 1882/83 and was to be contested by senior amateur teams from around the city. When the Football League was first formed, in 1888, the competition was for teams not included

in the League. Arsenal won the London Senior Cup in 1890, beating St Bartholemew's Hospital 6-0 in the Final, having beaten Clapton 3-2 with a late Peter Connolly goal after trailing 2-0 midway through the second-half. It remained the Club's most significant trophy until they won the FA Cup in 1930.

LOCAL LADS

Several players born and bred in Arsenal's home borough of Islington have gone on to represent the Club. However, not every Islingtonian made it in red and white; England international Joe Cole, born in the north of the borough in Archway, moved to west London to play for Chelsea.

But here are some local lads who did play for the Gunners; Charlie George, Jay Bothroyd, Ryan Smith, Dave Bacuzzi, John Halls, Eddie McGoldrick, Paolo Vernazza, Mark Flatts, Chris Whyte and Raphael Meade.

LOGIE, Jimmy

Born **Edinburgh, 23 November 1919**
Died **April 1984**
Arsenal appearances **328**
Arsenal goals **76**
International caps (Scotland) **1**

Logie was the mainstay of the Gunners' post-war success under Tom Whittaker. The fact Scotland's selectors only rewarded him one cap – in November 1952 – was met with utter bewilderment at Highbury, not least from his manager who understood the value of the midfielder's technique and passing ability.

A schemer in the Alex James mould, the little Scotsman inspired Arsenal to their 1948 title win. But unlike James, who lived long enough to see his compatriots' majestic form that season, he also had an eye for goal, netting 68 times for the Gunners in the league and a further 8 in the FA Cup.

For eight seasons he was a regular for Arsenal, playing at inside-forward, and set up both of Reg Lewis' goals in the 2–0 win over Liverpool in the 1950 FA Cup Final. His influence grew by the season and he was made vice-captain for the 1953 championship win, when he scored in a 3–2 home win over Burnley on May Day to clinch the title.

He ended up working on a newspaper stand in Piccadilly. Respected journalist Brian Glanville said, 'Today he'd be a millionaire.'

LOUGHBOROUGH TOWN

The Leicestershire outfit hold the odd distinction of inflicting Arsenal's record defeat – and being at the wrong end of the Gunners' biggest ever win. On 12 December 1896 Woolwich Arsenal were crushed 8–0 by Loughborough in a Division Two match. But they gained their revenge on 12 March 1900 when the Gunners ran out 12–0 winners in south London. This equalled the Club's overall record victory which came in an FA Cup match against Kent rivals Ashford United on 14 October 1893.

Oddly enough, on the day Loughborough beat Arsenal so convincingly, the Gunners also had to play an FA Cup fixture against Leyton Orient in east London. Arsenal's reserves played the tie – and won 5–0.

LUCKY ARSENAL

See **Boring, Boring Arsenal** on page 33

LUKIC, John

Born **Chesterfield, Derbyshire, 11 December 1960**
Arsenal appearances **293**

The Chesterfield-born goalkeeper was a hugely popular figure among the North Bank supporters. As the 1989/90 season drew to a close the fans made it their priority to persuade manager George

Graham to stick with Lukic instead of QPR goalkeeper David Seaman, whom he had been actively – and openly – pursuing for several months.

Lukic had picked up a Littlewoods Cup winner's medal in 1987 and a title in 1989, now an immortal member of the side that won that heroic 2–0 victory at Anfield where he oozed authority in the pressure cooker atmopshere of that balmy Friday night.

But Seaman came in and Lukic departed for Leeds, the club he had arrived from in July 1983 to displace the legendary Pat Jennings. He won another title with the Yorkshire club in 1992 and then returned to Highbury in 1996 as goalkeeping cover.

In October 2000 he became the oldest player in Champions League history when he played in a 1–1 draw at SS Lazio – two months short of his 40th birthday.

John Lukic enjoyed two spells at Highbury. He won a title in 1989, but was replaced the following year with David Seaman. Lukic returned south in 1996.

MACDONALD, Malcolm

Born **Fulham, London,
7 January 1950**
Arsenal appearances **107**
Arsenal goals **57**
International caps (England) **14 (6 goals)**

A heroic striker with the looks, skills and goals that, despite his truncated stay at the Club, made him a Gunners legend. Even his transfer fee from Newcastle United - £333,333 - was fittingly flamboyant when Terry Neill signed him in August 1976. With God-like status on Tyneside, his departure was received badly by the Toon Army who had not had a hero of such huge proportions since 'Wor' Jackie Milburn.

Cocksure and brimming with confidence, Supermac responded magnificently to the challenge of lifting the mid-1970s gloom around Arsenal, smashing 29 goals in his first season, including a hat-trick against his former employers in a 5-3 win. He continued where he left off the following season when he plundered a further 25 goals.

However, an arthritic knee began to take its toll - notably in the 1978 FA Cup Final defeat to Ipswich when he was virtually anonymous. His third season was interrupted by injury and he missed the 3-2 FA Cup Final win over Manchester United, but bravely returned two days later for the

Malcolm Macdonald is denied during a match against QPR at Highbury shortly after his move from Newcastle in 1976. Supermac was tragically forced to retire through injury while in his prime.

final league game at Chelsea. Typically he scored in a 1-1 draw, but it was to be his final professional appearance, as within weeks, he was forced to retire at the age of 28.

MAKITA TOURNAMENT

The Makita Tournament was a pre-season event which ran from 1988 to 1994. Arsenal made more appearances than any other side, winning three of the five competitions they contested. In 1988, Arsenal kicked off with a 4-0 win over Spurs - with new signing Paul Gascogine - at Wembley and ended up winning the tournament with a 3-0 win over Bayern Munich. New league champions Arsenal held on to the trophy the following year after beating Liverpool 1-0, although Sampdoria denied them a trio of wins when they won 1-0 in 1990. The tournament moved to Highbury the next season but, again, Sampdoria were the victors, beating Arsenal on penalties. The Gunners missed the next two tournaments, but were back for its last outing in 1994, Highbury hosting again as Arsenal beat Napoli 1-0 in the Final.

MAKITA TOURNAMENT 1988
all matches played at Wembley

First Round
Arsenal 4-0 Tottenham Hotspur

AC Milan 1-0 Bayern Munich

Second Round
AC Milan 1-0 Tottenham Hotspur

Arsenal 3-0 Bayern Munich

Winners
Arsenal (on superior record)

MAKITA TOURNAMENT 1989
all matches played at Wembley

Semi-finals
Arsenal 1-0 Porto

Liverpool 2-0 Dynamo Kiev

Third-Place Match
Dynamo Kiev 1-0 Porto

Final
Arsenal 1-0 Liverpool

MAKITA TOURNAMENT 1990
all matches played at Wembley

Semi-finals
Sampdoria 1-1 Real Sociedad
Sampdoria won 5-3 on pens

Arsenal 2-0 Aston Villa

Third-Place Match
Real Sociedad 1-0 Aston Villa

Final
Sampdoria 1-0 Arsenal

MAKITA TOURNAMENT 1991
all matches played at Arsenal Stadium

Semi-finals
Sampdoria 6-1 West Ham United

Arsenal 1-0 Panathinaikos

Third-Place Match
Panathinaikos 1-1 West Ham United
Panathinaikos won 3-2 on pens

Final
Sampdoria 1-1 Arsenal
Sampdoria won 3-2 on pens

MAKITA TOURNAMENT 1994
all matches played at Arsenal Stadium

Semi-finals
Arsenal 0-0 Atlético Madrid
Arsenal won 3-2 on pens

Napoli 2-0 Chelsea

Third-Place Match
Chelsea 1-0 Atlético Madrid

Final
Arsenal 1-0 Napoli

MALE, George

Born **West Ham, London, 8 May 1910**
Died **19 February 1998**
Arsenal appearances **314**
Arsenal goals **0**
International caps (England) **19**

'By the time Herbert had finished with me I was convinced that not only was I was a full-back but I was the best in the country.' George Male's words proved just what a great job Herbert Chapman had carried out on the cockney's game. Joining the Club as a left-half, the great Gunners manager moved him on to the right side of the defence where he formed a great full-back partnership with Eddie Hapgood, both for Arsenal and England. He made his debut in a 7-1 win over Blackpool two days after Christmas 1930, but didn't cement his place in the starting line-up for another two years after Chapman's innovative change in role for him.

A fanatical trainer, Male was one of the fittest players at the Club and was soon chosen by England. He was one of seven Arsenal players who turned out for his country in the Battle of Highbury match against World champions Italy in November 1934 (see Battle of Highbury on page 27).

Male won four titles and an FA Cup with Arsenal before becoming a physical trainer for the army in Palestine on the eve of the Second World War. By the time hostilities had ceased, Male was 35 - and had managed to squeeze in more than 200 wartime games for the Club - but still managed to play on until 1948, bowing out as he started, with a thumping win - 8-0 against Grimsby in May 1948.

Male stayed with the Club in various coaching capacities and as a scout until his retirement in 1975, and is the man credited with unearthing Charlie George.

Opposite Tom Whittaker (seated left) was appointed manager in 1947 as George Allison's replacement. Here he discusses the injury list with (left to right) trainer Bill Milne and assistants Jack Crayston - later Whittaker's successor - and long-serving Joe Shaw.

MANAGERS

Full List (entries in grey indicate caretaker manager)

Sam Hollis	August 1894 – July 1897
Thomas Mitchell	August 1897 – March 1898
George Elcoat	March 1898 – May 1899
Harry Bradshaw	August 1899 – May 1904
Phil Kelso	July 1904 – February 1908
George Morrell	February 1908 – May 1915
Leslie Knighton	May 1919 – June 1925
Herbert Chapman	June 1925 – January 1934
Joe Shaw	January – June 1934
George Allison	June 1934 – May 1947
Tom Whittaker	June 1947 – October 1956
Jack Crayston	October 1956 – May 1958
George Swindin	July 1958 – May 1962
Billy Wright	May 1962 – June 1966
Bertie Mee	June 1966 – May 1976
Terry Neill	July 1976 – December 1983
Don Howe	December 1983 – March 1986
Steve Burtenshaw	March – May 1986
George Graham	June 1986 – February 1995
Stewart Houston	February – May 1995
Bruce Rioch	June 1995 – August 1996
Stewart Houston	August 1996
Pat Rice	September 1996
Arsène Wenger	September 1996 – present

MANCHESTER UNITED

English football fans have watched with excitement at the thrilling power struggle between Arsenal and Manchester United over the past 20 years. The Red Devils proved to be Arsenal's main rivals for much of the George Graham era and all of Arsène Wenger's tenure in north London, although the rivalry goes back long before then.

United have twice beaten Arsenal 6-1 at Old Trafford; in 1952 and again in 2001. Other notable games include a 4-5 home defeat in 1958, which was the last game the Busby Babes played in England, and a superb 4-0 home win over George Best's United at the start of the 1970/71 Double-winning season. A 1-0 win over United in October 1990 sparked the now infamous Old Trafford brawl in which players from both sides scuffled before order was restored. Arsenal were docked points for their part in the incident.

Dennis Bergkamp secured Arsenal's first Premiership win against United in November 1995 and the Gunners beat United 3-2 at home and 1-0 on the way to the title in 1997/98, and a 1-0 win at Old Trafford in 2002, courtesy of Sylvain Wiltord's strike, sealed another Gunners title. In recent years Thierry Henry has proved United's nemesis, starting with a winning goal in 2000 at Highbury and netting twice in a 3-1 win in 2001-02.

United and Arsenal have also taken part in some memorable matches in cup competitions over the years. The first ever FA Cup clash between the sides ended in a 5-0 win for the Gunners in 1937 – a record win against United. Arsenal beat United 3-2 in the 1979 FA Cup Final, but four years later United gained revenge by knocking Arsenal out of both domestic cup competitions at the semi-final stage. In 1987 Arsenal won a bad-tempered fifth round FA Cup tie 2-1 at Highbury, although United stunned the Gunners three years later with a magnificent 6-2 win at Highbury in the Littlewoods Cup. United beat Arsenal in the FA Cup semi-finals of 1999 and 2004 – both Villa Park wins sandwiching a 2-0 Old Trafford FA Cup victory for Arsenal in 2003 – and the Gunners exacted perfect revenge in 2004/05, kicking off the campaign with a 3-1 win in the Charity Shield and then returning to Cardiff at the end of the season to beat United on penalties in the FA Cup Final after a 0-0 draw.

MANOR GROUND – Plumstead

Arsenal had two spells at 'The Manor' in Plumstead, first from 1888 to 1890, then returning in 1893 until the move to Highbury in 1913.

Royal Arsenal first moved from Plumstead Common to nearby Manor Field - later renamed the Manor Ground - shortly after the end of the 1887/88 season. The players had to use the nearby Railway Tavern pub to change into their strip while the pitch was notoriously muddy, with a large open sewer on one side. Wagons were borrowed from a nearby army base to house spectators. The Club's first match there was a 3-3 draw with Millwall.

After moving to the Invicta Ground for three years the Club opted to try the Manor again. A limited company was formed and 13 and a half acres of land - roughly the size of the Emirates Stadium site - was purchased for £4,000 with money raised from a share issue. A 2,000-seater stand was constructed and the ground had an overall capacity of around 20,000 in time for Woolwich Arsenal's (the Club had since changed its name and turned professional) Football League Division Two debut. A crowd of 10,000 watched the Club's first professional match - a 2-2 draw with Newcastle United, Walter Shaw scoring Arsenal's first-ever league goal after ten minutes.

In 1904, with Harry Bradshaw's side on their way to promotion to the top-flight, the Club erected a second stand, called the Spion Kop, named after the famous Boer War battle.

The last match played at the Manor Ground was on 26 April 1913 when Middlesbrough earned a 1-1 draw. Today the old site is home to an industrial estate roughly bound by Nathan Way, Griffin Manor Way and Hadden Road.

MARBLE HALLS

Few football stadiums in the world had such a grand entrance as Highbury, which fitted in with the Club's role as one of the 'elder statesmen' of English football. After walking up the old steps and through the doors of the stadium, a bronze bust of Herbert Chapman sat on a plinth, a reminder of the great man's vision and talents, which enabled the Club to construct such a palatial building - three years after his death - in the 1930s. On the marble floor was a magnificent motif of the old Club crest and to the left the staff entrance to the box office. The dressing rooms were directly to the right, past a sweeping staircase that led to the boardroom, the Club's administration offices, media and publications department and the directors' box.

Contrary to rumours that it would be ripped out and taken to the new arena, the original hall, which has stood since its construction in 1936, will remain as a reception area in the new Highbury Square residential complex.

In honour of the old hall, the Club maintained the tradition by constructing marble entrances to both Club Level and the Diamond Club at the new Emirates Stadium.

MARADONA

The Argentina legend is regarded by many respected judges as the greatest ever footballer - and he could have graced the Highbury turf. In his book, *Revelations of a Football Manager*, Arsenal boss Terry

Arsenal's world famous marble hall entrance with Herbert Chapman's bust in the background. It will remain to be seen for generations to come as part of the new housing development currently being built at Highbury.

Neill revealed that he made 'strenuous attempts' to bring the midfielder to England after an approach from former Sheffield United manager Harry Haslam in February 1982. Haslam had failed in an audacious attempt to take the youngster to Bramall Lane a few years earlier but had stayed friends with Maradona's family.

Several big companies were approached to help fund the deal and his wages, which, with add-ons, were expected to exceed £700,000 – a huge figure in the early 1980s. By April of that year a five-year deal was being put together, but negotiations between London and Buenos Aires broke down within days of the outbreak of the Falklands War. Maradona eventually moved to Barcelona, with whom he had signed a pre-contract agreement, leaving Neill 'terribly frustrated'.

Maradona, however, has become an Arsenal fan in his retirement. In 2004 he said, 'I do like Arsenal a lot, they're the best in Europe and Thierry Henry is a "Maradonian" player.' He met up with the first-team squad during a pre-season tournament in Amsterdam in 2006 and visited Emirates Stadium in January 2008 when he watched the Gunners beat Newcastle United 3-0. After the match he commented, 'When I'm in England I am an Arsenal fan – they tried to sign me once and I often wonder what might have happened... '

Nineteen-year-old Peter Marinello arrived at Highbury in January 1970 with a big reputation and a host of admirers. However, indifferent form and an extravagant lifestyle made his stay in north London a disappointing one and he left for Portsmouth three years later.

MARGATE

Woolwich Arsenal had an informal relation-ship with Kent League founder members Cray Wanderers, but the first official 'nursery club' agreement was not signed until the mid-1930s. When George Allison replaced the late Herbert Chapman as manager in 1934 he set up another 'special relationship' with Southern League outfit Margate until the end of the 1937/38 season. Its purpose was simple – to blood promising young players in a competitive environment.

Why Arsenal couldn't do that in their own reserve team was explained at the time by chairman Sir Samuel Hill-Wood: 'Our second team is at the head of the London Combination [league] and we dare not experiment with the team – it would only offend players hopeful of getting a medal... What we wanted was some club willing and good enough to teach our young players for us.'

Arsenal funded 60 per cent of the Margate players' wages and also paid for their Hartsdown Park pitch to be re-laid and reduced in size to the exact specifications of the Highbury surface. And the scheme was a success, with

several players breaking through to the Arsenal side, notably striker Reg Lewis, who scored both goals in the 1950 FA Cup Final win over Liverpool.

MARINELLO, Peter

Born **Edinburgh, 20 February 1950**
Arsenal appearances **43 (8)**
Arsenal goals **5**

Dubbed the Scottish George Best on his arrival from Hibernian for £100,000 in

January 1970, he immediately made a storming start with a brilliant individual goal on his debut against Manchester United at Old Trafford. But sadly, that was as good as it got. It seems all the pressures of life at a big city club were proving too much for the softly-spoken Scotsman. His form suffered and he missed virtually the entire Double-winning campaign.

His skills were not in doubt, but his temperament was another issue, and despite all Bertie Mee's desperate attempts to incorporate him in the first team, he ultimately proved an expensive failure with a cut-price move to Portsmouth in 1973. Marinello had struck 22 goals in 77 London Combination games, compared to just five goals in 51 first-team appearances - a statistic that tells it all.

MARINER, Paul

Born **Chorley, Lancashire, 22 May 1953**
Arsenal appearances **60 (10)**
Arsenal goals **17**
International caps (England) **35 (13 goals)**

Mariner's best years were clearly behind him when Don Howe swooped for the Ipswich striker in February 1984. A traditional targetman and excellent header of the ball, the England forward won just two more caps while at Highbury with his final international appearance coming in a goalless draw against Romania in May 1985.

At Highbury his first-team opportunites were becoming increasingly rare and he was even grateful to be drafted in as an emergency centre-back after an injury to David O'Leary. But in 1986 new manager George Graham wanted to cut the average age of the squad and Mariner was soon on his way to Portsmouth.

Since 1988 Mariner has lived in America where he has coached for several MLS sides.

MARWOOD, Brian

Born **Seaham, Co. Durham, 5 February 1960**
Arsenal appearances **60**
Arsenal goals **17**
International caps (England) **1**

Though his stay at Highbury was all too brief, the impact that this tidy winger made at Highbury was huge. George Graham parted with £600,000 in March 1988 to sign him from Sheffield Wednesday, in the main to feed Alan Smith with inviting crosses to feast on. It was an inspired move, as for the most part of the next season Marwood was vital to Arsenal's 1988/89 title-winning run. He scored important goals too, notably the winner against Newcastle United during the run-in. But that was his last game of the season due to injury, and it was the same story the next year until his time in London was up and he moved back to Sheffield to play for United in September 1990.

He later chaired the Professional Footballers' Association and is now one of the most intelligent and articulate media commentators in the business.

McLINTOCK, Frank (MBE)

Born **Glasgow, 28 December 1939**
Arsenal appearances **401 (2)**
Arsenal goals **32**
International caps (Scotland) **9**

It all came late for the inspirational Glaswegian, so often the loser, who went from zero to hero after a series of Wembley heartaches. McLintock lost four cup finals at the national stadium in the 1960s - two FA Cups with Leicester and two League Cups with Arsenal - before he finally got his hands on some silverware when he skippered the Gunners to the Inter-Cities Fairs Cup final at Highbury.

'At 29 I thought my football life was over,' he said, recalling Arsenal's shock defeat to Swindon in the 1969 League Cup Final. 'I was numb, shot to pieces.' It says everything about his indomitable character that he bounced back spectacularly to earn European and, a year later, Double domestic success. 'The man was incredible, the perfect captain,' says his former coach and neighbour, Don Howe. 'He always led by example.'

It was Howe who converted him from wing-half to centre-back after his arrival from Leicester for what was then a British record of £80,000 in 1964 and he went on to become club captain in 1967. But after two FA Cup Final defeats he handed in a transfer request, although later withdrew it after talks with his manager Bertie Mee.

After the Fairs Cup he led the Club to its first League and Cup Double in 1971 - finally picking up a Wembley winner's medal after seeing his side a goal down in extra time before fighting back to beat Liverpool, 2-1. McLintock hid his own disappointment to gee up his shattered side and it was those very qualities which deservedly saw him pick up the Football Writers' Association Footballer of the Year award.

He led Arsenal to their sixth Wembley final in 1972, which they lost to Leeds, and second place in the First Division the year after, before he was surprisingly sold to QPR in June 1973. It was a move he did not covet and it soured his relationship with a club that remains his one true love. 'I had nine smashing years as an Arsenal player,' he said later. 'But it didn't end well - once you have been an Arsenal player it is hard to get it out of your system.'

McNAB, Bob

Born **Huddersfield, Yorkshire, 20 July 1943**
Arsenal appearances **362 (3)**
Arsenal goals **3**
International caps (England) **4**

The straight-talking Yorkshireman turned down Liverpool to join the Gunners for

£50,000 in 1966 and gave nine years' sterling service at Highbury. Vocal both on and off the pitch, he was a member of the ITV panel for the 1970 World Cup, and still maintains that if he had been on the pitch England would not have blown their 2-0 lead to West Germany in the quarter-final. After an inspirational performance in the Fairs Cup Final win against Anderlecht, he had initially been in Sir Alf Ramsey's squad to travel to Mexico, but he was one of the players who were dropped when the final numbers were trimmed down. He never played for his country again.

The next season he missed just two games as Arsenal won the Double and stayed in the side until moving to Wolves in 1975. McNab now lives in the US, where he ended his playing days, and has business interests in LA and Mexico.

MEDIA

Here is a selection of Arsenal players who have gone on to forge careers of varying success in the football-mad media world:

Tony Adams (TV)
Charlie Buchan (newspapers)
Lee Dixon (TV)
Eddie Hapgood (newspapers)
Bernard Joy (newspapers)
Brian Marwood (TV)
Frank McLintock (TV)
Bob McNab (TV)
Charlie Nicholas (TV)
Niall Quinn (TV)
Alan Smith (TV, radio and newspapers)
Bob Wilson (TV)
Nigel Winterburn (TV)

George Allison, however, went the other way. He left his job as a BBC commentator to take over as secretary of Arsenal. He was appointed manager in the summer of 1933.

Bob McNab (far right) acrobatically clears off the line against Spurs as Pat Rice, Bob Wilson and Peter Storey look on in the last league match of 1970-71 season. Arsenal won 1-0 and took the league title. The Yorkshireman was, for a while, the most expensive full-back in world football.

MEE, Bertie (OBE)

MANAGER 1966/76
Born **Bullwell, Nottinghamshire,
25 December 1918**
Died **22 October 2001**

Arsenal's decision to appoint physio-therapist Bertie Mee as manager in the summer of 1966 looked strange on the outside. But the Gunners board knew what they were getting. Mee had taken over as physio from club legend Billy Milne in 1960 and watched from the inside as predecessor Billy Wright limped through four years of underachievement.

Mee – a winger for Derby County before injury cut short his career – knew there was a talented pool of players at his disposal. Allied with discipline, firm leadership and fresh coaching ideas, the good times would return to Highbury. For a former army sergeant, hard work was second nature and he carried out his job with military precision, employing top quality coaching staff in Dave Sexton and Don Howe, who would be his trusted right-hand man through the Club's most successful period for two decades.

His strong work ethic seeped its way into the Club's consciousness and a Highbury revolution had begun. Promoting youngsters John Radford, Ray Kennedy and Charlie George, and handing the captain's armband to Frank McLintock, Arsenal reached two successive League Cup Finals in the late 1960s and then beat Anderlecht to claim the Inter Cities Fairs Cup, on a stirring night at Highbury in April 1970.

The next season he steered Arsenal to a domestic Double to emulate Tottenham's 1961 achievements. In the title run-in, sensing history, he made a famous speech to the players after beating Stoke City in an FA Cup semi-final replay: 'I would not normally say this as a family man, but I am going to ask you, for your sakes and for

Bertie Mee sits outside Highbury with the league championship and FA Cup trophies on 30 May 1971.

the sake of this football club, to put your family second for the next month. You have the chance to put your names in the record books for all time.' They heeded his advice and became legends.

Arsenal lost the FA Cup Final the next season to Leeds United and came second in the league in 1973. Mee was criticised in some quarters for breaking up the Double team too early, notably letting McLintock leave for QPR, and he announced his resignation in 1976.

He recharged his batteries before joining Watford as assistant to Graham Taylor and unearthing the talented winger John Barnes. He was made an OBE in 1984 for services to football and stayed as a Watford director before retiring in 1991.

MEE'S DOUBLE WINNERS

Bertie Mee's side won few friends outside of north London, but his Double winners were as well-drilled and effective a team as to have ever graced the English game.

It was built, of course, on a solid base, with unflappable goalkeeper Bob Wilson's bravery and positioning complementing a defence superbly marshalled by skipper Frank McLintock, who organised his side with passion and common sense. In midfield the graceful George Graham prompted many of the team's attacks with Peter Storey providing the muscle when the going got tough. The industrious George Armstrong characteristically worked the wing, protecting his full-back and pumping the opponents' area with pinpoint crosses. John Radford led the line with authority – and goals – perfectly complementing partner Ray Kennedy and the creative genius of Charlie George, so often the winner at the back end of the season. The standard team line-up was: Bob Wilson, Pat Rice, Bob McNab, Frank McLintock, Peter Simpson, Peter Storey, George Graham, George Armstrong, Charlie George, Ray Kennedy, John Radford.

MEMBERSHIP

Since moving to Emirates Stadium Arsenal's membership figures have been extraordinary, with the number of fans signed up as official members standing at over 200,000, including more than 30,000 Junior Gunners.

There are various levels of membership at Arsenal ranging from Red to Platinum. Members receive a membership card and pack including DVD, Club yearbook and other Club memorabilia. They are also entitled to apply for tickets for various league and cup matches as well as friendlies.

MERCANTILE CREDIT TROPHY

The competition was held in the autumn of 1988 as part of the Football League's centenary celebrations with Arsenal beating QPR 2-0 and Liverpool 2-1 to earn a place in the Final against Manchester United at Villa Park. Just over 22,000 were there on 9 October to see goals from Paul Davis and Michael Thomas see off United 2-1.

MERCER, Joe

Born **Ellesmere Port, Cheshire, 9 August 1914**
Died **9 August 1990**
Arsenal appearances **273**
Arsenal goals **2**
International caps (England) **5**

The legendary left-sided defender spent 14 years with Everton before signing for Arsenal in 1946 for £9,000. As Gunners skipper he won titles in 1948 and 1953 – to go with the title medal he won with the Toffees in 1939 – although his finest hour came in 1950 when he finally won an FA Cup medal for Arsenal against Liverpool. It was all the sweeter as Mercer had stayed

living on Merseyside to run a grocery business and trained with the Anfield club while commuting to Highbury on match-days. He also skippered the side that narrowly lost the 1952 FA Cup Final to Newcastle and, addressing the post-match banquet, said, 'I thought the greatest honour was captaining England. It isn't – it was captaining Arsenal today.'

He retired in 1953, but changed his mind and returned the next season in his 40th year. However, a broken leg the following year finally brought down the curtain on a magnificent playing career. Mercer later managed Sheffield United and Aston Villa before guiding Manchester City to four trophies alongside Malcolm Allison. He was made an OBE and briefly managed England in 1974 following Sir Alf Ramsey's resignation.

MERGER

Woolwich Arsenal very nearly merged with Fulham just before moving to Highbury in 1913. Sir Henry Norris, who had bought the Gunners in 1910 and was on the board at Craven Cottage, wanted Arsenal to move to Fulham's ground to play alternate Saturdays, after becoming exasperated with the lack of support for the Club in south east London. But when that idea was shelved, he proposed a full-blown merger. Fortunately, the Football League blocked the move and Norris had to look elsewhere. After an extensive search, he decided to move the Club across to Highbury in north London.

MERSON, Paul

Born **Harlesden, London, 20 March 1968**
Arsenal appearances **378 (44)**
Arsenal goals **99**
International caps (England) **21 (3 goals)**

Another jewel from Arsenal's youth system who thrilled and frustrated Highbury crowds

for more than a decade before a thumping pay rise tempted him away from the Wenger revolution just as he began to show glimpses of his best form ever.

Capable of the unexpected, he broke into George Graham's side in the 1988/89 title-winning season and rewarded his manager with a series of super displays where his skills and strength brought him some spectacular goals. He scored ten times that season, made his debut for the England Under-21 side, and was voted PFA Young Player of the Year.

His long hair and rebellious image made fans see him as a latter-day Charlie George and he had the skills to match, winning the title in 1991 and the domestic double cup success in 1993, scoring with a swerving drive in the Coca-Cola Cup Final.

His post-match celebrations – pretending to swig pints of beer – gave an insight into his private life and the Club's drinking culture at that time. Before long he publicly admitted to various drink, drug and gambling addictions and he broke down in tears at a press conference, flanked by George Graham and vice-chairman David Dein.

He showed tremendous spirit to return in February 1995 and enjoyed a second wind, playing more than 100 consecutive games to impress new manager Arsène Wenger. But with the offer of a three-year deal on the table and England calling, Merson opted to move to Middlesbrough. 'I can't believe I did it. What was I thinking of? My biggest regret is leaving Arsenal,' a typically honest Merson has since told the official *Arsenal* magazine. It was also a great source of disappointment to Arsenal fans that he never joined the exclusive Hundred Club, when he left Highbury

having scored 99 goals for the Club. He now writes a typically forthright column for the magazine and also appears regularly on Sky Sports.

MILITARY CONNECTIONS

Arsenal's links to the military are most obviously seen in the Club's name and on its badge. The Royal Arsenal, where the Club was formed, manufactured and stored equipment for the British Army and Royal Navy.

Woolwich was the single most important military town in Britain at the end of the 19th century. In 1886 there were nearly 30 military units based in the area, including the Royal Military Academy and the Royal Artillery Regiment, but its history stretches back to the time of Henry VIII whose Royal Dockyard was sited there.

At the turn of the 20th century the terraces were often awash with the khaki

uniforms of servicemen and it was at the old Manor Ground where an English football institution was formed. Liverpool FC's Kop at Anfield is famous throughout the footballing world, but the first kop was actually at Arsenal's former home. In 1904, Arsenal opened a mound of terracing at the Manor Ground which regulars – many of whom were Boer War veterans – soon nicknamed the Spion Kop, which means 'look-out' in Afrikaans and was a hill in South Africa where 322 British soldiers were killed.

MILLENNIUM STADIUM

Also see **Cardiff** on page 43

The former Cardiff Arms Park has been a home from home for Arsenal since 2001. The FA chose to use the venue for the FA Cup Final and the Community Shield while the £757m Wembley Stadium redevelopment took place.

Opposite Paul Merson celebrates scoring against Sheffield Wednesday in the 1993 Coca-Cola Cup Final. 'The Magic Man' remains hugely popular with fans.

Right The Millennium Stadium in Cardiff is an impressive sight on FA Cup Final day in May 2003 as the Gunners prepare to take on Southampton. The journey to Cardiff became a familiar one for Arsenal fans during the early years of the 2000s.

Arsène Wenger's side reached the FA Cup Final that year – the first time the FA Cup Final had been held outside Wembley since the 1970 replay between Chelsea and Leeds United at Old Trafford in Manchester.

Arsenal went on to compete in the 2002, 2003 and 2005 Finals in the Welsh capital – winning all of them – while also appearing in four successive Community Shields since 2002, winning the trophy twice.

MITCHELL, Thomas Brown

MANAGER 1897/98
Born **Dumfries, circa 1843**
Died **August 1921**

The Scotsman became the Club's first professional manager after resigning from his post as secretary of the mighty Blackburn Rovers in 1896. After finishing tenth the previous season, Brown improved the playing staff and the team finished a creditable fifth at the end of his only season at Plumstead. But by then he had gone, resigning in March and later moving back to Blackburn where he stayed to his death in 1921.

MORRELL, George

MANAGER 1908/15
Born **Glasgow, circa 1873**
Died **Unknown**

Still the only Gunners manager to have been relegated, George Morrell oversaw the Club's big move from Plumstead to Islington in 1913. Appointed in February 1908, the 35-year-old Glaswegian arrived after a short but successful period at Greenock Morton. He bought in Alf

Common – previously the first £1,000 player in football history – to form a dream partnership up front with star striker Andy Ducat, but both were soon sold as cash-strapped Woolwich Arsenal dropped to the Second Division in 1912/13, winning just three league games all season. The two seasons before the First World War saw the Club remain in the second tier of English football, before Morrell resigned in 1915, signing off with a 7-0 win over Nottingham Forest.

MORROW, Steve

Born **Kilclenny, near Belfast, Ireland, 2 July 1970**
Arsenal appearances **52 (33)**
Arsenal goals **6**
International caps (Northern Ireland) **39**

Poor old Steve Morrow! No matter what else he achieves in football or elsewhere, he will always be remembered for a freak

Steve Morrow will always be remembered for his goal – and subsequent fall – at the 1993 Coca-Cola Cup Final.

accident on the Wembley turf on what should have been the greatest day of his career. He had just scored the winning goal in the 1993 Coca-Cola League Cup Final against Sheffield Wednesday and his Arsenal team-mates were all celebrating when skipper Tony Adams playfully picked him up and dropped him – breaking his arm.

But he made a full recovery from his sickening injury – and forgave his captain before the cast was even set – to star in the following year's Cup-Winners' Cup Final in Copenhagen as a deputy in the midfield for the absent John Jensen. It was his best performance in a Gunners shirt as Arsenal won the trophy against all the odds.

However, Morrow could never replicate that form on a weekly basis and when the Wenger era arrived his days were numbered and he followed former Arsenal coach Stewart Houston to QPR for £500,000.

MOSS, Frank

Born **Leyland, Lancashire,
5 November 1909**
Died **7 February 1970**
Arsenal appearances **161**
Arsenal goals **1**
International caps (England) **4**

The former Preston North End and Oldham Athletic goalkeeper signed for Arsenal in November 1931 for £3,000. He had reputedly caught Herbert Chapman's eye while the Gunners boss was scouting for another player and he immediately took over from Charlie Preedy in goal on his arrival at Highbury.

Moss was the undisputed No.1 for five years, a member of the famous side which won three successive titles between 1933 and 1935, and played in the controversial 1932 FA Cup Final defeat to Newcastle United. His most heroic hour came in March 1935 when he dislocated his shoulder at Everton but, in the days before substitutes, was forced to play on

for the full 90 minutes on the left wing. Amazingly, he scored in a 2-0 win.

The injury would be the beginning of the end and, after just five more games in the next two years, he retired at the age of 27. Moss later became the youngest manager in Heart of Midlothian's history, but resigned in 1940.

MURALS

There have been two murals associated with Arsenal in the last few years, both much maligned but never forgotten.

The first appeared when the North Bank terrace was demolished in the summer of 1992. The Club erected the now infamous mural to hide the work taking place behind it. The huge mural ran the entire width of the pitch – more than 70 yards – with a sea of painted faces staring out from it. The Club even placed speakers along the mural with crowd noise piped from the other three sides of the stadium to maintain the 'Highbury Roar'.

The debut of the 'Mural End', as the displaced North Bankers dubbed it, ended in a 4-2 home defeat to Norwich and its final 'appearance' was even worse – a 3-1 loss to Spurs.

When it was torn down Arsenal hoped for better luck. But the post-mural era could not have started in worse fashion – rotund striker Mick Quinn hitting an unlikely hat-trick as Coventry won 3-0 in August 1993.

In 2005, to mark the last season at Highbury, a 52-metre mural was unveiled in the main passenger tunnel at Arsenal Tube station. Thierry Henry, Robert Pires and Ashley Cole cut the ribbon on the mural, titled 'The Final Salute', which depicted the stadium's 93-year history and offered both a glimpse of the club's roots in Woolwich and its future at Emirates Stadium. Henry said, 'It's very fitting that the only football club to have a Tube station named after it should display such a wonderful interpretation of the club's history here.'

MUSEUM

Arsenal's old museum, situated in Highbury's North Bank, was a huge attraction both on matchdays and during the week. The spectacular new museum at Emirates Stadium, opened in the arena's Northern Triangle building, has even more exhibits along with some of the old favourites. Still given pride of place are the boots Michael Thomas was wearing when he scored the second goal in the 2-0 title-winning match at Anfield in 1989 and Charlie George's FA Cup Final shirt from 1971.

New exhibits at Emirates include the shirts worn by goalscorers Jon Sammels and Alan Smith in the 1970 Fairs Cup and 1994 European Cup-Winners' Cup Final victories respectively, along with medals, shirts and caps belonging to David O'Leary, Lee Dixon, Brian Marwood and others. Also on display is the customised trophy presented to the Club by the FA Premier League for remaining unbeaten throughout the 2003/04 season.

'The museum offers a chance to take in many exhibits kindly donated by former players who hold a special place in Arsenal's history,' explains the Club's historian, Iain Cook. The facility also features several exciting new attractions including an impressive Legends Theatre and more than a dozen interactive displays based on themes from Arsenal's proud history including 'Title-winning Managers', 'The Invincibles of 2004', 'The Arsenal Spirit' and 'Highbury'.

'In the past,' Iain adds, 'the museum has been graced by some surprise visitors. Dennis Bergkamp visited once with his wife and children – they seemed to enjoy it. And I remember the day Davor Suker signed for us, he was the leading scorer in the World Cup and a big name. I was conducting a tour and halfway through he tagged along with his wife and his agent. Davor was a smashing chap and didn't mind me introducing him to his new fans at the end. He signed many autographs and chatted away to everyone which was a nice bonus for them.'

The museum is open seven days a week, including matchdays.

Thierry Henry admires the impressive mural at Arsenal underground station, which was created to celebrate the Club's 93 years at Highbury.

MUSIC

Arsenal have sporadically featured in the pop charts. The Gunners' biggest hit to date was the 1998 FA Cup Final release, 'Hot Stuff', which reached No.9. Other songs have featured references to the Club, such as Aswad's 1994 single 'Shine', which praises Ian Wright and the Highbury crowd.

Here is a selection of songs with Arsenal connections:

'Good Old Arsenal' – Arsenal FC (1971)
'I Wish I Could Play Like Charlie George' – The Strikers and Selston Bagthorpe Primary School (1972)
'We're Back Where We Belong' – Arsenal FC (1989)
'Your Arsenal' – Morrissey (1992)
'Shouting for the Gunners' – Arsenal FC featuring Tippa Irie and Peter Honeygale (1993)
'Go West' – Pet Shop Boys' (1993)*
'Shine' – Aswad (1994)
'Hot Stuff' – Arsenal FC (1998)
'Tony Adams' – Joe Strummer and the Mescaleros (1999)

'Arsenal No.1/Our Goal' – Arsenal FC (2000)
'Bob Wilson: Anchor Man' – Half Man Half Biscuit (2001)

* This Pet Shop Boys cover of a Village People hit is not technically an Arsenal song – but the tune was adopted by Arsenal fans for the now famous '1–0 to the Arsenal' chant and thereby earns itself special status.

NAMES

Arsenal have had four official names since the Club's formation in 1886: Dial Square (1886), Royal Arsenal (1886/91), Woolwich Arsenal (1891/1914), Arsenal (1914/Present). They have also been known unofficially as 'The Arsenal' on and off since moving to north London in 1913.

NEILL, Terry

MANAGER 1976/83
Born **Belfast, 8 May 1942**
Arsenal appearances **272 (3)**
Arsenal goals **10**
International caps **(Northern Ireland) 59 (2 goals)**

The Irish centre-half moved to Highbury from hometown club Bangor and, despite limitations as a player, was made the youngest skipper in Arsenal's history at the age of 20, when Billy Wright was appointed as manager in 1962. He made his debut in December 1960 in a 1-1 draw with Sheffield Wednesday and became a regular for much of the decade. His leadership qualities also earned him the captaincy of his country, but injuries curtailed his progress at Highbury when Bertie Mee replaced Wright and he moved to Hull in July 1970.

In 1973 he succeeded Bill Nicholson at Spurs and three years later he made the move back to Highbury as Mee's replacement, also bringing back Don Howe as his No.2. His arrival sparked a golden era of Irish players at the Club, with stars from both sides of the border providing the heart of the side and Liam Brady the outstanding performer. He also broke the Club transfer record to spend £333,333 on Malcolm Macdonald from Newcastle, but injuries forced the England striker to retire in 1979.

Neill guided Arsenal to three FA Cup Finals in succession from 1978, winning just one - in 1979 against Manchester United. The following year Valencia beat the Gunners 5-4 on penalties in the European Cup-Winners' Cup final.

The fact was that Neill's side had peaked and he watched helplessly as Brady and Frank Stapleton moved to Juventus and Manchester United respectively in successive summers. His tenure came to an end late in 1983, after his last big signing, Charlie Nicholas, started poorly and Walsall won 2-1 at Highbury in the Milk Cup. He was replaced by Don Howe. He later opened sports bars in London and worked in the media, but never returned to management.

NEILL'S STARS

Terry Neill was unlucky to see his best players either underperform, retire early or leave before their prime. His biggest disappointment was that the prolific **Malcolm Macdonald** had to retire early due to a knee injury after less than three seasons at Highbury. It was felt that if he stayed fit, Arsenal could have challenged Nottingham Forest and Liverpool for the title. As disappointing was the early form of Neill's last major signing, **Charlie Nicholas**, from Celtic for £650,000, which is said to have contributed to Neill's sacking in December 1983.

But Neill's side still had a magnificent spine - and it was made in Ireland. **Pat Jennings** followed him from Spurs and gave fantastic service in goal for eight years. **David O'Leary** was one of the outstanding centre-halves of his generation and at the other end fellow Dubliner **Frank Stapleton** was a supreme all-round striker. And between those two was the jewel in the side, **Liam Brady**. The midfielder ran the Arsenal team in the late 1970s with poise, skill and consistency - and a magical left foot.

But the other home nations contributed too. England's **Graham Rix** starred on the left-hand side and **Alan Sunderland** had a habit of scoring vital goals up front with Stapleton. Neill also signed the outstanding full-back of his generation, **Kenny Sansom**, who remains the Club's most-capped player.

Terry Neill became captain of Arsenal in 1962 at just 20 years of age. He later returned to the Club as manager, lifting the FA Cup in 1979.

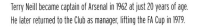

NELSON, Sammy

Born **Belfast, 1 April 1949**
Arsenal appearances **324 (14)**
Arsenal goals **12**
International caps (Northern Ireland) **51**
(1 goal)

A popular joker off the pitch and a whole-hearted, committed left-back on it, Nelson left an indelible mark on Highbury crowds in the 1970s, forming an all-Ulster full-back partnership with Pat Rice. He made his first-team debut in 1969 and was a patient understudy to Bob McNab, who left in 1975. Nelson became a first-team regular for the next five seasons, a virtual ever-present and played in the four major cup finals under Terry Neill. He was briefly suspended by the Club for dropping his shorts in celebration after scoring an equaliser against Coventry in April 1979 (he had scored an own goal earlier in the game), but it merely confirmed his standing as a North Bank favourite. He left for Brighton in 1981. He's now a regular after-dinner speaker and one of the former Arsenal players who work as guides for the Legends Tour around Emirates Stadium.

NEMESIS

Over the years there have been a number of players and clubs that the Arsenal fans have 'loved to hate'. Here are a number of 'arch villains' who always seemed to enjoy success when playing against the Gunners:

TEDDY SHERINGHAM
The former England striker has become an almost panto villain-type opponent to the Highbury crowd since the early 1990s. He has often admitted he doesn't like Arsenal and takes great pleasure in scoring against them and has done so while in the colours of Nottingham Forest, Manchester United, Tottenham Hotspur and Portsmouth.

VALENCIA
An unrivalled European nemesis – the Spanish side beat Arsenal on penalties in the 1980 Cup-Winners' Cup final and narrow defeats at their Mestalla home knocked the Gunners out of the 2001 and 2003 Champions League.

WAYNE ROONEY
Up to summer 2006, the England superstar had scored four goals against Arsenal – and three were decisive strikes. He exploded on to the scene with a 90th-minute winner to end Arsenal's 24-match unbeaten run in October 2002 – becoming the youngest ever Premiership scorer at 16 years and 360 days. He also ended Arsenal's 49-match unbeaten run by scoring one and setting up another for Manchester United in a 2-0 win at Old Trafford two years later. He did the same again with a brilliant performance in another 2-0 win over the Gunners in April 2006.

ROBBIE FOWLER
Another scouser who shot to prominence against Arsenal, Fowler scored the fastest ever Premiership hat-trick in a 3-0 win over the Gunners in 1994 – hitting all three goals in just 4 minutes and 33 seconds. Was it a fluke? The following season he notched up another treble in a 3-1 win over Arsenal at Anfield!

BRENTFORD
The League One outfit from west London have a superb record against the Gunners – and have lost a lower percentage of games against Arsenal than any other capital side. The Bees proved the Gunners' nemesis in the late 1930s, regularly winning at their Griffin Park home. They also did the double against Arsenal in the title run-in of 1937/38, by the skin of their teeth George Allison's side still managed to win their fifth championship. In ten matches between the clubs, Brentford have won five, drawn four – and lost just once.

NICHOLAS, Charlie

Born **Glasgow, 30 December 1961**
Arsenal appearances **184**
Arsenal goals **54**
International caps (Scotland) **20 (5 goals)**

'Champagne Charlie' was the glamour signing of the 1980s. A skilful, exciting showman on the pitch, a media darling and partying bachelor off it, he had a superb 1982/83 season which saw him score 50 goals for Celtic and win the Scottish Footballer of the Year and Scottish PFA Young Player of the Year awards. That form

Charlie Nicholas celebrates the equaliser against Liverpool in the 1987 Littlewoods Cup Final.

attracted huge attention when he revealed his desire to leave Scotland and he turned down Internazionale, Manchester United and Liverpool to move to Highbury in June 1983.

Much-loved on the North Bank, in truth he never fully lived up to all the hype and scored just 11 goals in his first full season. However, he was magnificent in the latter stages of the campaign and scored a memorable double in a 4-2 win at Spurs and then a brilliant individual goal in a 3-2 win in the return match at Highbury in April 1984.

He had a habit of scoring vital goals in big games, and his finest hour came in 1987 when he scored both goals in the Littlewoods Cup Final against Liverpool, but the next season he barely figured in the first team and he moved to Aberdeen in 1988.

Despite his indifferent four-and-a-half years in north London, he is fondly remembered for his occasional brilliance and rapport with the fans. Nicholas admitted he was concerned what the fans reaction would be when he returned in a Celtic shirt for Paul Davis' testimonial match in 1991, but he needn't have worried – the Arsenal fans gave him a tumultuous reception. He is now a forthright media pundit.

NICKNAMES

Every footballer has a nickname. Here are some of the most popular that were heard around the Club's Highbury home:

Willow - Bob Wilson
Chippy - Liam Brady
Willow - Steve Williams
Rodders - Tony Adams
Safe Hands - David Seaman
Merse - Paul Merson
Romford Pele - Ray Parlour
Titi - Thierry Henry
Albert Tatlock - Martin Hayes
Iceman - Dennis Bergkamp
Sunders - Alan Sunderland
Supermac - Malcolm Macdonald
Stroller - George Graham (as a player)
Gaddafi - George Graham (as a manager)
Snouty - Peter Storey

The Iron Man - Wilf Copping
Wee Alec - Alex James
One Chance - Tony Woodcock
Ceefax - Michael Thomas
Faxe - John Jensen
Nutty - Nigel Winterburn
Super Swede - Anders Limpar
Rocky - David Rocastle
Le Professeur - Arsène Wenger
Bobby - Robert Pires
Smudger - Alan Smith
The Horse - Oleg Luzhny
Noddy - Brian Talbot

NIGERIANS

Nwankwo Kanu remains a fans favourite long after departing for pastures new. But he was not the first Nigerian to call Highbury home.

In September 1949 the newly formed Nigerian national side embarked on a groundbreaking two-month tour of Britain and used Highbury as their training base. Huge interest was generated when the Africans arrived, mainly because they refused to wear boots and played in their bare feet. They played eight amateur sides around the country, but always came back to north London for the training facilities.

Gunners manager Tom Whittaker watched the tourists, but didn't feel compelled to take any of their players on trial. Goalkeeper Sam Ibiam later recalled: 'We played with bare feet in England. After the selection, they tried as much as possible to make us play with boots, but we were not used to it. We just threw them away.'

The Nigerian supporters club is one of the newest additions to the Arsenal family. Based in Lagos, it became an official supporters club in September 2005.

NIKE

The American sportswear giant moved into the English football market when it became Arsenal's sole kit manufacturer after taking over from Adidas in the summer of 1994.

Formed in 1971 the company takes its name from the Greek goddess of victory and also provides kits for Manchester United, Juventus, Barcelona and the Brazilian national team.

NO.2s

Behind every great manager is a superb assistant, always on hand with information, advice and a different point of view. Several of Arsenal's managers have been fortunate enough to have quality back-up. Here are five of the finest No.2s ever seen at the Club:

TOM WHITTAKER

Whittaker became Arsenal's first-team trainer in 1927 at the age of 29 and was often leaned on by manager Herbert Chapman for advice and support. When Chapman died in 1934, he and Joe Shaw steered the Club to another title before George Allison took over. Whittaker served under Allison until 1947 when he finally got the top job, winning two titles and an FA Cup before his early death in 1956, at the age of 58.

DON HOWE

The master tactician became first-team coach to Bertie Mee in 1968 and helped the Club to European and Double glory. Howe left in 1971 to take the reins at West Bromwich Albion and later coached Galatasaray in Turkey, before returning to Highbury to work as Terry Neill's No.2. It is no coincidence that his arrival coincided with an upturn in the Club's fortunes, with four cup finals in three years. He later masterminded Wimbledon's 1988 FA Cup win as right-hand man to former Gunners team-mate Bobby Gould.

THEO FOLEY

The perfect foil for hard taskmaster George Graham, the ebullient Irishman was Graham's trusted lieutenant at Millwall and followed him to Highbury in 1986. A popular figure with the players, Foley was an integral part of Arsenal's Littlewoods Cup success of 1987 and 1989 title win. But a year later he shocked the Club when he left to manage Northampton and later worked at Tottenham.

STEWART HOUSTON

After Theo Foley left Highbury, George Graham promoted the Scotsman to be his assistant. A tireless worker with a flair for coaching, he remained at the Club after Graham's departure and worked with new manager Bruce Rioch after a spell as caretaker boss. When Rioch left, he again took over temporarily, but left shortly before Arsène Wenger's arrival in 1996.

PAT RICE

An Arsenal man for the best part of 40 years, the Ulster-born defender brought up in north London was a youth team coach in the George Graham years, twice winning the FA Youth Cup, before he was the shock choice as Arsène Wenger's No.2 in 1996. Since then his local knowledge and passion have proved invaluable to the French manager.

NON-LEAGUE GUNNERS

Many Gunners began their careers in non-league football. **Eddie Hapgood** was signed from Northants minnows Kettering Town for £950 in 1927, while team-mate **George Male** started his football career in east London at Clapton. One of their contemporaries, Wales international half-back **Bob John**, played for Barry Town and Caerphilly before being signed up in January 1922 for a fee of £750.

In the 1950s **Jim Fotheringham** turned out for another Northants side, Corby Town, and **Jimmy Bloomfield**, a prolific scorer in his time at Highbury, was originally an amateur player with Hounslow Town in west London.

Arsenal signed striker **Alan Smith** in the early months of 1987 but loaned him back to Leicester City until the summer. He had originally been plucked from non-league obscurity by the Foxes from Midlands side Alvechurch before his big move to Highbury.

Ian Wright is the most recent former non-league footballer to play for the Club after starting his career at local club Greenwich Borough before moving to Crystal Palace and then Arsenal in September 1991.

Others, in recent years, have moved the other way too - 1971 Double-winning striker **John Radford** ended his career at Bishop's Stortford, later becoming their manager. While **Martin Hayes** - a title winner in 1989 - played for the likes of Crawley Town, Romford, Purfleet and Bishop's Stortford, before following in Radford's footsteps and taking over in the hot-seat at the Hertfordshire club.

NORRIS, Henry

A controversial figure in English football, as Arsenal chairman Henry Norris was the man responsible for Arsenal's move to north London - he engineered the relocation from Woolwich to Highbury in the summer of 1913 at considerable personal expense - and for hiring Herbert Chapman.

Norris was a colourful character. One of London's most renowned businessmen, he made a fortune in the property market, mainly in west London, where he was mayor of Fulham and Conservative MP for Fulham East. He was also, controversially, chairman of Fulham FC when he took charge of ailing Woolwich Arsenal. At once he proposed a merger of the two clubs, but the Football League dismissed the idea. He then launched a bid to move the Gunners to west London to groundshare at Fulham's Craven Cottage home, but that too was unsuccessful. So Norris opted to move the Club north of the river and, after exploring several sites, chose Highbury because of its large population, central location and excellent transport links.

Norris is infamous for persuading the Football League to promote Second Division Arsenal to the top flight in 1919, even though they had finished fifth in Division Two in the last full league season before football was suspended due to the First World War. A controversial move as they were promoted at the expense of several other clubs, including local rivals Tottenham Hotspur. This episode has remained a particularly sore point with Spurs supporters ever since.

Norris appointed Chapman manager in 1925, but was no longer there when Arsenal won their first major trophy, the FA Cup, in 1930. He was forced to step down a year earlier after a secret FA inquiry found him guilty of financial irregularities. He denied the accusation and unsuccessfully sued the FA for libel. He was banned from football and died in 1934 from a heart attack, aged 69.

NORTH BANK

The North Bank was the terrace behind the goal at the Gillespie Road end of Highbury which traditionally housed the hardcore Arsenal supporters. In its heyday roughly 20,000 fans could be accommodated under its dark cavernous roof, which was erected in 1935. Originally called the Laundry End, it first housed the Highbury clock, which Herbert Chapman had ordered for the fans' benefit, when the roof was added the clock was moved to the south end of the stadium.

The *Taylor Report* after the Hillsborough Disaster spelt the end of the old terrace and its final match was 2 May 1992 when Arsenal beat Southampton 5-1. It was demolished and replaced with the 12,263-seater North Bank stand (4,063 in the upper tier and 8,199 in the lower tier). It opened on 14 August 1993 for a match against Coventry City. The stand will be demolished and replaced with housing now the Club are at Emirates Stadium.

NOTTINGHAM FOREST

The east Midlands club claims two very big mentions in Arsenal's history. Firstly, the Gunners play in red because co-founder Fred Beardsley, a former Forest player, went back to his old club to ask for a set of kit for his new club. Forest kindly obliged and gave Arsenal an old set of their red home jerseys. Red has been Arsenal's main colour since. Secondly, nearly 30 years later, on 24 April 1915 Forest were the opponents for Arsenal's last game outside the top flight. Manager George Morrell - in charge the final time - saw his side give him the perfect send off as they ripped the visitors apart at Highbury with a 7-0 win in the old Second Division. Forward Henry King, in his final appearance for Arsenal, was the star of the day, scoring four goals to round off a prolific season.

O'LEARY, David

Born **Dublin, 2 May 1958**
Arsenal appearances **722**
Arsenal goals **14**
International caps **(Eire) 68 (1 goal)**

A Gunners stalwart, O'Leary resisted several lucrative moves away from Highbury to remain at the Club for 20 years. Signed as an apprentice in 1973, he made his Division One debut two years later under manager Bertie Mee. A classy centre-back, he was noted for his excellent positioning and elegant style of play.

In 1982 he was made Club captain by manager Terry Neill and went on to break several appearance records: he was the youngest person to play both 100 and 200 matches and he passed George Arnmstrong's all-time Club record of 621 first-team games in 1989 – scoring twice in a 4-3 win over Norwich in the process. He also holds Arsenal's all-time record for appearances: with 722 first-team games and over 1000 games at all levels.

He picked up a Littlewoods Cup winner's medal in 1987 and two years later won his first title, earning another in 1991. O'Leary ended his Arsenal career in 1993, winning the Coca-Cola Cup and then making his final appearance in the FA Cup Final win over Sheffield Wednesday in May the same year.

He later played for and managed Leeds United and was then manager at Aston Villa until July 2006.

OCH AYE! – Scottish Gunners

If it wasn't for a Scotsman, Arsenal Football Club would not be here today. Kirkcaldy-born David Danskin founded the Club in 1886 and much of the early side was made up of Scottish migrant workers who had headed down south to the factories of the Royal Arsenal for work.

But that is only one of many connections between the Club and Scotland. Some of the earliest managers were also from north of Hadrian's Wall: the likes of Thomas Brown Mitchell, Phil Kelso and George Morrell providing stability in the years before the Great War.

James Jackson – born in Cambuslang but brought up in Australia before moving back to Scotland – was Woolwich Arsenal's skipper in the Club's first ever season in Division One. **Roddy McEachrane** is another Scot who distinguished himself at the Club, staying for 13 years and making 346 appearances – without ever scoring a goal. He also holds the Arsenal Club record for the most appearances by a player without winning a cap or a medal.

Over the years some of the Gunners greatest players came from Scotland: **Alex James** – the fulcrum of the Club's 1930s glory years – made his name as a member of the Wembley Wizards side which humiliated England 5-1 at Wembley in 1928. **Jimmy Logie, Ian McPherson** and **Alex Forbes** – the current chairman of the South African Arsenal supporters club – were major stars of the post-war title-winning sides of 1948 and 1953. Striker **David Herd**, born in Hamilton, was a North Bank goalscoring hero in the late 1950s and was even replaced by the 'English Scotsman' – **Joe Baker**, Liverpool-born and an England international, but brought up north of the border and a Hibernian legend.

The 1971 Double-winners had a strong Scottish spine with **Frank McLintock** skippering a side which also contained goalkeeper **Bob Wilson** – born in Chesterfield to Scottish parents – **George Graham** and Glaswegian youngster **Eddie Kelly**.

However, since those days the influence from Scotland has dwindled, although there have still been some terrace favouites from the north: big defender **Willie Young** was a popular figure in the late 1970s and **Charlie Nicholas** provided some welcome flair in the 1980s.

On the playing front, the last Scots to pull on the red and white were **Paul Dickov** and **Scott Marshall** in the 1990s, but none have appeared for Arsenal in the new millennium. However, on the managerial front recent years have seen Graham return as manager in 1986 to kick-start a new era for the Gunners and his Scottish assistant Stuart Houston twice took on the role of

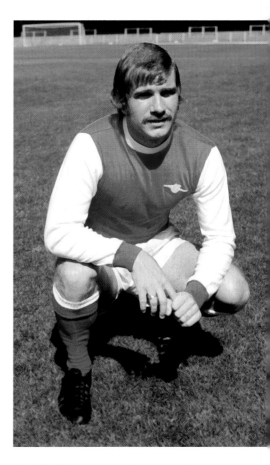

Och aye! Eddie Kelly is one of many Scots to have made an impact in Arsenal's long history.

caretaker manager at Highbury, either side of the appointment of former Scotland captain Bruce Rioch in 1995, a man who paved the way for Arsène Wenger's success with the signing of Dennis Bergkamp.

In total, more than 160 Scots have represented Arsenal.

OLD TRAFFORD

Since Alex Ferguson's arrival in 1986, Old Trafford has played host to some titanic matches between Manchester United and their closest rivals Arsenal. Ferguson's first match against the Gunners, a 2-0 win for United, ended the London Club's 22-game unbeaten run and saw David Rocastle shown a red card.

Controversy has never been far away in subsequent meetings in Manchester. A 1-0 Arsenal win in October 1990 was marred by a mass brawl which resulted in both sides having points deducted. Marc Overmars scored the only goal in a 1-0 win in March 1998 to put Arsenal on their way to their first Premiership trophy, and in May 2002, another 1-0 victory, courtesy of a late Sylvain Wiltord goal, sealed another Premiership title in a bad-tempered affair. In September 2003 there were more fireworks when Patrick Vieira was sent off and Ruud van Nistelrooy blasted a last-minute penalty over the bar as the sides drew 0-0.

Until then Arsenal's most memorable win at Old Trafford probably came in December 1985 when a Charlie Nicholas goal earned a 1-0 win for Arsenal - ending league leaders United's unbeaten start to the season. But United have also enjoyed some famous victories in recent years, notably a 2-0 win in October 2004 which ended Arsenal's 49-game unbeaten record. The Gunners' biggest defeat at the stadium came in February 2001 when United won 6-1 - a remarkable statistic as it was the only time Arsenal conceded any goals in a run of eight Premiership matches.

Arsenal have also played two semi-finals at Old Trafford: beating Spurs 2-1 in 2001 and then overcoming Sheffield United 1-0 in 2003.

OLDEST PLAYER

Jock Rutherford is the oldest player to have represented Arsenal after making his final appearance for the Club in a 1-0 home win over Manchester City on 20 March 1926 at the age of 41 years and 159 days. He had made his debut back in 1913 after moving south from Newcastle and was a regular in the old Division Two side, thus being in an elite band of players who turned out for the Club in south and north London.

Rutherford left Highbury to manage Stoke in April 1923, but soon returned south. In the summer of 1925 he announced his retirement, but changed his mind and stayed on at the start of Herbert Chapman's tenure to provide an experienced voice on the pitch. In all he played 232 matches and scored 27 goals for the Club.

His son John James Rutherford was also on Arsenal's books at the same time as his father, but he played just one League match for the Club.

Ole! Spanish Gunner - Jose Antonio Reyes signed from hometown club Sevilla in January 2004.

OLE! – Spanish Gunners

The Spanish influence at Arsenal has grown in recent years with former youth team player Francis Cagigao, now the Club's Spanish scout, helping open up new opportunities on the Iberian peninsula. Brought up in north London to Spanish parents, Cagigao helped unearth the talents of both **Cesc Fabregas** and **Jose Antonio Reyes**.

It is a strange irony that Lauren was almost the Club's first 'Spaniard'. His family moved from Cameroon to Andalucia when he was a youngster and he first signed as a professional with Sevilla. Despite dual nationality and approaches from the Spanish national team, he opted to represent the country of his birth.

In actual fact Jose Antonio Reyes (born 1 September 1983 in Utrera) was the first Spaniard to play for the Gunners after signing in January 2004 from hometown club Sevilla. A year later he became only the second player in history to be sent off in an FA Cup Final and he also featured as a substitute in the 2006 Champions League Final before moving to Real Madrid on loan, where he won the La Liga title. In 2007 he made his move to the Spanish capital permanent – signing for Real's city rivals Atletico.

Manuel Almunia (born 19 May 1977 in Pamplona) proved a reliable back-up goalkeeper to Jens Lehmann after signing from Albacete in 2003. He waited patiently in the wings – impressing whenever he was called upon for first-team action – before taking his chance in August 2007 after Lehmann was sidelined through injury. Almunia's form even led to talk of an England call-up after his own country ignored his efforts. On 4 April 2008 he was rewarded for his efforts by Arsenal when he signed a new long-term contract that runs until 2012.

Midfielder **Fran Merida**, (born 4 March 1990 in Barcelona) spent 2007/08 on loan at Real Sociedad and is tipped for a bright future at Emirates Stadium after making excellent progress. He signed a new long-term contract with the club in April 2008. 'He is an absolutely amazing player,' is Arsène Wenger's assessment.

Midfield schemer Jimmy Logie earned his only cap for Scotland against Northern Ireland on 5 November 1952 in a 1-1 draw in Glasgow.

ONE-CAP WONDERS

Brian Marwood was the last Gunner to make a solitary appearance for his country when he played in a 1-1 draw in a friendly against Saudi Arabia in Riyadh in November 1988, a match which also saw David Seaman's debut.

The following Gunners made their only appearance for their national sides while playing for the Club.

John Coleman	England	1907
Alex Graham	Scotland	1921
John Butler	England	1924
Alf Baker	England	1927
Herbie Roberts	England	1931
Bernard Joy	England	1936
Arthur Milton	England	1951
Jimmy Logie	Scotland	1952
Danny Clapton	England	1958
Jeff Blockley	England	1972
Jimmy Rimmer	England	1976
Alan Sunderland	England	1980
Brian Marwood	England	1988

ONE-NIL TO THE ARSENAL

In the 1939 movie *The Arsenal Stadium Mystery*, manager George Allison famously said, 'One-Nil to the Arsenal – and that's just how we like it!'

Skip ahead now to 1994 and the chant 'One-Nil to the Arsenal' was *derigeur* on the terraces. Sung to the tune of the Pet Shop Boys song, 'Go West', its origins have long been disputed. But a popular – and on the whole generally accepted – theory is that it was first sung during the European Cup-Winners' Cup run that season. Paris Saint-Germain, Arsenal's opponents in the semi-finals, sang a song to the same tune, 'Allez Paris Saint-Germain' and Arsenal fans quickly adopted it – anglicising the lyrics and bringing it back across the Channel.

Fittingly, Arsenal won the Cup-Winners' Cup final that season, 1-0 against Serie A side Parma!

ONE-NIL WINS

Arsenal have made a name for themselves for winning big matches by the narrowest of margins. Here are a few memorable – and important – victories by a solitary goal:

Arsenal 1–0 Hull City, FA Cup semi-final, March 1930
Arsenal 1–0 Sheffield United, FA Cup Final, April 1936
Arsenal 1–0 Tottenham, League Cup semi-final, November 1968

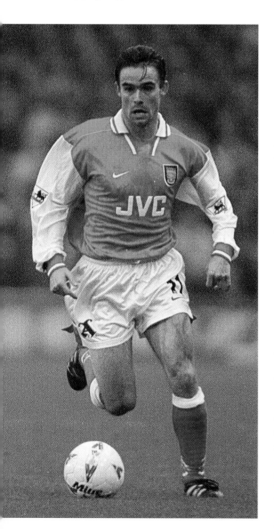

Marc Overmars scores the opening goal of the 1998 FA Cup Final.

Juventus 0–1 Arsenal, ECWC semi-final, second leg, April 1980
Arsenal 1–0 Liverpool, FA Cup semi-final, May 1980
Manchester United 0–1 Arsenal, Division One, October 1990
Liverpool 0–1 Arsenal, Division One, March 1991
Arsenal 1–0 Tottenham, FA Cup semi-final, April 1993
Arsenal 1–0 Paris Saint-Germain, ECWC semi-final, second leg, April 1994
Arsenal 1–0 Parma, ECWC Final, May 1994
Auxerre 0–1 Arsenal, ECWC quarter-final, second leg, April 1995
Manchester United 0–1 Arsenal, Premiership, March 1998
Arsenal 1–0 Southampton, FA Cup Final, May 2003
Real Madrid 0–1 Arsenal, Champions League 1st knockout stage, March 2006
Arsenal 1–0 Villarreal, Champions League semi-final, first leg, April 2006

OTHER ARSENALS AROUND THE WORLD

BEREKUM ARSENAL (GHANA)

A club situated near the border with Ivory Coast, it attained professional status in 1996 and is now a member of Ghana's Star Premier League, gaining four promotions to reach its country's top flight.

ARSENAL DE SARANDI (ARGENTINA)

Based in an area of Buenos Aires, the club was formed in 1957 and reached the top flight for the first time ever in 2002 under the guidance of Jorge Burruchaga, who began his playing career at the club in 1979 and scored the winning goal for Argentina in the 1986 World Cup Final. Arsenal's players sport light blue jerseys with a diagonal red band in honour of the two bigger clubs in the seaside suburb of Avellaneda – Racing (light blue) and Independiente (red). They play their games at the Estadio Julio H. Grondona, a 16,000-capacity stadium affectionately known as the 'Viaduct'. In 2007 'El Arse' beat Mexican giants Club America to win the Copa Sudamericana – the South American equivalent of the UEFA Cup.

ARSENAL KIEV (UKRAINE)

Originally the Russian army side, CSKA Kiev, the club changed its name to Arsenal in 2002 and is now a regular in the Ukraine Premier League. However, the club has always existed in the shadow of top city rivals Dynamo, traditionally the most successful Ukrainian club.

ARSENAL TULA (RUSSIA)

Like their counterparts from London, this side has big military connections as it is named after the munitions works for which the city of Tula – 300 miles south of Moscow – is famous. Tula play in the Russian first division and were one of the first clubs in the country to employ Brazilian players, now a regular practice among many clubs in Russia.

ARSENAL DO MINHO (PORTUGAL)

The nickname of Sporting Club de Braga, because of their distinctive team strip – red shirts with white sleeves.

OVERMARS, Marc

Born **Emst, Netherlands, 29 March 1973**
Arsenal appearances **143**
Arsenal goals **41**
International caps (Holland) **86 (17 goals)**

A flying left-winger with electric pace and an eye for goal, Overmars signed from Ajax Amsterdam in 1997. His speed earned him the nickname 'Roadrunner' in Holland.

After a shaky start at Highbury he became a sensation, scoring vital goals, including the only goal in a 1–0 victory at Manchester United in March 1998, which helped Arsenal win the title, and one in the FA Cup Final that year to secure the Double.

In the summer of 2000, he moved to Barcelona, becoming the most expensive Dutch player ever, but his time in Spain was interrupted by injury and he retired in July 2004. However, he returned to Arsenal and the new Emirates Stadium to take part in Dennis Bergkamp's Testimonial in July 2006.

PARKER, Tom

Born **Woolston, Hampshire,
19 November 1897**
Died **1 November 1987**
Arsenal appearances **294**
Arsenal goals **17**
International caps (England) **1**

The first ever Arsenal captain to win a trophy, Parker is still the holder of the most consecutive appearances in an Arsenal shirt honour.

Herbert Chapman signed the balding right-back from his hometown club Southampton in 1926 and he made his debut in April that year in a 4-2 victory against Blackburn Rovers, the start of his 172 successive games. He was soon made skipper and led the team out for their first appearance in an FA Cup Final in 1927, when Arsenal lost 1-0 to Cardiff. But Parker was back at Wembley as captain three years later when a 2-0 victory over Huddersfield Town gave the Club its first trophy, with the league title triumph following in 1931.

In 1933 he left Highbury for Norwich City where he served two spells as manager. He also went on to manage Southampton and ended his connections with football as the south-coast club's chief scout.

PARLOUR, Ray

See **Romford Pele** on page 171

PARTNERSHIPS

ALEX JAMES & DAVID JACK

Jack doesn't get the recognition he deserves because of James' legendary status in north London, but the duo were deadly together as the finest pair of inside-forwards in English football in the early 1930s.

GEORGE MALE & EDDIE HAPGOOD

The finest full-back pairing in English football in the interwar years, between them they played nearly 700 times for Arsenal and won more than 60 caps for England. Both were born leaders and equally calm under pressure, as well as being fanatically fit sportsmen.

FRANK McLINTOCK & PETER SIMPSON

The central defensive duo who provided a very solid base for the 1971 Double winners. The cultured and laidback Simpson was a perfect foil for the inspirational Scottish captain.

KENNY SANSOM & GRAHAM RIX

In the early 1980s Sansom and Rix enjoyed a superb understanding for both Club and country, with Sansom one of the first full-backs to overlap past his left-wing partner. The left side at Highbury and for the national team was never a 'problem position' with these two in the side.

LEE DIXON, STEVE BOULD, TONY ADAMS & NIGEL WINTERBURN

A remarkable four-man unit which lasted a decade and was the backbone of title wins in 1989, 1991 and 1998 and further triumphs in the FA Cup, the League Cup and the European Cup-Winners' Cup. Led by skipper Tony Adams, Steve Bould was the quiet enforcer alongside him in central defence, while in the full-back berths were the unerringly consistent Lee Dixon on the right and Nigel Winterburn on the left. Between them they clocked up more than 2,000 Arsenal appearances.

EMMANUEL PETIT & PATRICK VIEIRA

Many players have graced the Gunners' midfield over the years, but this is probably the finest pair of central midfielders to have worn red and white. The Gallic duo were the solid engine-room which sealed the 1998 Double and just weeks later they combined for Petit to score the third goal in France's 3-0 World Cup Final win over Brazil.

The ever-reliable skipper Tom Parker (left) talks to his opposite number, Newcastle's Jimmy Nelson, prior to a match on 19 March 1932 at Highbury. Joe Hulme scored to give Arsenal a 1-0 victory.

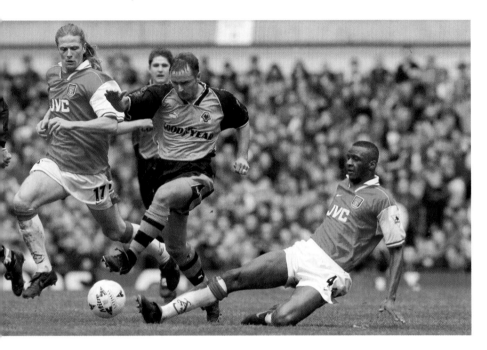

Emmanuel Petit (left) and Patrick Vieira (right) were a formidable midfield barrier during the 1997/98 Double-winning season. Here they combine during the 1-0 FA Cup semi-final over Wolves on 5 April.

PASSING GAME, The

Until the mid-1990s, Arsenal's style of play was a traditional source of criticism from rival fans. But when Bruce Rioch arrived in 1995, that perception began to alter. The signing of Dennis Bergkamp proved a catalyst for the winds of change about to blow through Highbury. It also signalled the new manager's intention to change the Gunners' playing ethos. David Platt was signed at the same time as the Dutchman to improve technique and skill in midfield. Rioch encouraged the players to play the ball through the middle and pass the ball with style rather than move it forward as quickly as possible from the defence, bypassing the midfield, as had often been the case before. Rioch left a year later, but aesthetically Arsenal had improved immeasurably.

Arsène Wenger was appointed manager six weeks after Rioch's departure and he continued the work the previous incumbent had started. Defenders Tony Adams and Steve Bould were encouraged to 'express themselves' by passing the ball on the floor and the two famously put that into practice when Arsenal won the title in 1998, combining brilliantly to show their attacking skills with Bould famously playing in his defensive partner to score against Everton in a 4-0 win to seal the title.

Since then Arsenal have earned a reputation as one of the best passing sides in Europe, with the likes of Bergkamp, Patrick Vieira, Robert Pires and Thierry Henry further enhancing Arsenal's standing as the most attractive team to watch in England.

PENALTIES

Arsenal have been involved in 14 competitive penalty shoot-outs in their history. The first was against Valencia in the 1980 Cup-

Winners' Cup Final, losing 5-4 after a 0-0 draw. Since that day the Gunners have beaten Millwall (1992), Sampdoria (1995), Port Vale (1998), West Ham (1998), Rotherham (2003), Sheffield United (2005), Manchester United (2005) and Doncaster Rovers (2005). Five shoot-outs have been lost: against Manchester United (1993 and 2003), Middlesbrough (1999), Leicester City (2000) and Galatasaray (2000).

Highbury only ever hosted one competi-tive shoot-out: in October 2003 the Gunners scraped past Rotherham 9-8 on penalties after a 1-1 draw in a Carling Cup tie. Sylvain Wiltord scored the decisive spot-kick – after missing the first penalty of the shoot-out.

Aside from shoot-outs there have been some memorable penalties in Arsenal's history... for both right and wrong reasons:

ARSENAL v STOKE CITY, FA CUP SEMI-FINAL, 1971
Arsenal trailed 2-0 to the Potters when Peter Storey pulled one back early in the second half. And he kept his cool to convert a late spot-kick past England keeper Gordon Banks to earn a replay and keep the Double dream alive.

ARSENAL v LUTON TOWN, LITTLEWOODS CUP FINAL, 1988
Arsenal led 2-1 with minutes to go when Nigel Winterburn stepped up to take a spot-kick which would seal the trophy. Andy Dibble saved his effort – and Luton scored twice to win 3-2.

ARSENAL v MANCHESTER UNITED, DIVISION ONE, 1991
Alan Smith completed his hat trick from the spot – sealing the Golden Boot in the process – as newly crowned champions Arsenal beat United 3-1 at a jubilant Highbury.

MANCHESTER UNITED v ARSENAL, FA CUP SEMI-FINAL, 1999
In the final minute with the scores level at 1-1, Dennis Bergkamp stepped up to put Arsenal through to a second successive FA Cup Final. But Peter Schmeichel parried his shot and United won 2-1 in extra time thanks to a wonder goal from Ryan Giggs.

ARSENAL v MANCHESTER CITY, PREMIERSHIP, 2005

Oh dear! Robert Pires and Thierry Henry tried to recreate an audacious Johan Cruyff penalty from 1982 for Ajax. Pires strolled up, attempted to pass to Henry, instead scuffing the top of the ball, and Henry stood bemused as a City defender hoofed it away to safety.

VILLARREAL v ARSENAL, CHAMPIONS LEAGUE SEMI-FINAL, 2006

Jens Lehmann saved a last-gasp spot-kick from Argentinian midfield star Juan Roman Riquelme to put Arsenal through to the Champions League Final.

ARSENAL v WIGAN ATHLETIC, PREMIERSHIP, 2006

Thierry Henry signed off at Highbury when he calmly slotted home from the spot to complete a hat-trick in front of the North Bank in the last ever match at the stadium.

ARSENAL v TOTTENHAM HOTSPUR PREMIER LEAGUE, 2007

With 19 minutes remaining, and the scores level at 1-1, Tottenham had a great chance to take the lead and seal their first away win against the old enemy in 15 years when they were awarded a penalty in front of their own fans. Manuel Almunia, however, denied Robbie Keane, and moments later substitute Nicklas Bendtner scored the Gunners' winner with his first touch.

PETIT, Emmanuel

Born **Dieppe, France, 22 December 1970**
Arsenal appearances **114 (4)**
Arsenal goals **11**
International caps (France) **63 (6 goals)**

The pony-tailed midfielder with a magical left foot joined Arsenal in June 1997, where he was reunited with his former manager at Monaco, Arsène Wenger. He arrived at Highbury as a utility man, playing either at centre-half or full-back, but Wenger switched him to a defensive midfielder and partnered him with fellow Frenchman Patrick Vieira. It was a dream duo, bringing instant success as the crucial axis of the Double-winning side of 1998.

The pair linked up again for France's World Cup-winning side that summer, with Vieira setting up Petit for the third and final goal in France's 3-0 win over Brazil in the final.

Petit left for FC Barcelona in 2000 as part of the deal that took Marc Overmars to the Nou Camp, but he returned to English football with Chelsea a year later. However, injuries took their toll and he announced his retirement from the game in January 2005.

PILL POPPERS

Manager Leslie Knighton came up with a novel way to improve results near the end of his tenure in 1925. The manager was approached by a Harley Street doctor in January that year, prior to an FA Cup match with favourites West Ham, who offered him some 'Courage Pills' to – in the doctor's words – 'tone up the nerves to produce the maximum effort'. Knighton, desperate for a win, agreed and gave each player a tablet an hour before the scheduled kick off. But 50 minutes later the game was called off due to fog. The players, however, were, in the words of Knighton, 'like a flock of lively lions'. All were raring to go – and wildly thirsty. The following Monday the same thing happened. Again, pills were administered, the game was called off, and the players experienced unusual side effects.

Four days later the game finally kicked off and the Arsenal players – buoyed by the pills – dominated from start to finish, but failed to score in a 0-0 draw. 'That night those pills created a riot,' recalled Knighton later, who admitted the thirst of the players became indescribably uncomfortable after the game.

The entire squad refused to take them for the replay and the game ended 2-2. The pills were not in evidence for the final game either as the players refused to have anything to do with them – and the Hammers won 1-0.

To this day, nobody knows what those pills contained.

PIRES, Robert

Born **Reims, France, 29 October 1973**
Arsenal appearances **238 (46)**
Arsenal goals **84**
International caps (France) **79 (14 goals)**

After an unhappy stay at Marseille Robert Pires moved to Arsenal in 2000 as a replacement for Marc Overmars – turning down an approach from Real Madrid at the same time. He had a shaky start in London, but marked his improvement by scoring the winner in the 2001 FA Cup semi-final against Spurs. The following season – despite missing the last two months of the campaign and the World Cup with cruciate ligament damage – he led the Premiership assist charts and was voted both FWA Footballer of the Year and Arsenal's Player of the Season as Arsenal won the Double. The next season he scored the winner against Southampton in the FA Cup Final – just days after scoring his first hat-trick in English football against the Saints at Highbury. He again excelled in the unbeaten 2003/04 season, by now acquiring a reputation for scoring in north London derbies which further endeared him to the fans. He won another FA Cup winner's medal in 2005 and came third in the Premiership scoring chart with 14 goals, but his form slipped in 2005/06 and his season ended on a low when he was sacrificed after 18 minutes against Barcelona in the Champions League Final after goalkeeper Jens Lehmann was sent off. Shortly after he signed for Villarreal.

PLATT, David

Born **Chadderton, Lancashire, 10 June, 1966**
Arsenal appearances **77 (31)**
Arsenal goals **15**
International caps (England) **62 (27 goals)**

The former England captain joined the Gunners from Juventus in the same week as Dennis Bergkamp and his work-rate and industry in the Gunners midfield was a large part of the Club's renaissance under

Bruce Rioch and Arsène Wenger. In his first season he impressed on the big occasion, including a man-of-the-match display in a 1-0 win over Manchester United. He also scored a brilliant winner against United two years later in a 3-2 Highbury win. After trophyless years at Crewe and Aston Villa and his stint in Italy, he realised a dream by winning English honours with Arsenal when he won the Premiership and lifted the FA Cup in 1998 before retiring from playing to take the reins at Sampdoria. He later managed Nottingham Forest and is now a media pundit and successful businessman.

PLAYER OF THE YEAR

The Arsenal Football Supporters' Club Player of the Year award has been won by some of the greatest players in the Club's history since Frank McLintock won the inaugural accolade in 1967. Thierry Henry is the only player to have won the award four times – Liam Brady and Tony Adams have won it on three occasions. Jens Lehmann became the first German to win the honour in 2006.

The full list of winners is as follows:

1967	Frank McLintock	1988	Michael Thomas
1968	John Radford	1989	Alan Smith
1969	Peter Simpson	1990	Tony Adams
1970	George Armstrong	1991	Steve Bould
1971	Bob Wilson	1992	Ian Wright
1972	Pat Rice	1993	Ian Wright
1973	John Radford	1994	Tony Adams
1974	Alan Ball	1995	David Seaman
1975	Jimmy Rimmer	1996	Martin Keown
1976	Liam Brady	1997	Dennis Bergkamp
1977	Frank Stapleton	1998	Ray Parlour
1978	Liam Brady	1999	Nigel Winterburn
1979	Liam Brady	2000	Thierry Henry
1980	Frank Stapleton	2001	Patrick Vieira
1981	Kenny Sansom	2002	Robert Pires
1982	John Hollins	2003	Thierry Henry
1983	Tony Woodcock	2004	Thierry Henry
1984	Charlie Nicholas	2005	Thierry Henry
1985	Stewart Robson	2006	Jens Lehmann
1986	David Rocastle	2007	Cesc Fabregas
1987	Tony Adams	2008	Cesc Fabregas

PLAYERS' HANDBOOK

On the first day of pre-season every professional player at the Hertfordshire training ground is given a little red handbook giving guidance and advice on how to conduct themselves, as well as laying down a few rules. The first page is headed, 'You are an Arsenal Player' and reminds the player it is a 'point of honour' to be 'perfectly balanced' and maintain an 'excellent mental and physical condition'.

Contact details are included for the management of the Club and a list of 16 basic rules is provided. They include Rule 11, which reminds the player that he cannot incur expenses on behalf of the Club without prior permission, and Rule 15, which politely reminds every-one that smoking is banned at various Club premises. Finally, players are reminded that they are expected to conduct themselves at all times in a manner that maintains the good name of the Club.

PLAYING SURFACE

Arsenal spent £15,000 on undersoil heating in 1964 – one of the first English clubs to install such a system. It allowed many games to go ahead that would other-wise have been called off, especially in the winter. But during the 1988/89 season the pitch drew huge criticism when it deteriorated rapidly during the title run-in, ending up covered in sand and strewn with huge divots. The entire pitch was reconstructed that year and since then it has won numerous plaudits, firstly under multi-award-winning groundsman Steve Braddock, and now current head grounds-man Paul Burgess (who took over in September 1999) and his assistant Paul Ashcroft (see Groundsman on page 101). The Highbury playing surface was generally recognised as the best in England.

In October 2005 the Club invested in a new artificial lighting system to ensure the

Former England captain David Platt arrived at Highbury alongside Dennis Bergkamp in July 1995.

DAVID PLATT (CONTINUED) – PREMIERSHIP – THE FULL RECORD

pitch remained in the finest condition. Created by Dutch company SGL, the complex system controls all the factors that contribute to the growth of the pitch: light, temperature, water, air and nutrients, and had already been successfully tested in the Netherlands by PSV Eindhoven.

In January 2006 Mr Burgess turned his attentions to the new Emirates Stadium. 'Of course, we're proud of the quality of the pitch at Highbury,' he said when he took delivery of the system. 'I have great support from Arsène Wenger and the Arsenal board of directors, who have always acknowledged my work. With the help of the latest technology I know we will maintain a pitch consistency at Emirates Stadium that will be the envy of the Premiership.'

PLUMSTEAD COMMON

Arsenal played their first formal fixture on Plumstead Common in January 1887 against Kent neighbours Erith. The Gunners won 6-1 and stayed there for a year until moving to nearby Manor Field, renamed the Manor Ground. The area is still a public space, bounded to the north by Old Mill Road and to the south by Plumstead Common Road. To the east lies Winn's Common.

Arsenal's 12th Premiership campaign was their most impressive to date. The Gunners went the entire season unbeaten and won the title at White Hart Lane, following a 2-2 draw with Tottenham.

PREMIERSHIP – The Full Record

1992/93

P	W	D	L	F	A	Pts
42	15	11	16	40	38	56

1993/94

P	W	D	L	F	A	Pts
42	18	17	7	53	28	71

1994/95

P	W	D	L	F	A	Pts
42	13	12	17	52	49	51

1995/96

P	W	D	L	F	A	Pts
38	17	12	9	49	32	63

1996/97

P	W	D	L	F	A	Pts
38	19	11	8	62	32	68

1997/98

P	W	D	L	F	A	Pts
38	23	9	6	68	33	78

1998/99

P	W	D	L	F	A	Pts
38	22	12	4	59	17	78

1999/2000

P	W	D	L	F	A	Pts
38	22	7	9	73	43	73

2000/01

P	W	D	L	F	A	Pts
38	20	10	8	63	38	70

2001/02

P	W	D	L	F	A	Pts
38	26	9	3	79	36	87

2002/03

P	W	D	L	F	A	Pts
38	23	9	6	85	42	78

2003/04

P	W	D	L	F	A	Pts
38	26	12	0	73	26	90

2004/05

P	W	D	L	F	A	Pts
38	25	8	5	87	36	83

2005/06

P	W	D	L	F	A	Pts
38	20	7	11	68	31	67

2006/07

P	W	D	L	F	A	Pts
38	19	11	8	63	35	68

2007/08

P	W	D	L	F	A	Pts
38	24	11	3	74	31	83

PRESS OFFICE

Arsenal's media department has gradually grown since it was set up in the 1996/97 season when the FA's Clare Tomlinson – now a presenter on Sky Sports – was appointed as a dedicated press officer. Until then, the press contacted individuals at the Club for interview requests and Club news.

Over the years the department – which currently has six full-time staff – has taken on greater responsibility with the Club's profile increasing rapidly. It handles interview requests, which come from all over the world, and holds a press conference before every match for TV, radio and the print media. It offers training to all young players to prepare them for the media glare and oversees all the Club's publications. In recent seasons it has worked hard to promote other aspects of the Club away from the playing side, such as the growing community work and the construction of Emirates Stadium.

PRIMORAC, Boro

Born in Mostar in Yugoslavia (now Bosnia) on 5 December 1954, Boro Primorac won 18 caps as a solid central defender for the former Yugoslavia during the 1980s, captaining the side during their successful 1982 World Cup qualifying campaign. In March 1997 he was appointed as Arsenal's first-team coach, having formerly worked for Cannes and Valenciennes in France and Grampus Eight in Japan.

PROFESSIONALS

The Club were the first south of Birmingham to turn professional – just five years after they were formed. In 1891 a motion was carried at the AGM to embrace professionalism, a proposal made by Jack Humble in a bid for the Club to keep its best players. It was carried by a large majority of members, but was unpopular with the London FA, which fanatically opposed professionalism and forced the Club into exile. Woolwich Arsenal were banned from playing in all competitions except the FA Cup and friendlies. However, just two years later they became the first side from London to be elected to the rapidly expanding national Football League, being granted a place in Division Two.

PROMOTION

Arsenal have not played outside the top flight of English football since 1915 and have only enjoyed two promotion-winning campaigns – although the second one is strongly debated (see Norris, Henry on page 154).

In 1903/04 Woolwich Arsenal gained promotion from the Second Division after finishing runners-up behind Preston North End, winning 21 of their 34 league games and scoring a whopping 91 goals in the process – 29 more than the champions.

The Gunners spent nine seasons in Division One before relegation came in 1913.

In 1914/15 the Club, now in north London, finished fifth and when professional football resumed after the First World War in 1919, the Gunners were elected to Division One after chairman Sir Henry Norris exerted his influence on the Football League, when it announced it was expanding the number of clubs in the top division.

PUBLICATIONS

The Club produces three main publications:

THE MATCHDAY PROGRAMME

This is produced for every first-team home game in all competitions. In 2005/06 it reached a record pagination of 84 pages with exclusive Club news, regular features, competitions and a Junior Gunners section. It has exclusive articles from the manager Arsène Wenger and skipper Thierry Henry. It also features extensive news on the reserves, Academy and Ladies sides.

ARSENAL MAGAZINE

This is a monthly publication which has been produced 'in-house', editorially, since 2002. Regular columnists are comedian and actor Paul Kaye, former player, coach and manager Don Howe and ex-player Paul Merson. Other contributors include respected journalist Brian Glanville, who wrote Cliff Bastin's autobiography over 50 years ago, and former players Lee Dixon and Charlie George. There are a host of regular articles such as 'Perfect Ten' and a monthly diary written by striker Theo Walcott as well as in-depth interviews with first-team players. There is also an extensive Junior Gunners pull-out section. In 2007, the magazine was re-designed with the help of Oxfordshire-based agency Cre8.

OFFICIAL HANDBOOK

This has been produced at the beginning of every season for more than 80 years, covering every single aspect of the Club for the forthcoming campaign. It features biographies on every player, statistics, extensive Club information, profiles of coaching staff and reserve players, and a review of the previous season.

PUBS

Arsenal's short move to Emirates Stadium means fans will barely have to change their pre-match routine (the new stadium is approximately 800 yards from Highbury).

The Club's location in a central London borough means it possibly has the best choice of pubs. Here are some of the better ones within a ten-minute walk:

St Paul's Road, N1: Alwynne Castle
Canonbury Place, N1: Canonbury Tavern
Upper Street, N1: The Famous Cock Tavern
Stroud Green Road, N4: The Old Dairy, The Worlds End
St Thomas's Road, N4: Auld Triangle
Seven Sisters Road, N4: The Twelve Pins
Station Place, Finsbury Park, N4: The Gaslight
Blackstock Road, N5: The Gunners, The Arsenal Tavern, The Woodbine, The Bank of Friendship, The T-Bird
Drayton Park, N5: The Drayton Arms
Holloway Road, N7: Tommy Flynns, Herbert Chapman's, The Coronet, The Bailey, The Lord Nelson, The Old Kings Head

QUACKS

The remarkable Dr Kevin O'Flanagan is well known to older Gunners fans after spending four years with the Club in the immediate years after the Second World War. But three other doctors have also represented the Club.

The first medical man at Arsenal was goalkeeper Dr Leigh Richmond Roose, a Welsh international who played 13 games for Woolwich Arsenal at the Manor Ground in 1911/12. The eccentric doctor was popular among fans and refused to wash his 'lucky shirt' which he wore underneath his goalkeeping jersey.

Dr James Paterson had two spells at Highbury in the 1920s. He set up a practice in nearby Clapton in 1924 after spending four years at Arsenal, before enjoying a return to play in Herbert Chapman's first season.

Dr James Marshall was a Scotsman who arrived from Glasgow Rangers for £4,000 in the 1934/35 season, playing four games during the campaign.

Dr Kevin O'Flanagan, however, remains a truly astonishing sporting figure. He played 16 matches for Arsenal between 1945 and 1949 as a winger, with moderate success. Though he remained an amateur throughout his career - mainly playing for the reserves at Highbury - he also worked at a north London hospital. His remarkable sporting talent saw him represent Ireland at both football and rugby and he was also a keen athlete. He later became a doctor in the Irish Olympic set up and worked for the Sports Medical Council.

QUARRELS

Arsenal's competitive nature has occasionally contributed to some bitter falling outs with opponents. Midfielder Steve Williams memorably tried to take on the entire Watford side after a shock FA Cup defeat at Highbury in 1987, while Ian Wright's personal battles with players and officialdom alike took up thousands of column inches in the national press. Here are three big quarrels in more detail:

LAZIO 1970

'We provided too much good wine,' said Lazio director Dr Giambartolomei, trying to diffuse the situation after the post-match banquet between the Roman side and Arsenal's players. The first leg of the Fairs Cup tie in 1970 had ended 2-2, but the real battle happened after the final whistle when players got involved in a mass brawl after an Italian had set upon Ray Kennedy. Players from both sides took part in the scuffle and, despite Lazio protesting their innocence, UEFA were not fooled and fined them. Bertie Mee dismissed any idea that the second leg should be cancelled and two weeks later Arsenal did their talking on the pitch with a 2-0 win.

NORWICH 1989

David O'Leary's record 622nd appearance came against high-flying Norwich City in November at Highbury. The Canaries side helped form a guard of honour for the Irishman prior to kick-off - but all niceties evaporated at the first whistle. The match culminated in a mass brawl - as Arsenal won 4-3 in the last minute thanks to a contentious penalty - and both sides received huge fines for their part in the fighting.

MANCHESTER UNITED FOR THE PAST 20 YEARS

A 21-man brawl at Old Trafford in 1990 was a mere hors-d'oeuvre for a period of bad feeling between the players of Arsenal and United. Although some people claim that an argument between Nigel Winterburn and Brian McClair after the latter had missed a penalty in an FA Cup match at Highbury in 1987 sparked the animosity.

But whatever the reason for it there have been several examples of serious tension between the players of the two clubs. Ian Wright and Peter Schmeichel had several public spats in the late 1990s, while Martin Keown and Ruud van Nistelrooy shared a mutual dislike for each other in several hot-tempered matches after the Dutchman's arrival at Old Trafford in 2001. And skippers Patrick Vieira and Roy Keane also famously

Quincy Owusu-Abeyie: the former Ajax youngster showed promise before leaving for Spartak Moscow.

clashed live on camera while in the Highbury tunnel prior to a game in February 2005. However, both often made public their admiration for the other despite the occasional cross word and crunching tackle.

QUINCY, Owusu-Abeyie

Born **Amsterdam 15 April 1986**
Arsenal appearances **8 (15)**
Arsenal goals **2**

He joined Arsenal from Ajax in September 2002, but despite immense promise failed to make an impact and, after just 23 appearances – mainly in the Carling Cup – and two goals, the Netherlands Under-21 striker departed for Spartak Moscow for an undisclosed fee in January 2006 and is currently on loan with Celta de Vigo.

QUINN, Mick

Talksport presenter, *Celebrity Fit Club* winner and successful racehorse trainer… Mick Quinn has many hats. And he also holds the honour of being the only opposition player to score a Premiership hat-trick at Highbury. His treble came on the opening day of the 1993/94 season in a shock 3-0 win for Coventry City. Gianluca Vialli also scored three for Chelsea at the old stadium in 1998 in a Worthington Cup tie.

QUINN, Niall (MBE)

Born **Dublin, 6 October 1966**
Arsenal appearances **81 (12)**
Arsenal goals **20**
International appearances (Republic of Ireland) **91 (20 goals)**

The tall Irish striker scored on his debut for Arsenal against Liverpool in December 1985 and averaged a little under a goal every four games as a peripheral first-team player. He enjoyed a fine campaign on George Graham's arrival the following year, earning a Littlewoods Cup winner's medal and playing 35 times, scoring eight goals and setting up numerous others. But his opportunities were dramatically reduced with the arrival of Alan Smith from Leicester City at the end of that season and his Highbury career would never reach such heights again. He made 81 starts in four and a half years before Manchester City came knocking in March 1990 and he moved to Maine Road for around £800,000.

At international level it was a different story, however, and he became the Republic of Ireland's all-time leading scorer with 21 goals in 91 appearances. That figure was surpassed in 2004 by Robbie Keane.

He later moved to Sunderland and was awarded an honorary MBE after donating the proceeds of his testimonial to charity. Since his playing days ended in 2003 he has forged a career as one of the few genuinely know-ledgeable, eloquent football pundits. He also wrote a critically acclaimed auto-biography that was nominated for the William Hill Sports Book of the Year award in 2002.

Quinn has been equally successful since hanging up his boots, taking over as chairman of Sunderland after leading an Irish consortium to buy the club. After an initial spell also managing the Black Cats, he appointed former inter-national team-mate Roy Keane who led the club into the Premier League at the first attempt.

Niall Quinn (centre) holds aloft the Littlewoods Cup in 1987 with the help of captain Kenny Sansom (left). The Irish striker spent five years in and out of the first team before leaving for Manchester City in 1990.

RACING CLUB DE PARIS

On 11 November 1930, Racing Club de Paris, the French capital's top team, hosted Arsenal for a friendly – a fixture that would become a regular one over the next 32 years. That day the Gunners won 7-2 with Jack Lambert scoring four times.

The encounters were originally conceived by Arsenal manager Herbert Chapman and his French counterpart Jean Bernard-Levy as a means of raising money for veterans of the First World War, and the matches were therefore played on, or near to, Armistice Day. Chapman was so involved in the project he even took a flag and ran the line for the inaugural match.

The fixtures gave Chapman's team celebrity status on the other side of the Channel, with several of the leading players given nicknames in the local sporting press. Cliff Bastin became *Le Feu d'Artifice* ('The Firework'), Joe Hulme was *L'Anguille* ('The Eel'), while Alex James' wizardry earned him the title *La Miracle* ('The Miracle').

In all the teams met 26 times (Arsenal won 21 of the encounters), with the only interruption coming between 1939 and 1945, the span of the Second World War. From 1948 onwards the two teams competed for the Jean Bernard-Levy Cup. The two sides met for the last time in 1962 with Arsenal winning 3-0 in Paris.

RADFORD, John

Born **Hemsworth, Yorkshire, 22 February 1947**
Arsenal appearances **482**
Arsenal goals **149**
International caps (England) **2**

John Radford was a long-serving striker and stalwart of the Double-winning season who joined the Club as a teenager and became one of the few players to have scored more than 100 goals for the Club.

He made his debut in 1963 as a 16-year-old and still holds the record as the youngest Gunner to score a hat-trick, netting his treble against Wolves before his 18th birthday in 1965.

He left Highbury in 1976 and played for West Ham and Blackburn before managing and playing for non-league outfit Bishop's Stortford.

Radford is now one of the former Arsenal stars who accompany visitors on the Legends Tour of Emirates Stadium.

RADIO

Arsenal can lay claim to being the most important club in the broadcasting world for a number of notable firsts.

On 22 January 1927, the BBC broadcast its first ever live match for its wireless listeners from Highbury in the 1-1 draw with Sheffield United. Charlie Buchan had the honour of scoring the first 'live' goal before Billy Gillespie levelled for the Blades. The *Radio Times* printed a diagram of the pitch divided into a number of squares so that listeners could follow the ball. The commentator placed the ball by saying it was 'in square 3' or 'in square 5', which is claimed by some to have spawned the phrase 'back to square one'. The match was to be described by Mr HBT Wakelin with 'local colour' provided by Mr CA Lewis. A review in the *Manchester Guardian* said, 'With the chart before one, it was fairly easy to visualise what was actually happening and the cheers and the groans of the spectators help considerably the imagination of the listeners.'

That season the FA Cup Final was also broadcast live for the first time and, again, Arsenal were involved, although it was Cardiff who were the victors at Wembley, taking the cup to Wales for the only time to date after a 1-0 win.

Arsenal launched its own radio show in 2005 available exclusively to subscribers of Arsenal TV Online on the Club's website. Dan Roebuck provides previews, news and full match commentary on every game home and away. A host of former Arsenal players regularly join Dan on the show, including Kenny Sansom, Stewart Robson, Paul Davis, Terry Neill and Nigel Winterburn.

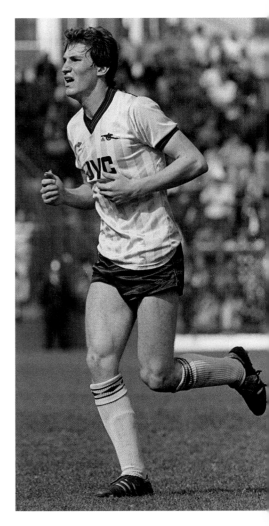

Now a frequent guest on Arsenal radio, Stewart Robson was one of the most promising young Gunners in the early 1980s.

READ ALL ABOUT IT

Arsenal's local newspaper, the *Islington Gazette*, has been covering the Club since it moved to the borough from south east London in the summer of 1913 and the paper hands out a Player of the Year award each season. Former reporter John Cross is now a football journalist on the *Daily Mirror*.

The *Highbury & Islington Express* – an offshoot of the popular *Ham & High* series in Hampstead – also covered the Club from 1996 until its closure in 2004. Gareth A Davies, who writes for the *Daily Telegraph*, was the first journalist for the paper to cover Arsenal followed by sports editor Richard Clarke, who later 'transferred' to Highbury to take charge of arsenal.com (see Website on page 199) and is now managing editor of Arsenal Broadband.

The *Islington Tribune*, part of the *Camden New Journal* stable of independently run newspapers, also has a lively Arsenal section.

For Greater London the *Evening Standard* covers the Club extensively. Actor and author Tom Watt is the Club's 'friend' on the radio in the London area and can be regularly heard on BBC Radio London 94.9FM.

RECORDS

Here is a selection of miscellaneous records and overall English/European club records set by Arsenal or by Arsenal players:

Most Champions League appearances
Thierry Henry - 70

Most European appearances
Thierry Henry - 78

**Consecutive clean sheets
by any side in the Champions League**
10 - achieved in 2005/06

**Successive top-flight wins in one season
by an English club**
13 - achieved in 2001/02 (beat previous record of 11 achieved by Spurs in 1960/61)

**Successive top-flight wins overall
by an English club**
14 - spanning 2001/02 and 2002/03 (beat previous record of 13 achieved by Spurs in 1960)

**Longest unbeaten away sequence
by an English side in Premiership**
27 - 5 April 2003 to 24 October 2004

**Longest unbeaten home sequence
by an English side in the Premiership**
33 - 7 May 2003 to 1 February 2005

**Most top-flight matches in one season
by an English club**
70 - 1979/80
(42 Division One,
11 FA Cup,
9 Cup-Winners' Cup,
7 League Cup,
1 Charity Shield)

**Most away points in a Premiership season
by an English club**
47 - 2001/02

**Most FA Cup Final appearances
by an English club**
17 (record held jointly with Manchester United)

**Successive championship wins
by an English club**
3 - 1930/31, 1931/32 and 1932/33
(record held jointly with
 Huddersfield Town 1923/24, 1924/25, 1925/26,
 Liverpool 1981/82, 1982/83, 1983/84
 and
 Manchester United 1998/99, 1999/2000, 2000/01)

Fewest goals conceded in a Premiership season by an English club
17 - 1998/99

Lowest Championship-winning points total by Arsenal
54 - 1952/53

Most consecutive seasons in top-flight by any English side
81 - 1919/20 to present

REDACTION

REDaction is a cross section of Arsenal fans who have implemented a series of initiatives to improve the atmosphere at Highbury. After consultations with the Fans Forum and the Club, the organisation has worked on several activities on matchdays and has been responsible for banners, the popular singing section and pre-match entertainment. Other successes have included fancy dress days, when they managed to persuade hundreds of fans to dress up for the final league game of the season.

In 2005 the Club allocated REDaction a budget to help in their efforts, and various fanzines and the official Arsenal website have publicised their activities.

RELEGATION

The Gunners were never relegated while playing at Highbury, and have only tasted its bitterness once in their entire history. Back in 1912/13 Woolwich Arsenal finished bottom of the table with a total of 18 points after only three wins in 38 matches, scoring 26 goals and conceding 74, and were relegated to Division Two. That summer they moved to Islington. Two Second Division campaigns followed at their new Highbury home, but in 1919 they were elected back into Division One – and have stayed in the top flight ever since.

REYES, Jose Antonio

See **OLE! - Spanish Gunners** on page 157

Opposite Loyalty personified - club stalwart Pat Rice spent nearly two decades at Highbury as a player, appearing in five FA Cup Finals and winning the Double. He is now Arsène Wenger's trusted right-hand man.

RICE, Pat

Born **Belfast, Ireland, 17 March 1949**
Arsenal appearances **527**
Arsenal goals **13**
International caps (Northern Ireland) **49**

The Ulsterman, who grew up in north London after his family moved across the Irish Sea when he was a child, walked into Highbury off the street and asked for a trial in 1964. He got it and, despite limited talents, his willingness to work hard was spotted early on. Rice grafted and grafted to improve his game and it paid off when he became the regular club right-back for a decade, winning the Double in 1971, captaining Arsenal for three seasons and appearing in five FA Cup Finals. He was also capped 49 times by Northern Ireland.

A natural motivator, Rice demanded toil and sweat from his team-mates right up to his departure to Watford in 1980. At Vicarage Road he began his coaching career under Graham Taylor and returned to Highbury as a youth team coach in 1984. He was briefly caretaker manager in 1996 prior to Arsène Wenger's arrival and was retained by the Frenchman as his No.2, providing local wisdom and knowledge during the French revolution of the past decade, and becoming one of a select band to have had a role in three Doubles in separate decades.

RIOCH, Bruce

MANAGER 1995/96
Born **Aldershot, Hampshire, 6 September 1947**

The former Scotland captain arrived at Highbury in the summer of 1995 after a successful spell at Bolton Wanderers to take over a club that was reeling from months of turmoil following the departure of George Graham. A tough disciplinarian, much like his predecessor, his first job was to strengthen the squad – and his ambition was evident when he enticed Dennis Bergkamp and David Platt to Highbury. Optimism was sky high and the season started positively.

Results were an improvement on the previous campaign and, notably, he began to change the style of football, ushering in a more continental passing game which has since become the norm. The only clouds on the Highbury horizon were a public spat with star striker Ian Wright and Rioch's apparent refusal to sign a contract tying him to the Club.

However, with the quality on the pitch significantly enhanced, the season ended in a flurry with a 2-1 win against his former club ensuring UEFA Cup football the following season. But just days after finally signing a contract he was dismissed as the Gunners board identified a new man to take the Club forward – Arsène Wenger.

RIP – Gunners Who Died Young

This is a list of players and managers who passed away tragically young:

George Armstrong, aged 55 in 2000
Bob Benson, aged 33 in 1916
Alexander Caie, aged 36 in 1914
Tommy Caton, aged 30 in 1993
Herbert Chapman, aged 56 in 1934
Andy Ducat, aged 56 in 1941
Niccolo Galli, aged 17 in 1999
Alex James, aged 51 in 1953
Jack Lambert, aged 38 in 1940
Joseph Powell, aged 26 in 1896
Sidney Pugh, aged 24 in 1944
David Rocastle, aged 33 in 2001
Tom Whittaker, aged 58 in 1956
Paul Vaessen, aged 39 in 2001

RIVALS

Arsenal have had a number of intense rivalries through the years. Here are some of the reasons why:

TOTTENHAM HOTSPUR
Undoubtedly Arsenal's number one rival due to the short distance (approximately 4 miles) and rich history between the two clubs. The north London derby remains one of the biggest club matches in world football.

CHELSEA/WEST HAM UNITED
The two other major London clubs have provided spirited competition over the years with inter-war crowds in excess of 70,000 flocking to Arsenal v Chelsea matches – the biggest crowds between any two London clubs.

HUDDERSFIELD TOWN
The two clubs were traditional rivals well into the 1950s after Arsenal poached Terriers' manager Herbert Chapman in 1925. At the time Town were the leading club side in England and remained a major force for another 30 years.

LIVERPOOL
The most successful side of the north against the most successful from the south – the rivalry culminated in Arsenal's 2-0 title-winning win at Anfield in 1989.

MANCHESTER UNITED
The biggest rivals of the past 20 years, Arsenal and Manchester United have been the two most successful English club sides since the early 1990s and that has been reflected in some memorable contests between the two.

LEEDS UNITED
Arsenal's biggest adversaries during the Bertie Mee years of the late 1960s and early 1970s, United beat Arsenal in Wembley finals in 1968 and 1972, but lost the title to the Gunners in 1971.

RIX, Graham

Born **Doncaster, 23 October 1957**
Arsenal appearances **463**
Arsenal goals **51**
International caps (England) **17**

A left-winger who joined Arsenal as an apprentice in 1974 and was one of a number of youngsters drafted into the first team on Terry Neill's arrival in 1978. A Graham Rix cross provided the winner for Alan Sunderland in the 1979 FA Cup Final but a year later he missed the crucial penalty as Valencia won the Cup-Winners' Cup in a dramatic shootout.

The disappointment toughened him up and he blossomed into the one of the Club's key players in the early 1980s, earning him a place in England's 1982 World Cup squad in Spain. He was given the club captaincy a year later at the age of 25, but a series of injuries to his Achilles tendon affected his progress and he lost his place when George Graham arrived in 1986. Rix figured occasionally before he was loaned to Brentford and eventually moved to Le Havre on a permanent deal in 1987. He later played for Dundee and Chelsea, coaching the latter under Gianluca Vialli and then going on to manage at Portsmouth, Oxford and Hearts.

ROCASTLE, David

Born **Lewisham, London, 2 May 1967**
Died **31 March 2001**
Arsenal appearances **258 (17)**
Arsenal goals **34**
International caps (England) **14**

Until his childhood pal Ian Wright arrived in the late summer of 1991, David Rocastle was the most exciting talent at Highbury since the days of Liam Brady and Malcolm Macdonald. A powerful man who would have been suited to the superfit, technically sound Premiership of the new Millennium, Rocky was a player who had it all. Perfectly balanced, strong as an ox and blessed with ballet-like feet that could dazzle crowds and leave defenders in a twist.

Given his debut by Don Howe in 1985, his flair and strength was an instant hit with the fans, who named him the Player of the Year in 1986. Along with his contemporaries Tony Adams, Martin Hayes, Michael Thomas and Niall Quinn he jumped from the youth ranks to the

Graham Rix escapes the attentions of Steve Foster (left) in a match against Brighton & Hove Albion at Highbury in 1983. Rix's cultured left foot earned him 17 England caps.

same No.7 shirt Rocky wore – scored and dedicated his goal to his predecessor.

Many of the current side had played with him, and his son Ryan was chosen as Arsenal's mascot for the FA Cup Final in May 2001. Arsenal fans also remembered Rocky in April 2006 when his family were invited to the 5–0 win over Aston Villa, a game which was designated David Rocastle Day by the Club. (See also Charities on page 50).

ROMFORD PELE – Ray Parlour

Born **Romford, London, 7 March 1973**
Arsenal appearances **467**
Arsenal goals **32**
International caps (England) **10**

Dubbed the 'Romford Pele' by the fans, Ray Parlour was one of Arsenal's most consistent midfielders in a Highbury career that straddled the George Graham, Bruce Rioch and Arsène Wenger eras. He made his debut in a 2–0 defeat at Liverpool in January 1992 – and promptly conceded a penalty when he fouled Ronnie Rosenthal. He won an FA Cup medal in 1993, but also experienced several off-the-field disciplinary problems before breaking into the side on a regular basis in the 1994/95 season.

When Arsène Wenger arrived in 1996, he was expected to be shown the door. Instead he blossomed under the Frenchman, winning a Double in 1998 and earning the Man of the Match champagne for his performance in the FA Cup Final.

He was capped by England the next year and continued to perform in the Gunners' engine-room alongside Patrick Vieira, excelling in big matches. He scored a hat-trick away at Werder Bremen in the UEFA Cup and was oustanding in a 3–1 defeat of Juventus in the Champions League. He scored a stunning 30-yard goal in the 2002 FA Cup Final against Chelsea and won two more title medals before moving to Middlesbrough in 2004. He later played for Hull City.

first team as George Graham's Young Guns exceeded expectations in 1986/87, winning the Littlewoods Cup and finishing fourth in the First Division. His steady improvement continued as the decade wore on and he won title medals in 1989 and 1991, and made his way into the national side, although a loss of form saw him omitted from the 1990 England World Cup squad.

There was shock among the fans when Graham sanctioned his move to Leeds United for £2m in 1992, but maybe he saw something others didn't. Injuries to his knee and hip had taken their toll and he never scaled such heights again, turning out for Manchester City, Chelsea, Norwich and Malaysian outfit Selangor. It speaks volumes for his honesty and personable nature – always making time to sign autographs and talk to fans – that the followers of all those clubs remember him with affection.

In February 2001 he revealed that he was suffering from non-Hodgkin's lymphoma, a cancer which attacks the immune system. He underwent chemotherapy but died the following month. On the day news emerged of his death, Arsenal hosted Tottenham at Highbury. A minute's silence was impeccably observed and, fittingly, Robert Pires – wearing the

Ray Parlour and Thierry Henry lift the Premiership Trophy in May 2002.
It marked the end of a triumphant week as 7 days earlier Parlour had
scored a 30-yard strike in a 2-0 FA Cup victory.

ROYALTY

Arsenal's royal connections go back to its fledgling days in Woolwich during the Victorian era, when even the Club's name was preceded by the word 'Royal' for a couple of seasons, much like Real Madrid and Royal Antwerp.

In December 1932 HRH The Prince of Wales, later to become the Duke of Windsor, visited Highbury to officially open the new West Stand, before being introduced to the players and then watching the Gunners beat Chelsea 4-1.

According to reports from his homeland the late King Olav V of Norway, who passed away in 1991, was a keen Gunner who enthusiastically supported his side from afar. More recently Prince Harry, unlike his Aston Villa-supporting brother William, has followed Arsenal and was spotted on the North Bank wearing an Arsenal hat and scarf. But he is not the first British royal to support the Club. While Chelsea may be more local to the house of Windsor, the Queen Mother is believed to have followed Arsenal because of her admiration for Denis Compton, who played for the club in the post-war years.

The Duke of Edinburgh has visited Highbury on several occasions on royal duty and even had to fill in for his wife in October 2006 when she was forced to pull out of the official opening of the new Emirates Stadium due to a muscle strain. But Her Majesty made it up to the Club when she invited the entire first-team squad to Buckingham Palace the following April. Midfielder Cesc Fabregas, wide-eyed with astonishment, later revealed that the Queen is, in fact, a secret Gunner, 'It seems the Queen follows football and she told us she was an Arsenal fan,' said the Spaniard, clearly impressed with the reigning monarch's knowledge of the beautiful game. 'She appeared to definitely know who I was and we exchanged a few special words.'

SAFE HANDS – David Seaman

Born **Rotherham, Yorkshire,
19 September 1963**
Arsenal appearances **405**
International caps (England) **75**

The £1.3m fee paid to QPR for Seaman made him the most expensive goalkeeper in the world in the summer of 1990, but within the first weeks of the new season the Arsenal fans were in no doubt it was money well spent. The Gunners won the title the following May and many believe Seaman's astonishing performance in a 1-0 win at Liverpool, when he made several world-class saves, clinched it. It was the start of a glorious career in which he won further titles in 1998 and 2002, as well as four FA Cups, a Coca-Cola Cup and a European Cup-Winners' Cup in 1994, when, along with his defensive colleagues, he gave possibly a career-best performance to keep out Parma.

Seaman earned a reputation as a master at saving penalties after superb shoot-out displays against Millwall and Sampdoria. In Euro 96 he became a national hero for his performances. He remained England's No.1 until the 2002 World Cup, when he was beaten by a freak Ronaldinho winner in the quarter-final against Brazil.

Despite criticism, he continued to win medals at Arsenal. Perhaps his best ever save was his last, when he clawed out Paul Peschisolido's header in the 2003 FA Cup semi-final against Sheffield United to put Arsenal through to a third successive final. His appearance in the Cardiff showdown – a 1-0 win over Southampton – was his final game for the Gunners after 13 years. He moved to Manchester City, but retired shortly after due to a recurring shoulder injury. Seaman remains an English footballing legend.

SAN SIRO

Two of Arsenal's greatest triumphs have come at the 85,000-seater home of Internazionale and AC Milan. Arsenal stunned the normally miserly Internazionale defence with a five-goal salvo that marked Arsène Wenger's biggest ever win on the continent. The famous San Siro was silenced when two goals from Thierry Henry and one each from Fredrik Ljungberg, Edu and Robert Pires secured a 5-1 win in the Champions League in November 2003.

In March 2008 they produced another remarkable away win at the stadium when they beat holders AC Milan 2-0 in the

Edu in action during the 5-1 win against Internazionale at San Siro. The Brazilian scored Arsenal's fourth.

Champions League courtesy of goals by Cesc Fabregas and Emmanuel Adebayor. It also avenged a 2-0 defeat at the stadium 13 years previously by the same opponents in the European Super Cup.

SANSOM, Kenny

Born **Camberwell, London,
26 September 1958**
Arsenal appearances **394**
Goals **6**
International caps (England) **86**

The south Londoner arrived from Crystal Palace in August 1980 in a swap deal which took striker Clive Allen and goalkeeper Paul Barron in the opposite direction as a replacement for Sammy Nelson in the left-back berth.

Over the next eight years with the Club, he cemented his reputation as one of the finest full-backs in world football, becoming Arsenal's most capped player and finally winning the trophy his class and consistency deserved when he skippered the side to Littlewoods Cup success in 1987.

He had made his England debut in 1979, but his international career ended, as did his time with Arsenal, in 1988, when his relationship with manager George Graham soured and the captain's armband was handed to Tony Adams.

Sansom moved to Newcastle and on his return to Highbury in black and white the next season had a goal disallowed for offside. He later played for QPR, Coventry, Everton, Brentford and Watford. He is now an increasingly popular media pundit and also one of the former Arsenal stars who accompany visitors on the Legends Tour of Emirates Stadium.

SANTIAGO BERNABEU

In February 2006 this magnificent stadium was the scene of one of Arsenal's greatest

ever triumphs. Thierry Henry scored a brilliant second-half winner after a mazy run that took him past four Madrid players to earn the Gunners a 1-0 win in the UEFA Champions League at the home of ten-times European champions Real Madrid. It was the first time an English club had beaten the Galacticos on their home patch.

SCHOOLBOYS' ENCLOSURE

This was the name given to the stretch of terrace in front of the north half of the East Stand at Highbury which was reserved for children until the early 1990s. Many young fans had their first taste of Highbury in the paddock, which had cheaper admission than other areas of the ground, before moving on to the North Bank or Clock End in their teens.

SCORING, SCORING, SCORING

Arsenal hold the record for the longest run of consecutive games in which they scored – a magnificent 55-match run which began with a 3-2 defeat against Southampton in the last ever game at The Dell on the final weekend of the 2000/01 season. The next game they drew a blank in was the following December when Manchester United won 2-0 at Old Trafford. In between the Gunners had netted at least once in every Premiership game of the 2001/02 title-winning season and the first 16 league games of the 2002/03 season.

A 3-0 win at Charlton on 14 September 2002 eclipsed Manchester City's 66-year record of scoring in 44 consecutive top flight games – and also set a new Club record of 27 unbeaten league matches, beating the previous record of 26 from 1990/91. The entire run also beat the previous English league record of 46 scoring games set by Chesterfield from 1929 to 1931.

SEAMAN, David

See **Safe Hands** on page 173

SELLEY, Ian

Born **Chertsey, Surrey, 14 June 1974**
Arsenal appearances **60**
Arsenal goals **2**

Tipped for a bright future at Highbury, Selley earned Under 21 caps for England after making his Arsenal debut in 1992 and joined a select group of European winners with an outstanding performance in midfield against Parma in the 1994 Cup-Winners' Cup final. George Graham described him as a 'cool kitten' but a broken leg against Leicester in 1995 cruelly halted his progress and he was sold on to Fulham for £500,000 where he suffered another leg break. Later had spells with Southend and Wimbledon before moving to Woking.

SEMI-FINALS

Arsenal have appeared in a total of 25 FA Cup semi-finals, an English record that leaves them one ahead of Manchester United. Arsenal also equalled United's record of reaching five successive semi-finals between 2001 and 2005, winning four of those games. Their first appearance came in 1906 when Newcastle beat Woolwich Arsenal 3-1 at Stoke. The following year they lost again at the same stage; 3-1 to Sheffield Wednesday at Birmingham's St Andrew's. Arsenal's first successful semi-final came in 1927 when Southampton were beaten 2-1 at Stamford Bridge.

The full record is as follows:

1905/06	Woolwich Arsenal 0-2 Newcastle
1906/07	Woolwich Arsenal 1-3 Sheffield Wednesday
1926/27	Arsenal 2-1 Southampton

Arsenal met Stoke City in the FA Cup semi-final for two consecutive years in the early 1970s and both ties went to a replay. In April 1972 the replay was at Goodison Park. Stoke took the lead through a Jimmy Greenhoff penalty but Charlie George equalised before John Radford (centre) beat Stoke keeper Gordon Banks for the winner.

1927/28	Arsenal 0–1 Blackburn Rovers	1970/71	Arsenal 2–2 Stoke City	(2nd replay)	Arsenal 1–1 Liverpool
1929/30	Arsenal 2–2 Hull City	(replay)		(3rd replay)	Arsenal 1–0 Liverpool
(replay)			Arsenal 2–0 Stoke City	1982/83	Arsenal 1–2 Manchester United
	Arsenal 1–0 Hull City	1971/72	Arsenal 1–1 Stoke City	1990/91	Arsenal 1–3 Tottenham Hotspur
1931/32	Arsenal 1–0 Manchester City	(replay)		1992/93	Arsenal 1–0 Tottenham Hotspur
1935/36	Arsenal 1–0 Grimsby Town		Arsenal 2–1 Stoke City	1997/98	Arsenal 1–0 Wolverhampton
1949/50	Arsenal 2–2 Chelsea	1972/73	Arsenal 1–2 Sunderland		Wanderers
(replay)		1977/78	Arsenal 3–0 Orient	1998/99	Arsenal 0–0 Manchester United
	Arsenal 1–0 Chelsea	1978/79	Arsenal 2–0 Wolverhampton	(replay)	
1951/52	Arsenal 1–1 Chelsea		Wanderers		Arsenal 1–2 Manchester United
(replay)		1979/80	Arsenal 0–0 Liverpool	2000/01	Arsenal 2–1 Tottenham Hotspur
	Arsenal 3–0 Chelsea	(replay)	Arsenal 1–1 Liverpool	2001/02	Arsenal 1–0 Middlesbrough

2002/03	Arsenal 1-0 Sheffield United
2003/04	Arsenal 0-1 Manchester United
2004/05	Arsenal 3-0 Blackburn Rovers

The Gunners have also appeared in the League Cup semi-finals on ten occasions - winning five and losing five.

The full record is as follows:

1968	Arsenal 3-2 Huddersfield
	Huddersfield 1-3 Arsenal
	(Arsenal won 6-3 on agg)
1969	Arsenal 1-0 Tottenham Hotspur
	Tottenham Hotspur 1-1 Arsenal
	(Arsenal won 2-1 on agg)
1978	Liverpool 2-1 Arsenal
	Arsenal 0-0 Liverpool
	(Liverpool won 2-1 on agg)
1983	Arsenal 2-4 Manchester United
	Manchester United 2-1 Arsenal
	(Manchester United won 6-3 on agg)
1987	Arsenal 0-1 Tottenham Hotspur
	Tottenham Hotspur 1-2 Arsenal
	(2-2 on agg)
	(replay)
	Tottenham Hotspur 1-2 Arsenal
1988	Everton 0-1 Arsenal
	Arsenal 3-1 Everton
	(Arsenal won 4-1 on agg)
1993	Crystal Palace 1-3 Arsenal
	Arsenal 2-0 Crystal Palace
	(Arsenal won 5-1 on agg)
1996	Arsenal 2-2 Aston Villa
	Aston Villa 0-0 Arsenal (aet)
	(Aston Villa won on away goals)
1998	Arsenal 2-1 Chelsea
	Chelsea 3-1 Arsenal
	(Chelsea won 4-3 on agg)
2005	Wigan Athletic 1-0 Arsenal
	Arsenal 2-1 Wigan Athletic
	(Wigan won on away goals)

SEVEN SISTERS ROAD

This is the main road link between Arsenal and bitter rivals Tottenham Hotspur. The road was built in 1833 and runs from the A1 in Holloway - Arsenal heartland - to the A10 in Tottenham.

SHAW, Joe

Born Bury, Lancashire, 7 May 1883
Died September 1963
Arsenal appearances 326
Arsenal goals 0

Shaw joined Woolwich Arsenal in 1907 and spent nearly half a century with the Gunners watching the Club change from a small south-east London outfit to the biggest club in the world. He was the first choice left-back for seven seasons, staying with the Club when it moved to Highbury and later succeeding Percy Sands as skipper. In 1921 he became the third player in the Club's history to play 300 games.

After retiring from playing, he became first a coach, and then manager of the reserve side and was caretaker manager after the death of Herbert Chapman in January 1934 helping the Club win a third title. He later went back to the reserve side and was assistant to Tom Whittaker after the war, retiring in 1956 after 49 years with the Club.

SHOPPING

Arsenal's move to Emirates Stadium brought with it a fantastic new shopping experience for fans. 'The Armoury', reflecting the Gunners Woolwich Arsenal heritage, is a massive 10,000 square feet store situated on the west flank of the stadium. The brainchild of retail guru George Davies, the man behind the rise of Next, George at Asda, Per Una at Marks & Spencer, the store is divided into distinct sections, including a Nike area, a gift area, a clothing area, a children's area and even a bed area. One of its most impressive features, not visible to the customer's eye but a vital tool for staff, is the advanced 'electronic point of sale', which allows the club to see at a glance the amount of stock remaining throughout the store, as well as at the smaller 'All Arsenal' outlet in the Northern Bridge building and its sister shop 'The World

of Sport', the Arsenal store, Finsbury Park which is re-opening in summer 2008 after extensive refurbishment.

In addition to these outlets, the Gunners home shopping facilities via Club brochures and the Internet is becoming an increasingly large part of the Club's retail arm as global support continues to grow rapidly.

SMITH, Alan

Born Bromsgrove, Worcestershire, 21 November 1962
Arsenal appearances 345
Arsenal goals 115
International caps (England) 13 (2 goals)

'Smudger' will always be remembered for a stunning 25-yard volley which beat Parma in the Cup-Winners' Cup Final of 1994. But in a career that spanned eight years at Highbury he proved that he offered much more than that single goal. An exceptional header of the ball, who rarely lost possession and worked as tirelessly as anyone, he also found time to find the back of the net with deadly regularity.

Signed from Leicester in 1987, he won the golden boot in the title years of 1989 - scoring at Anfield in the decider - and 1991, and hit four on his European debut in a 6-1 win over Austria Vienna. His goalscoring suffered when Ian Wright arrived, but he enjoyed one final hurrah in Copenhagen - when Wright was out through suspension - before injury forced his retirement the following year having clocked up 115 goals at Highbury. He is now a respected football writer and broadcaster.

SOCCER SCHOOLS

Closing in on its 20th year, the Arsenal Soccer School began as a local course for North London youngsters, but due to its

Joe Shaw (back row, third from left) spent 25 years as a player and a further 24 years as coach and assistant manager at Arsenal. He signed for Woolwich Arsenal in 1907, and was still first-choice full-back when the team moved to Highbury in 1913, playing in the first match at the new stadium on 6 September 1913 against Leicester before which this photograph was taken.

phenomenal success has now moved outside Greater London and, more recently, the UK. The courses have been carefully planned by some of the Gunners senior coaching staff, specializing in coaching and development sessions, covering skills and technique for children of all abilities aged five to fifteen. As well as London and the Home Counties, there are now courses across most of the south of England from Kent to Gloucestershire.

Tens of thousands of youngsters have benefited from the Gunners special coaching methods and it has also been taken across Europe and beyond to Africa and the Middle East. Arsène Wenger says, 'We now have a truly global presence spanning four continents. We are extremely proud of our soccer school programme and that it helps so many youngsters to play football "the Arsenal way".'

SPARTA PRAGUE

The Czech Republic side has a special connection with Arsenal. When Sparta president Dr Petric visited Woolwich Arsenal in 1906, he liked the Gunners kit so much he took a set home. The team abandoned their former striped jerseys and have worn the new colours ever since.

The current Sparta strip is a dark redcurrant colour, and club historians believe this closely resembles the Arsenal kit of the time, which is why a similar strip was worn for the last season at Highbury.

Sparta's Letna Stadium also witnessed Arsenal history in October 2005 when Thierry Henry scored twice to become the leading goalscorer in Gunners' history by surpassing Ian Wright's record of 185 goals.

Current Arsenal midfielder Tomas Rosicky is an ex-Sparta player – and he scored the first goal in a 3-0 over his former employers in a Champions League qualifier in August 2007. The Gunners beat city rivals Slavia later that season, 7-0 – their best ever home win in European competition.

SPONGING FOR A LIVING

Arsenal have an unrivalled record for long-serving physiotherapists for both Club and country. Since 1927 five of the physios have loyally served for more than ten years at Highbury – with two going on to have greater success as managers of the Club.

TOM WHITTAKER (1927/47)
Herbert Chapman is seen as a great footballing revolutionary, but Whittaker was equally visionary in the treatment room. Ironically a knee injury sustained while on an FA tour of Australia cut his playing career short in 1925, but after brilliantly diagnosing his own problem, he decided to study physiotherapy.

Whittaker made sure Highbury was equipped with all the latest medical equipment and his keen appreciation of modern manipulative methods made him a first port of call for men and women from across the sporting spectrum. An Indian Maharaja even visited Highbury in desperation, having been unable to use his arm for two years. Whittaker cured his ailment.

He had immense pride in serving England as trainer, and was the man with

the sponge for the infamous 3-2 win over Italy at Highbury in 1934, when seven Arsenal players were in the England starting line-up.

Whittaker remained trainer for 20 years until he was given the job as Arsenal secretary-manager.

WILLIAM 'BILLY' MILNE (1947/60)
A Scottish wing-half who started out at hometown club Buckie Thistle and moved to Highbury in 1921. He made 124 appearances for Arsenal before a broken leg ended his career in 1927.

Herbert Chapman kept Milne on due to his fanatical fitness regime and kept him on as assistant trainer to Tom Whittaker. He became physio after the war when Whittaker took the top job and despite his Banffshire roots he proudly took up a

In August 2008 Gary Lewin took up the post as permanent first-team physiotherapist for the England national football team after 22 years as the physio at Arsenal. His years of loyal service made him a popular figure at the Club and chants of 'There's only one Gary Lewin,' were commonly heard from the stands during home games.

physio's role with the England team. 'Billy' stayed at Highbury until his retirement in 1960 aged 65 when he was replaced by Bertie Mee. He died in 1975.

BERTIE MEE (1960/66)
The former army sergeant took the physio's job at Highbury in the summer of 1960 after impressing the Club with his work as a rehabilitation officer at the nearby Camden Road Centre. He quickly earned a reputation as a first-class trainer – and a stickler for discipline – among the players. Arsenal shocked the soccer world when, as with Tom Whittaker 19 years before, they appointed their physio as manager six years later. He was initially caretaker boss, but was quickly given the job on a permanent basis and went on to win the Fairs Cup and the Double within five years.

FRED STREET (1971/84)
The friendly, bald-header Londoner had worked with Bertie Mee in hospitals during the 1950s and worked at the Camden Road Centre after Mee left to take the physio's job at Highbury. Mee persuaded him to take the physio's job at Stoke in 1969 and when coach Don Howe took George Wright with him to West Brom, Mee invited Street back down to London. Like Whittaker and Milne before him, the FA asked the Highbury board to release Street for international duty, and he served for two decades under England managers Don Revie, Ron Greenwood, Bobby Robson and Graham Taylor.

GARY LEWIN (1986/2008)
Gary Lewin became the Club's youngest ever physio in 1986 at the age of 22. He had been a goalkeeper at Highbury but, as with Whittaker, Milne and Mee before him, injury cut short his playing days and he embarked on a career in sports medicine. And after precisely 1,205 matches in total as Arsenal's first-team physio, ending at the Stadium of Light in Sunderland in May 2008, Gary, who had also been part-time physio for England for more than a decade, was appointed as the first full-time head of physiotherapy to the Football Association.

SPONSORS

Arsenal Football Club have had four major sponsors: Electronics company JVC is the Club's longest serving sponsor having teamed up with Arsenal in 1981/82 and finally ending its shirt deal in 1998/99. Computer games company Sega/ Dreamcast became the Club's second sponsor for the start of the 1999/2000 the campaign and remained so until the end of 2001/02 Double-winning season. Telecommunications giant O2 joined up with Arsenal in 2002/03 and remained with the Club up to the end of the final season at Highbury, 2005/06. Airline Emirates signed a record £100m sponsorship deal in October 2004, which began in the summer of 2006 when the Club moved to Emirates Stadium. The deal also means the slogan 'Fly Emirates' will adorn the Arsenal shirt for the next eight years.

SPORTSMAN GROUND

This was the name of Royal Arsenal's home for the 1887/88 season after the Club moved from nearby Plumstead. It was situated on the edge of Plumstead Marshes and was an old pig farm. The Gunners only stayed there for one season because of the lack of facilities, moving to the Manor Ground in the summer of 1888, just south of the current Belmarsh high-security prison.

STADIUM TOURS

More than 150,000 people have already taken a look behind the scenes at Emirates Stadium on an official tour of the arena. Due to the Gunners' massive support worldwide and the impact of the new arena, the tours have become a major tourist destination for football-loving visitors to the capital. Fans have the opportunity to see all the areas that are crucial to the team on a matchday – from a walk down the players' tunnel to a seat in the first-team dressing room.

On standard tours, you can visit the Directors Box and the press conference facilities. The club also offers a Legends Tour of the stadium, with a former Arsenal star accompanying fans on the tour. Among those who regularly join supporters are Charlie George, Sammy Nelson, Eddie Kelly, John Radford, Kenny Sansom, Paul Davis and Perry Groves.

And as an additional bonus, all tours include a visit to the club's museum.

STAPLETON, Frank

Born **Dublin, Republic of Ireland, 10 July 1956**
Arsenal appearances **299**
Arsenal goals **108**
International caps (Rep of Ireland) **70**

A classy, intelligent striker who made his debut in 1975 and became yet another star from the then prolific Irish pro-duction line, Stapleton formed a lethal partnership with Malcolm Macdonald in 1976/77 and was top scorer for the following three years, before enduring thewrath of the North Bank when he decided to leave for Manchester United for £900,000 in 1981.

Stapleton won two FA Cups at Old Trafford until moving to Ajax Amsterdam in 1987 and turned out for Bradford City while becoming the leading scorer for the Irish national side with 20 goals, a record since surpassed by Niall Quinn and later Robbie Keane.

STOREY, Peter

Born **Farnham, Surrey, 7 July 1945**
Arsenal appearances **501**
Arsenal goals **17**
International caps (England) **19**

A midfielder enforcer in the Roy Keane mould, Peter Storey made few friends outside Highbury for his abrasive take-no-prisoners style. He made his debut in 1965 against Leicester as a full-back, capable of playing on either flank, but Bertie Mee saw more potential for him in the thick of the action and he was converted to a defensive mid-fielder. He was capped 19 times by England manager Sir Alf Ramsey and won the Fairs Cup and the league and Cup Double, staying until 1976 when he was transferred to Fulham.

STRONG, Geoff

Born **Kirkheaton, Northumberland, 19 September 1937**
Arsenal appearances **137**
Arsenal goals **77**

Since the war it could be argued Arsenal haven't had such a deadly two-pronged attack as Geoff Strong and Joe Baker. The big Geordie scored on his Gunners debut in 1960, aged 23, against his local side Newcastle United. He signed for the Gunners after completing his national service and greedily scored goals, equally deadly with either foot or head. The pair hit 56 between them in 1963/64 season, but Strong became disgruntled with the lack of trophies at Highbury and moved to Liverpool in November 1964 where he satisfied his desire for medals under Bill Shankly.

SUNDERLAND, Alan

Born **Mexborough, Yorkshire, 7 January 1953**
Arsenal appearances **277**
Arsenal goals **91**
International caps (England) **1**

Alan Sunderland earned himself iconic status in the eyes of Arsenal fans on a sweltering hot May afternoon at Wembley in May 1979. The Yorkshireman's late winner, when Manchester United had appeared to have all but snatched a draw

from the jaws of defeat in the FA Cup Final, ensured the game is remembered as one of the greatest ever finals.

Signed from Wolves in 1977, 'Sunders' was never prolific, but his cunning and guile regularly set up scoring chances for others, and he had a particular liking for the FA Cup, also scoring the quickest ever semi-final goal against Liverpool in 1980, getting on the scoresheet with just 13 seconds on the clock.

A solitary – and much prized – England cap came in 1980.

He became a publican when he retired and now lives in Malta, where he managed local side Birkirkara FC. He also appears on English TV occasionally as a media pundit.

SUPER SWEDES

There have been several notable Swedes at Highbury – with five representing the club up to the end of the 2007/08 season. **Anders Limpar** became the club's first modern-day foreign star when George Graham signed him from Cremonese in 1990. His impact was immediate with a string of match-winning performances and he cultivated a close relationship with the adoring North Bank.

After Limpar's departure to Everton, **Stefan Schwarz** arrived from Benfica and spent one promising season with the Club, scoring a vital free-kick against Sampdoria in the Cup-Winners' Cup, before leaving for Fiorentina in Italy.

Fredrik Ljungberg, like Limpar, enjoyed a wonderful rapport with the fans from the moment he made a scoring debut against

Manchester United in 1998. During nine seasons with the club, he won two title medals and three FA Cups -netting in the 2001 and 2002 Finals – before moving to West Ham in 2007.

Goalkeeper **Rami Shabaan**, born in Sweden to an Egyptian father and Finnish mother, played five times for the club after arriving from Djurgardens in 2002 – including a Champions League away win against Roma and a 3-0 home win in the north London derby. After a loan spell at West Ham he moved to Fredrikstad in his home country in 2006 and has since been capped by the Swedish national side.

Seb Larsson joined the Arsenal Academy in 2001 and made his first-team debut against Manchester City in 2004. He played three league matches for the club before moving to Birmingham City permanently after a loan period.

SUPPORTERS

Arsenal has a huge fanbase that now extends to all four corners of the globe.

The Club's heartland remains Holloway, Finsbury Park, Highbury, Archway and Finsbury, coupled with the home counties of Essex, Hertfordshire, Bucks, Middlesex and Bedfordshire, as many Londoners moved out to the provinces in the years following World War Two.

English football's enduring popularity has meant Arsenal have always had pockets of fans in areas such as Scandinavia and the Middle East. But with the Premiership going global on a massive scale in the 1990s – and Arsenal enjoying their longest spell of success since the 1930s – fans soon stretched in great numbers all over the British Isles. With swathes of foreign players joining the Club, notably French and African, and satellite television sending Arsenal matches across the planet, it saw Arsenal's popularity increase sharply.

Now, rather than a north London club, Arsenal are truly global. A 2005 report commissioned by Granada Ventures – Arsenal's commercial partners – claims Arsenal have a worldwide fanbase of around 27 million fans, making it the third best-supported club on the planet.

Opposite Alan Sunderland's finest hour. The striker (far right) turns away after scoring a dramatic last-gasp winner in the 1979 FA Cup Final at Wembley as Manchester United goalkeeper Gary Bailey (left) and defenders Jimmy Nicholl and Gordon McQueen look dejected.

Right We love you Freddie: Fans' favourite Fredrik Ljungberg wheels away after scoring a goal. In August 2006 the proud Swede was named captain of his country.

SUPPORTERS' CLUBS

Arsenal currently has around 90 official supporters' clubs around the world, but the figure is growing almost on a monthly basis. By the end of 2005 there were 19 in Great Britain, Northern Ireland and the Republic of Ireland had 35 and the rest were overseas.

The main supporters' club was formed at the beginning of the 1949/50 season and has produced a monthly magazine – *Gunflash* – since January 1950. Before he died in 1980, founder Richard Jones told journalist Vince Wright, a regular contributor to *Gunflash*, 'I thought it was about time that a club of Arsenal's standing had a supporters' club, so I called a meeting at Islington Town Hall one Sunday. The response was very encouraging with about 600 people turning up and we've not looked back.' The Club has always enjoyed close links with the supporters' club, located behind the old North Bank stand in St Thomas's Road, with former goalkeeper Bob Wilson as its president.

Many overseas supporters' clubs are extremely active and make regular trips to Highbury, particularly the Iceland and Denmark associations, who have large numbers of enthusiastic followers. Since 2004 Arsenal have organised several inter-club football tournaments on the pitch with supporters from several continents travelling to Highbury. The first year the Milton Keynes branch emerged victorious and in 2005 Hastings won the tournament as the number of entrants more than quadrupled.

In 2001 Arsenal employed a full-time supporters liaison officer. Since 1978 she had worked in a similar role at the FA.

Left Swedish winger Anders Limpar became the first major foreign player to succeed at Highbury when George Graham signed him from Italian club Cremonese in 1990. His pace, close control and ability to score important goals endeared him to the fans on the North Bank.

Right George Swindin stretches to paw the ball away and deny Newcastle United striker Jackie Milburn in the 1952 FA Cup Final.

SWINDIN, George

MANAGER 1958/62
Born Campsall, Yorkshire, 4 December 1914
Died 27 October 2005
Arsenal appearances 297

Recognised as the finest uncapped post-war goalkeeper in England, Swindin won title medals in 1938 and 1948. Brave and with solid arms to repel the hardest of shots, Swindin was in goal for the 1950 FA Cup success, a 2-0 victory over Liverpool, but left after his 39th birthday in February 1954 to become player-manager at Peterborough.

Four years later he succeeded Jack Crayston as Arsenal boss but, after a promising third-place in his first season, Arsenal slipped into mediocrity again. He left in 1962 and went on to manage Norwich, Cardiff, Kettering and Corby before running a garage in Northants until his retirement.

SWISS GUNNERS

Arsenal provided the Swiss national side with its central defensive duo for the 2006 World Cup:

PHILIPPE SENDEROS
Born Geneva, Switzerland,
14 February 1985
Arsenal appearances 103 (13)
Arsenal goals 4
International caps (Switzerland) 31
(3 goals)

Born to a Spanish father and a Serbian mother, the 6ft 1in defender captained Switzerland to the 2002 European Under-17s Championships and then turned down a host of top clubs to move to Highbury. A burly defender not too dissimilar to Steve Bould in his pomp, Senderos finished both 2004/05 and 2005/06 seasons as a first-team regular, but also suffered a loss of form and injuries. Senderos, who speaks five languages, has become a rock at the heart of the Swiss defence and in 2006 was named Swiss Player of the Year.

He continued to impress as a solid deputy for first choice centre-halves William Gallas and Kolo Toure and, during an extended run in the side in second half of the 2007/2008 campaign, he passed the 100 appearances mark for the Gunners as he prepared to play his part in Switzerland's ultimately unsuccessful Euro 2008 campaign.

JOHAN DJOUROU
Born Ivory Coast, 18 January 1987
Arsenal appearances 42 (6)
Arsenal goals 0
International caps (Switzerland) 17 (1 goal)

Djourou is forming a strong bond with compatriot Senderos for both Club and country. Born in the Ivory Coast but brought up in Switzerland, the defender arrived at Highbury from Swiss outfit Etoile-Carouge and was a member of the Swiss European Under-19s Championship squad in 2004. He played in the Carling Cup on several occasions before making his full Premiership debut for Arsenal in the 7-0 victory over Middlesbrough in January 2006, playing alongside Senderos. He made his international debut in March of that year again playing alongside Senderos. Djourou spent an impressive loan spell at Birmingham City in the first half of the 2007/08 season before his manager recalled him to the Gunners squad in January 2008 as defensive cover.

Swiss timing: Philippe Senderos (left) celebrates a goal with compatriot Johan Djourou.

TALBOT, Brian

Born **Ipswich, 21 July 1953**
Arsenal appearances **316**
Arsenal goals **49**
International caps (England) **6**

The tireless midfielder starred for hometown club Ipswich in their 1978 FA Cup Final win over Arsenal before moving to Highbury the following January for £450,000.

He became the first player to win the trophy with two different clubs in successive years in 1979, scoring in Arsenal's 3-2 win over Manchester United at Wembley.

Talbot netted in the semi-final against Liverpool a year later to set up a third appearance in the final in as many years, and continued to score frequently in his remaining five years at Highbury, averaging roughly one in every six games.

He occasionally scored spectacular free kicks while continuing to snap at the heels of opposing midfielders in his role patrolling in front of the back four.

He left for Watford in 1985 and later managed Aldershot, Rushden and Diamonds, and Oxford United.

T

Arsenal's Brian Talbot celebrates after scoring and giving his team a 12th minute lead over Liverpool during their third replay of the FA Cup semi-final match at Highfield Road, Coventry, on 1 May 1980.

TAPSCOTT, Derek

Born **Barry, Wales, 30 June 1932**
Died **12 June 2008**
Arsenal appearances **132**
Arsenal goals **68**
International caps (Wales) **14 (4 goals)**

Barry Town forward 'Tappy' Tapscott - one of 16 children - had no idea where he was heading to when he reached Paddington Station in April 1954 until his manager Bill Jones produced two underground tickets to Arsenal. 'I couldn't believe I was signing for the biggest club in the country,' he recalls.

But he certainly knew where the net was, scoring 68 times in his four years at Highbury, including two on his debut against Liverpool (on the same day a broken leg ended Joe Mercer's career) and twice ending the season as the Club's leading scorer.

Arsenal sold him for £10,000 to Cardiff in 1958 - making an £8,000 profit - where he scored more than a 100 goals before retiring in 1970. Sadly, Tapscott died in June 2008.

TEENAGE KICKS

There have been a number of talented teenagers who have made an impact at the Club:

Andy Ducat (19)
He scored twice in the 4-3 win over Newcastle on Christmas Day 1905.

Cliff Bastin (17)
Snapped up from Exeter after just 17 games for the Grecians and thrown straight into the Arsenal side, he held the Club's leading scorer record for more than 50 years.

Gerry Ward (16)
Still the youngest Arsenal player to appear in the league at the age of 16 years and 321 days against Huddersfield Town on 22 August 1953.

John Radford (17)
Made his debut aged 17 years and 28 days in 1963 - and hit a hat-trick against Wolves aged 17 years and 315 days, still the youngest ever treble scorer in an Arsenal shirt.

Eddie Kelly (18)
Glaswegian midfielder scored a blistering effort in the 1970 Fairs Cup Final a month before his 19th birthday.

Charlie George (19)
Exploded on to the scene with a double goal salvo in Fairs Cup semi-final against Ajax in 1970. Months earlier he was sent off against Glentoran in the same competition.

Ray Kennedy (18)
Scored the vital away goal in 1970 Fairs Cup Final. Also a Double-winner two months before his 20th birthday.

Liam Brady (17)
Made his league debut in 1973 aged 17 and was a first-team regular the following season, forming a midfield partnership with England star Alan Ball.

Paul Vaessen (18)
Scored the winner against Juventus in Turin in the Cup-Winners' Cup semi-final in 1980.

Stewart Robson (17)
Made his debut a month after his 17th birthday in December 1981 and was a first-team regular before his 18th. Seen by many at the time as a future England captain.

Tony Adams (17)
A born leader who made his first-team bow aged 17 at home to Sunderland in November 1983 and within four years was an England defender and the Club's youngest ever captain.

Niall Quinn (19)
Scored on his debut against champions-elect Liverpool in December 1985.

Ray Parlour (18)
Broke into the first-team as a teenager at Liverpool in 1992 and became the last link between the Graham and Wenger eras after a trophy-laden Highbury career.

Teenage Kicks: Theo Walcott, 17, became the youngest player to appear for England's senior side before he had even turned out for the Gunners' first team.

Jermaine Pennant (15)
Signed from Notts County when he was still only 15 and became youngest-ever Arsenal player in 1999 when he played against Middlesbrough in the Carling Cup aged 16 years and 319 days.

Cesc Fabregas (16)
Took Pennant's crown as the youngest Arsenal debutant when he played against Rotherham aged just 16 years and 177 days. Also the youngest goalscorer in Arsenal's history.

Theo Walcott (16)
Snapped up for a world-record fee for a teen-ager of a minimum £5m in January 2006, he became the youngest ever player to appear for England, making his debut in May the same year against Hungary at Old Trafford 75 days after his 17th birthday - before he had made a first-team start at Highbury.

TESTIMONIALS

Testimonials are traditionally awarded to players who give ten years' unbroken service to a Club, although the first ever Arsenal testimonial was a tribute match for defender Bob Benson, who died after a game at Highbury in 1916. In total, Highbury hosted 23 testimonials... and the first game at Emirates Stadium was also a testimonial, for Dennis Bergkamp. David O'Leary and Tony Adams are the only two Gunners to have been awarded two testimonials.

THE LIST IN FULL:

Bob Benson's Widow Benefit Match,
6 May 1916
Arsenal 2-2 Rest of London Combination

Jack Kelsey Testimonial, 20 May 1963
Arsenal 2-2 Glasgow Rangers

George Armstrong Testimonial,
12 March 1974
Arsenal 1-3 FC Barcelona

Peter Storey Testimonial, 9 December 1975
Arsenal 2-1 Feyenoord (Neth)

Peter Simpson Testimonial, 9 October 1976
Arsenal 1-2 Tottenham Hotspur

John Radford Testimonial, 10 May 1977
Arsenal 5-0 Hajduk Split

Pat Rice Testimonial, 22 November 1977
Arsenal 1-3 Tottenham Hotspur

Ted Drake Testimonial, 11 September 1979
Arsenal 2-0 Fulham

Sammy Nelson Testimonial,
25 November 1980
Arsenal 0-0 Glasgow Celtic

Pat Jennings Testimonial, 8 May 1985
Arsenal 2-3 Tottenham Hotspur

David O'Leary Testimonial,
5 August 1986
Arsenal 0-2 Glasgow Celtic

Graham Rix Testimonial,
13 October 1990
Arsenal 2-5 Tottenham Hotspur

Ray Kennedy Testimonial, 27 April 1991
Arsenal 1-3 Liverpool

Paul Davis Testimonial, 30 July 1991
Arsenal 2-2 Glasgow Celtic

David O'Leary Farewell Match,
17 May 1994
Arsenal 4-4 Manchester United

Tony Adams Testimonial, 13 August 1994
Arsenal 1-3 Crystal Palace

Alan Smith Benefit Match,
10 November 1995
Arsenal 2-0 Sampdoria

Paul Merson Benefit Match, 8 May 1996
Arsenal XI 8-5 International Select XI

Nigel Winterburn Testimonial, 13 May 1997
Arsenal 3-3 Glasgow Rangers

Lee Dixon Testimonial, 8 November 1999
Arsenal 3-1 Real Madrid CF

David Seaman Testimonial, 22 May 2001
Arsenal 0-2 FC Barcelona

Tony Adams Testimonial, 13 May 2002
Arsenal 1-1 Glasgow Celtic

Martin Keown Testimonial, 17 May 2004
Arsenal 6-0 England XI

Dennis Bergkamp Testimonial,
22 July 2006
Arsenal 2-1 Ajax Amsterdam

THOMAS, Michael

Born **Lambeth, London, 24 August 1967**
Arsenal appearances **206**
Arsenal goals **30**
International caps (England) **2**

Michael Thomas will go down in the annals of soccer history for scoring the injury-time goal at Anfield on 26 May 1989 which gave Arsenal a dramatic title victory.

A full-back converted to a midfielder, it was a highpoint he would never reach again. A long Highbury career looked a certainty, but fell out with manager George Graham shortly after, his performances suffered and his days were numbered in north London.

Ironically he moved to, of all places, Liverpool, after winning another league title medal in 1991 - where he scored in the 1992 FA Cup Final success over Sunderland, and he wound down his career with stints at Middlesbrough, Benfica and Wimbledon.

TIME CAPSULE

Arsenal have filled a time capsule, on view to supporters at Emirates Stadium, with nearly 40 items - 25 of which have been chosen by supporters. Memories and mementoes from Highbury past and present in the capsule include an original David Rocastle shirt, a captain's armband worn by Tony Adams and a replica model of Highbury.

The fans chose the following items:
1. A list of all Arsenal players ever.
2. Tony Adams' captain's armband.
3. A piece of Highbury turf.
4. Every Arsenal home shirt.
5. A replica model of Highbury.
6. A piece of marble from the Marble Halls.
7. An aerial picture of Highbury.
8. A Highbury flag.
9. A record of all matches played at Highbury.
10. A picture of Ian Wright's celebration after his record-breaking goal.
11. A video of the history of Arsenal from 1886 - present.

12. A history of the Club crest.
13. A shirt signed by the current squad.
14. Pictures of all Arsenal managers.
15. Pictures of all captains in sequence.
16. A video montage of memorable moments in the Club's history.
17. A replica of the clock from the Clock End.
18. A copy of a newspaper from the day the capsule was buried.
19. A picture of the old North Bank crowd.
20. A picture or replica of all trophies won.
21. A Highbury match ticket.
22. David Rocastle's shirt.
23. A guided tour of Highbury on video.
24. A picture of the famous back four.
25. A fans' message book.

TOP FLIGHT

Arsenal boast the proud record for the longest uninterrupted spell in the top flight of English football. The Club's last league game outside the top division was a 7-0 home win over Nottingham Forest in April 1915. The 2008/09 season was the 82nd consecutive campaign Arsenal had begun in the top tier. Everton are some way behind in second place having stayed in the top division since 1954. Before the Gunners, Sunderland were the holders of this record. They were elected into the football league in 1890, becoming the first team to join after the Football League's birth in 1888, and stayed in the top flight until 1957/58.

TOTTENHAM HOTSPUR

Arsenal's biggest rivals are situated just four miles north, up the Seven Sisters Road. Formed in 1882, Spurs have traditionally been one of the biggest clubs in England and are one of only four clubs to have won the Double. They have won two titles - the last in 1961 - and were the first English side to win a European trophy in 1963.

There is no love lost in games between Arsenal and Spurs with time failing to diminish a fierce rivalry. The Gunners have played them on 151 occasions, with the first

meeting between the two sides a friendly on 11 November 1887. Royal Arsenal trailed 2-1 with 15 minutes to go when the match was abandoned due to bad light. The first league match between the two clubs was in the First Division, on 4 December 1909. Arsenal won 1-0, but Spurs only became their main rivals when the Gunners moved to Islington in 1913.

Of those 151 games, Arsenal have emerged victorious 63 times while Spurs have won 49. David O'Leary holds the record for most appearances against Spurs with 35 in 18 years, while Gary Mabbutt is Spurs' record-holder with 31.

First competitive match against Spurs
4 Dec 1909 (h - Manor Ground, Plumstead) won 1-0 (Lawrence)

Biggest home win over Spurs
5-1 (20 Oct 1934 - league) (Drake 3, Beasley, Evans (og))

Biggest away win over Spurs
6-0 (6 March 1935 - league) (Kirchen 2, Drake 2, Dougall, Bastin (p))

Biggest home defeat to Spurs
0-3 (14 December 1912 - league)
0-3 (27 February 1954 - league)

Biggest away defeat to Spurs
0-5 (25 December 1911 - league)
0-5 (4 April 1983 - league)

TOURE, Kolo

Born **Bouake, Ivory Coast, 19 March 1981**
Arsenal appearances **257 (28)**
Arsenal goals **13**
International caps (Ivory Coast) **57**
(13 goals)

The Ivorian defender with the big smile and electrifying pace is, for many, the unofficial captain of the side. Arriving from his native country in 2002, he was initially thought of

as a utility man and was played in midfield, defence and even as an attacker. But he soon settled as a centre-back partner to Sol Campbell and won the FA Cup in 2003 followed by the title the next season. In 2005 he earned another FA Cup winner's medal and has rarely been out of the side since then. He also played a big part in Arsenal's run to the 2006 Champions League Final - scoring the winner in the home leg of the semi-final against Villarreal. He has been a regular for his country since 2000.

TRADEMARKS

Some players added their own trademarks to their kit and style:

Alex James - baggy trousers
The little Scot was known throughout the country for his long shorts, made famous by various drawings of James by popular cartoonist of the time, Tom Brewster.

Denis Compton - slicked-down hair
Legendary Middlesex cricketer and Arsenal winger was outstanding with bat and ball, but his slicked down jet-black hair earned him the title the 'Brylcreem Boy'.

Alan Ball - fancy footwear
The midfield star donned his now legendary white boots as part of an advertising deal in the early 1970s.

George Armstrong - long arms
Long-serving winger George Armstrong regularly ran up and down the line while grabbing the cuffs of his long sleeves.

Charlie George - long locks
Rebellious George arrived at Highbury with a popular Mod skinhead cut, but became famous for his trademark long, floppy hair in the 1970/71 Double season.

Charlie Nicholas - lovely legs
The Scottish striker was a 1980s pin-up and sent female pulses racing further by pulling his already short shorts up and folding them over at the top.

Trademarks: Denis Compton (left) sports his famous 'Bryclreem Boy' hairstyle as he lines up alongside brother Leslie.

Sleeves
Since the 1930s the team always takes to the field with all players wearing the same style shirt – even down to the length of their sleeves, which is decided by the Club captain.

Metropolitan Police Band
For many years the marching band would entertain the Highbury crowd at half time. For the final match at Highbury in May 2006 the band returned along with police tenor Alex Morgan, who regularly sang for the Highbury crowds until the early 1980s.

TRAINING GROUND

Until 1961, the Arsenal players used to train at Highbury, running around a cinder track which encircled the pitch, playing on a shale surface behind by the Clock End and lifting weights in the stadium gym. The Club then moved its training operation to the former University College of London's Student Union site in London Colney, Hertfordshire.

That has since been replaced by a state-of-the-art 143-acre training centre in adjacent Shenley. The centre has ten full-size pitches – two of which have undersoil heating – maintained by former Highbury head groundsman Steve Braddock's team and it stages youth team matches and reserve friendlies. Arsène Wenger was a key figure in the development of the centre, working with his coaching and medical team to design the contents and layout of the building.

Indoors the facility boasts six changing rooms, a steamroom, a swimming pool with adjustable floor, gymnasium, treatment rooms, massage baths and restaurant. In addition to the playing and coaching staff, two full-time gardeners, ten groundstaff, four catering staff, three building supervisors and the manager's secretary/youth secretary are all based at Shenley. At the start of the 2004/05 season, a dedicated press briefing building was opened at the site.

Thierry Henry – stockings suspended
The French striker sparked a craze by pulling his socks up over his knees, since copied by school children and many opponents.

TRADITIONS

While Arsenal has cemented its position as a forward-thinking football club, it also prides itself on its traditions – here are some of the most celebrated:

Roast dinners
A traditional English roast has been served in the directors' lounge before all Sunday fixtures since the Second World War.

Floral welcome
Flowers in the colours of the opposition team are displayed in the boardroom at every match.

Carol singing
One of the lesser-known traditions, youth-team players are forced to sing a selection of Christmas carols to first-team players and Club staff in the training ground canteen every yuletide.

Goalkeeping jersey
For more than 50 years, when the club reached a cup final, the goalkeeper's jersey was washed before the game. It was a superstition that dated back to the 1927 FA Cup Final when goalkeeper Dan Lewis blamed his shiny new jersey for his mistake, when the ball slipped out of his grasp and over the line for Cardiff City's winner.

Clapping all four corners
Herbert Chapman insisted that the team applauded all sides of the stadium when they ran out on to the pitch. It remains so to this day.

Side by side at cup finals
When Arsenal played Herbert Chapman's former side Huddersfield in the 1930 FA Cup Final, the two sides took to the field side by side out of respect for the manager, sparking a cup tradition that is still followed today.

TRANSFER MILESTONES

Arsenal were once called the Bank of England Club and although most financial details of transfers are now kept under wraps that hasn't always been the case.

In 1925 Herbert Chapman caused uproar when he proudly paid £2,000 for 34-year-old Sunderland striker Charlie Buchan – and an extra £100 for every goal he scored in his first season at Highbury. He scored 20, doubling his fee. Chapman made Bolton forward David Jack the first five-figure player in world football in 1928 when he paid £10,890 for his services, nearly double the previous record. Chapman even got the Bolton's representatives drunk on gin and tonic to stop the price from escalating even higher.

Bryn Jones was another world-record signing at Highbury in 1938, when Arsenal paid Wolves £14,000 for the Wales international – sparking disgust in the House of Commons as well as the national press. Bob McNab's £50,000 fee to Huddersfield was an English record for a full-back in the autumn of 1966, while Alan Ball's transfer from Everton in December 1971 for £220,000 broke the overall English record made nearly two years earlier when West Ham's Martin Peters signed for Spurs for £200,000.

In 1990 George Graham made David Seaman the most expensive goalkeeper in world football when he paid QPR £1.3m for him. And Arsenal joined the big league for outfield players again in 1995 when the £7.5m deal to buy Internazionale's Dennis Bergkamp was, briefly, the most expensive deal in English football.

Theo Walcott became the world's most expensive teenager when he signed from Southampton in January 2006 for an initial £5m, which could rise to £12m depending on the England striker's success.

TRANSPORT LINKS,
Getting to Emirates Stadium

By Train/Underground...

If coming from central London, then the nearest underground station is Arsenal on the Piccadilly line, just a five-minute walk from the ground. Holloway Road station, west of the stadium, cannot be used before or after matches due to insufficient capacity. Other tube stations in walking distance of the stadium are Finsbury Park (Piccadilly/Victoria lines) and Highbury & Islington (Victoria Line). Drayton Park station is situated next to the stadium, but only has a limited service.

By Bus...

Bus numbers 43 and 271 from Upper Street stop on the Holloway Road (A1) directly next to the south and west flanks of the stadium. The number 4 runs between Islington and Archway and stops within five minutes of the ground on Blackstock Road.

By Car...

Head south on the A1 from Golders Green for about six miles, until you see Holloway Road tube station on your right. Take the next left at the traffic lights into Hornsey Road and the stadium is in front of you. There is little parking at the stadium or nearby streets and a residents' only parking scheme operates around the stadium on matchdays, so you will need to park some distance away and walk.

TRAVEL CLUB

The Arsenal Travel Club has provided coach, train and air travel for tens of thousands of fans to away games, domestically and across Europe spanning three decades. Before the Club set up its own 'in-house' facility, fans would use services provided by the official Supporters Club, through organisations like David Dryer Travel, or go under their own steam. Membership of the Travel Club has grown over the years and reached a peak of 4,819 by the end of the 2007/08 season.

TV

Arsenal were the first team to be covered by live TV cameras, probably because of Highbury's proximity to the BBC's Alexandra Palace studios. The Club arranged a special friendly between the first team and a second XI at Highbury on 16 September 1937. And independent television's first live game also involved Arsenal, with the nation's cameras following them to Bedford Town's Eyrie Ground in the hope of a major upset. The first game had finished 1-1 at Highbury, Arsenal fortunate to level late on, but there was no upset in the replay as the Gunners won the FA Cup third round tie 2-1 on 12 January 1956.

Eight years later, on 22 August 1964, the Gunners had a starring role in the first match ever featured on BBC's *Match of the Day*, although they lost their Division One clash at Liverpool 3-2. Arsenal's first live Sky match was also at Anfield, goals from Ian Wright and Anders Limpar gave the Gunners a 2-0 win over Liverpool on 23 August 1992 as Arsenal registered their first win of the season.

Today, the *Arsenal TV Show*, produced exclusively for the Club, is an inter-national three-hour programme with all the latest news and views, including exclusive interviews, footage and all the action from Gunners matches. It is sold to 60 countries around the world, including Netherlands, Mexico, France and Bulgaria and is hugely popular in the Far East, where in Japan alone it attracts 4 million viewers ever week.

There is also an *Arsenal TV Online* show available to subscribers of Arsenal.com, with coverage of press conferences, post-match interviews, highlights shows of every game and streams of pre-season friendlies.

Arsenal TV

In January 2008 Arsenal launched their own television channel available across the UK and beyond on satellite. In partnership with Input Media, it airs live from state-of-the-art studios inside Emirates Stadium from 5 p.m. on weekdays with a range of live shows and features. Actor and author Tom Watt, who wrote an acclaimed book about his passion for Arsenal's old North Bank terrace, *The End*, hosts a live fans forum every week and other regulars include former Gunners Stewart Robson, Paul Davis, Kenny Sansom and John Radford. Bob Wilson also hosts his own show talking to former players, there are also dedicated programmes on Arsenal Ladies' and the Academy's latest prospects. All reserve games are shown live and exclusively.

UEFA CUP CAMPAIGNS

Arsenal have entered the UEFA Cup on six occasions:

1978/79 - THIRD ROUND
The Gunners' first ever UEFA Cup tie saw Frank Stapleton score in a 3-0 home win over Lokomotiv Leipzig. He hit two more in a 4-1 win the second leg in East Germany. Arsenal travelled behind the Iron Curtain again in the second round when they lost 2-1 against Yugoslavian giants Hajduk Split. But a Willie Young goal in the return at Highbury put Arsenal through to a third-round clash with another Yugoslavian side, Red Star Belgrade. A 1-0 first-leg defeat in Belgrade gave the Gunners hope, but they could only draw 1-1 in the second leg in front of 41,451, going out 2-1 on aggregate.

1981/82 - SECOND ROUND
In the first round Panathinaikos of Greece were comfortably beaten 3-0 on aggregate and Belgian minnows KFC Winterslag looked easy opponents in the second. But the Gunners went down 1-0 in the first leg and, despite goals from John Hollins and Graham Rix earning a 2-1 win at Highbury, the Gunners crashed out on away goals.

1982/83 - FIRST ROUND
Spartak Moscow handed Arsenal a Highbury lesson - and it could have been so different. Goals from Stewart Robson and Lee Chapman in the opening 13 minutes had given the Gunners a 2-0 lead in Moscow, but

Frank Stapleton enjoyed Arsenal's first ever UEFA Cup tie against Lokomotiv Leipzig - he netted at Highbury and hit two more in the return leg.

the Soviets came back to win 3-2 with Yuri Gavilov scoring a last-gasp header. Back at Highbury hopes were high, but Spartak ruthlessly tore Arsenal apart, winning 5-2 and earning a standing ovation on the final whistle. Then coach Don Howe, however, still maintains Arsenal were a little unlucky: 'We played really well that night. They were superb, but honestly, on another night it could have been a different story.'

1996/97 - FIRST ROUND

Stefan Effenberg starred for the German team Borussia Mönchengladbach in a 3-2 win at Highbury in the first leg, but two weeks later, with new manager Arsène Wenger on the Arsenal bench, Paul Merson pulled the tie level with a stunning strike before Borussia pulled away to win 3-2 again - and 6-4 on aggregate.

1997/98 - FIRST ROUND

A year later another disappointing European campaign ended at the first hurdle. PAOK Salonika won 1-0 in Greece and Arsenal could only earn a 1-1 draw in the Highbury return - Dennis Bergkamp scoring his first European goal in red and white - as PAOK went through 2-1 on aggregate.

1999/2000 - RUNNERS-UP

Arsenal joined the competition in late 1999 at the third round stage after going out of the Champions League. First opponents Nantes were beaten 6-3 on aggregate and the Gunners then hammered Spain's champions-elect Deportivo La Coruña 5-1 at Highbury to go through the fourth round 6-3 on aggregate. In the quarter-finals Werder Bremen were blown away 6-2 on aggregate after a Ray Parlour hat-trick earned a 4-2 win in Germany.

In the semis RC Lens stood between Arsenal a first European final in six years. Dennis Bergkamp's strike gave Arsenal a slender 1-0 advantage to take to northern France and Thierry Henry and Kanu netted in a 2-1 win to send Arsenal to a Copenhagen showdown with Galatasaray SK.

The Turks proved tough opponents, but when talismanic midfielder Georghe Hagi, a bewitching presence on the night, was sent off for hitting Tony Adams, Arsenal had the advantage. The game went to extra time and the Gunners searched for the Golden Goal; Marc Overmars, Thierry Henry and Martin Keown all blowing chances to win it. Galatasaray held out for penalties - and luck was on their side as Patrick Vieira and Davor Suker both missed from the spot as the Turks won 4-1 in the shoot-out.

UNDERGROUND

Gillespie Road station on the Piccadilly Line was one of the carrots that enticed Arsenal to Highbury in 1913. It made the Gunners the most easily accessible club in English football, with trains taking less than 15 minutes from King's Cross station and just a few minutes longer from the West End.

On his arrival at Highbury in 1925, new manager Herbert Chapman was impressed. As Arsenal became more successful, the inventive Yorkshireman commented how good it would be to rename the station after the Club. After all, thousands were flocking to the Highbury ground each week via the station. In 1932 extensions to Arnos Grove in the north and Hounslow and South Harrow in the west brought thousands closer to the Club. Chapman began a campaign to get the name changed. London Underground was reluctant at first, but as the Club's fame grew, it bowed to the manager's persuasive powers. The decision meant tens of thousands of maps, signs and booklets had to be destroyed and replaced, and on 5 November 1932 Gillespie Road became Arsenal Station.

In 2005, a 52-metre mural was unveiled in the station tunnel commemorating Arsenal's 93 years at Highbury. The station, like the Piccadilly Line, celebrated its centenary in 2006.

UNSUNG HEROES

The list of unsung heroes at any football club is a long one. Here is a small selection of those associated with the Gunners:

BILLY MILNE
For 39 years, starting in the early 1920s, Milne was a club stalwart as player, assistant trainer and physio.

ALF BAKER
Played every position for Arsenal, was occasional skipper and served the Club for 11 years as a player before finally earning a winner's medal in 1930. Was later a scout at Highbury.

PERRY GROVES
A much-ridiculed £70,000 striker, but earned two league titles a and League Cup medal in the late 1980s and early 1990s.

RONNIE ROOKE
Scored a remarkable 68 goals in 88 league matches between 1946 and 1949.

GEORGE ARMSTRONG
A flying winger during the 1960s and 1970s, he quietly got on with his job for 13 years without ever being a star. Later worked as the youth team boss.

BRIAN MARWOOD
Only had a fleeting stay at Highbury, but his wingplay was immaculate in the 1988/89 title-winning season.

ANDY LINIGHAN
Uncomplaining despite playing second fiddle to Adams, Bould and Keown for six and a half years in the early 1990s.

MARTIN HAYES
Scored 24 goals in the 1986/87 season, including 12 penalties.

IAN ALLINSON
Scored vitals goals from the bench in the 1980s - including a memorable FA Cup goal at Spurs.

UPPER STREET

This is Islington's main high street and also the start of the A1 which leads into Holloway Road in the north of the

Unsung heroes: Alf Baker (back left) proudly lines up with the rest of the 1930 FA Cup-winning squad. The squad in full: (back row, left to right) Alf Baker, Jack Lambert, Charlie Preedy, Bill Seddon, Eddie Hapgood, Bob John; (middle row, left to right) Herbert Chapman, David Jack, Tom Parker, Alex James, Tom Whittaker; (front row, left to right) Joe Hulme, Cliff Bastin.

the colourful Scot lurched from one disastrous display to another, only occasionally offering a glimpse of his true talents, and often becoming the fallguy for yet another defeat.

An easy target for the crowd, Ure's shortcomings were ruthlessly exposed and in the 1990s wounds were reopened when Nick Hornby was critical of him in his book, *Fever Pitch*. He left Highbury for Manchester United in 1969. Away from the pitch, however, he showed himself a more than capable TV personality, becoming a favourite on popular BBC show *Quiz Ball*.

USA

Two Americans have played for Arsenal in recent years: Frank Simek and Danny Karbassiyoon, who both turned out for the first-team in Carling Cup games before moving to pastures new. Missouri-born right-back Simek skippered the reserve side and played once for the first team in a 5-1 win over Wolves. He transferred to Sheffield Wednesday in 2005. Left-sided defender Karbassiyoon, born in Roanoke, Missouri, marked his debut - against Manchester City in 2004 - with a goal, but failed to make a Premiership appearance and left for Burnley in 2005.

Former Gunners Steve Morrow and Paul Mariner both forged careers in US soccer. Mariner has lived in the United States for nearly 20 years and is the current assistant coach at Major League Soccer outfit New England Revolution. Morrow spent two years with MLS side Dallas Burn before returning to the UK.

borough. It also marks the heart of Islington where Arsenal's many trophy parades over the years have ended at the town hall. The street contains many fashionable shops, pubs, restaurants and theatres - it is home to the famous Hope & Anchor pub, the King's Head theatre pub and the Screen on the Green cinema. Upper Street is served by two tube stations, Angel in the south and Highbury & Islington in the north.

UPSETS

Some cup days to forget, when Arsenal failed against lower league opposition:

QPR (Div 3) **2-0 Arsenal** - FA Cup, 3rd Rd, 1921
Walsall (Div 3 North) **2-0 Arsenal**
- FA Cup, 3rd Rd, 1933
Arsenal 1-2 Norwich City (Div 3 South)
- FA Cup, 4th Rd, 1953

Northampton Town (Div 3 South) **3-1 Arsenal**
- FA Cup, 3rd Rd, 1958
Swindon Town (Div 3) **3-1 Arsenal (aet)**
- League Cup Final, 1969
Arsenal 1-2 Walsall (Div 3) - Milk Cup, 4th Rd, 1983
York City (Div 3) **1-0 Arsenal**
- FA Cup, 3rd Rd, 1985
Wrexham (Div 4) **2-1 Arsenal** - FA Cup, 3rd Rd, 1992

URE, Ian

Born **Ayr, Scotland,
7 December 1939**
Arsenal appearances **202**
Arsenal goals **2**
International caps (Scotland) **11**

Signed for £62,500 - a world-record fee for a centre-half in 1963 - from European Cup semi-finalists Dundee, Ure was seen as the man to return Arsenal's defence to its past glories. Instead,

Ian Ure (right) braces himself as he attempts to block a powerful shot from former Gunner David Herd, playing here for Manchester United, in a Division One clash at Highbury on 23 September 1963. Ure himself would move to the Old Trafford club six years later.

However, one ex-Gunner played in the US and remains there almost 30 years after leaving Britain. Double-winning full-back Bob McNab tried his luck in the fledgling NASL with San Antonio, but after briefly returning to north London to play for Barnet, moved to Canada to coach Vancouver Whitecaps. He now lives in California where he is a property developer – and even helped Karbassiyoon's passage to Highbury after having a chat with Arsenal chief scout Steve Rowley. 'I mentioned to Steve it may be worth coming over and taking a look at him,' explains Bob. 'Steve liked the look of him and he made it over to London Colney. He played up front but was converted to left-back and didn't look back.'

Bob's daughter, Mercedes, is now a famous face across the 'Pond' – she is a successful actress and model and has appeared in shows such as *Buffy The Vampire Slayer* and *Dawson's Creek*.

VAESSEN, Paul

Born **Bermondsey, London, 16 October 1961**
Died **8 August 2001**
Arsenal appearances **41**
Arsenal goals **9**

The name Paul Vaessen is synonymous with a famous night in Turin in 1980 when Arsenal became the first club for a decade

– and the first ever English side – to beat Juventus on their own ground in European competition.

Vaessen's last-minute header snatched a 1-0 win and propelled Arsenal into the final of the European Cup-Winners' Cup. Vaessen, on as substitute for David Price, said years later, 'I'll never forget the silence when I scored. The firecrackers, the drums, the chanting all stopped. It was eerie... We made up for it in the bar afterwards. The champagne was out. We sang and laughed. The adrenalin buzz was fantastic. A few of the lads were driving around the hotel grounds on a tractor at four in the morning without a stitch on.'

But his joy was short-lived. Vaessen suffered a severe knee injury and was forced to quit football two years later having made just 41 appearances for Arsenal. He had personal problems after retiring and tragically died in 2001 at the age of 39.

VALENCIA CF

Over the years the Spanish club have emerged as Arsenal's European nemesis.

In 1980, they beat the Gunners on penalties in the European Cup-Winners' Cup final. Arsenal drew 0-0 at the Heysel Stadium before Liam Brady and Graham Rix failed from the spot in the resulting penalty shoot-out.

In 2001, John Carew's header knocked Arsenal out of the Champions League on away goals in the quarter-finals after Thierry Henry and Ray Parlour had given the Gunners a 2-1 lead from the first leg.

The Norway international striker struck twice more at the Mestalla Stadium in March 2003 to inflict a 2-1 defeat on Arsène Wenger's men and deny them a place in the last eight of the same competition.

VAN BRONCKHORST, Giovanni

Born **Rotterdam, Netherlands, 5 Feb 1975**
Arsenal appearances **39 (25)**
Arsenal goals **2**
International caps (Netherlands) **77**
(4 goals)

The left-sided utility man, equally comfortable in defence or midfield, was signed from Glasgow Rangers in 2001, but never made the impact he or the Club had hoped for once he moved south of the border. Injuries and fierce competition on the left flank from Ashley Cole restricted his appearances, although he played enough games to earn a title medal in 2001/02. Barcelona continued their long tradition of employing Dutchmen when they took him on loan in 2003 and the move was soon made permanent.

He started for the Catalans in their 2-1 Champions League Final win over Arsenal in May 2006.

Teenage striker Paul Vaessen scored one of the most famous goals in Arsenal's history, but injury cut short his career.

VAN PERSIE, Robin

Born **Rotterdam, Netherlands, 6 August 1983**
Arsenal appearances **84 (49)**
Arsenal goals **43**
International caps (Netherlands) **24**
(7 goals)

The 2002 Dutch PFA's Young Player of the Year arrived from Feyenoord in May 2004 after turning down PSV Eindhoven to move to England. Touted as the long-term replace-ment for his compatriot Dennis Bergkamp at both club and international level, and after a shaky start with his discipline, van Persie's strength, skill and eye for goal have come to the fore, scoring numerous goals including two stunning efforts in the 2005 FA Cup semi-final win over Blackburn.

He won the prestigious Player of the Month award in November 2005 after scoring six goals in just four starts and has also forced his way into the Netherlands starting line-up.

His fine form continued in 2006/07 and he ended the season as the Club's top scorer despite missing the last four months of the campaign through injury. His stay at Arsenal has continued to be injury-hit – but on his day it is clear that the Rotterdammer is one of the most precocious talents in European football.

'VICTORIA CONCORDIA CRESCIT'

The Gunners' Latin motto first appeared on the Arsenal crest in the first matchday programme of the 1949/50 season.

It had emerged a year or so earlier when Harry Homer, the programme editor of the day, coined the quotation to sum up Arsenal's title-winning 1947/48 campaign.

The choice of 'Victoria Concordia Crescit', which translates as 'Victory grows out of harmony', so impressed the Club it was officially adopted by Arsenal and featured on the Club crest until 2002.

VICTORIES,
Record wins in all competitons

BIGGEST HOME WIN OVERALL
12-0 (v Loughborough Town (h),
12 March 1900, League Division 2)
12-0 (v Ashford United (h) 14 Oct 1893,
FA Cup, 1st Rd)

BIGGEST AWAY WIN OVERALL
7-0 (v Standard Liege (Bel) (a), 3 Nov
1993, Cup-Winners' Cup, 2nd Rd)

BIGGEST HOME WIN IN THE LEAGUE
12-0 (v Loughborough Town (h),
12 March 1900, League Division 2)

BIGGEST HOME WIN IN
THE TOP DIVISION
9-1 (v Grimsby Town (h), 28 Jan 1931,
League Division 1)

BIGGEST AWAY WIN IN THE LEAGUE
7-1 (v Aston Villa (a), 14 Dec 1935,
League Division 1)

BIGGEST HOME WIN IN
THE PREMIERSHIP
7-0 (v Everton (h), 12 May 2005)
7-0 (v Middlesbrough (h), 14 Jan 2006)

BIGGEST AWAY WIN IN
THE PREMIERSHIP
6-1 (Middlesbrough (a) 24 April 1999)

BIGGEST HOME WIN IN
ALL EUROPEAN COMPETITIONS
7-1 (v Dinamo Bacau (Rom) (h),
18 Mar 1970, Fairs Cup, 4th Rd)

BIGGEST AWAY WIN IN
ALL EUROPEAN COMPETITIONS
7-0 (v Standard Liege (Bel) (a),
3 Nov 1993, Cup-Winners' Cup, 2nd Rd)

BIGGEST HOME WIN IN
UEFA CHAMPIONS LEAGUE
5-1 (v Rosenborg (Nor) (h), 7 Dec 2004,
Group Stage)

BIGGEST WIN IN
UEFA CHAMPIONS LEAGUE
AT WEMBLEY
3-1 (v AIK Solna (Swe), 22 Sep 1999,
Group Stage 1)

BIGGEST AWAY WIN IN
UEFA CHAMPIONS LEAGUE
5-1 (v Inter Milan (a), 25 Nov 2003,
Group Stage 1)
4-0 (v PSV Eindhoven (a), 25 Sep 2002,
Group Stage 1)

BIGGEST HOME WIN IN
THE FA CUP
12-0 (v Ashford United (h) 14 Oct 1893,
FA Cup, 1st Rd)

BIGGEST AWAY WIN IN
THE FA CUP
7-1 (v Burnley (a), 20 Feb 1937,
FA Cup, 5th Rd)

BIGGEST HOME WIN IN
THE LEAGUE CUP
7-0 (v Leeds United (h), 4 Sep 1979,
League Cup, 2nd Rd)

BIGGEST AWAY WIN IN
THE LEAGUE CUP
6-1 (v Scunthorpe Utd (a), 25 Sep 1968,
League Cup, 2nd Rd)
6-1 (v Plymouth Argyle (a), 3 Oct 1989 ,
Lge Cup, 2nd Rd)

BIGGEST WIN UNDER
ARSÈNE WENGER
7-0 (v Everton (h), 12 May 2005,
Premiership)
7-0 (v Middlesbrough (h), 14 Jan 2006,
Premiership)

VIEIRA, Patrick

Born **Dakar, Senegal, 23 June 1976**
Arsenal appearances **409**
Arsenal goals **33**
International caps (France) **105 (6 goals)**

Cape Verdian by blood and Senegalese by birth, the France international found his footballing home in north London where his performances and leadership illuminated Highbury for nine trophy-laden years.

The midfielder captained Cannes at 19 before he was snapped up by AC Milan. But after just two appearances at the San Siro Arsène Wenger rescued him with a move to Highbury and, from the moment he made his debut as a substitute against Sheffield Wednesday in 1996, the Arsenal faithful realised a very special talent was in their midst. Vieira's stamina and physical strength allowed him to settle quickly in the Premiership, while his composure, passing and technique added exciting attacking options to the team.

He made his debut for France in 1997 and formed a dream Gunners partnership in midfield with compatriot Manu Petit as Arsenal won the Double in 1998. He also won a World Cup-winner's medal that summer, setting up Petit for France's third goal in a 3-0 victory in the final against Brazil.

His disciplinary problems were often highlighted by the media – a problem he largely curtailed without receiving much credit outside north London – but his success continued with a Euro 2000 win with France and a second Double with Arsenal in 2002. He was promoted to Club skipper when Tony Adams retired in 2002, but missed Arsenal's 2003 FA Cup Final win through injury. However, in 2003/04, he captained the side on the historic unbeaten league season and had to deflect strong rumours he was leaving for Real Madrid that summer.

But after the 2005 FA Cup Final, when he scored the winning kick in the penalty shoot-out against Manchester United, he finally left

A jubilant Patrick Vieira parades around the Millennium Stadium with the FA Cup trophy in May 2005.

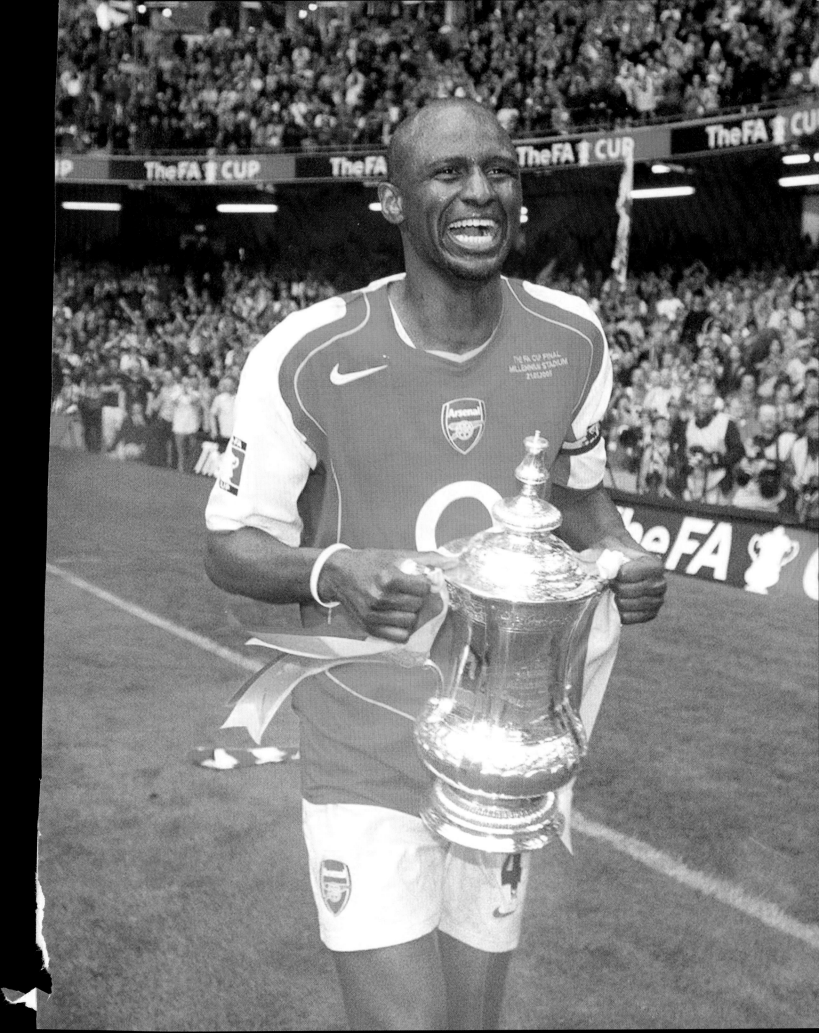

for Juventus. His last game at Highbury had ended in suitable fashion; the Frenchman scoring in a 7-0 win over Everton. Vieira had written his place in Highbury folklore as one of Arsenal's most successful captains. He quickly returned to Highbury to a rapturous reception in the quarter-finals of the UEFA Champions League in March 2006 – but was outshone by his replacement Cesc Fabregas in Arsenal's 2-0 win.

VILLA PARK

Aston Villa's palatial home in Birmingham has hosted some of the Gunners' greatest games – and, of course, some heart-breaking defeats.

In the league, 1935 saw Ted Drake score all seven for the Gunners in a 7-1 win over the Villans and Tony Woodcock smashed Villa's ten-month unbeaten home record with a five-goal haul in the Gunners' 6-2 win in 1983. The Gunners' first post-war away league win came at Villa with a 2-0 success in September 1946, while more recently Robert Pires' brilliant lob over Peter Schmeichel secured a vitally important 2-1 win in March 2002 on the way to the Double.

In the FA Cup there has been mixed success at the old stadium – with Manchester United proving a Villa Park nemesis. Arsenal beat Manchester City 1-0 in the 1932 FA Cup semi-final and a 2-0 semi-final replay win against Stoke in 1970 sent the Gunners to Wembley, but the following season the two sides drew 1-1 at the same stage of the competition. United, however, have beaten Arsenal three times at Villa Park in semi-finals; 2-1 in 1983 and, famously, in 1999 when Ryan Giggs scored the winner for ten-man United; and 1-0 in 2004, courtesy of Paul Scholes' strike.

VOICE OF ARSENAL

Matchdays wouldn't be matchdays without our brilliant host Paul Burrell. The popular Brummie has been the Club's DJ since 1991

and is now a regular fixture – with fans turning up early to catch his unique entertainment prior to kick-off.

'I used to be compere at Caesar's Palace in Luton and got to know people like Pat Rice and Liam Brady,' explains Paul. 'Then one day Ken Friar rang me up and asked if I would like to come down to Highbury to provide the pre-match entertainment – and I'm still here now!'

Paul's first game was a 1-1 draw with QPR in August 1991 and since then he has established himself as the best in the business. But his job changed dramatically when the Jumbotron screens were introduced in 1994. 'Until then, I came with a bag of singles and did my thing, but when the screens were installed it became more of a TV show. Now there are adverts and I have to liaise with others as to when I'm "on air".

'Before it was a one-man job, but now it is a big team effort, with lots of people working behind the scenes.'

Now he interviews Arsène Wenger before every game and acts as the 'voice of Arsenal' right up to kick-off, playing musical requests and meeting and greeting fans and opponents. 'It has always been on an informal basis. I have no contract, just a hand shake, and that suits me fine. It's a brilliant job to have,' he adds.

WADE, Joe

Born **Shoreditch, London, 7 July 1921**
Died **12 November 2005**
Arsenal appearances **86**
Arsenal goals **0**

Few players have shown the sort of loyalty that Joe Wade did to Arsenal. The left-back joined the Club as an amateur in 1944 and turned professional the following year. He stayed 12 years at Arsenal, but was largely kept out of the first team by the likes of Walley Barnes, Laurie Scott and Lionel Smith. As a result he amassed more than 300 reserve appearances. Barnes broke a leg in the 1952 FA Cup Final and, the following season, Wade took his opportunity.

He played 40 league games as Arsenal won the title and the next season was appointed skipper. He led the side in Moscow against the famous Dynamos side and also toured in Brazil, Portugal, Germany and France. In 1956 he became player-manager at Southern League Hereford, renaming his new house 'Highbury'. His success at Hereford prompted an approach from Spurs to join as coach – he turned them down. Joe stayed in Hereford after his retirement, opening a sports shop and briefly managing the Club again in 1971.

WALCOTT, Theo

Born **Stanmore, Middlesex, 16 March 1989**
Arsenal appearances **33 (38)**
Arsenal goals **8**
International caps (England) **1**

Theo Walcott became the most expensive 16-year-old in British football history when he joined Arsenal in January 2006 after just 13 appearances for Southampton, netting five times. He was fast-tracked into the England Under-17s side and scored five goals in nine matches in 2004/05. He then made history when he became the youngest player to turn out for the full England side when he made his debut against Hungary at Old Trafford on 30 May 2006, at the age of 17 years and 75 days, beating Wayne Rooney's record. Generally recognised as the most exciting English talent to emerge since Wayne Rooney, Walcott is a striker with electric pace, a cool head and unlimited potential.

His first Gunners goal came in a 1-2 loss to Chelsea in the 2007 Carling Cup Final and Walcott enjoyed a consistent 2007/08 campaign as he established himself in Arsène Wenger's squad, finally exploding into life when he netted a super double in a 7-0 win over Slavia Prague. He also struck a brace in a 2-2 draw at Birmingham in February and ended the season impressively by scoring the winner at Sunderland. But his most memorable moment came when he ran 80 yards to set up Emmanuel Adebayor's goal in a 2-4 Champions League loss at Liverpool, drawing favourable comparisons to a certain Diego Maradona.

WALL, Bob

There are few club staff who will ever be able to match the loyalty of Bob Wall. Born just a mile away from Arsenal, at Manor House, in February 1912, he joined the club in 1928 as personal assistant to then Secretary-Manager Herbert Chapman.

Wall held many posts at Highbury including Box Office Administration Manager and Assistant Secretary while also impressing in the military after joining the Territorial Army in the summer of 1939. He was stationed in Gibraltar during hostilities and rose to the ranks of Brigadier-Major.

On his return to Highbury he succeeded John Peters as Assistant Secretary in January 1950 and was appointed the club's first sole Secretary in 1956 after the death of Tom Whittaker, the last Secretary-Manager before the jobs were split.

Wall wrote a book about his experiences at the Club in 1969 entitled *Arsenal from the Heart* before he retired in March 1977 - after nearly 50 years service to the Club - and was given a place on the Board of Directors until his death on 23 March 1981, aged 69.

WAR AT HIGHBURY

No club made greater sacrifices than Arsenal during the Second World War, 42 of the Club's 44 professional playing staff served King and Country, and nine were killed in action. Highbury, itself, was vital for the war effort in London. The stadium was used as a first aid post and ARP (Air Raid Precautions) Centre and was manned by Cliff Bastin and Tom Whittaker, although Whittaker later joined the RAF and became a squadron leader, earning an MBE for his service on D-Day. Bastin had failed his army entrance examination due to his poor hearing (he was practically deaf), but it did not stop a radio station in Italy claiming the striker had been captured by the Italian army. He was, in fact, on duty at Highbury at the time of the alleged capture.

The stadium was not allowed to be used for wartime matches so Arsenal had to play their 'home' games at White Hart Lane, using a variety of guest players such as Stanley Matthews, Stan Mortensen and Bill Shankly.

Arsenal still excelled in unofficial war competition with the League South A Division title in 1940, the London League in 1942 and Football League South league and Cup Double in 1943, the Gunners beating Charlton 7-1 at Wembley in the Cup Final.

Back at Highbury, the stadium had become a target for German bombers due to its importance in the war effort and it was bombed on several occasions with the North Bank roof destroyed and terracing at the Clock End badly damaged in 1942.

Arsenal returned to a patched up Highbury in the summer of 1946, kicking off the new season against Blackburn Rovers on 4 September - seven years after its last Division One match.

WEBSITE

Arsenal.co.uk was launched at the beginning of the 1997/98 season and in June 1999 was relaunched as Arsenal.com. There are three dedicated reporters employed on the site, which is a joint venture between Arsenal and ITV.

In April 2006 Arsenal.com registered a record 2 million unique users - quadruple the number for the same period in 2003 - with two-thirds of those from outside the UK. It averages approximately 28 million page impressions a month and has sister sites in Chinese and Malay. Voted Sports Website of the Year in 2005, it is consistently in the top 40 sports sites in the world.

WELSH GUNNERS

There have been a number of significant Welshmen in Arsenal's history.

Powys-born skipper **Caesar Llewellyn Jenkyns** was the Club's first-ever international player when he played against Scotland in 1896. **Bob John**, signed from Caerphilly, was Arsenal's pre-war record appearance-maker with 470 games between 1922 and 1937. When manager Herbert Chapman arrived in 1925 his first choice goalkeeper was Glamorgan-born stopper **Dan Lewis**, who played in the 1927 FA Cup Final but fumbled a weak shot to hand the winner to opponents... Cardiff City. Troedyrhiw-born left-winger **Charlie Jones** won a trio of title medals in the early 1930s and Wales international midfielder **Bryn Jones** became a world record signing at £14,000 from Wolves in 1938.

Welshmen were the first Gunners to play in a World Cup; giant goalkeeper **Jack Kelsey** and midfielder **Dave Bowen** played for Wales in the 1958 competition in Sweden. Kelsey, from Swansea, was the Club's No.1 for much of the 1950s - and considered world-class by many neutrals - and after retiring stayed on to manage the Club's merchandise shop. Maesteg-born Bowen skippered Arsenal at the end of the decade and was also the first Gunner to appear in a major European final, turning out for a London XI which lost 8-2 on aggregate against Barcelona in the Inter-Cities Fairs Cup in 1958. **Derek Tapscott**, signed from hometown club Barry Town in 1953, was one of Arsenal's most prolific strikers, smashing 68 goals in just 132 games before moving to Cardiff in 1958.

Peter Nicholas, from Monmouthshire, signed from Crystal Palace in 1981, making 80 appearances in red and white and scoring three goals, as well as becoming Wales captain before returning to Selhurst Park two years later. At the time he was the record Wales appearance-maker with 73 before being beaten by Neville Southall. Powerful striker **John Hartson** was the last major Wales international player to turn out for Arsenal, hitting 17 goals in 55 starts, including a goal in the 1995 Cup-Winners' Cup Final.

In recent years the Arsenal youth set up has provided Wales with two starlets: Cardiff City's Rhys Weston and Under-21 striker Adam Birchall, now at Mansfield Town.

WEMBLEY

Arsenal's first trip to the national stadium in April 1927 ended in a 1-0 defeat in the FA Cup

Final against Cardiff, but they returned three years later to beat Huddersfield Town 2-0 and claim a first major trophy for the Club.

In total, Arsenal have contested 13 FA Cup Finals at Wembley, winning seven and losing six. The Club has also played two FA Cup semi-finals at Wembley, losing 3-1 to Spurs in 1991 but gaining revenge over their local rivals two years later with a 1-0 win courtesy of a Tony Adams header.

The Gunners have also featured in five League Cup Finals at the stadium, winning two and losing three. Arsenal also beat Charlton 7-1 in the Football League South Cup Final at the national stadium in 1943, with Reg Lewis scoring four goals.

As well as contesting a number of Charity Shield matches at the old stadium down the years, Arsenal adopted Wembley as their home for Champions League fixtures in 1998/99 and 1999/2000. The decision gave more fans an opportunity to watch the Gunners - with gates averaging more than 71,000 - but results were disappointing with three defeats in six group matches.

WENGER, Arsène

MANAGER 1996-present
Born **Strasbourg, France, 22 Oct 1949**

On his appointment in September 1996, the notoriously fickle English media was greatly unimpressed. 'Arsène Who?' screamed more than one tabloid, accompanied by a picture of the studious-looking unknown Frenchman. It speaks volumes that more than a decade on, many informed judges - and those same journalists - believe Wenger has taken Herbert Chapman's place as the greatest manager in Arsenal's history. What has taken place at Arsenal since 1996 has been nothing short of a miracle.

After all, he is the only manager to win three titles for the Club, and has won four FA Cups, taken the Club to their first Champions League Final and master-minded the move from Highbury to Emirates Stadium. His fitness regime and strict dietary controls had, by their own admissions, extended the playing careers of ageing defenders such as Nigel Winterburn, Tony Adams, Steve Bould and Lee Dixon. Wenger has upped the ante with his dedication to attacking, free-flowing football. Highbury saw the level of entertainment rise to new heights,

especially in the title-winning seasons of 1997/98, 2001/02 and 2003/04.

His reputation for unearthing un-realised potential is second to none in world football. Patrick Vieira was plucked from AC Milan's reserves, Thierry Henry was all set to move to Udinese on loan when Wenger intervened, Robert Pires had a wretched season at Marseilles when he arrived at Arsenal... all three have since been Arsenal Players of the Year. His global connections have brought in players such as Nicolas Anelka, Kolo Toure, Emmanuel Eboue and Cesc Fabregas for nominal fees. Anelka reputedly left for Real

Arsène Wenger was virtually unknown when he came to England in 1996. His incredible impact on the Club, like Herbert Chapman's, will still be felt long after he leaves.

Madrid for £22.5m - more than 40 times the fee Arsenal paid Paris Saint-Germain for him. It is deals like these that have given rise to Wenger being dubbed 'The Miracle Maker'.

Wenger's achievements have been noted far and wide. He has been awarded the Legion d'Honneur - France's highest award - an honourary OBE and the Freedom of the borough of Islington. And it was only fitting that the greatest Arsenal manager since Herbert Chapman led the countdown at the last game at Highbury before the Club moved on to bigger and better things at Emirates Stadium.

WEST STAND

Originally built in 1932 at a cost of £50,000, the new West Stand was officially opened in December of that year by HRH Prince of Wales before a 4-1 victory over Chelsea. It was billed as the grandest stand in Britain. Designed by architects Claude Waterlow Ferrier and Walter Binnie, it was the first stage of a project that would give Highbury its distinctive Art Deco style. The stand replaced the former open bank of terracing that had stood at Highbury since 1913. Its original capacity was approximately 21,000, with 4,000 seats in its upper tier and room for 17,000 standing spectators in the lower tier.

In the 1960s the majority of the lower standing section was converted into seating for 5,500 fans, while a small standing 'paddock' was maintained at the front until 1993, when it was replaced with more seats, lowering the total capacity of the stand to 10,942.

In the latter part of 2006, work commenced on converting the stand into homes as part of the new Highbury housing development. It remains a listed building.

WHITE HART LANE

The home of Arsenal's local rivals was also the venue for two of the Gunners' greatest triumphs. In 1971, Arsenal headed to White Hart Lane needing a win or a goalless draw to pip Leeds United to the championship. With thousands locked outside, Ray Kennedy's late header and a clean sheet took the title to Highbury. In 2004 Arsène Wenger's men arrived in N17 needing just a point to clinch the Premiership crown. Early goals from Patrick Vieira and Robert Pires put Arsenal in charge and, although Spurs snatched a point, the Gunners ended the day with another league title.

The most goals in a north London derby at the ground were scored in the 5-4 Arsenal Premiership victory at White Hart Lane on 13 November 2004. The biggest winning margin was 6-0 to Arsenal on 6 March 1935, when Alf Kirchen scored twice on his Gunners debut.

Tottenham have beaten Arsenal 5-0 at home on two occasions - Christmas Day 1911 and April 1983 - the latter was revenge for a memorable 5-0 Arsenal win at the Lane in December 1978 when Alan Sunderland scored a hat-trick and Liam Brady curled in a stunning effort to sink Spurs. In recent years Kanu also scored a brilliant individual effort to secure a 3-1 away win in 1999.

WHITTAKER, Tom (MBE)

MANAGER 1947/56
Born **Aldershot, Surrey, 21 July 1898**
Died **24 October 1956**
Arsenal appearances **70**
Arsenal goals **2**

Tom Whittaker served Arsenal with great distinction for nearly 40 years as player, trainer and manager. He joined the Club in 1919 after serving during the First World War, but made just 70 appearances as a wing-half, scoring twice, before a knee injury forced his retirement in 1925. He immediately embarked on a physiotherapy course and became Herbert Chapman's trusted right-hand man and Club trainer, revamping much of the training regime and becoming one of the first people in football to emphasise the importance of a sensible diet for players. After Chapman's death in 1934 he continued to serve under his successor, George Allison, and also became a trainer for the England national team.

During the Second World War he served as an ARP warden at Highbury alongside Cliff Bastin and later became an RAF pilot, earning an MBE for his service.

When hostilities ended, the genial Whittaker was back at Highbury as trainer and within two years was appointed secretary-manager when Allison retired. He led the club to league titles in 1948 and 1953 and the 1950 FA Cup, but with the Club's fortunes on the wane Whittaker died suddenly of a heart attack on 24 October 1956. He was 58.

Former player Jack Crayston, who served as his assistant, said tearfully the next day, 'In all my years with the Club, I never heard him say an unkind thing.' And his former skipper Joe Mercer added, 'I know of no one who had so many friends.'

WHITTAKER'S STARS

After the ravages of war, it was Whittaker who faced the unenviable task of rebuilding a Club that had dominated the 1930s. And when **George Male** retired in May 1948, it ended all playing connections with the Herbert Chapman era. **George Swindin** was the undisputed No.1 for much of his rein, before being ably replaced by **Jack Kelsey** in goal. Veteran defender **Joe Mercer**, a footballing superstar, was drafted in and proved a lynchpin for the next seven seasons with the highly-motivated **Walley Barnes** providing more steel to the Arsenal defence. The irrepressible **Jimmy Logie** was the midfield schemer who faced obvious comparisons to pre-war hero **Alex James**, while strikers such as **Reg Lewis** - who netted 33 times in 1947/48 - **Doug Lishman, Ronnie Rooke** and **Cliff Holton** banged in the goals that helped bring two league titles and the FA Cup to Highbury during the Whittaker years. In his latter years, Whittaker caused a sensation with his last major star signing when he bought former England striker **Tommy Lawton** from Brentford in 1954 – but the move wasn't a success and the glory years were coming to an end.

WIGAN ATHLETIC

Wigan were Arsenal's last ever opponents at Highbury on 7 May 2006. They had never played at the old stadium since their formation in 1932 – but ended up playing there twice in five months. In January, Athletic lost 2-1 in the Carling Cup semi-final second leg, but went through on away goals courtesy of a last-minute strike from Jason Roberts. But Arsenal gained their revenge on their Highbury bow with a 4-2 win – despite Wigan leading 2-1 at one stage. The 2,000 Wigan fans present for that historic match were each given a commemorative blue T-shirt for the occasion.

WILLIAMS, Steve

Born **Hammersmith, London,
12 July 1958**
Arsenal appearances **119 (2)**
Arsenal goals **5**
International caps (England) **6**

Steve Williams was destined to play in red and white – his parents, both from Holloway, met and fell in love on the North Bank. Signed from Southampton in December 1984, 'Willow' was never shy to voice an opinion and became a leader both on and off the pitch, with contempt for anyone not willing to spill blood for the cause.

But as well as being a dogged battler, he also had the ability to control the pace of a game almost at will, with fine vision and technique. He was one of the senior members of George Graham's 1987 Littlewoods Cup winners, but left a year later for Luton Town after a rumoured

falling out with Graham when he was dropped from the 1988 final.

Williams' verdict on the matter? 'Absolute rubbish – I never once had an argument with George. Arsenal is my club and it was *always* an honour to pull on the red and white.'

WILSON, Bob

Born **Chesterfield, Derbyshire,
30 October 1941**
Arsenal appearances **308**
International caps (Scotland) **2**

A courageous goalkeeper and the first line of defence during the 1971 Double season, Wilson remains one of the most popular players ever to have turned out for the Gunners. He made his debut in 1963 while still an amateur and schoolteacher in nearby Holloway and was offered a professional contract a year later.

A disastrous 1969 League Cup Final appearance proved a character-building experience and he was a fundamental part of the 1970 Fairs Cup win over Anderlecht and then the Double success a year later. Wilson was famed for his fanatical training routine and lack of goalkeeping gloves, preferring to play with bare hands to further add to his reputation as one of the most fearless custodians in Europe. He was also called up by Scotland due to his parentage, becoming the first English-born player to represent the Scots for a century.

He retired in 1974 and embarked on a successful career as a TV presenter. Wilson also continued as a goalkeeping coach at Highbury from the 1980s through to the new millennium, and still remains a part of the Arsenal scene.

Despite his magnificent career, Willow's life has been tinged with sadness. Two of his brothers died in action during the Second World War, and his daughter Anna died, aged 21, from leukemia in December 1998. In the past few years he has devoted much of his time to the Willow Foundation, a charity set up in her memory, which has been backed by many Arsenal players past and present.

WILTORD, Sylvain

Born **Neuilly-sur-Marne, France,
10 May 1974**
Arsenal appearances **124 (51)**
Arsenal goals **49**
International caps (France) **92
(26 goals)**

Wiltord arrived at Highbury from Girondins Bordeaux in August 2000 having shot to prominence just weeks before when he scored a 94th-minute equaliser in the European Championships Final against Italy. Though a quick and direct striker, Wiltord never quite cemented his place in the team, starting many games from the bench or on the wing. The highlight of his Arsenal career was scoring the winner against Manchester United at Old Trafford which clinched the 2002 Premier League title. He let his contract run down after the 2004 title triumph and moved back to France with Lyon, where he has since won two title medals.

WINTERBURN, Nigel

Born **Nuneaton, Warwickshire,
11 December 1963**
Arsenal appearances **584**
Arsenal goals **12**
International caps (England) **2**

Signed from Wimbledon in 1987, Winterburn started his Highbury career as a right-back before switching flanks as a replacement for Kenny Sansom at the beginning of the 1988/89 season. He stayed in his new position for almost 13 years.

Though he infamously missed a penalty in the Littlewoods Cup Final defeat to Luton in 1988 he was a title winner in May 1989 at Anfield. By then firmly established as the Club's number one left-back, he earned another title medal in 1991 and FA and League Cup-winner's medals in 1993, before the

Bob Wilson, in typically determined pose, prepares to defend a corner. His bravery and obsessive training was legendary at Highbury.

famous back four's finest hour – their stunning defensive display in the 1994 Cup-Winners' Cup Final against Parma.

When Arsène Wenger arrived in 1996, Winterburn and his other ageing defensive colleagues benefited greatly from the Frenchman's new fitness regime, increasing his shelf life by several years as he won a third title medal in 1998 and another FA Cup. Tenacious, hard-working and highly-motivated, except for a brief blip in the early 1990s – including a well-publicised spat with a fan – Winterburn was consistency personified and became a terrace hero for his bravery.

He improved into his mid-30s, but was dislodged by the silky Silvinho in 1999 and made the short trip to West Ham in 2000, where he impressed the Upton Park crowds for three more years up to his 40th birthday, before retiring and embarking on a career as a football pundit.

Despite his reputation and a reliable and tenacious full back he won only two England caps during his long career.

WM FORMATION

Herbert Chapman proved a trailblazer yet again when his Arsenal side introduced the WM formation in the mid-1920s to counter a change in the offside rule in 1925. The change reduced the number of opposition players that an attacker needed between himself and the goal-line from three to two. This led to the introduction of a centre-back to stop the opposing centre-forward, and tried to balance defensive and offensive playing.

The formation became so successful that by the late-1930s most English clubs had adopted it. Today the formation is described as 3-2-5 or 3-4-3.

WOODCOCK, Tony

Born **Nottingham, 6 December 1955**
Arsenal appearances **164**
Arsenal goals **68**
International caps (England) **42**
(16 goals)

Arsenal's premier striker of the 1980s turned down the likes of Juventus, Manchester United and Liverpool to move to Highbury in the pre-season of 1982. Manager Terry Neill spent £500,000 on the 26-year-old to bring him home from West German side Cologne. In four seasons at Arsenal he averaged a little under a goal every two games, earned himself nearly 20 more England caps and, when firing on all cylinders, electrified Highbury crowds with his pace and predatory instincts.

His finest hour in a Gunners shirt came in October 1983, when he scored five goals in the opening 48 minutes of a 6–2 away win at Aston Villa, their first home defeat in nearly a year. That season would prove his most productive, 'Woody' chalking up 21 goals in 37 games. But he would never fully recapture the form that made him such an effective member of Brian Clough's European Cup-winning side of 1979 and he moved back to Cologne for £140,000 in 1986.

He later became director of football at Frankfurt before returning to the UK in 2003 to set up a sports and media business with Viv Anderson.

WOOLWICH

Woolwich, the birthplace of Arsenal Football Club, is situated in south east London. In late 1886 a group of workers at the old Woolwich Armaments Factory decided to form a football club. Initially it was called Dial Square, but its name soon changed to Royal Arsenal and, eventually, Woolwich Arsenal. Shortly after the Club moved to Highbury, it became known simply as Arsenal.

The London Development Agency is currently redeveloping the 76-acre site where the factory once stood and, in honour of its rich footballing tradition, a commemorative plaque was unveiled by Arsenal director Richard Carr in October 2005. The site will play a key role in the rejuvenation of the Thames Gateway in the next few years – and Mr Carr urged Gunners fans to pay a visit to the area and remember its huge part in the Club's history. He said, 'Although the Club played at Highbury from 1913 onwards, the time between 1886 and 1913 is an extremely important period in the foundation and early development of our Club. It is a wonderful gesture by the LDA to produce this fantastic memorial plinth to commemorate the birthplace of Arsenal Football Club.'

The original arch incorporating the famous clock dial – which inspired the Club's original name – has been retained as a listed structure.

WRIGHT, Billy (CBE)

MANAGER 1962/66
Born **Ironbridge, Shropshire,**
6 February 1924
Died **3 September 1994**

An English football legend, Billy Wright won 105 caps for his country and made 541 appearances for Wolves. He became manager of his boyhood heroes Arsenal in 1962, but failed to haul the Club out of its malaise after a promising, goal-filled beginning to his Highbury tenure. Under Wright Arsenal never finished higher than seventh and in his final season as low as 14th. With a heavy heart the board chose to dismiss the hugely popular manager and he left management to work in the media as head of Sport for ATV and Central Television.

Wright is still fondly remembered by older figures at the Club and is credited with giving many of the 1971 Double-winning side their first-team chances. He was married to Joy Beverley of singing group the Beverley Sisters and he was made an inaugural inductee of the English Football Hall of Fame in 2002 – eight years after his death.

WRIGHT, Ian (MBE)

Born **Woolwich, London,**
3 November 1963
Arsenal appearances **288**
Arsenal goals **185**
International caps (England) **33 (9 goals)**

Ian Wright remains one of the most natural goalgetters to have ever worn the red and white. In seven remarkable Highbury years the cocksure south Londoner turned himself into a Gunners legend with a stunning goalscoring rate – and irrepressible win-at-all-costs style. One of the game's great characters, 'Wrighty' scored a hat-trick on his league bow at Southampton and won the Golden Boot at the end of his first season at Arsenal, 1991/92, with another treble in the return fixture at Highbury in the final game to be played in front of the original North Bank on the last day of the season.

Wright was the Club's top goalscorer for his first five years and helped the Gunners to double domestic cup success in 1993. A year later his goals proved vital as Arsenal reached the Cup-Winners' Cup Final, but Wright was in tears when he was banned from the showpiece match after picking up a booking in the semi-final win over Paris Saint-Germain. It was one of his many run-ins with officialdom as his competitive edge often got him into trouble. But in 1995 he scored in every match up to the semi-finals as Arsenal reached the final of the same competition for the second successive season.

In September 1997 he finally beat Cliff Bastin's 50-year Club goalscoring record with a hat-trick in a 4–1 win over Bolton. But he injured a hamstring a couple of months later which ruled him out of the rest of the season and, although he was named as a substitute in the FA Cup Final against Newcastle United, he did not play. However, he had done enough to finally get his hands on a title medal. After a glittering career in which he became the darling of the North Bank he moved to West Ham in the summer of 1998, before ending his career with spells at Nottingham Forest, Celtic and Burnley, and retiring in 2000.

X-RAYS

As a Club Arsenal has always tried to provide the best medical treatment for players, with Highbury, the training ground in Hertfordshire, and, latterly, Emirates Stadium, housing some of the most sophisticated equipment to aid recovery. Tom Whittaker ensured that Highbury was one of the first football stadiums to have its own X-ray facilities. Today, the Club always has a mobile X-ray unit available on matchdays in case of serious injury, and since 2003 state-of-the-art defibrillators have also been on site for all matches.

Back in the 1930s, players used to receive ultra-violet light treatment as it was thought the UV rays could help accelerate recovery from injury. Since those days, however, that theory has been dismissed by most leading medical figures.

But it's not all mod cons for physiotherapist Gary Lewin. At Highbury an old wooden cabinet remained in the medical room from the day it was built until Lewin and his team vacated it for the new Emirates Stadium in the summer of 2006. The cabinet housed a collection of old medical journals and plastic mannequin parts displaying the make-up of leg muscles and tissue... an invaluable tool for any physio.

YELLOW

For the best part of half a century Arsenal's traditional away colours have been yellow with blue trim. It seems likely that the tradition began when Arsenal wore gold shirts for the FA Cup Final in 1950, a colour which proved hugely popular with the fans. A slightly amended yellow strip was introduced gradually during the decade, before becoming standard second strip by 1960. Subsequently some of the Club's most famous victories have come in yellow, including both the 1971 and 1979 FA Cup Finals and,

most famously, the 1989 title won at Anfield against Liverpool.

Arsenal also occasionally wore yellow at Highbury, for example, when they beat Torino in 1994 en route to the Cup-Winners' Cup Final.

YOUNG, Willie

Born **Edinburgh, 25 November 1951**
Arsenal appearances **236**
Arsenal goals **19**

A monster of a defender, 'Big Willie' is one of the few men to have successfully made the move down the Seven Sisters Road from Spurs to Arsenal. However, following his transfer the Edinburgh-born stopper was, for a period, a hate figure among both sets of fans, a dreadful debut against Ipswich almost culminating in a punch-up with an irate Arsenal fan outside the ground. But he soon channelled his natural aggressive streak positively on the pitch, partnering the Rolls Royce-like David O'Leary at the heart of the defence in a classic good-cop, bad-cop double act.

Ironically it was against his former employers, in the north London derby, that Young finally won over his new fans, his head colliding with goalkeeper Jimmy Rimmer's knee only for him to continue the game, swathed in blood-soaked bandages and cutting a heroic figure. 'The fans knew at that point Spurs meant nothing to me anymore,' he claimed.

He would go on to play in three successive FA Cup Finals – gaining a winners' medal in 1979 – and the ill-fated Cup-Winners' Cup Final the following year, a campaign in which he would score some vital – and rare – goals en route to Brussels.

Brian Clough's Nottingham Forest was his next destination just before Christmas 1981 after he fell out with manager Terry Neill over a pay dispute. He would admit later that he regretted leaving the Gunners – clashing with Clough on several occasions – and came close to returning,

Willie Young (centre, right) in action against West Bromwich Albion on 16 August 1980. The red-headed defender had a horror start to his Arsenal career after signing from rivals Tottenham Hotspur, but the Highbury faithful soon warmed to his never-say-die spirit.

only for Arsenal's interest to cool. He wound up his playing career with stints at Norwich, Brighton and Darlington, before becoming a successful publican and restaurateur in Nottinghamshire.

YOUNGEST GUNNER

Cesc Fabregas became Arsenal's youngest ever first-team player on 28 October 2003 when he played in a 1-1 draw against Rotherham in the League Cup third round match. When the former Barcelona youngster took the field that night at the age of 16 years and 177 days, he took the record from Jermaine Pennant, who made his debut aged 16 years and 319 days in the same competition four years earlier at Middlesbrough. It was a great night for the Club with five other players also making their debuts: Justin Hoyte, Jerome Thomas, Gael Clichy, Graham Stack and substitute Ryan Smith. Arsenal went through 9-8 on penalties.

Fabregas went on to score in the 5-1 win over Wolves in the fourth round 35 days later – breaking another record by becoming Arsenal's youngest goalscorer at the age of 16 years and 212 days.

YOUTH CUP, The FA

Arsenal made their first FA Youth Cup Final appearance in 1965, but were beaten 3-2 on aggregate by Everton. Since then they have reached six more finals – and won them all. Charlie George (1966), David Hillier (1988) and Ashley Cole (2000) are three young